Branded
Conservatives

Politics,
Media &
Popular Culture

David A. Schultz, *General Editor*

Vol. 12

PETER LANG
New York • Washington, D.C./Baltimore • Bern
Frankfurt am Main • Berlin • Brussels • Vienna • Oxford

Kenneth M. Cosgrove

Branded Conservatives

How the Brand Brought
the Right from the Fringes
to the Center of American Politics

PETER LANG
New York • Washington, D.C./Baltimore • Bern
Frankfurt am Main • Berlin • Brussels • Vienna • Oxford

Library of Congress Cataloging-in-Publication Data

Cosgrove, Kenneth M.
Branded conservatives: how the brand brought the right
from the fringes to the center of American politics / Kenneth M. Cosgrove.
p. cm. — (Politics, media, and popular culture; v. 12)
Includes bibliographical references and index.
1. Conservatism—United States—History—20th century.
2. United States—Politics and government—20th century. I. Title.
JC573.2.U6C67   320.520973'09045—dc22   2006101457
ISBN 978-0-8204-7465-6
ISSN 1094-6225

Bibliographic information published by **Die Deutsche Bibliothek**.
Die Deutsche Bibliothek lists this publication in the "Deutsche
Nationalbibliografie"; detailed bibliographic data is available
on the Internet at http://dnb.ddb.de/.

Cover design by Lisa Barfield

The paper in this book meets the guidelines for permanence and durability
of the Committee on Production Guidelines for Book Longevity
of the Council of Library Resources.

© 2007 Peter Lang Publishing, Inc., New York
29 Broadway, 18th floor, New York, NY 10006
www.peterlang.com

Printed in the United States of America

for Erin

Acknowledgments

This work would not have been possible without the major contributions of a number of people and institutions. I am deeply indebted to all of them. Any failings in the manuscript are, of course, mine alone.

Without Pam Balch's encouragement and support, this would have never happened. At a time when I thought that I had a good idea, she made it possible for me to find out for sure. Without Pam Houston, I would not have been physically or mentally able to write nor would my thinking on the topic crystallized as quickly as it did during 2003. Erin Cosgrove contributed significantly by listening to my ideas, providing literature, criticism, insight, and suggestions. It was Erin who, in response to my repeated query of "why do you think that they'd do that?," suggested that the marketing literature might be very useful in understanding the Conservative movement that was very much my interest at the time that the project started. Her punishment, of course, was to sit through endless questions and read numerous evolving drafts as the project developed.

I would like to thank the members and instructors of the Salzburg Seminar's American Studies Center Seminar 26 that dealt with presidential leadership and media for providing insights and literature that proved valuable. I am indebted to Lance Bennett, who took the time to read the earliest version of this idea when it was still a study of the Clinton Impeachment, as well as to John Berg and Chris Bosso, who saw the second version of it at the 2003 New England Political Science Association Meeting. Thanks to Bruce Buchannan and those members of the audience who gave me very useful feedback when the third version was presented at the 2003 American Political Science Association Meeting. Phillip John Davies gave me an outlet and incentive for getting the first version of the Iraq Chapter written for his wonderful "Elections Ahead" conference in 2004.

I would like to thank Phyllis Korper and Peter Lang Publishing for being very patient as I struggled through a difficult year and a half while trying to work on this. I would particularly like to acknowledge David Schultz for providing numerous editorial and literature suggestions.

A number of my professional colleagues made generally useful suggestions and contributions to the project. All of my professional colleagues were very helpful, but specific contributions to the project were made by: John Berg, Anne Cammisa, Quinn Dickerson, Melissa Haussman, Judy Dushku, Agnes Bain, Clint Maffett, and Marsha Marrotta, made this a better work and helped me to finish it. Special thanks are due to Brian Roberts who was able to help rescue these files from a crashing hard drive at one very late stage of the process and to Kathi Maio for her sage advice in a few areas. I would particularly like to thank Nathan Shrader for his insights and efforts to make this a better piece of work. Special thanks to Michael Mushlitz of WGBH Boston.

All of these people and institutions greatly contributed to the work and I will always be deeply in their debt.

Table of Contents

A Crash Course in Branding

In 1964, few people would have predicted that the Conservative movement would occupy the central position in American political life that it did from 1980 onward. Many political scientists were arguing that the end of partisanship as a meaningful force in American politics was nigh during the 1970s and early 1980s. This was wrong, however, because it was at this time that the Republican Party dominated by Conservatives began to market its candidates by making significant use of branding. This book is about the key element of the Conservative marketing strategy and its impact on American politics: the use of a brand strategy by the Conservative movement. Conservatives have employed brands to sell their candidates in much the same way that many businesses use brands to sell products to consumers. Both use brands because they are powerful tools with which a marketer can cut through the noise of a crowded marketplace.[1] There is a significant difference between a brand deployed to promote a consumer product and one employed to promote politicians. That brands are, as Naomi Klein (2000) has noted, a somewhat totalitarian concept is of little relevance when it comes to selling products, and can be problematic for selling politics.[2] When it comes to selling political candidates, parties, and issues, we can see how this tendency poses a significant threat to democratic discourse in general and substantive discussion about public policy in particular.

The brand strategy is the tool that Conservatives have used to build their movement from 1964 until the present. Building a brand story that is consistent in terms of content is a very important aspect of branding. This is because the story around the brand helps the audience know whether or not it should be interested in the product being promoted by the brand. The brand story gives the product an identity that can be quickly communicated to the audience and is a key way of explaining what a given product is to an audience and to build its identity.[3] As Schweiger and Adami show in the European case, there is considerable evidence to support the idea that brand strategies can be applied to and be effective in politics.[4]

Conservatives have made good use of the brand strategy because they have always gone to great lengths to show that their brand promises have been kept and, if not, have worked to reposition their brands. They have not only branded themselves, but their opponents as well, and, in both cases, have done so through the use of a few core aspects into which line extensions can be placed. They have been doing so for a long time and, as we see, have built a number of brands that resonate in specific ways with specific audiences. This book argues that Conservatives have used branding in the way noted above and have used it to turn their movement into one that has taken over the Republican Party and shifted American politics in a rightward direction.[5] The brand that they have built has become the movement's public essence[6] and, in that sense, constitutes part of what Newman calls their political image.[7]

This work argues that, in addition to selling candidates in the mass media, Conservatives have branded all aspects of their movement in order to create lasting relationships with very specific audiences in the way in which Turow (1997) notes has happened throughout American business and society. Branding has become a key tool during the last decade or so because targeting, a process of reaching some audiences while driving away others, has broken society into many niches.[8] This trend began in the magazine business and spread outward into other forms of media and, eventually, into other areas of American life.[9] An example is provided by the 2004 Bush campaign's pursuit of Hispanics because this clearly was an effort to "build market share" in a "fast growing segment" faster than the Democrats could.[10]

The Conservative brand employed to promote a large number of products, not just candidates, was aimed at a few focused constituencies first and then, gradually expanded to reach other segments consistently with target marketing and is distributed through a number of channels other than mass media.[11] This targeting has had the net effect of producing a politics that, like much of the American media, is aimed not only at reaching some audiences but also at driving away others.[12] A tool through which this is accomplished is signaling, which allows marketers to split customers into narrow audiences in order to speak specifically to them, show that they were establishing "different kinds of emotional as well as commercial relationships with different kinds of customers," express their interest in specific audiences by trying to speak to them across a variety of media, and by building relationships with other kinds of marketers to show consumers that they were related by "shared values, activities and interests."[13] Just as media companies have specific formats that serve as their brand,[14] Conservatives too have a brand that is also quite specifically constructed. As media companies put on programming that is outrageous and capable of generating buzz in support of their brand while attracting or repelling specific audiences, so do Conservatives produce political products and brands that some audience segments find to be wonderful while others find them to be utterly repellant.[15] The Conservative brand is very much in keeping with the notion of being a package that people in specific audiences see as reflecting their identity.[16]

One Conservative example that we will see is the idea of the "Reagan Conservative"; that is, people became Republicans because of Ronald Reagan.[17] A case in point is provided by George W. Bush's 2004 campaign manager Ken Mehlman, who said,

> I'm a Reagan conservative is what I call myself. I got attracted to the Republican Party based on the Cold War, obviously. I'm 38 years old, so I came of age politically in the late '70s, early '80s.[18]

Ronald Reagan greatly resembles the results of the branding that companies are doing in the era of target marketing because, just as do cable television companies that have a few leading figures and signature shows,[19] so does Reagan fill this role for Conservatives. Reagan's 1980 election could be seen as proof of the fragmenting nature of the American public as well as the impact of targeted marketing techniques on American political life.[20]

Turning Reagan into a brand and building a line extension between him and George W. Bush exactly resembles the branding work done by cable television companies and it produces the same reaction. Just as the MTV, the ESPN, or the Lifetime networks are not for everyone and, indeed, some people will find themselves highly offended by the programming presented on these channels, so too Conservatism isn't for everyone and some people may find themselves highly offended by its message. On the other hand, like these television channels, Conservatism appeals to large numbers of people in very specific audiences and can do quite well as a result. As we see later in this work, a second example of this phenomenon is provided by the Clinton impeachment because some people believed deeply in it while others were totally turned off by it. Conservatives experienced great success with those audiences that liked it but didn't do nearly as well with other segments.

Conservatives do not hope to reach every audience with their brand—they are trying to reach the right audiences and to keep them—and the brand is the key tool through which this can be accomplished.[21] For them, as for many American businesses, brand loyalty can be built through a direct marketing program in order to encourage their continual use of the product.[22] The tandem of branding and relationship marketing is relatively new in business and politics because, beginning in the mid-1980s, businesses began to pay more attention to their current customers and on attracting more like them than they did to broadening their products' audience.[23] The reason for this, I argue, is that Conservatives have found that, as American companies do, it is much more effective in terms of yield to send targeted messages aimed at keeping current customers over a lifetime than it is to send mass media messages to attract new ones.[24]

The direct marketing that Conservatives do is close to corporate direct marketing because it is usually based on very sophisticated databases and, as a result, allows the marketer to efficiently target the right customers rather than simply issuing general appeals.[25] The result of this, in a national sense, has been to move from a primarily mass society and culture to more of a disconnected series of niches that converse with each other and, possibly, with overlapping lifestyle niches but not other segments of the society.[26] A clear example of this can be found in the Bush 2004 strategy.

The point to building and using a brand in such a direct, targeted environment is that it generates customer loyalty and, in turn, can result in the purchase of a number of products over a consumer's lifetime. Instead of moving customers through a line of cars, foods, or electronics sharing the same brand name over a lifetime, Conservatives use their brands to move them through a family of political products. It is possible to make the College Republicans move onto the Young Republicans and then into a number of Conservative interest groups while purchasing a variety of interest group and think-tank products before settling into a variety of lifestyle niches in which one can remain and converse with people just like themselves.[27]

This has led to the development of what Turow terms the image tribe because discussions take place solely within it rather than spreading out to reach other parts of the society.[28] A person can graduate from the College Republicans to the Young Republicans, purchase a variety of conservative interest group and media products along the way before moving into one of several specific lifestyle niches (termed image tribes) in which s/he can remain and converse with those just like themselves rather than the bulk of the populace.[29] It is the brand and the target, as well as mass marketing supporting it that are the key elements behind the Conservative ascendancy in the United States over the past thirty years. Simply, Conservatives are not trying to get all Americans to like or vote for them but, rather, are trying to get the right audiences to like them, buy their products, and support their candidates lifelong not just during a single electoral cycle.[30]

Having attracted the right audience, Conservatives use a number of communicative channels to build and to reinforce loyalty to their brands. These include talk radio, conservative opinion journals, cable television, the Internet, and direct mail in addition to mainstream broadcast media. As Moore and Slater (2003) explain in the case of Karl Rove:

"Bill Israel was a teaching assistant with Rove one semester and recalls him instructing how negative campaigning can turn voters quickly and decisively. 'It's better to narrowcast,' Rove said in class one day explaining the technique of passing powerful messages to small groups without stirring the larger public. 'Radio is really good for a negative attack,' he said, 'because it's tough to figure what the opposition is doing. The only thing worse to face is mail.' 'Direct mail,' Rove assured, 'is immune from press coverage.'"[31] The targeting of which Turow writes is close to these sentiments because through it specific messages can be passed to specific audiences so that nobody else really sees but that, consistent with his argument, they can then endlessly discuss among themselves.

Part of my point is that Conservatives have used branding in an environment in which partisan affiliations overall are weakening to do just this and, as a result, have a devoted audience for their political products to which they can regularly turn. This, in turn, reduces the number of new customers that they must reach for their products come election time. Should they succeed in reaching new customers or audiences, the Conservatives will work to build lasting relationships with them as described earlier. We can see this in the 2004 Bush campaign's targeting of and relationship building with three new audience segments for the Conservative message.

One of the key ways through which they do so is direct marketing because the whole point is to reach out to these audiences and build their loyalty.[32] This, in turn, is an efficient thing to do for a campaign or an interest group, just as it is for a company, because it is cost-effective to hold onto one's best performing audience segments while ignoring or actively trying to drive away others because they may not produce the value over time that makes their pursuit worthwhile.[33] One of the key ways in which they have done so is through the use of extensive relationship marketing. The relationship marketing that they do is in tune with Turow's argument because it is personalized and is tailored to suit the activities and interests of each of their customers.[34] This is reflected in the 2004 Bush campaign which had specific relationship-building programs for farmers, hunters, and women to name but three lifestyle audiences. The communication can be more personalized, as the author experienced first hand, by being on the Bush–Cheney 2004 mailing list. Each of the communications opened with a personalized greeting and was very much targeted toward the region where I had lived and the interests expressed when joining the list. It is, however, no more democratic a tool than is the brand itself because all of the power in the relationship stays with the marketer rather than flowing at all to the customer.[35]

This book looks at the brand as used by the Conservative movement, just as outlined, to build loyalty within its target audience segments, to expand those by appealing to the fast-growing undecided voter group, to build a network of well-supported political institutions, to promote polices, to win elections, and to define their opponents. Thus, it pays much attention to the contents of the brand and how new topics are extended into it again and again. The Conservatives have used branding to build a strong movement, as well as to quickly familiarize their target audiences with new organizations, issues, and candidates. The overall effect has been to create a movement that enjoys deep loyalty within its targeted audiences and a series of political brands that hold lasting value or equity. They do not simply use these brands at election time; rather, they use them on a regular basis to promote all sorts of things and to reinforce relationships with the audiences. This book will present a series of cases that show the ways in which Conservatives employ branding and the benefits that they have derived from doing so. Its focus is the brand rather than the techniques through which brand or political image is built.

Chapter 1 provides an explanation of branding. Chapter 2 examines the recent history of the United States and the Conservative movement in order to show branding's key role in contemporary American politics. Chapter 3 analyzes Ronald Reagan as a marketer and as a brand. This is because he has filled both functions for the Conservative movement. Chapter 4 looks at the Clinton scandals as an exercise in branded marketing. Chapter 5 looks at the contract with America, an exercise in differentiation as well as an example of why keeping the brand promise is so important. Chapter 6 looks at the way in which the George W. Bush administration branded the War on Terror, then created a line extension between it and an invasion of Iraq. Chapters 7 to 9 examine the way in which the 2004 Bush campaign used the brand strategy across media types to win an election that it should have had considerable difficulty winning. We will close in Chapter 10 with some thoughts on the overall impact that this style of politics is continuing to have on American democracy. That it did so was a testament to the power that the brand and targeted appeals have in contemporary American politics.

The brand strategy's use has let Conservatives produce a consistent message about themselves to their audiences, to reposition that message when necessary, and to build lasting relationships with their audience targets as we have just seen. It has enabled it to produce politics and politicians that fit a consistent brand story, with limited two-way communication featuring a lot of emotion, strong language, and potent pictures but little discussion of substance. While other consumer marketing techniques have contributed to this rise, insofar as they make the public aware of and loyal to the brand, this work argues that it is the brand strategy that has moved the Conservatives from the fringes of American political life to the center.[36] Its use by Conservatives is equally worth examining because it has facilitated the development of an entire movement, as well as the ideas, institutions, and individuals associated with that movement. Conservatism is, as we see, a very successful social movement as Lisa McGirr (2001) argues and part of the reason for its success is that its leaders have constantly made efforts to communicate with their audience going back to the earliest days of the modern movement as Schoenwald (2001) shows.

While this politics has served the Conservative movement very well, it is not at all clear that it has served the people or the government of the United States nearly as well. The branded politics that Conservatives have brought to the United States has resulted in the election of candidates, development of an independent media, and establishment of a large number of think tanks who owe their success to the feelings that they can produce in the public, rather than the substantive impact of the policies that they propose or the soundness of their analysis of current events. The best case in point is the man whom, we see, Conservatives have turned into a heritage brand for their movement: Ronald Reagan. Reagan helped to popularize the Conservative movement on the national stage using a political strategy that very much resembles branding. Large numbers of average Americans have, as a result, voted for politicians who enact policies that work against their substantive interests because of the highly visible, emotive way in which this policy has been presented to them. The reasons being the benefits of the policy are highly visible while its costs are not, because these policies have been bundled into a larger story about socio-cultural issues with which many of them identify have been repeatedly delivered to them in a very focused way and this is keeping with the brand strategy because, as Turow notes, the brand becomes something that the audience sees as part of their identity.[37]

The brand strategy has become a key part of the Conservative movement's success because the movement was developing at exactly the same time that consumer marketing techniques were improving and as an ethos of consumerism was taking hold across the country.[38] For a new movement to present its candidates, using the same techniques to that being used to sell other kinds of products, was an entirely logical occurrence. Richard Viguerie noted this in his 2004 book with David Franke by saying that he began working on finding ways to sell Conservatism to the American public because nobody else was, and that to do so, he spent a lot of time reading the consumer marketing literature in order to apply its teachings to the marketing of Conservative politics.[39] Through a process of trial and error, Viguerie learned how to make product marketing techniques work. As he put it, "One of the first things that I learned with Young Americans for Freedom, for example was: *stick to your brand* [italics appear in the original) (to use commercial terminology) (parenthesis appears in the original]."[40] This he figured out by doing a mailing that focused on the activities of Young Americans for

Freedom on a college campus and another on its work to elect Goldwater that made a pitch for funding.[41] The letter that worked better was the one that focused on fighting battles against the Left on college campuses, as Viguerie and Franke put it, "*That was our brand. That was our market.* [Italics original] I had not understood branding, and the importance of the image that your potential customers or donors have of you."[42] Whereas Conservatives have been using a brand strategy since the movement's early days on the national stage, all that has really changed is that some of the personalities and issues involved in specific campaigns have come and gone, while their core brand story has remained essentially unchanged. This makes it exactly like the successful corporations of recent decades of whom Klein tells us: "For these companies, the ostensible product was mere filler for the real production: the brand. They integrated the idea of brand into the very fabric of their companies."[43] As these above-noted Viguerie quotes and the cases in this book show, the Conservative movement has used the brand strategy in exactly this fashion.

Branding works in politics for the same reason that it works in all consumer marketing; it provides people with a shortcut to understand the products being sold to them.[44] As Klein notes, the brand serves an educative function and through its use "the corporate 'personality' uniquely named, packaged and advertised had arrived."[45] We can see the power of the brand in the following two examples. First, what comes to mind when you think of safe cars? The answer, as it is with the vast majority of Americans, is probably Volvo. Volvo is an example of a successful brand because it has created an association in the public mind between the company's product and one aspect of the brand story promoting that product. Volvo built public awareness of this aspect of its product through the creation and repetition of a brand story over a long period of time. Volvo is a successful brand because while the car may have styling issues, it keeps the promise that it is made for being safe.[46] This is the power of simplicity because Volvo's brand focuses on a single word.[47] The public understands the Volvo brand because of a public relations campaign that has both positioned the product and presented it in narrative terms to the audience through a wide variety of advertising and free media.[48] Volvo has developed a logo and some slogans with which consumers are familiar in support of its brand. They show the audience that Volvo's promise of safety is being kept.[49] The Volvo brand is very effective because one word sums up its characteristics or attributes.[50]

A second example of a successful brand is Nike.[51] When I mentioned the word, three things probably popped into your head. They were the phrase "Just Do It," and a visual image of a swoosh stripe, and some feelings about or toward the brand.[52] As Zyman and Miller note, the imagery built around a brand is used to set a brand apart, attract the right audience to it, give that audience a set of feelings about using and being affiliated with it; a way to build relationships in the customer's mind between brands as well as between brands and other social entities with which the marketer wants their brand associated; and one key way to shape the audience target perceptions of and relationships with the brand.[53] Nike has been successful because it has stuck with its core business: athletic equipment.[54] It has avoided the trap of adding product lines to things that are not associated with fitness. For example, there are no Nike designer jeans or Nike coffee Given that the public associates Nike with the manufacture of fitness equipment, a move in other directions may have the ability to damage the value of the brand. A brand is most valuable when it retains its focus on promoting its core products. Whereas it may seem that a brand could be expanded to appeal to all audiences, it really cannot because trying to do so will make the brand's meaning unclear and drive down its worth.[55]

Brands can either die or lose the attention of a desired audience.[56] This has happened to Volvo and it has responded by extending its brand by altering its product line slightly in order to appeal to a younger audience. In order to appeal to this new audience, Volvo brought out smaller, sportier models than it had once made and repositioned itself as being "for life" instead of being "for safety." Volvo's actions in this example show how a slight adjustment in a brand story can attract new audiences to the product and allow new products in the line to be introduced to the consumer.[57] This can be a tricky proposition because companies often upgrade their products while deemphasizing their initial difference and lose market share as a result.[58] In addition to building brand loyalty, businesses and politicians must try to find new audiences for their products. Nike and Volvo work to attract new customers for their products by trying to appeal to younger audiences (who do not have established brand loyalties) and by delving into those audience segments that fit their current consumer profile. To survive, brands must either attract new audiences for their products or add new people to their current audience[59]

As Viguerie notes,[60] the early Conservative marketers found that their branded appeals resonated more strongly with some audiences than with others. While the initial Conservative audience was older and well heeled, the movement has repositioned its brand since then to appeal to younger and more diverse audiences. Conservatives have done this by engaging in highly organized youth marketing campaigns; by targeting specific undecided audiences; and, as we saw above, by using the brand to build a lasting relationship with them. In this, Conservative branding functions very much like how audiences are sold by media outlets to advertisers because, in both cases, the end result has been a claim that a special relationship exists in which this becomes the product of choice for large swaths of the audience.[61]

The audience demographic that the marketer is trying to reach is a key aspect in building the brand.[62] Conservatives have branded their candidates, issues, and movements. Their brand tells a story, makes promises, is specifically positioned to appeal to targeted audiences, and is supported by a variety of public relations techniques including consumer advertising. Conservatives have used brands to efficiently communicate with their target audiences, to keep those audiences from questioning the Conservative story and position on issues as they emerge, and to develop a legion of faithful consumers for their various products. Branding has done for Conservatives what it did for Nike or Volvo. Just as it did for these companies, the brand strategy helped the Conservative movement to teach the public about its products, build a bigger and more loyal audience for those products, and move the producer from small to big player status in their industry. The use of the brand strategy means that Conservatives are, as we see, trying to win the fight over time even if they do not win every battle in it.[63] The brand strategy makes Nike a leader in the footwear trade, Volvo dominant in the safe car category, and Conservatives a much bigger player in American politics than it would have seemed possible in 1960.

While various Democrats have mounted single-shot campaigns to brand themselves, the party has not successfully mounted such an effort in the same long-term way that Conservatives have and, as a result, their party suffers from communicative problems. Further it is not clear that the Democrats have as focused or as large a number of lifestyle niches at which they can target market their brand in the way that we saw Conservatives could in the earlier explanations. Since the Conservative movement has consistently used the brand strategy during its dominance of the Republican Party, the public understands what that party believes in, that it has come to dominate several issue categories, that the movement has Ronald Reagan as its public face, and that the net upshot has been to give the public a good sense of who is in the party and if they should be in it.

Republicans have been working with branding for over forty years and, as a result, they now begin each election cycle with an enormous advantage over their opponents who must develop a new marketing strategy each time. In short, brand strategy has given the Conservatives the advantage of speed.[64] Since the Democrats have not mounted a consistent effort to brand themselves, they have not built the same identity within the audience that Conservatives have. It is not always clear what the Democrats stand for, to whom they are talking, or that individual Democrats are in any way part of a larger political force. In short, they have not used brand strategy to define their movement or the future that it is proposing for the country in the way that Conservatives have.[65]

Branding has transformed the Conservatives into a majority within the Republican Party and for this reason this work speaks of Conservatives instead of Republicans because that party has simply become the vehicle through which Conservatives market their ideas.[66] Brand strategy, in turn, has helped Conservatives gain control of the presidency for all but eight years during the period from 1980 to 2008, the House of Representatives from 1994 onward, and the Senate for much of the same period.

While this has been good for Conservatives, it poses a major threat to our traditional understanding of participation in a democratic society.[67] In a representative democracy, a normal expectation is that the citizens are active participants in and observers of public affairs. The brand turns that relationship on its head because it offers the public a set of issues and leaders that are packaged for consumption.[68] The voice of the citizen is neither necessary nor encouraged in a branded politics beyond the extent to which citizens consume a given political product and, on some occasions, tell their friends about it. The second problem is that branding undermines the need for the citizen to really have much information about the facts of the government's activities or the implications of the policies being proposed by political leaders. Instead of sober assessments of the policy and leadership options available to it, the brand encourages the public to take the shortcut of buying into a story and a packaged version of events. The implication of the brand is that its continued use will produce the kind of politics without citizens[69] and in which the public is reduced from a participant in a democratic process to a consumer of a branded political product.

Brands and Conservatism: A Happy Marriage

In order to make the point that Conservatives have enjoyed great success because they brand, it must first be noted that American politics in the contemporary age has shifted from one based on grassroots organization to one based on the use of mass marketing techniques.[70] One of the key techniques used to market politics is the brand. Some argue that brand is a product of blurring ideological distinctions in the United States, but I argue that, in addition to using it to attract undecided voters, Conservatives have used it to build an identity to which their audiences have become loyal.[71] Second, it is necessary to answer the following question: what is branding and how does it fit into a marketed politics? First, branding fits into a marketed politics because it is a key part of most product marketing campaigns aimed at consumers in the United States. Companies brand their products, just like politicians, parties, and interest groups brand because of the noisy, crowded marketplace in which they find themselves. Producers use brands in this environment because they efficiently summarize a product and its features, help to differentiate one product from another, and can give the consumer a strong emotional attachment to a given product that can last for years.

Second, a branded politics fits the highly individualistic, empathetic, experience-oriented, and lifestyle-defined culture found in the contemporary United States.[72] Brands have great power in an age of niche marketing in which people self-identify as members of specific lifestyle groups. They are tools that let marketers tell their audience that the company too is a member of their community or that use of the product will confer membership in that community. They are not, however, fully democratic because they do not allow for the recipient to participate in the development of their contents. What the target gets to decide is whether they are interested in buying into the branded political product or not. All else is determined by the people mounting the marketing campaign supporting the brand.[73]

Third, branding works well to set one product apart from the others in a crowded, competitive marketplace. There are more products and more kinds of products available now than ever before. Branding can teach the public about the product, what its unique selling proposition is, and can set it apart from other similar products in a way that gets the public to purchase it[74] and can best be described as "a more efficient way to sell things."[75] A successful brand story can help a company build enduring customer loyalty that extends across generations and through several product cycles.[76] This is exactly what Conservatives have used it to do: sell their movement, their candidates, their policies, and their institutions.

In politics, branding is useful because there are now more groups churning out more information about politics, politicians, and public policy than ever before in the United States and there are more media outlets through which these groups can get their message out.[77] Conservatives have used branding to set themselves apart from their fellow Republicans and from their Democratic opponents. The first step to building a successful brand is to differentiate oneself from one's competitors.[78] Conservatives have done so and, as a result, their movement has a clear identity for themselves, their issues, and their candidates that neither the liberal Republicans nor the Democrats have been able to create for themselves. At the same time, Conservatives have used branding as a shortcut that lets them explain their issues and candidates to the public more quickly.

Fourth, brands allow marketers to reach and build relationships with a target audience. There are few mass audience events in the United States anymore. All other events attract niche audiences that marketers can study through segmentation tools like the PRIZM system.[79] The use of brand strategy makes perfect sense for politicians because brands are a way to target specific audience segments and build loyalty within them over a long period of time.[80] Brands are tools that can be adjusted to show a target audience that the underlying product fits with their lifestyle and that the target audience should be interested in that product. Thus, it is important for a brand to have a story that fits the lifestyle experience that it is purporting to tout and to be sure that the story is appropriate for the community being targeted. Conservatives, as we will see, have built such a narrative.

Fifth, brands are visual in two ways. First, every brand has a logo or visual image associated with it. For example, Pillsbury has the doughboy, Volkswagen has the letters v and w interlaced within a circle, and Coca-Cola has its name famously written in script across its label.[81] Given the emphasis on the visual image that has developed in American politics since television came on the scene, it should hardly be surprising that political brands have developed the same kinds of visual stimuli to make their point that other kinds of consumer products have developed.[82] The second way that branding is a visual phenomenon is that it puts pictures into the heads of the audience targets.[83] Not only can the audience supply the meaning for this picture but it can also be supplied by the repetition of the brand story and proof that the promises made in the brand story have been kept.

Sixth, branding has also produced a core audience for Conservatism that is not likely to be dissuaded from support even in the face of the movement's obvious failures. The audiences that buy into branded Conservatism will always support it, as long as the failings appearing before their eyes can be explained away as the fault of those elements of American life that Conservatism's brand story has demonized. Thus, in addition to being a tool to reach the fast-growing independent or undecided voters,[84] I argue that Conservatives have used branding to create lasting relationships in order to reduce their dependence on the former. The brand quickly explains how each Conservative product it is supporting fits into the overall product line. As a result, the Conservatives have used branding to produce strong attachments to their political products, reinforce partisan loyalty, and move their audience targets through a variety of products over the course of a lifetime much as do commercial marketers.

Doing so offers them the potential to tap into a more dedicated, deeper audience and reduces, in turn, their need to attract as many undecided voters. We can see this in the sometimes noted point that Conservative voters seem to be less amenable to factual persuasion than are other voters. Since they buy into a branded politics, the facts are not nearly as important to them as are the feelings that they hold about the party, its candidates, and its issues.[85]

That the brand has become a tool of political communication is not surprising when we consider the importance of the visual image and the ethos of consumerism in modern American culture. In other words, branding is one of the tools that has come to be used to sell politics in what Neil Postman (1986) termed the videographic age[86] and of which Cohen (2003) has written. In the contemporary American political system, the public generally perceives little difference between candidates and parties.[87] Conservatives have solved this problem with their core audience as noted earlier and have used the brand strategy to differentiate themselves from Democrats with persuadable audience targets. This kind of thing goes well beyond what Jamieson (1996) examined in her wonderful study of presidential advertising because it involves communication across a wide variety of channels toward very specific audiences.[88] Brands can be supported by advertising, but as we just noted, there are a wide variety of communicative channels for distributing them and achieving brand loyalty. Before moving onto an examination of how a branded politics works, it is important that we have a clear sense of what a brand is and what it is not.

But What Is a Brand?

A brand builds images in people's minds about a product or, for our purposes, politicians or public policies. It is both objective and subjective, given meaning by the marketer and by the consumer. It is an important communicative tool that allows people to understand the person, product, or issue in question ideally in the way that the marketer wants it to be seen. It has great value in modern America because, as Ries and Ries (2002) put it, "the power of a brand lies in its ability to influence purchasing behavior. But a brand name on a package is not the same as a brand name in a mind."[89] It is powerful because it can communicate a lot of information quickly and, by doing so, helps simplify the choices that people have to make in a confusing world.[90] It is somewhat like the symbols of which Murray Edelman (1964) wrote when he noted that symbols have the capacity to sum up an event or series of events in the political world for the public. The difference between a brand and a symbol is that a brand is something that is specifically designed to do this, often through the extensive use of market research; is intentionally disseminated through a wide variety of channels to make sure that the public understands its content, certain aspects of which can be emphasized over others depending on the circumstances and audience at hand; and can be built into something of lasting value. It is like a symbol because it sums up an event, but not like one whose meaning is developed by social or elite consensus about an event, because its meaning is the result of a specific intent on the part of the producer to tap into beliefs held by the audience and associate their product with those beliefs.[91] The audience may have a good deal to do with ascribing meaning to an event and then turning that into a symbol but, in the case of brands, the audience need only decide if it likes the brand story that a more elite group has designed for its consumption.

Brands differ from symbols because brands have specific stories that marketers develop in order to show the target that the product fits with their beliefs. Marketers construct the brand to tell a specific story and make specific promises. The story and promises are important ways in which marketers try to produce appropriate feelings about the product among the audience. For example, while Pearl Harbor and the Vietnam War produce specific sets of feelings among Americans, it is mostly because of the symbolic meaning of these events as people have agreed upon them. The Nike brand and logo, however, have a strong chance of producing exactly the feelings in the targeted group that the marketer intends.[92] The brand story and promise are constructed in a way that allows them to tap into what is already in the prospect's mind.

The Conservative brand, its supporting story, and promise do for Conservatives what branding does in general: lets them teach the public about their product and the way that it differs from other available ones in the crowded marketplace. The need to differentiate becomes more important over time because generally the earliest brands to fill a market category tend to end up dominating that category, especially when they are able to focus to the point that their brand becomes a generic term for the entire category.[93] Being first or nearly first allows an entrepreneur to own the category in which they are working and this gives other entrepreneurs the problem of finding a market niche.[94] Branding is one key way through which differentiation can be accomplished.[95] Positioning is a device through which marketers define the dialogue and outline the area of the market in which they wish to compete.[96]

Those who did not want to differentiate could either become faster at distributing a similar product or develop a similar product with some unique features.[97] Through branding, goals could be accomplished, a kind of fellowship could be built between products, and the overall category could be made stronger.[98] We can see why so many politicians, organizations, and policies are now branded as Conservative and why the Democrats will have a difficult time claiming the mantle of centrism or moderation for their own use. In the former case, more conservative political infrastructure and communicative structure emerged as it became clear that there was a marketplace to support it. In the second case, the marketing problem that the Democrats have had with their rightward shift is that they run into territory already occupied by Conservatives who can correctly claim that they were there first and that the Democrats have arrived late to the party or, even worse, are dishonest.[99] The second impact that Conservative positioning has had on Democratic definition efforts is that its use has enabled Conservatives to narrow the focus of the public debate and public impressions about Democrats to a few topics that have generally amounted to an emphasis on liberalism.[100]

The brand strategy has become more important in all sorts of product marketing, including politics, during the last couple of decades not only because of a competitive marketplace but also because of a faster lifestyle, dual career couples, longer commutes, and longer workdays.[101] As Lance Bennett showed,[102] several of these factors were directly related to the decline in social participation that Putnam noted and of which it was suggested above the impetus for political branding comes. The need to be efficient and to have a device to highlight specific parts of the story of a politician, organization, or policy's story is driven by the decline of a mass market in the country. Brands are useful devices because relevant aspects of their story and promise can be mentioned to specific audiences.[103] Brands are one way through which marketers differentiate their products from one another. The importance of differentiating one product from others has become more important as the number of products on the market and the amount of background noise in American life have increased.[104] By building a highly recognizable brand, the product marketer saves time in the future because it will no longer be necessary to educate the public about every aspect of an individual product or even about new products other than to say that the new product is related to the established ones.[105] Conservatives clearly do this when introducing new candidates and proposals and their organizations will generally take great pains to explain how they have some relationship to one of the brands in the product line. Brands are useful marketing tools because they save time for the consumer as Travis notes.[106] This is because the brand and its story have familiarized consumers with the product, its story, and its promises.[107] Unbranded products, and politicians for that matter, must overcome an initial education and public skepticism phase with which branded products do not have to deal.

A brand can give someone who has little time information that can be used to help to decide which product to buy. Since the brand has been built over time and we know that it keeps its promise, we can buy a product without doing much research about it. Branding allows a movement to build a reputation about itself with the audience and perceptions about it within that audience. Delving into a theme that parallels one of the chapters of this book, Travis (2000) notes,

> Just look at President William Jefferson Clinton. Consider him for a moment as a brand. Despite a very good performance record, his reputation as "Slick Willie" appears to be written on a slate that he can never wipe clean. It started in the primaries and continued to dog him even before he came a cropper with his second-term indiscretions.[108]

Like all brands, the Clinton one built on the aspects of the product that serve the marketer's ends. As we see later, in the Clinton case, his opponents consistently worked with the negative aspects of his character and sought to always point out incidents that supported these perceptions within their targeted portion of the electorate. Other examples that proved Mr. Clinton was a man of low character came to be included in the anti-Clinton marketing campaign but nothing that ever stressed the good aspects of Mr. Clinton appeared in it. Doing so would have reduced the effectiveness of the brand story being developed by Conservatives around Mr. Clinton.

This is because brands are particularly effective with consumers who are either totally unsophisticated about a given product or know only a bit about it. This is an apt description of the level of knowledge that most Americans presently have about politics. A brand strategy is ideally suited for this environment because it quickly gives the public a sense of knowledge about, attachment to, and trust in a given political product. Just as it does in other aspects of American consumer culture, political brands give voters a sense that they have enough information to make an informed decision about a political product.

Brands and Archetypes: A Deeper Meaning

Brand strategies work in American politics because they fit with modern American culture. Contemporary culture does not work with analytical approaches to politics nor does it encourage its targets to be analytical in their political outlook. Like other types of marketers, those selling politics seek to establish connections with their prospects and those building brands try to establish enduring connections. As Mark and Pearson (2001) have noted, "today the brand has become a repository, not merely of functional characteristics, but of meaning and value."[109] The most successful brands have become what they term "archetypes."[110] Successful brands and products are so because they sum up such archetypical meaning for the viewer, they have a symbolic meaning that is much deeper than the product being sold.[111] Brands have had to take on archetypical meanings for much the same reason as political candidates have had to brand themselves in recent years: huge increases have taken place in the number of competitors in the marketplace for most products just as huge increases in the number of voices and ideas vying for the public's attention in the political arena have taken place.[112] They go on to note that brands that had acquired such strong meaning were more valued from the investor community's perspective because the brand is able to become "a consistent enduring expression of meaning—essentially becoming a brand icon" in its own right.[113] Brands become archetypes because they serve the deep needs in the customer's psyche. They argue that archetypes "signal the fulfillment of basic human desires and release deep emotions and yearnings."[114] They draw upon the work of several scholars in the field of psychology, most notably Abraham Maslow.[115] As they put it, "archetypes mediate between products and customer motivation by providing an intangible experience of meaning."[116] The concept of archetypal brands that they explore in consumer product marketing is equally applicable to politics. We can see this in the meaning that Conservative marketers have given to the movement when presenting it to their target audience. By establishing and advancing the story, Conservatives make their brand stronger and cement their relationship with the audience, as well as the audience's relationship with them.

Building these kinds of strong connections is particularly important in a society like the modern United States that, as we saw earlier, has been slowly fracturing into a number of much more focused lifestyle niches.[117] The importance of the brand and especially of archetypal brands has expanded in the United States because the former social consensus has been filled by entertainment and marketing businesses.[118] The upshot being that,

> we are creating meaning without managing meaning. It is no wonder then that the public appetite for meaning, particularly archetypal meaning is so strong that archetypal brands, in the form of personalities, public figures and corporate officers are fervently embraced and defended.[119]

Conservatives regularly work with several of the archetypal categories that Mark and Pearson have developed. They are explorer, hero, outlaw, regular guy, caregiver, and the ruler. We can see this in the way that the 2004 Bush campaign was able to present its candidate as a regular guy, in the way in which government reduction has been presented as both a chance to let people take care of their own needs and be freer (explorer), as well as in the way in which it has been presented as being contrary to the wishes of the liberal elite (transforming it into an outlaw archetype). We can see it in the way in which Ronald Reagan was branded as a combination of the explorer, hero, and regular guy archetypes best symbolized by the numerous pictures of Reagan either wearing a white cowboy hat, riding a horse or both. It has been with these archetypes that the Conservative movement has had its best success in building brands that can win elections. On the other hand, it has experienced setbacks when it has worked with the ruler archetype (as with the case with the first President Bush). By building brands that work with cultural archetypes, the Conservative movement is able to build a strong bond with its audience, quickly fit new individuals and issues into its marketing strategy, and quickly give its audience a sense of what the movement is both all about and what it wants this time.

Brands work not only because they are shortcuts to knowledge but also because they are able to produce product images and identities, as well as strong feelings in their target audience.[120] As Daryl Travis (2000) has pointed out, the value of the brand lies in the emotions with which people associate it. Travis's argument to businesses is that, in a real sense, the brand is the business and that brands carry a high level of what he terms emotional equity.[121] The same point is true of political campaigns and candidates. Those that use brand strategies can develop a lasting message to which people respond emotively rather than analytically.[122] A person with strong feelings about a branded politician, organization or policy will be very difficult indeed to shift from his or her position via the use of factual analysis. Quoting Scott Bedbury, a former Nike and Starbucks employee who now works as a consultant, Travis notes that a brand functions like a story and that new products can be introduced by building fellowship with older products when he says,

> A great brand is a metaphorical story that's evolving all the time. This connects with something very deep—a fundamental human appreciation of mythology. People have always needed to make sense of things at a higher level. We all want to think that we are part of something bigger than ourselves. Companies that manifest that sensibility in their employees and consumers invoke something very powerful.[123]

That political campaigns attempt to build "metaphorical stories that's evolving all the time" is obvious. Consider how Bill Clinton told his personal story in a way that fitted it into deeply held American values, Ronald Reagan regularly referred to the country as a "Shining City on a Hill," and George Bush presents himself as an average guy with strong values just like Reagan did.

Once these brand stories make an emotional connection with the public, the facts do not matter unless there are obvious examples in which reality does not match the brand story. For example, Democrats have neither been able to convince the public of the imprudence of the Bush fiscal policy nor been able to inflict a political cost for the failure to find weapons of mass destruction in Iraq because the consequence of these failures is not very visible in the first case, and the Bush team changed its point of emphasis on Iraq from finding weapons of mass destruction to building freedom (a conservative archetype) and fighting terror overseas instead of at home. In the case of Hurricane Katrina, the administration suffered tremendous political damage because it presented the public with a highly visible case in which Bush's brand promise could clearly be seen not to have been kept. A second example is provided by the comparison between the Clinton and the Iran-Contra scandals. In the former case, Republicans were damaged; however, they used their brand to change the public's focus. In the latter case, consistent with the argument above, Conservatives supported Clinton's impeachment while most of the country thought that the case being used as its base was inappropriate.[124] In the Iran-Contra case, it was obvious that whatever the White House's good intentions regarding the promotion of democracy in the hemisphere and fighting communism were, the Reagan administration had acted in a way that was not consistent with its brand story, was damaged, but found a way to reposition its brand. While there were a number of other cases in which the Reagan administration had acted in ways that were ethically and legally questionable, they were not nearly visible enough to put the lie to the brand story in quite the same way as the high visible Iran-Contra scandal did.

Building the metaphorical story is a way for marketers to establish a connection with the audience. By working with archetypes, marketers can help the prospect build strong feelings about the brand. As Travis notes, consumers develop deep feelings about the brands that they purchase[125] and associating a product with a favorable set of emotions constitutes one way to better sell it. As Travis notes, the brand is about what people think and feel more than they do about the product itself.[126] As he nicely put it, "a brand is made in your head and heart . . . brands are sold one at a time, and they are sold by F-E-E-L-I-N-G-S."[127] Creating a set of favorable feelings in the prospect's mind can have the effect of creating "customer evangelists."[128] Once the customer develops a favorable set of feelings about the brand, the company will benefit from the sense of loyalty toward and ownership of the product on which a company can trade for years to come.[129] As we see American politics has become about the kinds of feelings around which brands are built and can become archetypes.[130]

We can see this in the way in which Conservatives have run campaigns around issues like gay marriage and abortion that, while about policy on some level, are for the bulk of the population more about feelings than substance. Issues are only useful in such a politics to the extent that they support the overall feelings promoted by the brand. Should voters become positively inclined toward a brand, then it would be wise for politicians of the party that first promoted that to affiliate themselves with it. This is exactly what has happened in the Republican Party. Voters have the working understanding and feeling for the Conservative brand that they also have for commercial brands. These feelings have been reinforced and employed to elect Republican candidates via the use of multilevel marketing techniques in the 2004 election and, to some extent, the Contract with America.[131] In the commercial world, a powerful brand has the potential to greatly enhance sales.[132] Political brands have the ability to win individual elections, build movements, and perpetuate that movement over time. Travis notes that a brand really is "an unwritten contract of intrinsic value, an expectation of performance, a covenant of goodness with its users, is predictable, is an unwritten warranty, is a mark of integrity, is a presentation of credentials, is a mark of trust and reduced risk, is a reputation, is a collection of memories, and can be more than the sum of all of these parts."[133] This is particularly what has happened with the term Conservative over the last two decades but has, by extension, been applied to a host of political products in the movement's line.

As Schoenwald's 2001 book shows, it took Conservatives a long period of time to move from their position at the end of World War II to the one in which they currently sit. The benefit of this long gestation period is that the public is well educated about and some parts of it strongly attached to Conservative politicians and policies that make up the brand. Conservatives have developed a hard-core audience for whom little factual analysis is required to know what the Conservative policy is made up of, who the Conservative candidate is, and what the Conservative organization promotes is correct. That this has created a situation in which a group of political elites have found a means through which they can secure their candidates' election and get their desired policies onto the national agenda is clear when we consider how brands and the stories supporting them are built.

Branding: Framing's Next Level

While political scientists have devoted a great deal of time to the ideas of frames and pseudoevents, they have not devoted nearly as much attention to the concept of branding. Serious students of politics and the casual observer can benefit from learning about the ways in which the branded politics found in America works. There are a number of reasons why this is so. First, many political consultants come from a consumer marketing background and understand their activities in those terms. Second, the brand is the key tool that has allowed Conservatives to easily introduce different candidates, policies, and organizations to the American public. Third, without this understanding, it will be difficult for political scientists to fully understand how Conservative politics works in America.

It is important to note what political science has correctly figured out in order to show how the branding concept could augment these understandings. Thus, our tale about the Conservative brand strategy would not be complete without examining the concept with which most political scientists are most familiar: the frame. The framing concept can augment our understanding of the way in which branded politics works and, by doing so, improve our understanding of the ways in which participants in the political spectacle try to hit their audience targets. While branding is not, per se, framing, the two concepts can work symbiotically to enhance our understanding of the way in which Conservatives have built a successful movement and created loyalty within their audiences. In order to show how this can be, we need to know how a brand is similar, differs from, and can work with a frame. Brands tend to develop strong essences and enduring equity. Frames, on the other hand, can have enduring meaning but do not usually enjoy the kind of lasting value that a brand can develop over time. Second, while frames can inadvertently develop an essence or some value, brands gain these things through the hard work of their designers. This distinction leads to the third difference between frames and brands: the analysis of frames usually deals with the way in which the audience understands the frame and less with the way in which the political marketer shaped its contents (see, for example, Jamieson and Waldman, 2003). This is because branding is the technique used by the organization promoting a political product, whereas a frame is the means through which the target audience sees the event.

While political scientists understand that message discipline is important in campaigns, they seem not to understand the ultimate goal of it: build a brand, fitting something new into an established brand or emphasizing a specific aspect of a brand at a given moment in time or to a given audience. We can see how politicians understand the value of a brand and the key role that repetition and adjustment to circumstances plays in making it successful or to reposition it when we remember the many problems to which the Bush tax cuts were presented as the solution during the early part of the first George W. Bush administration. At various times they served as a cure-all for a consumer spending slump, economic slowdown, and the effects of a major terrorist incident. Seventh, branding is about a lot more than free and paid media coverage. It is about building an enduring identity around a product line. When we look at the way in which the contemporary Conservative movement presents itself and its ideas to the public, we can see that there is much more involved than buying advertising and a daily quest for free media coverage. There is the creation of a branded product that will endure even after the individuals, organizations, and policies for which the brand is currently in use have left the national stage. The development of branded political products has been one of the key means through which Conservatives have developed lasting relationships with those segments of the electorate whose votes they rely on to win office.

A frame can be a single shot or deal with a single issue but it rarely takes on equity and essence as does a brand. Advertising, particularly over a lengthy period of time, is the most common way that product marketers build up an essence around and equity in their brands, but brands can be pushed through a wide variety of marketing channels. As Bennett shows, companies are delighted to take advertising in the form of news coverage and will send out video news releases and b-roll (pictures without an accompanying soundtrack), in some cases, along with scripts for local reporters to read.[134] Just as is true for politics, corporate brands are built by much more than advertising. Just like politicians, private concerns stress the value of repetition in order to build a brand that the consumer will develop either a favorable feeling toward or a sense of ownership about. For example, the anti-Clinton campaign was much like any other kind of brand-based marketing campaign because it was rolled out segment by segment. It failed because, as noted above, it could not convince a general audience to buy into its narrative. Branding efforts can fail if the brand story is not correctly told, if the branded product is not sufficiently differentiated from rivals or if the brand loses its focus.[135]

A better way to understand how the framing and branding concepts can work together is provided by Kathleen Hall Jamieson and Paul Waldman in their fine book *The Press Effect* (2003). Applying the frames-and-lenses approach that they employ, we can see that what frequently is framed and seen through the viewer's lenses are brands. The frames-and-lenses model is a rough equivalent to the frame of reference that product marketers employ to encourage their customers to think about a product in a given way.[136] A brand's frame of reference or competitive framework is intended to help the customer figure out what the product is and what other products it could take the place of while still meeting their needs.[137] Framing is, as just noted, an important part of the branding process because it allows marketers to fit their product into the consumer's world and provide a clear understanding to them about what the product is, what it does, what is unique about it, and how it differs from other available products even if it is like them in some ways. Like other kinds of product marketers, political marketers adjust aspects of their brands to fit into specific subject areas about which the target audience cares at any given moment. Sometimes the marketer can raise a subject, sometimes the media can, sometimes the target audience can, but the point is that when a subject comes up, some political marketers have a brand that they can insert into the discussion. By fitting the brand to the current frame of reference, the marketer makes it easier for the audience to understand how the subjects, candidates, policies, and organizations being sold at the time solve the problems of the moment.

Another very useful study that outlines the way in which framing works with the brand strategy is George Lakoff's 2004 work *Don't Think of an Elephant!: Know Your Values and Frame the Debate*. In addition to describing the way in which frames work and their importance in setting the terms under which debates and marketing campaigns can be conducted, he is also implicitly explaining the importance of having a clear brand story when selling issues. Lakoff's key contribution is to note the good use to which Conservatives have made of building a set of value-based frames around which they market themselves.[138] One example of the way in which Conservatives have employed values to make their points is provided by Karl Rove's speech to the 2005 Conservative Political Action Conference in which he argued that Conservatives were successful because "we are defending time honored values"[139] and that "Conservatives have long known that political liberty depends on a healthy social and moral order."[140]

What Lakoff does not do in his book that Rove did in his speech is move on to draw a clear link between these values and Conservative public policy proposals. Rove did it in the next line of his speech by arguing that Bush was working

> to strengthening society's key institutions: families, schools, communities. And he
> is committed to protecting those mediating structures so important to our free-

dom, like our churches, our neighborhood and private groups, the institutions that shape character, that provide our young with moral education. That is why this president supports welfare reform that strengthens families and requires work. That is why he supported and our movement supports adoption and responsible father-hood initiatives. That is why he is committed to building a culture of life and uphold-ing the dignity of every human person, and seeks a world in which every child is welcomed in life and protected in law (applause).[141]

Rove then extended the brand story to show specific Conservative con-stituencies exactly how they were benefited by their support for Conservative politicians and policies:

And that is why he's provided unprecedented support for religious charities that provide a safety net of mercy and compassion. And it is why this president sup-ports the protection of traditional marriage against activist judges; why he signed legislation that insists on testing, high standards and accountability in our pub-lic schools; and why he's helped foster a culture of service and citizenship.[142]

Having both reiterated the link between the brand story's promises being made and kept, Rove then closed by reminding the audience about what the end goals of their movement and the administration were in personal terms, much as we see Ronald Reagan once did:

He believes in these things because he knows that they will lead to a society that is more compassionate and free and decent and stronger and better. And we are attempting to match that with a spread of liberty abroad because we must show that we are worthy of liberty at home.[143]

We can see how values form the basis of the Conservative brand through the above, as well as the ways in which Conservatives link their policies and politicians to specific aspects of the brand story at any given point in time. What this passage from Karl Rove shows is just what Lakoff points out in his work and what was mentioned above: these value-based frames become political brands because they tap into the deep feelings that a target audience holds about the subject matter.

The passage above shows how Conservatives build narratives that tap into larger narratives, the meaning of which is provided in some part by the audi-ence, and that the political products marketed by Conservative politicians have some kind of relationship to these things. What the Rove quote further shows is that, while frames and values are keys to political success, they only matter in-so-far as they can be built into something that resonates with and builds loyalty within the audience. The passage above shows exactly how Conservatives moved from broad value-based frames to brands and used those to create a successful social movement. Conservatives do not just do things on an ad hoc basis; their frames and rhetoric are part of an overall marketing strategy that includes a narrative. In this, the value-based frames that Lakoff speaks of fit well with the brand strategy.

For progressives and others outside the Conservative movement, the path to political power does not just consist of a matter of building a better marketing strategy and rolling that out to a few more segments in order to capture enough votes to win an election. Instead, these movements must do as Conservatives have done by using frames in order to shape the debate.[144] The Conservatives have developed a set of value, or archetypal brands to put into the frame. The path to political power for progressives and others rests a good bit more on finding frames, narratives, and personalities about which brands can be built; employing contrast marketing techniques to accentuate the difference between brands; showing the audiences that promises made have been kept; that it consists of just finding more personable candidates, more activists, new marketing techniques; and having more money with which to run public relations campaigns. Mary Matalin, speaking on "NBC News' Meet the Press" on November 14, 2004, explained the progress that Conservatives had made in recent decades in winning elections:

> But there's also a generational thing going on here as well. It started about in the '60s but accelerating in the '80s when I came to town with President Reagan, the Democrats controlled every level of government and now the Republicans control the Senate, the House, the governors, and most importantly the legislative chambers. It's 50–50 now, which is the bench. And in the Democratic Senate chamber, 15 of the—a third of the Democratic senators are from red states. So those people—Bush increased his margins in the red states. He also increased his margins exponentially in the blue states, in New York, in Massachusetts, in New Jersey, in Rhode Island, in Hawaii, in Connecticut.[145]

It is the brand story and the years of repetition of that brand story that enables Conservatives to present themselves, their candidates, institutions, and issues in a way that has built enduring loyalty to them. The brand story that does so rests upon a set of values and is understood through a series of frames that is provided by both voters and political marketers. Otherwise, the voters will have a difficult time understanding what a party stands for, what its values are, and how those have been consistent over time. This is exactly the situation in which the Democrats, who have not made lasting use of the brand strategy, and the Republicans, who have, currently find themselves.

Frames and brands are not hostile concepts; rather, they are symbiotic. The frame is one of the key building blocks for the brand without which the branded strategy that Conservatives have ridden to political glory would not work nearly as well. Since the audience sees the world outside themselves through a series of frames, political marketers fit their branded messages into those frames to have their greatest impact.

Conservatives have been able to develop a strong relationship with specific parts of the electorate because of the brand equity that they have built around their products. Conservatives have had this success because they have turned individuals and broad areas of their issue agenda into brands to promote their political fortunes, as well as their policy agenda.[146] Two examples of Conservative branded individuals are Ronald Reagan (now the heritage brand for Conservatism) and George W. Bush (a.k.a., W). Branding individuals lets the Conservative movement put a happy face on its products, helps to personalize its products, and, by fitting these individuals into a populist character, have encouraged large segments of the public to feel that their interests are served by Conservative politicians and to think that Conservative politicians are just like them. Conservatives also like to work with branded policy proposals and generally have experienced good success in doing so when they have had branded individuals promoting branded initiatives. Three examples are the Reagan revolution (Ronald Reagan), the Contract with America (Newt Gingrich), and the War on Terror (George W. Bush), and sometimes one is used to sell the other. For example, Grover Norquist has been quoted by the television program *Frontline* as saying that George W. Bush ran in 2000 "standing on political structures that had been built, but standing directly next to Reagan in terms of worldview"[147] in 2000.

These people speak to an audience that knows them, is usually favorably disposed toward them, and, thus, trusts their judgment when new persons and things are introduced. Conservatives brand to promote domestic and foreign policies, candidates, all sorts of political organizations, and their political opponents. In the following chapters we see the various ways in which Conservatives have done so. For now here are some examples: the response to 9/11 was branded as the "War on Terror," a coordinated campaign to gain a majority in the House of Representatives was branded the "Contract with America," and a branded individual, W also known as George W. Bush, was able to win two terms in the White House in large part by talking about personal attributes.

Conservatives have used the branding technique to market their domestic policy as well. They have presented their plans for changing the national government's role in education (the No Child Left Behind Act), old age pensions (Strengthening Social Security), and dramatic changes in the structure of American economic life (as Reaganomics or Economic Growth and Opportunity depending on the Conservatives in question). Doing this efficiently promotes policies and builds relationships. For example, during the Bush years, the White House Web site has regularly contained links to the branded initiatives being promoted by the administration. When clicked on, these links opened to a page of material promoting each branded initiative.

Given that branding has such power and has been used to good effect in politics, it is important for students of politics to understand the concept and how it works. Conservative politicians use branding for exactly the same reasons that we noted other kinds of product marketers use it. Like their commercial marketers, politicians face a large number of competitors for public attention. The number of media channels through which a brand can be distributed is greater now than it once was.[148] The brand is a useful tool in a fragmenting media environment.[149] This is exactly the kind of environment in which commercial marketers have made effective use of the brand strategy and we should not be surprised to find that the political movement that has made the most use of it has been more successful in this environment.

Conservatives have gotten much better at the use of consumer marketing techniques in politics since their early days; some even argue that they perfected their use in 1980.[150] Since Conservatives have worked with marketing and branding strategies for such a long time now, their brands have developed considerable equity and this means that it is easier for Conservatives to reach voters than is the case for Democrats. This saves time for Conservatives that can, in turn, be applied to figuring out what aspects of their own brand to emphasize in a general election, figuring out how to brand their opponent or both. One piece of evidence that supports this is that the Conservative scores on National Election Studies feeling thermometers have not dipped below 55 during the period from 1984 onward whereas the liberal scores on the same indicator have not risen above 55 during the same period.[151]

We can see the value of branding and the way in which it is capable of building up consumer brand loyalty when we consider the fact that a Bush or Dole has been on every Republican presidential ticket since 1976. Having these familiar individuals on the ticket saves the party time because the voters to whom they are pitching their partisan products are already familiar with and trust them. The same can be said for the consistency with which the Republican Party has worked with what it has termed a conservative issue agenda over the last thirty years. When Conservatives work with new issues and candidates, they do so by fitting them into the established brands they have built in a few key areas. By doing this, new issues and personalities can be sold quickly, something that the unbranded Democrats cannot do. In short, the brand strategy allows the Conservatives to take a line extension approach as new candidates and policies need to be promoted and build loyalty within their targeted audiences.[152]

The Republican Party, Think Tanks, and Interest Groups Brand Because . . .

In addition to candidates, political parties, interest groups, and office holders all brand public policies and political activities at present.[153] In order to understand from where the impetus to brand comes from, we need to look at the nature of the modern political party, the contemporary interest group, and the think tank. All three of these kinds of organizations rely heavily on their ability to sell people things in order to stay in business and, as a result, it is reasonable to suggest that a product marketing model and a branded strategy are easy means through which this goal can be accomplished.

Regarding the political party and electoral process, it is reasonable to consider voters to be akin to consumers and politicians to be equivalent to manufacturers in the present American system.[154] Political parties exist to serve the needs of politicians.[155] Thus, branding and marketing become important activities for both parties and politicians. The voters can be thought of in this construction as the receivers of these messages. Electoral outcomes at the presidential level since 1988 have shown no national consensus on either issue salience or partisan identification. It is true that, relative to a half-century ago, there are more individuals who self-identify as Conservatives and regional shifts have clearly taken place. Aldrich's breakthrough lies in focusing on the role of the party as organization and in government. By doing so, he effectively allocates a consumer role to voters.[156] The next step for such organizations is to adopt a marketing model as was noted above and the step beyond that would be to adopt a branding strategy, something that we have seen political parties do.

Branding helps parties build unique identities for themselves and their products that differ from other parties'. It is for this reason that branded appeals are often made by using a good deal of contrast marketing and position-ing.[157] Branding lets parties, interest groups, and think tanks present their ideas quickly to a public that does not always pay attention between elections, as well as in a way that will activate those parts of the audience that pay atten-tion all the time but might not always participate.

We can see why Conservatives brand when we look briefly at the Clinton scandals. By developing the Slick Willie brand, the Republican Party was able to (1) offset its losses of the national security and economic issues that have traditionally put them into office, (2) draw a sharp contrast between par-ties at exactly the time that the Democratic Leadership Council was trying to reposition the Democrats as a party of Moderates, (3) provide a basis upon which the Contract with America might be sold, (4) provided Congress with a rationale for opposing Mr. Clinton's proposals, (5) hold onto their audience share, (6) allow a wide variety of Conservative organizations to teach the public about and differentiate their products from one another, and (7) to attract support from voters who might have always agreed with the Conservative message but had done so passively. Simply, it allowed both the core audience for the Republican Party and much of the public to see what the Republicans were against and the Democrats for, at first appeared to position the Republicans on the popular side of the debates and shifted the public discussion toward the cultural and symbolic issues that favor Republicans more than Democrats.

By thinking of voters as consumers, we can better understand the way in which a branded politics works in the United States. The electorate is divided into two or more less stable groups of partisans and a quickly grow-ing third group that is not enrolled in any party.[158] Within the undecided group are people who lean to each of the parties. The trick for the party, then, is to turn some of them from undecided voters into party supporters while reinforcing relationships with the established audience. Needless to say, a brand built upon items about which the voter has strong feelings might be enough to do the trick.

As we will see, the 2004 Bush campaign employed exactly this strategy to increase turnout among undecided voters who leaned toward it and the members of the new markets within which it was trying to expand. While par-tisans also respond to branded product marketing campaigns, years of brand building has probably already made them loyal. Thus, parties marketed their branded products to their partisans because it is a way to reinforce the brand story, increase brand loyalty, and increase the chances that votes and political support will be forthcoming when needed. The way in which the parties are attempting to reach their target audiences is via the use of highly visual, dramatic, and graphic appeals that are often tightly scripted.[159] While these appeals may chase a lot of the audience away from consuming either product, they have the happy effect of motivating some people to buy the product. This fits nicely with Schier's (2000) argument about activation strategies[160], particularly when the marketing imperatives and techniques that we have seen in this chapter are added to it. Steven E. Schier's *By Invitation Only: The Rise of Exclusive Politics in the United States* (2000), examines the use of activation strategies by interest groups to encourage the membership to join a group, then become politically active on its behalf. What Schier is really talking about, in large part, is the way in which interest groups use brand-based marketing campaigns to encourage citizens to do these things.

Two other prominent American political forms, interest groups and think tanks, also market and brand themselves. They do so in order to get enough members to stay in business, as well as to gain attention for their ideas among decision makers and to attract financial support from grant makers. Those interest groups that cannot limit the supply of goods that their good work obtains, that cannot compel people to join as a condition of professional licensure, and that do not provide an obvious economic benefit in exchange for participation have to market and brand themselves and their ideas in order to survive. That interest groups market themselves in order to survive is implicit in most of the interest group politics literature, especially in the exchange theory of interest group behavior made famous by Robert Salisbury and noted in the context of political campaigns by Newman.[161] If an exchange is to take place, then the consumer end of the exchange must be made aware that such a thing is possible, be told how they would benefit personally, and be shown how their efforts could help the cause.

Like most kinds of institutions that cannot ration benefits, all sorts of interest groups rely on making people feel that they are doing the right thing by participating; giving people stuff in return for their contributions, and in organizing mass activities so that the supporters feel that they really are part of a group.[162] A final scholarly work, Theda Skocpol's *Diminished Democracy: From Membership to Management in American Civic Life* (2003), outlines the structural transformation that has taken place in American society and politics that created the conditions under which a branded politics could develop. All of these fine works miss something and it is the brand strategy and product marketing model's importance.

Like interest groups, think tanks are heavily dependent upon outside funders for their survival. Writing in *The Transformation of American Politics: The New Washington and the Rise of Think Tanks*, David Ricci (1993) noted the centrality of marketing within modern American politics.[163] Ricci examined think tanks as a policy grist mill from which politicians could gather ideas to be used to further their political and ideological goals. There are two other components to the marketing done by think tanks. The first of these is the marketing that think tanks must do to donor organizations in order to stay in business. The second is the marketing to the public that think tanks do in order to get financial support, to gain political support for their ideas, and to show their donors that they are getting what they pay for.[164] Think tanks do this by issuing a variety of publications to a variety of audiences, by hosting events that earn media coverage, by producing their own audio and video news releases to media outlets, and by providing their experts as guests to media around the nation.[165] Like interest groups, some think tanks pursue more of a branded strategy than do others. Ideological think tanks are more dependent upon branding and marketing to survive than are those associated with a particular industry or trade association. Thus, we should not be surprised that the think tank brand names with which we are all familiar are the ones that have built clear brand identities.

The brand strategy has been an important tool through which Conservatives have sold their policy proposals. Branding is an important tool through which this can be done because it offers the opportunity to try to change the public's area of concentration about a given subject. As the Iraq War marketing campaign shows, a marketer will sometimes try to switch from the discussion of one aspect of the brand to another in response to the reception that the original presentation received in the marketplace. The Bush team sold the domestic security aspect of the War on Terror brand because this was the area in which Republican candidates enjoyed an advantage over their Democratic rivals in the run-up to the 2002 congressional elections, as well as because such an emphasis fit the most important concerns in the American public's mind at the time.[166] The brand strategy was also a key part of the way in which the public was sold on the Afghan War as is clear from George Tenet's analysis of how the conflict should be presented to the American public in which he said, "We need to brand these folks as outsiders" in order to sell the war to the American and Afghan public.[167] In addition to working with the above-noted outsider theme, he proposed two other aspects out of which to build a narrative: First, reminding everyone about the successful CIA effort to drive the Soviets out of Afghanistan in the 1980s. Second, underscore that the United States had no desire for territory or permanent bases in the region.[168]

Conservatives have, in short, applied the brand strategy to promote all sorts of policies, including national security policy. Branding can work to sell public policies for the same reason that it can work to sell cookies in a crowded supermarket. The branded product stands out on the shelf of choices because the consumer has heard about it before. Conservatives generally use the brand strategy to set up a binary choice between their preferred option and other, less favorable choices that favor their point and suggest dire consequences if their preferred option is not adopted. Two examples of the way in which Conservatives do so in office are the Bush administration's creation of a line extension between its Iraq invasion and the War on Terror brand that it had built and its early second-term Social Security privatization plan that was marketed under its ownership society brand. In the first case, the Bush team was able to define the public's and Congress's choice as being one between a preemptive invasion or an almost certain second terror attack on U.S. soil. As a result, the Bush team helped Conservatives gain seats in the congressional midterm elections and built support for its planned Iraq invasion. Its branded Social Security initiative failed because the Bush team was never able to define the debate as a choice between its branded product and immediate disaster, was never able to show the public how its proposal was better than the numerous other available alternatives that also seemed capable of dealing with the issue, nor could it convince people that disaster would come soon if no action was taken on this issue. A brand works best when it explains how buying its product could help the consumer and avoid disaster. In the former case the Bush team was able to show how its proposal did so and won while in the latter it was not able to do so and lost.

Conservative elected officials work with friendly interest groups and think tanks to sell branded politics to the American public. These branded policies are usually sold in ways that make them appear to be in the interest of the majority of the population, have some clear connection between the brand essence and the way in which the policy supposedly would work, but seldom mention how those pushing the initiative would benefit themselves. Two examples from the Bush administration, one to limit the amount of and kinds of damages in civil suits and the other to change the tax code, show how this is so. The Common Sense Legal Reform proposal was developed with considerable input from tobacco companies seeking protection against litigation.[169] The Bush administration was interested in this both because it had received considerable backing from that industry and because its passage would represent a blow to one of the major supporters of the Democrats: trial lawyers who would lose work and fees as a result of the changes.[170] By positioning and branding these significant changes as "Common Sense Reform," the proposal's supporters both positioned it in a way that made direct opposition difficult, gave it a brand designed to appeal to average Americans, and came with a number of horror stories about juries awarding large damages in cases when they probably should not have done so, but never really talked about who was behind the proposal or the ways in which these proponents would benefit from its enactment. A second example of this was the Bush tax cuts for the same reasons as above. One of the smartest things that the administration did to both sell the branded policy and show that that brand promise of lower taxes had been kept was to send most Americans a check to demonstrate this. As Waldman (2004) notes,

> The Bush tax cuts actually did have one populist element: it sent $300 to every person with income-tax liability, essentially a pre-payment of the reduction they would later receive. Although most people might not remember, the idea was actually proposed by Congressional Democrats once they realized a tax cut was inevitable. But Bush quickly realized that the $300 checks could be an effective way of distracting people from the fact that most of the tax cut's benefits went to the wealthy.[171]

Not so much a distraction, this Democratic gift offered the Bush administration an opportunity to demonstrate to its audience that there was a relationship from the W brand and the tax checks that had just been received. It showed that the brand promise made by W in particular and Republicans in general of lower taxes or "tax fairness" was being kept. They also had the effect of obscuring the way in which the Bush tax cut actually was distributed but altering public perceptions is one of the uses of the brand in politics. In this case, people perceived that they had received the tax cut that Mr. Bush had promised; he positioned himself to claim credit for it and, by doing so, was able to demonstrate that what people had voted for was what he was doing.

A Top-Down Activity

One of the things that we must acknowledge is that branded politics is fundamentally a politics driven by elites.[172] Branding is one of the key tools through which public opinion can be encouraged to echo elite opinion in the way in which Key argued that public opinion does.[173] The difference between Key's argument and the brand strategy is that the public does have some input into forming the brand and, through its responses, can dictate the life of the brand, as well as the aspects of it that receive prominent mentions in the marketing campaigns supporting them. Branding and brand building fit Key's argument because they involve the extensive measurement of public attitudes by political elites in order to shape a message that can then be distributed through a variety of channels to the target audience. The elites do the research that decides what the contents of the brand will be and figure out to whom the branded political product is to be sold. The way in which the public gets to participate is in the techniques used to build the brand such as surveys and focus groups.[174] Like all brands, political ones are heavily dependent on the response of the audience for their success. Audience response, then, is the other key way through which the public has some input into the contents of the brand. A brand that fits with the public's understanding of how the world works; that taps into their needs, wants, and desires; or one with which the audience develops a strong tie (as was true in the case of Coca-Cola which found that people were more tied to the brand than to the product based on the public outrage when the product's formula was changed in a very public way) will be successful while one that does not will not be so fortunate.[175] Branding and brand building are elite tools because they involve extensive measurement of and response to public attitudes that can be distributed through a variety of channels to the target audience. The brand story is repeated frequently in order to familiarize the public with it and to show the public that the branded product is something that they would like (or benefit from in the case of most public policies). At no point does the audience directly decide upon the content of the message but their response to it dictates its overall success or failure. Thus, it is important for the elite to have a clear sense of themselves, their product, and the brand that they are trying to shape.

Here too, Lakoff's work makes an important contribution and it is that the use of techniques like value-based framing show the weakness of a given political movement based on its use of what he terms Orwellian language.[176] Conservatives do this, he argues, not because they are strong but because they are weak.[177] That is to say that they use such language when they are promoting items on which the potential for strong public opposition exists.[178]

For Conservatives, this would be most of the time because, as poll after poll shows, a majority of the public does not agree with Conservatives on most substantive issues. One person's Orwellian language can be taken by others to be part of a brand strategy. This is, again, because Conservatives do not just employ these terms on an occasional basis. They do so in a way that gives them a long-term value, in a highly structured way that encourages the public to see only specific aspects of the substantive question under discussion, and in a way that ensures that their brands are framed such that it automatically puts them on the winning side of the argument. They incorporate the brand strategy in all of their communicative efforts because doing so reinforces loyalty to it and, by extension, to the movement behind it.[179] Since 9/11, this has been particularly true in the areas of social and economic policy questions and, not surprisingly, the Conservatives have spoken much less about those matters than they have about national security questions. When they do speak of the issues on which they do not side with the majority, they very much take the branded approach.

Conservatives have employed a brand strategy to shape the way in which the public thinks about all sorts of civic and social activities, as well as what the public thinks about the government itself. We can see this in the way in which years of Conservative brand building against "big government" really hid from view the significant reductions in public sector capacity that were so evident in New Orleans in the aftermath of Hurricane Katrina. Conservatives from Reagan forward never proposed making government so limited in capacity that it lacked the capacity to quickly and effectively respond to a hurricane, yet which has been the effect of their policies and these they have sold to the public in guise of limiting the power of the so-called big government.[180] Rather than argue that they are against individual rights, full citizenship for women, or individual choice, Conservatives first built a frame around their antiabortion stance that encouraged the public to place the needs of the fetus ahead of that of the mother, then built the prolife brand within that frame.[181] Consistent with the brand strategy, Conservatives have never extended their prolife position to opposition to capital punishment or the use of force to settle international disagreements. The prolife brand does not encompass those things because the frame around it is fetuses, not those other people who die at the hands of the state. One example of the way in which the prolife brand is used to promote controversial policies is provided by the Unborn Victims of Violence Act that was signed into law by George W. Bush on April 1, 2004.[182] While this act is aimed at additional punishments for those who commit crimes against pregnant women, it implicitly gives the unborn the rights of a citizen, a useful thing should the Conservatives actually ever decide to outlaw abortion. In these cases, Conservatives did not explain the downsides of these policies to the public, or in fact really explain their full effects, because doing so would have meant that the public would not have supported them.

By overwhelming majorities, Americans want the government to be fiscally responsible, have the capacity to solve important national problems, and support abortion rights in some form. What Conservatives use Lakoff's Orwellian language to do is to make sure that they respond to the concerns of their core audiences, encourage the rest of the population to think of these issues in highly specific ways, show that they are on the side of average people, and show that promises made are kept. In all of these cases we can see how the framing of which Lakoff writes is actually the foundational part of the Conservative brand strategy.

What's the Matter with Kansas? Conservatives and Brand Stories

Conservatives have several brand stories that are intended to show the public that what they want is in the voters' interest. They are (1) an emphasis on benefits to the individual instead of the health of the society. We can see this in the frequent incantation that "it's your money" when Conservatives talk about taxes and government spending and in Ronald Reagan's query to Americans during the 1980 election asking them if they were better off than had been the case four years earlier. In both of these examples, the nation's overall needs and well-being are not considered. (2) Presenting their movement as being for more individual freedom or believers in the wisdom of the public (this usually comes with a contrasting message that the Democrats favor more government control). This brand story is primarily employed in the economic policy area. Republicans do not use it to support abortion rights or the ability of homosexuals to legally marry. (3) Presenting their movement as being great believers in local control and states' rights. This was particularly true during the period up through the first George W. Bush administration. (4) Presenting themselves as strong patriots and advocates for the military. Republican marketing efforts and brands are heavily dependent on the images of nationhood, on the contents of the American civil religion or creed, and on giving the military very visible support. Essentially, their brand story is that they love the flag, America, and the strong military protecting her.

The goal of the Conservative brand strategy is to build lasting relationships with the target audience, as well as to get them to whatever is being promoted at any given time. Populism is a key aspect of the Conservative brand story. Simply, no matter how elite their background or skewed toward the top their policies are in reality, Conservatives present themselves as being like and representing the interests of average people. We can see this at the presidential level in the following example: George W. Bush and Ronald Reagan played the everyman role superbly and were elected twice.[183] George H.W. Bush was unable to do so in a convincing fashion and was defeated in his run for re-election. We can see in policy branding when we look at examples like the way in which the tax cuts passed during the George H.W. Bush administration were presented as "tax fairness."[184] These points of emphasis allowed the more elite aspects of Reagan and George W. Bush to be minimized in the public mind and blunted the argument made by Democrats that the Bush tax cuts were unfair due to the lopsided distribution of the benefits to the top income earners.

Ronald Reagan is the man around whom Conservatives have created a heritage brand and, having done so, they try to nominate presidential candidates who could play the role of president in exactly the way that Reagan played it. The extent to which these efforts had built loyalty within the audiences targeted by Reagan and the heritage brand's promoters was clear in the outpouring of response to Reagan's death that came from it. As Tim Wise noted just after the Reagan funeral, Reagan's real interests and constituency could be seen from the absence of African Americans who turned out to pay tribute to him in ceremonies in California and Washington.[185]

This proves the point that, through the use of brand strategy, Conservatives have created something that can be repeatedly used to market their candidates, institutions, and issues. The Reagan heritage allows Conservatives to tap into the positive feelings that much of the population still holds about him. The Reagan of the brand story is a creation aimed at tapping into the feelings held by the audience. Although the brand story is developed by the marketer it fits and resonates with the audience because it serves one of their psychological needs.[186]

Thomas Frank speaks of this in his book *What's the Matter with Kansas?*, a good portion of which examines some of the reasons behind the huge increase in support that Conservative candidates, most of whom are from that state's socioeconomic upper class, have come to enjoy in recent decades from some of the most socioeconomically downtrodden segments of that state's population. The explanation that Frank provides is consistent with branded politics because it centers heavily on value-based issues presented through a clear story. His best definition of the brand stories that Conservatives develop and the way in which they become a coherent whole is what he calls the plen-T-plaint. This he describes as a number of unrelated complaints that encourage emotive response rather than rational analysis:

> Aiming instead to infuriate us with dozens, hundreds, thousands of stories of the many tiny ways the world around us assaults family values, uses obscenities, disrespects parents, foments revolution and so on. It offers us no resolution, simply reminding us that we can never win.[187]

This device is really the Conservative brand story regarding social issues in the United States.

In its scope and intensity, it resonates with the world that the target audiences experience on a daily basis but never mentions economic matters nor, in particular, how much of the responsibility for these outrages lies at the feet of Conservative politicians and public policies.[188] Instead, as Frank notes, it lays the blame for all of these outrages at the feet of one of the most important brands that Conservatives have developed during their use of the brand strategy: the Liberals.[189] It is, as Frank notes, the Liberals as well who can be blamed for the failure by Conservative politicians to make any progress in cleaning up these outrages[190] despite the fact that Conservatives have enjoyed control of the national government for long stretches of the period since they started using the brand strategy in 1980.

The net effect of all of this is to produce a very coherent story that blames the Liberals for the nation's decline by emphasizing cultural issues rather than apportioning any blame to Conservative regulatory and economic policy in creating people's unhappiness.[191] What Frank describes as the plen-T-plaint is really the core brand story around which Conservatives have worked to reach the working-class audience of which he writes. This brand story would not work except for the fact that it is very much rooted in the day-to-day experiences of the audience that it is trying to reach and because it plays on things that are visible in the environment around them. The complaints about culture, for example, that Frank notes are highly visible while the impact of Conservative economic policy of which he speaks is not.

As we see later, the Democratic failure to develop an alternate brand story that pins much of the cause of these problems on the economic policy that produced them has been one of the key ways that the Conservatives have been able to ride a brand story about social discontent into office and into implementing public policies that reward the wealthy, as well as create the conditions under which the outrages take place in the first place. As Frank's work shows, the well-constructed brand story can shape public opinion in specific directions and reward those who make the best use of them.

Candidates, Issues, and Organizations Come and Go, but Brands Endure

The specific tools that marketers used to build commercial brands look a lot like the tools that political consultants use to build campaign messages, and in the case of Conservatives, political brands. Messages are developed, positions taken, polls and focus groups taken of the public, the marketer figures out what the target audience is, learns through research what its needs are, sets up the framework with which the competition will take place (e.g., if one is trying to sell a fax/copier, a question that must be dealt with is what products constitute the competition or in which category should this product compete), figures out what benefits the customer wants and tries to provide those (emotional versus functional), shows the link between the promised benefits and the way in which the product works, as well as what the audience wants.[192] This looks a lot like the process through which a political campaign develops its message because it is the same. The only difference is that, in commercial marketing, some physical product normally exists whereas in political marketing the end result is a set of proposals, organizations, and individuals. As we saw above regarding all brands, political brands are very much about feelings.

Brand building and distribution are not random activities, rather, a lot of thought, a good deal of sophisticated research, a lot of time, and a lot of money are expended in their creation. It is very important that the brand reaches the target audience, produces a response in it and at the same time develops a clear understanding within the audience that this brand is not like the others. Practically, this means that political branding involves a good deal of differentiating between political product and a lot of contrast marketing to make sure that the audience gets the differences between the political products being offered to it. Conservatives emphasize on the different aspects of an individual brand when they present it to different audiences. The key demographic groups for the Conservative product are in the 50–60 age category[193] and part of a much larger group that ranges in age from the late twenties to an overlap with the mature category (the "Boomers").[194] Since the Boomer category in particular likes a very hot, moralistic, message,[195] Conservative product marketers put a lot of spice into their brands. Doing this helps to attract the right audiences, get rid of other audiences, show that the Conservatives have clear positions about which they feel deeply, and attempt to make the audience respond with the desired type of emotion as we saw above.

Ways Branding Is Used

Just as in consumer marketing, message discipline is important in selling the brand and, hence, the product. This is particularly true when one is dealing with either commodity products or products that constitute discretionary purchases. The brand can include an overall icon or logo (such as either the image of "The Evil One" used interchangeably for Osama bin Laden and Saddam Hussein during the George W. Bush administration or to sum up an event as was the case during the "Clinton Scandals" or to sum up an issue of public policy as was the case for the "Axis of Evil" (nuclear proliferation and states of concern), the "War on Terror" (instead of a more difficult but focused operation launched specifically against Al Qaeda), and the "No Child Left Behind" (high-stakes testing and performance requirements for schools) education program enacted during the first Bush administration. In commercial marketing, the equivalent would be the Mercedes-Benz faceplate, the Nike swoosh, and the Microsoft logo. Like a solid political symbol, the logo and the brand that it supports help the target audience make sense of a confusing world or to feel that we belong to a specific social or consumer group. The political brands tend to fit the self-image that most Americans hold about themselves and their country. As a compassionate people, few Americans want to see children left behind; as believers in the essential goodness of their nation, few Americans have a problem with calling Osama bin Laden "the evil one;"

and given our historic love of a good moral crusade, nothing could be more appropriate for Americans than to be fighting the "War on Terror." The brand is the story and the logo is the visualization of the story out of which political products are built and sold to the American public.

Given that logos and brands convey images about products, companies use branding to favorably shape public attitudes toward their products and will sometimes try to depict their opponents' products in a way that moves public opinion in a more negative direction. Doing these things can increase one's own market share or, failing that, drive down a competitor's share. Either can be the means through which a company hits its quarterly sales figures. Given that election and policy marketing campaigns come with deadlines, political marketers have an incentive to behave in the same way. For example, during the 2004 election, many of George W. Bush's campaign commercials focused on very specific elements of what was wrong with John Kerry while speaking in glowing, but very general, terms about the positive attributes of George W. Bush. While Bush's favorability rating inched up only slightly, the decline in Senator Kerry's positive rating was a very important means through which Bush won in November.

Political brands can be built that shape the public discussion toward what the marketer considers to be a desirable topic and away from what the marketer considers to be an undesirable subject. As noted above, the Bush administration branded its response to the attack on 9/11 as a general "War on Terror" because it would diminish public expectation that Al Qaeda could be defeated or that Osama bin Laden would be captured, because it provided a context for doing a number of other things that the administration felt were desirable and because, as Jamieson and Waldman (2003) note, doing so blocked the development of a Pearl Harbor-like frame around that day's events that could have produced a serious inquiry into the failures that led to that day's events.[196]

Brands can give an individual policy an identity that the public can support even if they know little about the specific contents of the policy. In this, the brand is a postmodern device.[197] During the Bush administration two examples of this were the enactment of the "Patriot Act," that many observers argue sharply reduced the rights enjoyed by American citizens, and the "Medicare Modernization and Reform Act." In the former case, the policy proposes to do things that are patriotic whereas in the latter it proposes to modernize and reform a system that the public sees as rickety. These two examples illustrate the beauty of branding; that is, that the branded policies can be sold to the public by using terms that the public has been socialized to support. Few Americans would say that they are unpatriotic or against the reform and modernization of government programs. Thus, those who oppose such branded initiatives immediately start out on the defensive. They are positioned badly and, as a result, less likely to succeed. According to Ries and Trout,

> Positioning starts with a product. A piece of merchandise, a service, a company, an institution, or even a person. Perhaps yourself. But positioning is not what you do to a product. Positioning is what you do to the mind of the prospect. That is, you position the product in the mind of the prospect. So it's incorrect to call the concept "product positioning." You're not really doing something to the product itself. Not that positioning doesn't involve change, it often does. But the changes made in the name, the price, and the package are really not changes in the product at all. They're basically cosmetic changes done for the purpose of securing a worthwhile position in the prospect's mind.[198]

The combination of branding and positioning has made it difficult for Democrats to oppose Republican candidates and ideas either substantively or emotively during the last four decades. When combined with differentiation, the audience gets a clear impression of why picking one product over another would be a good thing.[199] Developing an effective brand and a strategically potent position can have the effect of putting some items on the agenda, keeping others off, and dictating the terms upon which the next election or policy marketing campaign will be fought. Branding in this way appears to be of particular value to interest groups and policy entrepreneurs. This is because they are seeking a place in the corridors of power when decisions are being made.

Branding is of particular value with the unfamiliar or with topics about which the audience can have passionate politics. While it is used to sell public policy and in electoral campaigns, its value is clearest in the latter. George W. Bush was a relative unknown in national politics prior to his run for the presidency in 2000. He was well positioned because of his famous name and, because his campaign used the brands that had been developed by Reagan and Gingrich, he was able to explain quickly to the voters who he was and what he stood for. The testimony to the power of branding in this example is that Bush was able to win the election despite the nation's peace and prosperity.[200] While the outcome of the election was close, Bush won and one key reason for this was that he used brand strategy to appeal to audiences who longed for the days of Reagan, and because of his personal attributes.[201]

Selling branded policies can be more difficult without a clear problem because a head-to-head comparison between ideas seldom takes place in a forum available to most of the public, there are more than two options available for the public to consider, and in many cases there will be a familiar status quo that it will be difficult to move the public away from.[202] The brand strategy encourages the creation of a visible crisis in order to succeed as was the case on September 11, 2001. The brand strategy works well in that situation and ones in which the public can be shown that there is a serious problem. In dealing with 9/11, the Bush team focused on a broadly constructed branded response, because doing so gave it a basis to sell much of its policy agenda. In contrast, Mr. Bush had a very difficult time selling his Social Security proposal during the early days of his second term because it was not clear if there was a problem with the current system, there were numerous other proposals on offer, and many of the proposals proposed by other players seemed to be simpler and of more direct relevance to the problem that Mr. Bush was proposing. Without a highly visible problem about which people have some feelings, the brand strategy will not work as well to sell policies.

The Goal of All This

The remainder of this work looks at the way in which Conservatives have used brand strategy to build their movement. The Conservative movement, as we saw, has been using a brand strategy to sell itself to the public and, as a result, these brands now have considerable equity and they have developed an audience that is very loyal to them. As a result this is available for all sorts of political entrepreneurs to make use of. This is done through the research techniques noted above, reinforced by a brand building and education campaign that takes place across media and has the effect of showing the public what the Conservative product is, how it suits their needs, and how it differs from other alternatives. Conservatives use product marketing tools to build their brand but, at the same time, their brands are fundamentally values based. As a result, the brand attracts the desired audiences, reinforces loyalty within it, and repels others. Such an approach not only is well suited to the presidential system in the United States but it is also a key tool through which all sorts of Conservatives have found and directed resources toward the appropriate markets. Conservatives are successful because they use the brand strategy to efficiently define their movement, the institutions associ-ated with it, and their opponents. Even Democrats like John Kerry, who have begun to appreciate the power of the brand in politics, have not devoted nearly enough time to building a single brand and then reinforcing it in the public mind via repetition.

Once the initial brand has been built and disseminated, then loyalty to it has to be built, and its product line can be extended as was noted above. Other items can be added to it. This is typical in corporate marketing cam-paigns. This is a particularly risky phase of any campaign because too many line extensions can dilute the value of the brand, render it entirely worth-less, or add products to it that are both financial and communicative failures. For example, in the Clinton impeachment campaign, in the end, there was no single scandal that the Conservatives could have used to encourage enough members of the general public and Congress to cross the chasm and support a removal. Instead, the number of scandals that they had employed to build the equity in their branded Clinton ended up being so diluted that they had no meaning and, hence, as far as most of the public was concerned, the Conservatives had no case upon which to base their impeach-ment drive. This is the problem of having too many simultaneous line exten-sions or what Ries and Ries call the "line extension trap."[203]

The problem of too many line extensions can lead the audience to ques-tion the quality of the product in question. As Ries and Ries[204] suggested, quality or making people believe that you have a quality product is a key means through which marketers sell their products. If people perceive that the product in question is of high quality then they will purchase it, invest in it, or support it at the ballot box. If they do not, they would not (and unlike corporations, political parties cannot compete on price).[205]

For example, consider the difference that perceptions of quality make in a political marketing campaign. The well-defined brand of the War on Terror allowed the Bush administration to focus on a single line extension of its bat-tle with Osama, the Evil One, and the war in Iraq. As I show in a later chap-ter, the administration built fellowship in the public mind between the events of 9/11 and the possibility of an attack either directly by or sponsored by Iraq using weapons of mass destruction. As a result, it was able to build a high level of popular support for an invasion of Iraq for which there was no real justification based on 9/11.

One of the key ways that it was accomplished was through the statements made by U.S. officials including the director of the Central Intelligence Agency, secretary of defense, secretary of state, and National Security Council advisor that Iraq probably had such weapons and would use them if given a chance. Consider, in contrast, the Clinton scandals. The marketing problems were simple: too many line extensions and the problem of credentials as well as too few endorsers whom the public felt were credible. We can see the difference in a focused line extension with a number of credible endorsers and an overextended brand with few credible endorsers. The difference simply was that Mr. Clinton stayed in office and Mr. Hussein did not.

*   The folling chapters present the cases in which the Conservative movement successfully used branding to move from a fringe movement to the center of American political life. We see how Ronald Reagan both branded his way to the White House and has become a heritage brand for Conservatism. We also see how Newt Gingrich used branding to capture a majority in the House of Representatives for the first time in forty years. We analyze the Clinton impeachment as a marketed event in general and as a branded event in particular. Doing so shows us how Conservative groups were able to mount a branded corporate campaign[206] and what the limitations to using such a strategy are. George W. Bush shows us how brands can be refocused to overcome a negative public impression, how to build fellowship between brands, how to brand public policies, and how a branded campaign can enable even an incumbent with what would traditionally have been thought of as a weak record in office to win reelection. Before doing so, we examine the changes within American society and the political system that created the conditions that have made branded politics possible.

Participation in Politics

Reorganization of American Media, Interest Groups, and Society

Introduction

Chapter 1 defined and outlined what branding is, how Conservatives have used it to advance their causes over a wide variety of campaigns and issues, as well as how the net effect of its use has been to transform the Conservative movement from a marginal, regional movement to one that occupies a central place in American political life. This chapter looks at the important changes that have taken place in American social organizations, the way in which Americans participate in politics, a reorganization of American media, a major structural transformation of the economy, and a dramatic reorganization of government.

The end result of these changes has been the creation of a more diverse but fractious election system and electorate that often focused on social issues that are ideally suited to form the basis of branding campaigns, the creation of a large number of organizations that use branding to sell their political wares, and to distinguish themselves a more open government that provides the subject matter on which the brand can be built and promoted, and a media that contains more outlets but fewer owners. Significant technological changes in the field of computer-driven direct mail, the development of talk radio, and the proliferation of the World Wide Web gave Conservatives more channels for their branded products than they had ever had in the past.[1]

The Conservative movement, in its present incarnation, organized during this period, capitalized on a series of policy changes to mobilize their supporters and, because of its relative youth, adapted quickly to new technology as it presented itself. The Conservative movement, as it should be noted, is a social movement that extends beyond a political party.[2] It can be thought of as being like a company, but one with multiple business units and not just a single one as scholars of political marketing have usually thought of political parties.[3] Conservatism developed during the eras of party marketers (1950s–1970s) and total campaigning.[4] The latter period is defined as "a total environment of politics" that eliminates the distinction between "campaigning and governing."[5] The Conservative movement, as we see in the subsequent chapters, is very much responsible for the promotion of such a politics; it should come as no surprise that the American case referenced by Nimmo is Reagan,[6] because Reagan was very much the product of a movement that saw itself as involved in politics on a continual basis. Conservatives had wandered in the American political wilderness for most of this period of Democratic dominance, sometimes being unable to capture a majority within their own party but found several different ways to popularize their movement.[7] One of these, I am arguing, is through the use of a brand strategy. In order to understand how they did so, we must first have a good sense of where Conservatism came from, how it was organized, and what it wanted.

Conservatism: Something New under the Sun?

Conservatism has been more aggressive in its use of branding and other consumer marketing techniques because, in its current incarnation, it grew up during the post-World War II American consumer boom. It is a coalition that is younger than its Democratic rivals and came of age during the rapid expansion of American consumer culture. As a result, it is not surprising that Conservatives use the techniques of the age in which their movement was born. Given its age, as well as the fact that the Democrats had driven much of the nation's politics from 1932 until at least the end of the 1960s, it was hardly surprising that Conservatives had a lot of material out of which to build their brands. The modern Conservative movement was in a weak, divided position from the 1930s through the 1960s.[8] Those who had survived the Depression period could be swayed by the movement's strong anticommunist position. The Conservative movement in its current form is something new under the American political sun and is very much a product of the 1960s.[9] As numerous scholars have independently shown, modern Conservatism is a lot different from its classical ancestor[10] and, for this reason, can best be understood as something new on the American political stage. The first major event that helped Conservatives take over the Republican Party was the 1964 presidential election cycle that saw Goldwater and his Conservatives begin the defeat of the socially and economically Moderate Rockefeller Republicans that would culminate with the Reagan Revolution.[11] Bill Rentschler (2000) quotes from a Nancy Reagan statement to him to show how Goldwater set the stage for the successes to come:

> In the 1950s it wasn't fashionable to be Conservative and it took men like Barry and my husband. They found they had a lot in common and made history by igniting the fire of the Conservative movement. They believed that the government should simply get out of the way. Barry started a crusade and handed the torch to Ronnie.[12]

Goldwater did a great deal to expand the audience for Conservative products and introduce it to what would become the core of the Conservative brand. Richard Viguerie and David Franke explain that this campaign was very important to the Conservative takeover of the Republican Party because it taught Conservatives how to raise money from the mass audience, and because it made Reagan into a star with whom the audience for the Conservative movement could relate.[13]

The key point from which to analyze the origins of the Conservative brand strategy begins during the late 1960s and ends with the election of Ronald Reagan in 1980.[14] Reagan, as we see in a subsequent chapter, was the man who brought the Conservative movement to power and is the man who was able to convince average Americans that it was okay to desert the

Democratic Party in droves. It is for this reason that Reagan has become a heritage brand in the Conservative movement and the point at which Conservative brand stories currently start. We can see this in the absence of all but four Republicans in the current party's brand story: Lincoln, TR, Coolidge (particularly during the Reagan administration[15]), and Reagan and, sometimes, this is reduced further to simply Reagan and Lincoln. Because this is a brand story, the way in which the individuals contained in it are presented is highly stylized. Lincoln saved the Union and provided freedom to the oppressed; TR has significant populist appeal because of his rough-riding and trust-busting; Coolidge has been used, including by Reagan, to justify limited government while Reagan has become the modern Conservative movement's heritage brand and is presented as being like Lincoln because he brought freedom to Eastern Europe. Consistent with the brand strategy, Conservatives have developed a stylized history for their movement and presented the nation's history in stylized ways designed to be visible and to produce strong feelings within the audience. Just as Reagan often made reference to John Winthrop's writings to sell his ideas, contemporary Conservative politicians often make reference to the Framers, especially Thomas Jefferson, to sell theirs. Doing so gives the movement and its brands much better credentials than a recitation of its recent history likely would.

The Conservative brand story in short stresses that the movement developed from a sense among average Americans that things were wrong in the nation. It centered on a hatred of communism, love for God and a desire for free enterprise. It arose during the 1950s and stepped toward success with the 1964 Goldwater campaign, and then wandered in the wilderness until Ronald Reagan mounted an unsuccessful challenge to Gerald Ford in 1976. While Conservatives were building their movement in the wilderness, Liberals in Washington were steadily worsening the nation's problems. Finally, the election of Ronald Reagan in 1980 brought the country back to its senses and Conservatives to power in Washington. The Conservative brand story contains a positive aspect of its origins that focuses on a figure that many Americans recall: Ronald Reagan. As Schoenwald[16] argues, Ronald Reagan was produced by an insurgent Conservative movement and was the first of the movement's leaders to win the White House. Thus, when most Conservatives speak of the individual around whom their movement is centered, they frequently cite the Gipper himself and it is for this reason that he is its heritage brand.

Although Reagan is the heritage brand, the Conservative movement is very much the product of split intellectual roots. These twisted origins have produced a movement that has made good use of and is well suited to employ the brand strategy because this early period shaped public perceptions about the movement and helped to unite it by the end of the 1960s.[17] One strand is very much about confrontation and is movement based whereas the other was focused on winning elections.[18] The result was to build a movement that was focused on a variety of activities and had a variety of organizations in place by the end of that decade[19] and was well suited to participate in the era of total campaigning that was developing, as noted above, as the movement was developing.

The movement has seen itself as an outsider at the highest levels of American politics and, as Sara Diamond has noted, has generally seen itself as an underdog.[20] These underdogs feel that they became politically active because they see their ideas and values as being under attack from the hostile secular culture and this perception has made the movement more aggressive.[21] This is why much of the early message Conservatives put forth was focused on either the rightness of its extremity or on making dramatic change once in government. The heat and aggression contained within their narrative was exacerbated in the movement's early years by its reactionary nature. Conservatism seemed to be always complaining, finding fault, and speaking with angry rhetoric, because it was reacting to changes that had been institutionalized by Democrats first through the New Deal and second through the Great Society programs.[22] Rather than describing their agenda to the public, the Conservative movement spent the period from Goldwater to Reagan pointing out the failures of Liberals, Democrats, and big government as it occasionally still does.

Given that it thought of itself as an underdog, outsider movement, it is hardly surprising the Conservatives felt that the institutions that were extant as their movement developed were biased toward Liberal Democrats. These perceptions gave Conservatives an incentive to create their own media, and social, intellectual capital-generating institutions.[23] The net effect has been to create a set of institutions that are within the movement's ideological sphere of influence, which have delegitimated the older institutions to the core audience and have been key means through which the brand is distributed in order to more effectively mobilize their followers. As a result, Conservative ideas have enjoyed wide distribution throughout American life.[24] The construction of this Conservative political infrastructure produced exactly the structure that would eventually be able to develop quickly and sell branded products to the public. The underdog mentality encouraged Conservatives to build institutions that are controlled by the movement, and it is these institutions that have proven to be ideally suited to distribute the brands that Conservatives subsequently built. The underdog mentality also encouraged Conservatives to adopt and make extensive use of new technologies. This is clearly stated in the title of Viguerie and Frank's book *America's Right Turn: How Conservatives Used New and Alternative Media to Take Power*.[25] In the book, they show how Conservative movement made good use of direct mail, alternative print media outlets, small publishing houses talk radio, and cable television to get their message out.

Conservatives have an easy time hitting their targets because the audience for the message is very focused. As numerous scholars have observed,[26] there are multiple strains of Conservatism and neo-Conservatism that boil down to an interest in either social or economic policy. Conservatives have developed a few aspects to their archetypal brand and fit current events and personalities into those as line extensions, and they are not hesitant to build fellowship between their core brands, its line extensions, and launched second and subbrands as circumstances have dictated. Their ability to do so is the result of their focused audience plus their independent distribution system. As a result, the Conservative movement has appeared to be much more unified than the Democrats even though, as we have seen, significant differences exist between the two kinds of Conservatives.

The brand strategy is one of the key tools that have forestalled the civil war between these elements that Lowi[27] foresaw. It kept them from focusing on their disagreements for three reasons: (1) specific aspects of the brand can be discussed with specific audiences, (2) Conservatives have developed powerful brands around the Liberals and Democrats, as well as around individual issues that help to present a clear threat to their audiences, and (3) brands encourage audiences to focus on specific aspects of an issue and, as a result, limit the chance that the audience sees whatever contradictions might exist within the movement's positions. Thus, the brand strategy solves the paradox that Lowi[28] raised about the incompatibility of the capitalist and moralist wings of the Conservative movement. Branding allows the economic Conservatives to hear about economic issues and the moral Conservatives to hear about moral ones. The brand strategy also means Conservatives can focus on hot button issues and personal traits instead of policy issues in order to sell their candidates. Without the brand strategy, it is doubtful that the Conservative movement would have risen to the prominence that it has attained in the United States.

In their brands and in their brand story, Conservatives like to give the appearance of solidarity, but much of this appearance is a direct result of the brand strategy's and the message distribution system's impact. Modern American Conservatism is very much a movement and continues to have a movement culture.[29] However, the Conservative movement's youth has not had the time to consolidate as a social movement in the way that Jeffery Berry noted that Liberal groups have done.[30] This lack of consolidation means that Conservative marketers can still present the movement, its members, and their values as under siege from the Liberals even though Conservative politicians have dominated at least one of the elected institutions of the American government since 1994 and the movement's representation in the Washington community has grown dramatically since 1980. Simply, the Liberal groups of which Berry wrote in 1999 have been in Washington for longer and are easy targets for inclusion as line extensions in the Conservative brand strategy.

The lack of consolidation in the face of these highly visible, institutionalized Liberal groups gives conservative entrepreneurs fodder for their brand-building activities because there will always be controversial Liberal policies about which to complain and, at the same time, they can continue playing up the insurgent nature of their movement. Even though Reagan was sunny and optimistic in his presentation of Conservatism, he and his successors have always stressed the insurgent nature of their movement. As scholars like Murray Edelman have noted,[31] the use of a threat is always a good organizing tool and, for our purposes, the Liberal brand that Conservatives have developed has been used to mobilize the movement's membership for several decades.

Conservatives have been able to sell themselves as outsiders because, geographically, they are not from quite the same places as are Liberals. As Schoenwald[32] and McGirr[33] independently show, this movement came from geographically distinct places for the most part when compared with that of Liberal activists. Until recently, its leaders and members were produced by very different institutions than their progressive rivals.[34] Conservatism has been much more a movement of the South, Southwest, middle section of the nation, and specific industries.[35] This means that historically its rhetoric has contained a good deal of anti-Washington, antigovernment, anti-Eastern, and anti-elite institutional rhetoric, all of which sometimes appears in their brand narrative.[36] It is visible with particular clarity in the brand that Conservatives have built around Liberals, especially when it comes to the Kennedys, the Clintons, and the Kerrys who have taken on the role of target for Conservatives externally that Nelson Rockefeller once occupied for them internally.[37] This fractured Conservative movement, which relies on marketing techniques to sell itself to the public and hold its contradictory wings at bay, would not have been able to come to power in the United States save for a large number of transformations that took place in the country from the end of World War II. These transformations are discussed in the following section.

The Consumer Republic Requires a Marketed, Branded Politics

As Cohen[38] shows, a cultural transformation toward consumerism has changed the way in which American politics and society work. So much so that as George H.W. Bush and Bill Clinton employed Reagan's economic policy, they "helped recast the Consumers Republic into what might be called the consumerization of the Republic, where consumer/citizens, still permeable categories in the political culture, increasingly related to government itself as shoppers in a marketplace"[39] to the point that "by the end of the twentieth century, citizen and consumer had become interlocking identities for most Americans."[40] That a branded politics slowly developed in the country should not be surprising in light of the ascendancy of consumerist values throughout the society. As Naomi Klein[41] and other observers have noted, the number of things upon which brands and logos have been slapped on in recent years has increased dramatically. Thus, it should come as no surprise that such a culture would produce politicians who sell themselves in the same ways as other kinds of commercial marketers. Nor should we be surprised that the techniques of public relations, including branding, have come to play a key role in American political life.[42]

As described by Robert Putnam[43] in *Bowling Alone,* when we couple branding with the decline in civic voluntarism as measured through active participation in community groups, another key part of the story of how American politics came to be branded politics becomes clear. Putnam argued that rather than engaging in activities that connected individuals to their communities and built social capital, Americans are spending more and more of their time in the isolated, passive pursuit of watching television. Thus, he suggested that both the level of social connectedness and the amount of social capital within the society decreased dramatically during the second half of the twentieth century. Given that, we should not be surprised that electoral politics and policy debates now take place more on television than at the grassroots. This, in turn, opens the door to a product marketing strategy heavy on branded individuals, issues, and movements both because the branding technique fits the video format and because it fits the society's consumerist values.

The brand has become more important in Conservative political marketing as the number of media outlets and different types of media outlets have increased in the post–World War II United States. This is, as noted above, because Conservatives have made such effective use of new media and marketing technologies as they have come on line. The brand has become more important in Conservative political marketing as the number and sophistication of public relations firms involved in political life increased during the second part of the last century. As Rampton and Stauber in their insightful work[44] note:

> The PR industry also orchestrates many of the so-called "grassroots citizen campaigns" that lobby Washington, state and local governments. Unlike genuine grassroots movements, however, these industry generated Astroturf movements are controlled by the corporate interests that pay their bills.[45]

As they note, much of the industry that is currently understood to be the public relations industry owes its origins to the ideas of Edward Bernays.[46] Bernays, as Rampton and Stauber argue, thought that through the use of what would come to be called public relations techniques social stability could be achieved.[47] Conservatives have used the brand strategy to achieve such stability in their own party.

As Rampton and Stauber show, Conservatives did a great deal during the Reagan years to refine the use of public relations techniques in government. They note the extent to which the administration used public relations techniques to try to build support for the Nicaraguan Contrast after the Congress had passed the Boland Amendment by creating a public diplomacy operation and quote Peter Kornbluth as arguing that it was "'America's first peacetime propaganda ministry" with the goal of using public relations and military psychological operations to "keep the media in line" and, as a result, limiting information that contradicted the administration's story from reaching the public and the Congress.[48] Given that this work is arguing that Conservatism has made good use of the brand as a movement, creating such an operation would be a logical way to bring the branding process into government.

The introduction of public relations strategies and firms into public affairs that they document took place from the Reagan years onward—a fact that fits with the argument made here because brand-building campaigns are a kind of public relations campaign and, given that many Conservatives come from corporate marketing and public relations backgrounds or, once they showed their skill on the campaign trail, became employed as consultants by corporations in search of political advice,[49] it is not surprising that some cross-pollination between the world of politics and the marketing of products took place.

Conservatives have used public relations to define their brand, their movement, and the future much in the way that, as Zyman and Miller suggest, a public relations campaign does for the brand[50] They suggest that a public relations campaign in support of a brand should focus on "the three Ds: define the brand, define the company, define the future."[51] In the case of Conservatives, the second D, of course, stands for defining the movement since there is no company but, as is always the case with brands, public relations campaigns are very useful in generating interest.[52] Public relations is important because it can tell the public about the brand story[53] and show people why they should or should not be interested in the product that it is supporting.[54] The result has been an increased interest in, coverage for, and loyalty toward the Conservative product just as they suggest can happen with a well-developed public relations campaign in support of a brand.[55] Thus, in studying the use of public relations techniques in Conservative politics, scholars have been examining one of the ways in which Conservatives have built their brand and created customer loyalty to it.

Both Kathleen Hall Jamieson and Lizabeth Cohen stress the impact of marketing techniques on politics. Jamieson does it via her brilliant work *Packaging the Presidency*. She examines advertising and its importance in promoting candidates but does not look at the role that branding plays in promoting candidates. Her work is an outstanding examination of presidential campaign advertising but, as I argue, even though some of the techniques that Jamieson rightly points out are used to promote public awareness of candidates, Conservatives also use them to build awareness of their overall brand rather than individual candidates in a single election. Cohen, especially in her conclusions, examines the impact that the ethos of consumerism is having on American society. One of her key insights is that the politics of the consumerist republic as she terms it have become much more about the interest of individuals than about the overall good of the nation.[56] It is this individualist orientation that really paves the way for a branded politics to take place because brand and the marketing associated with it are all about tapping into a set of feelings in the audience.

Branded politics is facilitated in the United States because, as the nation's consumerist mentality has grown, the number of things in American life that are branded has also increased. It should hardly be surprising that political candidates, issues, and movements have come to be sold using the same techniques that are used to sell colleges and churches in this consumerist republic.[57] Americans are both familiar with and responsive to branded marketing campaigns so it makes sense to those in public life. It was a series of large-scale socioeconomic changes that began with World War II and the New Deal and ended with the Great Society that gave Conservatives the material with which to work. The next section presents that material on an issue-by-issue basis and it is to that we now turn.

Social Changes Produce Conservative Issues

From 1932 through the late 1960s the United States changed profoundly as a nation. The Government became more involved in economic, social, and cultural life than it ever had been before. The New Deal introduced a number of economic reforms intended to tame the excesses of the marketplace based largely on the economic theory of John Maynard Keynes.[58] It included government intervention in the economy, a retirement age, and a major social insurance program (Social Security)[59] that could eventually become fodder for a branded campaign because it was highly visible and distributed benefits in a way that made people feel most attached to it. It also implemented a number of large-scale public works projects. In short, it established economic and regulatory models upon which the United States would operate at least until 1980.[60] The Conservative movement would eventually come to object to most of these programs based on cost, the taxation needed to support them, and the supposed economic costs of all the regulations that had been enacted.[61] The New Deal programs remained popular as long as more people benefited from them than paid for them,[62] meaning that it was very difficult for Conservatives to attack them until that point in time.[63]

The Conservatives, as Rush Limbaugh frequently did during the Clinton years and periodically during the 2004 election, term any new Democratic programs as part of a "Raw Deal" in an obvious attempt to remind people of why they tired of the Democrats in the first place. By the time Ronald Reagan came into office, enough flaws had been exposed in the New Deal models for the Conservative movement to give examples to support its brand story and with which to sell its reform proposals for years to come.

Conservatives also had a set of foreign policy issues around which they could build branded marketing campaigns by 1980. World War II and Cold War aftermath built the United States into a global military power that had alliance commitments and membership in a number of multilateral organizations. One of the bigger reasons that the Conservative movement attracted so many members during its early days was because of its strong anticommunism and its antipathy to the multilateral organizations, especially the United Nations.[64]

Anticommunism fit well into the Conservative argument for a strong national defense and for a potent sense of patriotism among the citizens. These two themes became more obvious parts of the brand strategy given the way in which the Vietnam War ended and the fractiousness that this ending produced at home. The Conservatives were unhappy with the way in which the Vietnam War ended and were suspicious of the softer approach taken by the left toward the USSR.[65] Instead, they honed a clear message that divided the world into two camps with the United States being on the side of freedom and justice versus the tyranny found under Communism.[66] Further, as Grover Norquist argued, anticommunism, as expressed through Reagan and Goldwater, was directly linked to confronting the growing power of the American state that did not respect its own citizens' rights.[67] The fervor with which Conservatives pursued these issues never waxed nor waned, but what did change was the audience's willingness to listen.

While the New Deal and Cold War may have provided the overall issues around which Conservatives organized themselves as the movement developed, there were a series of other transformations in American life that gave the movement steam and issues on which to market for years to come. Most of these took place during the time between Goldwater's nomination and Reagan's election.[68] We look briefly at the impact that each of these issues had upon the Conservative movement's branding strategy because each constitutes a key part of that strategy. We begin with the issue that allowed

Conservatism to expand out of its regional stronghold in California and the middle part of the nation: the civil rights revolution.

Civil Rights

One of the most dramatic changes that took place in the United States in the second half of the twentieth century was that involving the treatment of African Americans. This was a direct consequence of a media-savvy grass-roots movement led by the Rev. Martin Luther King. Its upshot was that the federal government enacted a number of policies intended to deal with this problem and its effects. The two program areas that would provide the Conservative movement with the basis upon which part of its brand might be built were the Great Society programs intended to provide economic and educational assistance to a mostly African American constituency (expanded welfare benefits and school busing to achieve desegregation to name two examples), and social benefits intended to ameliorate the impact of past discrimination (affirmative action and school busing to achieve integration).[69]

The Conservative brand story focuses on the Johnson administration's Great Society programs, racial strife in urban areas, and the policies that were enacted in support of racial integration, especially affirmative action and busing.[70] Busing and affirmative action policy resonated with both groups and were but two of the reasons why Conservatives were eventually able to sell their program to industrial, clerical, and lower management employees nationwide.[71] The upshot was to give Conservatives two new white working classes audiences, one in the North and one in the South[72] to which they could present their branded political products. While the Republican Party under Abraham Lincoln had fought a war to free African American slaves in the South, one hundred years later it would argue in favor of states rights. Over time, the Solid South of the New Deal transformed into the Solid Republican South and a Northern working class that reliably voted for Conservatives.[73]

The civil rights movement had a second major consequence that impacted the way in which Conservatives brand their ideas. The civil rights movement that showed a well-constructed grassroots movement that understood how to use media to explain itself could have a great deal of impact on public policy even if on the surface it seemed to have little power, no connections, and few prospects for success.[74] This encouraged other types of citizen groups to organize along the same lines.[75] The marketing opportunity for

Conservatives came because each of these groups spoke as did the civil rights movements in terms of rights.[76] Lowi argues that these rights claims around the issues of poverty, race, and women's rights moved the Democrats leftward and pushed some Democrats alienated by this shift into the Republican Party.[77] Conservatism gained a focused audience to which it could speak but a group that was rather large in numbers. The net effect of these grassroots rights movements on policy was thus:

> The Supreme Court was forcing to the forefront the whole set of highly controversial issues which would become the topic of the intensely politicized social/moral "values" debate—sexual privacy, birth control, criminal defendants' rights, school prayer, obscenity and, eventually, abortion and the death penalty.[78]

Thus, was the Conservative movement put into position to credibly claim that it was representative of the nation's traditional values as it continues to do.[79]

These rights movements modeled themselves on the King legacy to advocate for the rights of specific groups. An example of the lifestyle movements that came to prominence that helped to fuel the Conservative movement during the post-1960's period is the gay rights movement.[80] The gay rights movement offered Conservatives another chance to work with their traditional and family values aspect of the Conservative brand. This has been effective because the gay rights movement has been both successful and controversial. This movement and the way in which Conservatives have built a branded opposition to it are very similar to four other controversial issues on which Conservatives have used their traditional and family values brands: sex education, pornography, women's rights, and abortion.[81]

Other Rights-Based Claims

Two other offshoots of the civil rights movement that enabled Conservatives to employ a brand strategy around social issues were the feminist and youth culture movements.[82] The former featured dramatic departures in social roles for women while the latter featured radically different attitudes toward culture, sex, and drugs that existed among older generations. McGirr (2001) in her case study argues that abortion rights were of particular importance to Conservatives as they threatened religiously based beliefs about gender roles, played a key role in promoting Catholic-Protestant relations, and were a key organizing vehicle for the movement.[83] One of the biggest issues around which Conservatives have built brands is the question of abortion. It is the perfect issue for a branding campaign because there is a narrow public consensus about its legality, there are distinct opinions within specific segments of the population, and it comes with a set of high emotive visual images attached. This, in turn, opened the door to a warren of other controversial issues including those surrounding the legal status of women, the need for antigender discrimination legislation in employment and equality in compensation, and reproductive rights.[84] All of these issues continue to be used within the Conservative brand.

Youth culture helped further the Conservative brand strategy because it was so unlike the dominant culture of its day. This movement had developed gradually in major cities and on college campuses and seemed to have goals that were different from those of many Americans.[85] The movement grew in size because of opposition to the draft and the Vietnam War by many young people and others in the New Left.[86] The images provided by protesting women, minorities, and oddly attired young people gave Conservatives brand-building opportunities with which they continue to work forty years later and another opportunity to target the noneconomically motivated audiences. Conservatives have brought up their 1960's brand story when selling Ronald Reagan and George W. Bush, as well as when opposing Bill Clinton. This fight has played a prominent role in Conservative branding campaigns. The protesting hippie logo that Conservatives have developed around Democrats has also been used to suggest the weakness of that party's position on international issues, especially those involving the military.

Conservatives have used the legacy of the 1960s to build their general liberal brand, to build another brand out of the antiwar movement that was used to question the patriotism of both Bill Clinton and John Kerry. [87] An example of the way in which the legacy of the 1960s is used is provided by the script for a television advertisement produced by Swift Boat Veterans for Truth during the 2004 election. The ad, entitled "Any Questions?" repeatedly challenged John Kerry's integrity and raised questions about Kerry's postwar activities.[88] It used testimonials from a number of veterans who claimed that Kerry had lied before the Senate. The effect of spots like this one was to raise doubt in the public's mind about Kerry's war record in order to blow up the narrative his campaign had been building on the topic and, in the process, transform him into another truth-challenged antiwar hippie ala Bill Clinton and supposed Internet inventor Al Gore.

Conservatives have built a brand from the feminist movement, the most effective summation of which can be found in the term used for the movement by Rush Limbaugh: "Feminazi."[89] Elite feminists are, in this brand story, presented as trying to impose their minority agenda and, in the course of doing so, are making the majority radically change its behavior. In other words, as McGirr notes make women and men stray from their God-given gender roles, or as some Conservative pundits argue, simply hate men.[90] The legacy of the 1960s in general, and aspects of policy that was implemented during that time in specific, have greatly influenced Conservative branding efforts to the present day.

The upshot of the 1960s has been the creation of a brand about Liberals by Conservatives based in popular memory and actual events.[91] By doing this, Conservatives have positioned the Democrats as being responsible for all of the downsides to the 1960s without giving them any credit for that decade's accomplishments. Doing this has enabled Conservative marketers to remind their audiences why they became Conservatives and given them a vehicle through which recent Conservative successes might be contrasted against the historical failures of the Liberals in order to show younger voters that voting Conservative is the way to go. The Liberals are one of the oldest, most effective, and best understood of the Conservative brands. Its brand narrative is a simple tale in which Liberals cause America's problems as they have continually done since the 1960s. It was Liberalism that defeated America in Vietnam, promoted drug use, promiscuity, the decline of family values, and the diminution of traditional morality. This has been accomplished because of the youth culture's values, because of the creation of social programs that reward indolence or work as a poverty trap,[92] stifling regulations on business, high taxation rates, and a huge debt caused by overspending on social programs. As Lakoff [93] notes, there is a moral element to the Conservative positions on these issues, and, as a result, these positions are ideally suited for inclusion in the brand strategy.

Those who have contributed to the essence surrounding the Liberal brand include the Kennedy family, especially Ted Kennedy. Hollywood personalities and people in the entertainment business industry; those who support Democratic candidates or the social movements that arose on the left as a result of the 1960s; academics (but not those associated with Conservative institutions and think tanks); prominent mainstream media figures and media outlets (e.g., Dan Rather and the New York Times Corporation); feminist leaders such as Eleanor Smeal; prominent African American politicians; and religious leaders. Conservatives normally brand their Democratic opponent du jour as mere extensions of the Liberal line. A good example of the way in which the Liberal brand is applied to Democrats is apparent in the following passage written by Conservative author and humorist P.J. O'Rourke:

> When a Reagan Conservative says someone "means well," it is hardly a compliment. But when a Clinton liberal says someone "wants to do good" it is enough to excuse a Clinton (or two) [94]

This passage contrasts two of what have become Conservative core brands over the past decade and a half: the virtuous Reagan brand that provides the Conservatives with their heritage versus the Slick Willie brand that came to stand for all that was wrong with Democrats during the 1990s.

Conservatives have used branding to reduce all Democrats to the status of Liberals even when such is clearly not the case. Because they are all presented as one, the Conservative complaint about each Democrat is made simpler and faster than it would otherwise be. This is the way in which line extensions, fellowship, subbranding, and the creation of sibling brands augment the brand's power.[95] While each Democrat is given their own logo and brand, fellowship is also built between and sometimes included as line extensions in the Conservative brand story about Liberals. An example is provided by the way in which Reagan, and later G.H.W. Bush, turned Jimmy Carter into a logo for Liberal incompetence. The Carter brand was used in three elections and throughout the Reagan and Bush administrations in order to explain away current problems and to contrast whatever successes these two administrations claimed with Carter's failures. Doing so was the kind of exercise normally used to position brands.[96] The Clintons similarly were branded as Liberals, although in their case, the brand focused on morals, feminism, and race policy. The net result of these efforts was to build a line extension between these individuals and the Liberal brand built by Conservatives.

Conservative Brands

The Conservative movement produced its own versions of several of the movements that developed from the 1960s onward and its own sets of postmaterialist issues just as the Liberal groups did.[97] For example, Berry is primarily concerned with Liberal groups but he notes the influence of postmaterialism, especially in the form of Christian groups.[98] Conservative Christian movements are in many ways a reaction to the cultural transformation outlined above.[99] The Christian movement is also a key marketing channel through which Conservative brands are distributed; as Berry puts it, these "conservative citizen groups market themselves largely around the politics of abortion and other family value related issues such as prayer in public schools, vouchers for public schools, home-schooling, pornography, and moral decay exhibited in movies and on television."[100] Berry argues that the Democrats have been pulled in a demographically upscale direction by its citizen groups whereas the Republicans have been pulled away from these more upscale audiences because "it is the citizen groups of the right and not the left who are more attuned to the interests of those on the lower rungs of the economic ladder."[101]

The Conservatives have made the most of the cultural values aspect of its archetypal brand. Generally, Conservative Christianity's narrative states that the United States has enjoyed peace and prosperity for most of its history as a direct result of God's will. However, because of the society's decreasing commitment to Christianity, God is displeased and the United States is in danger of losing its privileged status as God's new chosen nation.[102] The Christian Right's complaints can be summed up as follows: this culture is too tolerant of immoral lifestyles and activities, has strayed too far from the traditional definition of marriage because of feminism, and has created a death culture because of its embrace of abortion rights.[103] It should be obvious how such movements could fit within the Conservative movement and how the use of the brand strategy could effectively mobilize them.

There are a variety of other kinds of lifestyle groups with which the Conservative Party has executed the brand strategy. One example is the National Rifle Association (NRA) that has used the brand strategy to both attract more members and mobilize them to participate in Conservative political campaigns. The NRA, as Robert J. Spitzer[104] notes, gradually became more political because doing so was good for its business. The NRA membership is a perfect demographic target for Conservatives because the demographics of its membership overlap the target audience for Conservative products.[105] The NRA, while usually not officially taking a partisan, has built a campaign based around the slogan that its members should "Vote Freedom First." In 2004, it endorsed George W. Bush for president.[106] The "Vote Freedom First" campaign includes a logo, slogan, publications, and bumper stickers. The freedom that is in question, of course, is the freedom to own firearms as the NRA says is guaranteed by the Second Amendment to the U.S. Constitution.[107]

While Conservatives built a number of successful brands, subbrands, and an attribute of the core Conservative around social policy matters, they were greatly advantaged by a profound shift in the U.S. economy away from an industrial, highly unionized economy in which the workers were tied through their representational organizations to the Democratic Party toward a service-based economy in which few workers were unionized and in which much industry had migrated to low wage, low tax, low regulatory open shop states.[108] All of these changes altered the strategic environment in which politics was conducted and issues over which politics is contested in a direction that advantaged Conservatives and accentuated the importance of branding.[109]

Major Economic Transformation Erodes the Power of Labor Unions

The economic transformation from an industrial, unionized workforce to a postindustrial, nonunion workforce advantaged Conservatives in four ways. First, labor unions declined in numbers if not immediately and this impacted politics over time.[110] Second, as workers saw their wages drop, the salience of the tax issue increased and, as we saw above, so did the Conservative ability to speak with social classes that used to be out of its reach.[111] Third, Conservative economic policies advantaged and disadvantaged specific audiences and industries and, it can be argued, increased the size of the constituencies that would respond to this aspect of their core brand.[112] While Conservatives have sometimes worked a class warfare aspect into their economic policy brand, its core aspect focuses on tax cuts and lower regulation as a way to spur economic growth.[113] These two themes recall the economic difficulties that the nation experienced during the late 1970s[114] and tapped into the cultural and economic aspects of the 1960s of which Conservatives have built a brand. Additionally, a focus on these two issues let Conservatives focus on the working-class and lower middle-class people who were most profoundly affected by the above-noted changes. These were useful because taxes had been increased to pay for the Vietnam War and Great Society programs, because there had been a protracted period of economic difficulty during the 1970s that impacted working and middle-class people directly, and because significant economic restructuring during the period affected these same two groups as Ruy Teixeira and Joel Rodgers show.[115]

The Conservatives have contrast techniques to amplify the impact of their tax cuts as an economic policy brand aspect. All Conservatives since Goldwater have worked to position themselves for lower taxes and Democrats for higher.[116] Given that this is a brand story, there is no comparison involved when Conservatives assert that taxes are too high, nor is any analysis of the proposed tax reduction on individual social classes ever provided.[117] Sometimes, as George W. Bush repeatedly did in the 2004 election, they provide their audience with examples of the ways in which recipients have spent their tax refunds to personalize the brand story and show that its promises have been kept. This even though most of the policies that Conservatives have put into place have actually made tax and economic conditions worse for many of the people to whom they market their accomplishments in this area.[118] The brand strategy is aimed at encouraging people to feel certain things and not to bore them with details.

Historical Images and Brand Building: The Conservative Advantage

Conservatives have built their brand upon the history of the United States since the 1960s. The perception that government is corrupt as a result of scandals delegitimates it in the public eye and makes it easier to sell an agenda based on the need for less government by which Conservatives usually mean the need for less economic regulation and less social spending. An emphasis on scandal has given the Conservative movement three negative logos with which to work: the promiscuous John F. Kennedy, the crude Lyndon Baines Johnson who first lied about and then botched the Vietnam War, and the incompetent Jimmy Carter best remembered for the Iran hostage crisis, a stagnant economy, an odd family, and a killer bunny rabbit.[119] These logos and their affiliation of these presidents with the lifestyle of the Left wing of the Democratic Party opened the way for the much newer Conservative movement to cloak itself in the symbols of the nation's tradition. These negative Democratic logos allow Conservatives to omit the fact that Richard Nixon was a Republican, to gloss over his terms in office entirely, or to lump him in with the other "failed" Liberal presidents of the period. Conservatives have used the brand strategy to blame Democrats for all of this and to extend all Democratic candidates into the Liberal brand regardless of their actual political beliefs.

While Conservatives have made hay by turning Democrats into logos that are then used to frame unfavorable comparisons, they also sometimes use them to sell Conservative products or to appeal to specific audiences. One example is the John F. Kennedy's 1961 tax cut that, as promoted by Conservatives, showed the wisdom of supply side economics. Ronald Reagan frequently mentioned that he had been a great supporter of Franklin Roosevelt and the New Deal but then went on to argue that he had not left the New Deal Democratic Party, instead the Democratic Party had left him. By doing so, Conservatives attempted to show those voters thinking about switching parties that it was not just a good idea, but entirely understandable given where the Democratic Party had gone since the Kennedy administration. The next chapter examines the way in which Conservatives have transformed Ronald Reagan from a movement leader and president of the United States into a heritage brand for the movement, as well as the basis upon which many of the movement's other brand stories are built. It should not be surprising that Conservatives love Reagan so much because he is the individual who brought the movement to power and who was able to get its moral and economic movements to set aside their differences.

Reagan as a Marketer and as a Brand for Conservative Movement

While Conservative themes and Conservative ideas had made a lot of head-way with the voters since 1964, the turning point in the Conservative revolution did not take place until 1980. In that year Ronald Reagan was elected to the presidency. This is important to our story for eight reasons. First, Reagan was a Conservative movement leader who brought a slew of Conservative activists to Washington.[1] Second, in many ways, the whole point to having Reagan lead the Conservative movement was to generate interest in and support for the movement first in California and then in the rest of the nation.[2] Third, the 1980 Reagan campaign was the first to employ fully a product marketing model to present itself.[3] Fourth, Reagan was very much the product of a top-down driven campaign to sell Conservatism.[4] Fifth, the Reagan brand in particular tapped into a sense of nostalgia within the nation.[5] Combs (1993), in many ways, rightly describes the narrative that the administration turned into its brand story and the aspects of which the overall Reagan brand was composed. I am arguing that what Reagan's team was up to was not really mythmaking but rather brand building because it and subsequent generations of Conservative marketers have repeatedly tapped into the same emotions within their audience targets, often using Dutch himself to do so.[6] As a result, the brand built around Reagan has transformed the way in which Conservatives sell themselves to the public.[7] Sixth, the Reagan era is important for subsequent Conservative marketing because Reagan and his time in office have been turned into a brand with which contemporary Conservatives try to build fellowship in order to sell their current products. Seventh, in order to recapture the marketing success that they enjoyed with Reagan, Conservatives have tried to find candidates to play the role of Reagan. The most notable example on the national stage at present is, as many observers note and we will see, George W. Bush who did just this in 2000 and again in 2004. Eighth, Reagan had a strong grasp of the importance of the symbolism of the Executive Branch and its or his own performance skills to turn in a good job in the public presidency.[8] In sum, these reasons explain why Reagan and his administration have become the basis upon which a heritage brand is being built.

Finding people to reprise the Reagan role has been difficult. Reagan had strong media skills, a well-honed sense of the concerns of average Americans, a sense of how to sell products based on his GE years, and rock-solid Conservative credentials. Reagan's skill sets have proven to be very difficult to replicate and, so far, only George W. Bush has really had some success in trying to play the Reagan role. Most Conservative candidates have lacked either the personal touch that Reagan had or his media and sales savvy or both. Such candidates have solved this problem by presenting themselves through the lens of the everyman, populist, aspect of the Reagan brand because doing so provides visual proof of the argument, sometimes made by Reagan himself: that most Americans agreed with his and the movement's beliefs.[9] Reagan as a Conservative leader saw himself as working to help "the forgotten American, the man in the suburbs working sixty hours a week to support his family and being taxed heavily for the benefit of someone else."[10] This is the basis of the populist aspect of the Conservative brand in general and the Reagan brand in particular.

Reagan's administration pioneered the branded politics that Republicans have mastered during the past three decades.[11] The Reagan brand has been built as a result of Reagan's media operation and sales ability.[12] Reagan's staff clearly understood the way that brands could sell ideas. One of Reagan's biggest accomplishments was to sell Conservative ideas and values in ways that the American public liked.[13] For this reason alone, it would be worth examining Reagan in a work on branded politics; but there is a second reason to pay special attention to him. This chapter looks at Reagan as a marketer and as a brand because he has filled both functions for the Conservative movement. Given that few politicians have the unique skills that Reagan had, I argue that Conservatives have kept him alive by building a brand about him, using it as the heritage brand for their movement, and applying specific aspects of it to specific situations as befits a modern political marketing campaign.

Ronald Reagan is the most important single figure in the modern Conservative movement. This is so because he brought the Conservative movement and its ideas to the pinnacle of power and because he made Conservatism acceptable to and popular with the public.[14] It is hardly shocking that Conservatives would wish to use him as a heritage brand given the fact that his original purpose was to sell a top-down driven movement to the public.[15] All of his Republican successors have tried to present themselves as being just like average folks and as being on the side of small town, traditional, American values. For example, George H.W. Bush claimed to be a big fan of pork rinds, Country Western music, and car racing. Bob Dole resigned the Senate in order to "go home to Kansas" during the 1996 campaign and George W. Bush had allowed the everyman role to seep into all aspects of his public persona.[16] Indeed, the prevalence of the Reagan brand is such that a book was recently published entitled *Why I Am a Reagan Conservative* that was edited by Michael Deaver (2005).

Why Use Reagan in This Way?

Conservatives have tried to turn Reagan into a brand specifically because today so many of their candidates are very much unlike Reagan himself. They are representative of the upper class and see dealing with their more downscale fellow Conservatives as a necessary evil in order to hold power.[17] Ronald Reagan was very much a product of the American Midwestern working class who had made good in California.[18] Reagan's humble, small town roots stand in contrast to the more elite backgrounds of many Conservative activists and politicians, especially those from the Bush family. Also, the emphases on the positive feelings associated with Reagan personally and, by extension, with the Reagan brand go a long way toward minimizing the more downbeat feelings that most Americans would have if the substantive impact of Conservative policies were fully explained to them.

Conservatives work with Reagan in a way that has created a brand that is aimed at producing positive feelings and impressions of national success. One of the reasons why they have been so successful in doing this is because the people promoting this brand story firmly believe in it themselves. In the Reagan brand story, the man restored the American economy by cutting taxes and regulation, invigorated the nation's senses of patriotism and morality, and single-handedly won the Cold War. We can see these themes in the words of Orrin Hatch speaking about the link between his and Reagan's political careers:

> When I decided to run and fight for conservative values, I discovered that I wasn't alone. On the Pacific Coast, a Governor in California was leading a gathering Conservative revolution that would soon invade the Potomac. We believed the answer lay in lower taxes, less government, fewer regulations, less centralized power, and a wiser use of power that must be exercised on behalf of the people.[19]

After outlining what Reagan stood for, Hatch then moved on to note how these things were very much in keeping with the nation's traditions and made an appeal based on the importance of the individual. The individualistic appeal was a key part of the way in which Reagan had been marketed as a candidate, and the emphasis on the well-being of the individual has continued to be a key part of the Reagan brand story as the passage above clearly shows.

Reagan's successors have sought to brand him in order to establish their own credentials quickly with those who voted for the man or came of age during his administration. Conservatives have worked to build the brand by naming as many things as possible after Reagan in order to increase the number of impressions that their version of him receives and, by doing so, to create a Reagan who can stand shoulder to shoulder with the historical giants of the presidency like Abraham Lincoln. Once placed in the national pantheon of heroes, Reagan could be used to sell Conservative policies for decades to come.

Conservatives seek to use Reagan as a heritage brand instead of Abraham Lincoln or Theodore Roosevelt for several reasons. First, many voters remember Reagan in office or have seen a video of Reagan or heard about the Conservative version of his heroic achievements. Second, there are literally mountains of video and audio of Reagan as president. Third, Reagan spoke in the sound bytes on which media feed and marketing campaigns run while TR and Lincoln spoke in the flowing prose of what Neil Postman called the typographic age in his seminal 1986 work *Amusing Ourselves to Death: Public Discourse in the Age of Show Business*. Fourth, Reagan was a Conservative movement leader in a way that Lincoln or TR could not be said to have been. Fifth, by turning Reagan into a brand, the legacy of TR and Lincoln can be reinterpreted for current audiences, who know little about these earlier Republican icons, to share the values of modern Conservatism. Sixth, by turning Reagan into a heritage brand, Conservatives can continue to take advantage of the Reagan campaigns and his administration's marketing efforts. Reagan is the heritage that differentiates the Conservative product from other political options and this is one of its most important uses in brand building.[20] Through the creation of the Reagan heritage brand, Conservatives have been able to incorporate Republican icons into their current marketing campaigns and to present the public with a consistent populist narrative.

The creation of the Reagan brand has allowed Conservatives to offset the archetypal advantage that Democrats gradually acquired in the popular narrative of American history from the 1930s onward. At the time of Reagan's election in 1980, Democrats were able to speak to a pantheon of leaders who had served during the age of electronic communication, which included Franklin Roosevelt, Harry Truman, and the Kennedy brothers. Democratic candidates could tap into a large archive of audio and video sound bytes of these candidates if they were so inclined. Republican Conservatives, on the other hand, had no such icons in the media age. Richard Nixon was a stain upon the party because of Watergate, Ike was neither blessed with good media skills nor a Conservative, Barry Goldwater was loved by Conservatives but seen as too extreme by most of the voters, and, as noted earlier, Lincoln and TR were useful as stories but not in marketing campaigns. With such material to work, it is not surprising that even Reagan himself spoke more about those Democratic icons than he did about those who had led his own party during its White House service. Reagan was very fond of FDR, and his repeated references to FDR allowed him to reinforce his New Deal credentials[21] and were a visible way to show the older segments of his target audience that their feelings were caused by that party and that they could do as Reagan had done by switching to the Republicans.[22]

By attempting to turn Reagan into a heritage brand, Conservatives have built a device through which they can rapidly familiarize voters with new policies and personalities, as well as build an overall brand story for the Conservative product line that can be attached to any issue. Instead of mordant discussions of taxes and spending or defense priorities, Conservatives can sell themselves and their ideas as being heirs to the great man's legacy. What Conservatives are trying to do with Reagan is commonly done by product marketers eager to teach the public about new products and how they relate to the older, more familiar, product line.

Heritage Brands and Their Uses

Building heritage brands is nothing new in the product marketing world. My argument is that what Republicans are doing with Reagan is making him into the heritage character for their brand much as Trout and Rivkin argue Kentucky Fried Chicken did with Colonel Sanders, General Mills did with Betty Crocker, and Quaker Oats did with Aunt Jemima.[23] The way in which Conservatives use Reagan is consistent with the idea of heritage in branding because he is the man who brought Conservatism to the center of American life and therefore can be considered to be the political equivalent of the above-noted commercial characters that first popularized their brands.[24] The heritage brand is a tool with which trust can be built and by using it one product differentiated from another[25] and it is so because history is one tool that can make people feel good about their purchasing decisions.[26] Heritage is important because it puts products into a line, it is a history that binds generations, can be a tradition that is passed down, and, as a result, ensures generational continuity.[27] Companies that lose their heritage "literally break a trust bond, abandon people who have counted on that link generate passivity and create emotional numbing."[28] Heritage in brand can be a way to show longevity and this can be taken by the customer to be a form of leadership in its own right.[29] Further, the heritage brand is of use as a differentiation tool because it emphasizes a specific set of traditions and cultures.[30] The heritage is something that can be updated to fit present circumstances, built into a narrative about a product, and can consist of a number of things from physical setting to country of origin to location to the fact that one has always opposed something to family ties or the location of a business in a community.[31]

What conservatives have done is to apply this principle to politics. Heritage brands have the power to define the current products to the consumer.[32] A heritage brand has considerable value because they establish credentials that increase audience confidence in the product being sold.[33] It does so because it establishes brand heritage that is "the most important property of all" and helps give the brand its meaning to the consumers.[34] Examples of heritage meanings could include family or seasonal habits, positive memories, something that is well known, something that is consistent, and something that turns you into an expert or connoisseur.[35]

The Reagan brand does this for Conservatives because it shows that theirs are the old values of a small town America that had become lost to an urban Liberalism. The Reagan brand speaks of an idyllic past as is the case when the man's personal history as a small town lifeguard in Dixon, Illinois, is mentioned[36] and this very much fits with the definition and uses of heritage brands that were presented above.[37] We can see this same emphasis on the Midwestern, small town aspects of the Reagan brand in George W. Bush's speech at Reagan's 2004 funeral:

> When the sun sets tonight off the coast of California, and we lay to rest our 40th President, a great American story will close. The second son of Nell and Jack Reagan first knew the world as a place of open plains, quiet streets, gas-lit rooms, and carriages drawn by horse. If you could go back to the Dixon, Illinois of 1922, you'd find a boy of 11 reading adventure stories at the public library, or running with his brother, Neil, along Rock River, and coming home to a little house on Hennepin Avenue. That town was the kind of place you remember where you prayed side by side with your neighbors, and if things were going wrong for them, you prayed for them, and knew they'd pray for you if things went wrong for you. The Reagan family would see its share of hardship, struggle and uncertainty.[38]

This passage shows exactly how the Conservatives have distilled in Ronald Reagan's personal story the various elements of the brand story that they had been building about themselves and their opponents from the 1960s through the 1980s. The small town, traditional values aspect of the Reagan heritage brand helps to establish where the movement physically comes from, much as Russian origin does for vodka or Belgian origin does for monastic ales.[39] Conversely, location can be used as a heritage to show that if something came from a certain place, it could not be any good.[40] One can see this in politics in the way in which John Kerry and Michael Dukakis both found their origins used against them by members of the Bush family running on the Reagan heritage.[41] The Reagan brand fits the heritage category because Conservatives have worked consistently to present the 1980s as a very good time in America while giving Reagan full credit for bringing a sense of optimism to the nation, restoring its patriotism, rebuilding its military, and igniting an economic boom. In short, he is the perfect politician out of which to create a heritage brand.

Reagan's personal traits are the key to the heritage brand.[42] There are four marketing rationales for this: (1) Reagan had significant electronic media skills, (2) Reagan was a marketer himself, knew how to appeal to people and ended up personally popular as a result,[43] (3) Reagan had a consistent message that did not change over time,[44] and (4) Reagan understood the populist nature of the role that he was playing.[45] Reagan could play this role well because he had a strong sense of himself as being an average person and of representing the interests of average people.[46] The creation of the everyman character as well as the emphasis of Reagan's Midwestern roots were quite intentional[47] and made good sense given the Midwestern origins of many California conservatives.[48]

Reagan, unlike many of the Conservative candidates and political marketers who have worked to turn him into a heritage brand, did have an authentic but tenuous tie to the backgrounds of the people who made up the rank and file of the Conservative movement and, as Frank (2004) has noted, such authenticity is important in Conservative marketing. It is no wonder that the candidates and marketers from more privileged backgrounds have worked to turn him into a brand because by doing so they insulate themselves from charges that theirs is really the top-down driven movement that it is, in reality, becoming.[49] The Reagan heritage brand is built around Reagan's personal traits and public attitudes toward those that, through the power of line extensions, can be bestowed upon other Conservative products. We can see how Reagan's personal background is emphasized as the source of this trust in George W. Bush's remarks at his funeral:

> Along the way, certain convictions were formed and fixed in the man. Ronald Reagan believed that everything happened for a reason, and that we should strive to know and do the will of God. He believed that the gentleman always does the kindest thing. He believed that people were basically good, and had the right to be free. He believed that bigotry and prejudice were the worst things a person could be guilty of. He believed in the Golden Rule and in the power of prayer. He believed that America was not just a place in the world, but the hope of the world.[50]

This shows the power that a brand story can have, because glossed over were the numerous downsides to the actual Reagan administration.[51]

Reagan is the ideal candidate to be made into a heritage brand because his administration was so focused on creating a favorable climate of public opinion in office and afterwards about itself, Conservatives, and the nation.[52] Reagan, for example, knew full well how to tap into the strong position with Conservative Christians and military supporters that the 1960s had bequeathed to the Republican Party.[53] Because of this and his clever stage-craft, he was seen as a strong leader who made the country feel good about itself after the Vietnam experience and was able to appeal to his audience's psychological needs by making them feel better about themselves and the country.[54] The ability to produce specific feelings in the audience is, as we saw in Chapter 1, one of a brand's core functions.

Conservatives have built the Reagan heritage brand in order to hold their movement together and forestall partisan civil war.[55] The Reagan brand does so because he is the one movement leader who ever really held the moralist and economic wings of the party together.[56] The Reagan heritage brand could do for Conservatives again what Reagan did for them in the first place—make them acceptable to the voters. Reagan was movement leader but also a pragmatic populist who frequently found himself articulating much of what his core audience felt and this put him in a very different place than the one in which the most Conservative elements of the movement find themselves vis-à-vis the electorate.[57]

Reagan is of use to Conservatives as a heritage brand because his public persona was so different from those of other Conservative leaders and because of his media savvy. Reagan was optimistic, fiercely patriotic, and forward looking.[58] He was popular and his skills, background, and personal traits allowed him to create relationships with his audience targets in a way that subsequent Conservatives could not do without building fellowship between him and themselves. Few subsequent Conservative candidates have possessed these things in the way that Reagan did. The first President Bush could not hide his patrician background, had a problem with diction, and lacked Reagan's common touch. The second President Bush simply had a problem with diction. Conservative congressional leaders have lacked Reagan's optimism and ability to take the heat out of the Conservative message. Reagan is the only Conservative who has combined these things; thus, making him into a heritage brand to cover the deficiencies of the current products.

Conservatives use Reagan as a heritage brand for the same reason that commercial marketers like to use heritage brands: they quickly establish the credentials of new products by enabling them to tap into the marketing work that had been done in the past. By building the Reagan heritage brand,

Conservatives have gained an ability to present their target audience with a consistent face and role for the president, to hold their movement together, and to present a happy face to the public. Thus, the Reagan heritage brand is one of the keys to the success of the Conservative movement, without which either the movement would fracture or it would become more extreme in its public face.

Building Reagan into a heritage brand is a smart thing to do given that he was the man who told Americans that it was okay to leave the Democrats to vote for Republicans, as he himself had done as a result of what he perceived to be a leftward shift in the Democratic Party. Making the man who convinced a large number of Americans to leave the Democrats and become Republicans into their heritage brand lets contemporary Conservatives remind this audience why the switched in they first place and reiterate the importance of voting Republican today. Building Reagan into a heritage brand also means that Conservatives gain a foundational story into which any number of new brand aspects, extensions, and new brands can be placed. In other words, by doing this, Conservatives would gain the ability to justify new polices by referring to older ones and to introduce new candidates by making reference to their similarities to Reagan. Reagan can be used as a brand to market subsequent Conservative candidates because he led their movement to the center of American political life. The Reagan brand works with swing voters because it is value based and because its everyman aspect is quite populist in contrast to the Liberal brand. Reagan's sunny personality and use of humor also serve as a nice counterpoint to a movement that has a popular image focused on its most extreme elements and on the heat that is used in its brand stories.[59] As a result, he could say the same things as the other Conservatives but did so in a way that made Conservatives happy but did not alienate the rest of the public. This pleasantness was an important tool that Reagan used to his advantage.

The Conservatives have tried to move the Reagan heritage from brand to archetype. They have done this by repeatedly asserting that Reagan's real legacy is that he won the Cold War and expanded freedom around the globe. Writing in his edited volume on Reagan Conservatives, Michael Deaver put it bluntly "History will record Reagan as the man who beat the communists without firing a missile, freed countless humans from the yoke of tyranny and changed the way America looked at itself."[60] Ken Mehlman's comments in the same book, which draw a link from Winston Churchill in World War II to Ronald Reagan in the Cold War to George W. Bush in the War on Terror, show how the Conservatives use the Reagan brand to give the current leaders and policies credentials on national security issues:

> And in the 21st Century we again face a threat and a choice, Do we take the path of Reagan and Churchill to confront international aggressors, stop dictators who threaten their neighbors and bring terrorists wherever they gather? Or do we adopt the false hope of peace though appeasement only to leave our children and future generations with a much larger and more dangerous threat? Conservatives understand the mandate of freedom and that it calls us to the path of resilience. This calling has never been more urgent than now, in the presidency of George W. Bush. Under his leadership, we rise to write the next chapter in freedom's story one whose peaceful ending depends—as always—on our renewed commitment.[61]

The quoted text above shows the extent to which the Reagan, with which Conservative political activists want to work, is very much the Reagan of the brand story. To argue that the Reagan administration played no role in producing the problems that the United States faces in the early twenty-first century is at best self-serving and to claim that the Reagan administration stood for freedom everywhere on an equal basis is likewise misleading. For example, consider the way in which Reagan's role in the Iran-Contra affair was dealt with during his administration. Simply, because this issue was causing problems, the administration repositioned away from Central America to begin discussing the need to negotiate with the USSR[62] and it was Reagan's role in bringing an end to the Cold War that the heritage brand speaks. Turning Reagan into a heritage brand is wise because he introduced a generation to Conservative politics, he was the first Conservative who most Americans liked, and, in many ways, is still the movement's public face. Reagan brought a whole new audience to Conservative politics, and subsequent generations of Conservative marketers have wisely played on that initial relationship by building fellowship between their candidates and policies and the Reagan heritage brand.

Conservatives have tried to reinforce the public's impression that Reagan is a major figure among presidents through a coordinated effort to name as many things as possible after him—put him on U.S. currency or put his image on Mount Rushmore. The net effect of doing so would be to generate more impressions for the Reagan heritage brand, as well as to move the Reagan brand story itself from a matter of assertion to a matter of established fact in contemporary history. Again, the Reagan that is being lionized is not the Reagan of fact but the Reagan created in the marketing campaigns and in the scripted administration.

One of the purposes of a heritage brand is to establish a relationship between the known commodity and its line extensions as was noted above. Conservative marketers have placed a great emphasis on relationship building much as commercial marketers do.[63] Thus, we can see how the Conservatives have gone about building Reagan into a heritage brand, as well as the advantages that the brand strategy conferred upon their candidates come election time. As Viguerie and Franke (2004) note, building lasting value is most important for movements that wish to endure,[64] and, given the transformational nature of what Conservatives were up to, such would have been a logical undertaking.[65] By building a heritage brand and placing it on display in as many places as possible, Conservatives are really trying to both take advantage of their past marketing efforts and build a brand capable of recruiting younger people to the Conservative cause for the next several generations. They can use Reagan in this way because they have been brand building for so long.

Reagan has been developed into a heritage brand because much of what the Reagan team did in 1980 to get its man elected still works and because Reagan was the first Conservative to get elected, he retains great value within the Conservative movement.[66] Republican candidates regularly take cues from the Reagan playbook. To cite but one trivial example, George W. Bush's response to a question uttered during the 2000 presidential election that Jesus was his favorite thinker had been Ronald Reagan's response to a question by journalist David Frost about who his favorite historical figure was.[67] Conservatives will invoke the Reagan name to justify their current policy positions. For example, Susskind reports about a meeting between Vice-President Cheney and Treasury Secretary Paul O'Neil that made direct reference to Reagan to justify the Bush tax proposals. The context is that of a conversation about the impact that some of the proposed reductions would have on the national debt:

> O'Neil jumped in, arguing sharply that the government is "moving toward a fiscal crisis" and then pointing out "what rising deficits will mean to our economic and fiscal soundness." Dick cut him off. "Reagan proved deficits don't matter. . . . He was speechless. Cheney moved to fill the void. "We won the midterms. This is our due."[68]

In this example, the Reagan brand story (that Susskind notes Reagan himself had pragmatically moved away from during his time in office) was used to justify the enactment of a tax plan that was both skewed toward the top end of the party's economic constituency and threatened to place the nation billions of dollars further in debt.

Republican candidates, no matter how patrician, try to play the same kind of everyman character that Reagan played. The average guy or everyman position allows them to contrast themselves and their down-to-earth behavior with that of the Liberal elite.[69] We saw this in 2000 and 2004 when the Bush campaigns did this to Al Gore and John Kerry[70]; in 1988, when George Bush Sr. did it to Michael Dukakis[71]; and once again in the latter stages of the Clinton impeachment when Henry Hyde tried to present himself and his House colleagues as being "blue collar type people."[72] Doing this lets Conservatives show the voters that they share their concerns and interests and to deflect discussion about their personal backgrounds and net worth.

The Reagan heritage brand is of great value to the organizations that make up the rapidly institutionalizing Conservative movement in Washington. These organizations have sought to make use of the heritage brand by building fellowship between Conservative organizations, Conservative policies, and the Reagan brand whenever possible. Reagan is used whenever necessary to sell current policy positions. Reagan's history is used by Washington think tanks and other entrepreneurs to sell everything from tax cuts to calendars. Through its use, the Conservative movement is able to develop contrasts between its positions and candidates against both Liberal Republicans and Democrats. The Reagan brand is frequently used to reemphasize the core principles of the Conservative movement and to emphasize its broad themes. It is used by a variety of Conservative politicians and groups because it allows them to explain what they are for to the public, builds fellowship with a popular ex-president, and allows them to mask their own shortcomings.

The Key to the Conservative Brand

Ronald Reagan is a good foundation upon which a heritage brand can be built because he spoke with conviction about Conservative ideas and to a conservative audience as one of them because he was one of the movement's leading public figures during the 1960s and was able to represent the Conservative movement in a way that the majority of the public found to be acceptable. This was not something that Conservatives like Barry Goldwater had been able to do.[73] Reagan's public persona allowed him to preach the Conservative gospel without scaring Moderate voters away[74] and he did so in a way that was highly convincing because he genuinely looked like he believed all that he was saying and this makes him the ideal candidate to brand.

There are two distinct Reagan administrations: the one that was in the White House for eight years and the one that lives on in the Conservative brand story.[75] This first tends to be much more mixed, has a lot more input from Reagan's critics, deals with the entire administration and is broader in its analysis than the highly sanitized brand story. A good example of this is provided by the economic policy because Reagan Conservatives have a very different sense of an argument about that than many other people.[76] As is the case with all kinds of brands and brand stories, as long as the promise made in them appears to be kept then the facts of any matter do not count for much. Only when the brand promise is not kept will the facts really begin to matter. Thus, Reagan's real accomplishment in office and use now are the same. He shows us how important building a brand is for a political movement.

The Reagan brand essence did not delve deeply into any given policy issue. Rather, it sought to produce a set of emotions as we saw above and as is consistent with the use of a brand strategy. While Democrats and the media criticized Reagan's alleged lack of knowledge about public affairs, this was beside the point because the brand strategy was enabling his administration to produce the desired feelings within its target audience. What the Reagan administration was most concerned about was the creation of positive public feelings about and loyalty toward their man.[77] Such a goal is very much in keeping with the brand strategy because as long as the public only sees the positive and it appears the brand story is being kept, the brand will prosper. For this reason, Reagan remained personally untainted while many in his administration were in legal difficulty. This was another reason why Reagan remained so popular with a large swath of the American public even as he implemented policies that were not in their interest. Simply, because it looked like Reagan was above reproach and interested in pursuing the interests of the everyman that he claimed to, and there was no obvious evidence to visually show that he was not doing so, the Reagan brand could thrive.

Reagan, consistent with the way in which Conservatives have used the brand strategy, pursued policies that, on the surface, appeared to be in the interest of the bulk of the population. For example, Reagan would happily discuss how cutting taxes would benefit people but he would never delve into the more rigorous question of who would benefit most and who would pay for this decision in exactly the same way that George W. Bush would do two decades later.[78] This was made possible because, as was noted above, he spent years learning how to play the everyman role. Even though the United States national debt expanded dramatically during the Reagan years and many, including some members of the subsequent Bush administration, felt that they directly caused a deep recession during the late 1980s and early 1990s, this was no problem for the Reagan brand because these failures visibly happened on somebody else's watch.

The Reagan brand has been able to escape blame for the failures that took place during the administration because Reagan's team positioned him to avoid it while placing it squarely on others.[79] This frequently meant blaming either the bureaucracy as a whole, individuals within the administration, or most frequently the core Conservative brand—the Liberals in Congress. Tip O'Neil became something of a parliamentary opposition leader during the Reagan years in order to blunt the media advantages of the presidency.[80] The Reagan team made good use of positioning and contrast techniques much in the way that we see Newt Gingrich did to argue that their man was on the side of average Americans while the Democrats represented an alphabet soup of Liberal interest groups and other undeserving social elements. When things went well, it was the result of the Reagan policies and when they did not, it was the fault of the Liberals in Congress. The brand strategy that was formulated during the Reagan years enables Conservatives to do so while minimizing the damage that gaffes cause, as was shown in the aftermath of the Iran-Contra scandal.[81] It is little wonder that the result has been the creation of a brand that continues to linger even after the man at the center of it has gone.

Building the Reagan Heritage Brand

Conservatives have built Reagan into a heritage brand because he was the one Conservative whom Americans had grown truly comfortable enough with that they trusted him and building trust in new products is, as noted above, one of the heritage brand's key functions. Additionally, as we have seen, Reagan was the ideal candidate to be turned into a heritage brand because he was the person who had attracted a large number of former Democrats to the Republican Party and lured Moderate to Conservative Democrats to vote for him, the so-called Reagan Democrats.[82] For these reasons, Reagan was the ideal candidate out of whom a heritage brand could be built and, by doing so, Conservatives could take advantage of the good marketing and goodwill that had been done in support of the original product.

Without Reagan in office, Conservatives were going to have a difficult time institutionalizing their movement. Their first problem popped up in the form of George H.W. Bush. He was not part of the Conservative movement and, had coined the phrase "voodoo economics" to describe Reagan's economic policy, and many Conservatives suspected that his was a Paul on the road to the West Wing type of conversion. In addition to having his regional roots in New England, George H.W. Bush was clearly a product of the American upper class, something that Reagan had not originally been nor were many of the people who had become Conservatives because of Reagan either. Micklethwait and Wooldridge (2004) capture the essence of these feelings when they write that, once Bush left office, some Conservatives talked about the "Bush Clinton years"[83] as a piece. As Dick Armey put it:

> When Ronald Reagan left for California on January 20, 1989, George Bush was left with more assets than any president in history. A thriving economy. A world awakening to a new freedom. Socialist ideas in disgrace . . . Seeing liberalism in its death throes, voters turned to George Bush [H.W.] and said, "Finish it off!" Instead, they got a reversal of the Reagan revolution.[84]

From a Conservative perspective, it was not unreasonable to see how the election of George Bush signified an enormous setback for the movement and, over time, a possible return to its role on the fringes of American life because

> to Armey and his allies, the 1988 campaign made clear that Bush was no Ronald Reagan. When Bush was denounced as a wimp on the cover of *Newsweek* or dismissed as "every woman's first husband" on the late-night talk shows, the liberal media were merely saying publicly what many conservatives muttered privately. For a time it looked as if Michael Dukakis could take advantage of this.[85]

Building Reagan into a heritage brand was one way to keep the Conservative movement's profile high in the public, limit Bush's ability to move the party's agenda back to the center, and to keep the contrast alive against the Liberals that had served Conservatism well since the late 1960s. Were Bush able to move the party back to the center then it would lose a significant amount of its ability to build effective brands.

That the patrician Bush ended up as president and as a one-term president showed that there was no way to make sure that Conservatives could regularly find candidates who had the numerous skill sets that Reagan possessed. It also showed that lots of people could use the Reagan playbook and aspects of the brand that Reagan had developed to win the presidency.[86] In the case of George H.W. Bush, his bow to the everyman role involved professing his love for pork rinds, country music, and car racing at various times during the 1988 election and while in office. Additionally, Bush worked with the patriotism theme of the Reagan heritage brand by making an issue out of the flag and the pledge of allegiance, by using country singer Lee Greenwood's song "I'm Proud to be an American" as the campaign's theme song, and by working with the cultural issues of archetypal Conservative brand. Bush used the brand strategy by taking a highly visible cruise around Boston Harbor in order to show that his opponent could not manage his own state and to remind Conservatives skeptical of Bush's roots of exactly which state that was.[87] The Reagan branding effort and the brand that had been built around Reagan were used in the George H.W. Bush campaign.[88] If George H.W. Bush could make use of Reagan in this way, then so could a lot of other Republicans and Conservatives.

My argument is that the heritage brand really was built once Reagan left the national stage during the 1990s. Given his illness, there was little chance that he could continue to function as an active movement leader and pitchman for Conservative causes but, given that he had built up a great relationship with the public and a very favorable reputation within the movement, building him into a brand would allow Conservatives to continue making hay out of him even though he had already left the stage. While Reagan's literal death would not occur for another ten years, his death as a public figure really took place during the middle 1990s. After this, Conservatives have gradually built him into a heritage brand.

Like all of the Conservative brands, the Reagan one was built by the creation of a brand story and essence, the focus of which can be adjusted to fit the interests of a variety of audiences. The brand story includes Reagan's everyman aspects, his personal history, his ideological beliefs, and his public policy successes. His policy successes include ending the Cold War, growing the economy, and changing the nation's mood as well as its self-image. This brand has been built by the same kind of loose network that built the Slick Willie brand. A few individuals, some interest groups and think tanks, as well as some media outlets have preached the gospel of Reagan in every available format and attempted to give him credit for every possible current success. They have sought to inject the Reagan legacy into contemporary debate, to mention it to their targeted constituencies at appropriate times, and to generate as many impressions as they can for the brand by telling its story and naming as many things as possible after Reagan. The point of these efforts is to accentuate the positive about Reagan in order to build a favorable brand essence about him.

Generating Impressions, Building Memorials

One of the ways that Conservatives have disseminated the heritage brand is through the creation of memorials to Reagan. Conservatives have mounted an organized effort to memorialize Reagan in as many places and in as many ways as possible.[89] The first reason for doing so is because of the obvious attachment Conservatives have for Reagan and legitimate belief in the significance of his accomplishments. The second, I am arguing in a way consistent with the marketing literature, is to promote Reagan as a heritage brand, through which other Conservative products and, indeed, other kinds of products, might be sold. The organized campaign to memorialize Reagan can be considered as a form of brand building. A variety of things, from the Florida Turnpike, to the biggest federal building in Washington, and Washington's National Airport to a mountain in New Hampshire have already been named after him.[90] The memorials, of course, stress the brand story that Conservatives are promoting and are a way of generating impressions for it and, by association, with the Conservative movement.

This naming binge is turning Reagan into an archetypical brand for Conservatism in much the same way that John F. Kennedy and Martin Luther King became archetypes (but not brands because they have not had the marketing apparatus placed behind them that Conservatives have placed behind Reagan) for the Democrats during the 1960s.[91] Both these men had a large number of public projects named after them immediately following their deaths (in Kennedy's case the former Idlewile Airport in New York bears his name and just about every city of any size in the United States has a street named after Dr. King who also has a national holiday celebrated in his honor). The Reagan Legacy project Web site comes complete with a list of sites named after Reagan in the United States, as well as in Hungary, Ireland, Poland, Grenada, and the Marshall Islands.[92] The bulk of these are in Illinois and California but there is something named for Reagan in about half of the states. It has proposed putting Reagan's image on American currency, encourages citizens to lobby their elected officials to increase the number of things named after Reagan, and is working to have Reagan honored by the states on his birthday.[93] Even if some of these things are of little physical consequence, it can be argued that they serve to generate impressions for the Reagan brand much as purchasing naming rights on sports stadiums does for corporations.

Many Conservative organizations market themselves using the Reagan brand. For example, consider the case of the Young America's Foundation that owns Rancho del Cielo and uses this affiliation in its marketing efforts. It uses the facility to promote the Conservative cause through its Reagan Ranch program that "fosters the virtues of individual freedom, limited government, patriotism and traditional values"[94] in young people. Following Reagan's death, this organization created a Web site to memorialize Reagan and allowed those who logged onto it to share their memories of the president, played a song entitled "I Remember," and made a number of fundraising appeals to preserve the ranch.[95] The Ronald Reagan Presidential Foundation established its own Web site after his death, where it contains a moving synopsis of Reagan's funeral events, asks for donations to keep his legacy alive, lists the businesses that were the library's official licensees at the time, and links to its catalog, which offers a variety of products including a trademarked line of clothing and accessories named after Reagan.[96] These are very much in keeping with the argument that heritage can be established based on a location and becoming an enduring part of a community.[97]

Washington-based think tanks and interest groups have also tapped into the Reagan heritage. One example is provided by the Heritage Foundation's Reagan Memorial Briefing Room that contains a wide variety of information about him.[98] Doing so is both a way to memorialize a man who really did yeoman work to advance the Conservative cause while at the same time tapping into the considerable brand equity that exists as a result of the work that his own team and subsequent Conservative marketers have done.

Reagan Heritage Logos and Brand Story: Their Use by George W. Bush

The aspects of the Reagan brand fit the core Conservative brand. They are (1) Reagan as everyman, (2) Reagan as Patriot, and (3) Reagan the Liberator.

These are in keeping with Reagan's regional background, personal traits, and target audience interests and have a clear sense of truth to them. The second aspect of the Reagan brand that has been turned into a logo is that of Reagan as patriotic leader. This was a point of emphasis when Reagan was presented either surrounded by the symbols of state or institution or in a situation that stressed them. The third aspect, Reagan the Liberator, places Reagan as Cold War victor. The Republican Party is working to build fellowship between Reagan and Abraham Lincoln. The relationships between the two are as follows: (1) Reagan and Lincoln both remade the shape of the federal union and (2) Reagan and Lincoln both set large numbers of people free. This theme came up repeatedly at his funeral and was most eloquently stated by Lady Thatcher who said that "With the lever of American patriotism" Reagan had "lifted up the world" and went on to list a number of cities in the former eastern bloc before arguing that "the world mourns the passing of the great liberator and echoes his prayer: God bless America."[99]

The linkage between Reagan and Lincoln is intentionally being developed. Lincoln was commonly referred to during the period after his assassination as the Liberator as well. To drive the point home, Conservatives have changed the name of the Republican Party's annual dinner from "The Lincoln Day Dinner" to the "Lincoln-Reagan Day Dinner" and have named their Washington headquarters the Ronald Reagan Center. House Conservatives have proposed a monument to Reagan that would put him in physical proximity to Lincoln on the National Mall because he had "helped restore the American people's faith in our system of government and returned pride in being an American" in the words of one of the cosponsors of a bill that would grant Reagan an exemption to the twenty-five-year waiting period for memorials.[100] Doing this would place the Reagan brand in the category of archetypal brand, cement the impression of the Reagan brand that Conservatives are selling firmly in the public mind, and allow future Conservative candidates to use the Reagan heritage brand to point out how they are just like the man who made America great again.

Reagan was not above blaming his immediate predecessor for the nation's problems, would also regularly invoke Jimmy Carter as a logo for all that the Conservative movement had been complaining about since the 1960s, and would regularly contrast his own strong leadership with Carter's weaker style. George W. Bush and his team have clearly employed this element of the Reagan brand themselves. This has particularly been the case since 9/11.

After that date, Bush has regularly appeared surrounded by the symbols of state, with service personnel, and with those who have lost loved ones either on that day or in the wars since then. By presenting himself as patriotic leader and surrounding himself with these constituencies, Bush has ensured that the audiences before which he appears are supportive (the military has to stand at attention and applaud at his speeches because he is their commander) and the physical settings emphasize the point that he is leading a nation involved in a conflict against "evil" much as Ronald Reagan was in confronting the U.S.S.R.

The contrast between the claims and behavior of Ronald Reagan and George W. Bush show the difference between the original and a line extension. Contrast the Reagan as cowboy brand aspect of the original with that of George W. Bush, the second ranch owner to recently occupy the White House. It appears that Bush's team decided to use the cowboy portion of the Reagan brand given that Bush bought his ranch in 1999.[101] The problem with tapping into this aspect of the Reagan brand has been one of authenticity given the differences between the two men's ranch activities. Regardless, by adopting the cowboy aspect, Bush is able to tap into the equity that the Reagan brand has built with the audience segments that he is targeting. They are united in their use of the brand strategy, but a large part of the way in which George W. Bush has used branding is through the use of Reagan as a heritage brand and, as a result, his administration has been able to tap into years of brand building by Conservative activists, organizations, candidates, and marketers.

Reagan the Brand

Ronald Reagan is a good choice to be a Conservative heritage brand because (1) his public performances contained the key Conservative brand aspects of anticommunism, family, faith, freedom, and patriotism, (2) many Americans liked Reagan personally even if they did not always like what he did in office and, a lot of Americans do remember the 1980s as a good period in the nation's history, (3) Reagan was and remains well known as an optimistic leader to many Americans not only because of his service as president but also because of his prior careers as an actor and a product pitchman and (4) The American public had high levels of trust in Reagan until the Iran-Contra scandal hit and Reagan's team was able to reposition their brand by moving on to negotiating with the Soviets as we saw above. After that he and his supporters moved to limit the amount of damage that Reagan's public image suffered by shifting the subject on to negotiating with the U.S.S.R.[102] and, ultimately, into claiming the collapse of the U.S.S.R. and the end of the Cold War as his great accomplishment. Because he has been transformed into a branded individual, there is no mention made of the numerous policy and ethical failures that took place during his administration.

The sum of these efforts can be seen in the points of emphasis presented in the Reagan Presidential Funeral during June 2004. Reagan was mourned as a patriot, populist, nice guy, and Great Liberator of Eastern Europe, and winner of the Cold War. He was not a millionaire film actor whose political career was supported by a coterie of wealthy supporters, who tolerated corruption in office, dictatorship in the Third World, and was by all accounts somewhat unaware of the activities of the government that he was in charge of. As we shall see in subsequent chapters, the Reagan heritage brand played important roles in the Clinton impeachment, the Bush 2000 electoral strategy and its priorities in government, and the marketing in support of the contract with America. We should not underestimate the extent to which the former party of Lincoln has, in fact, become the party of Reagan. As noted above, the chances of another politician who possessed Reagan's full range of communicative and marketing skills coming along anytime soon is remote, the Conservative movement is as fractious as it has always been and the validity of Reagan's agenda is hardly a settled matter outside of the voter niches who either supported him in life or, if too young to have done so, certainly would have if given the chance. It is for these reasons that the Reagan brand was developed and for these reasons it has been deployed during the last decade and a half. In the next chapter we turn to an examination of the way in which Conservatives dealt with Ronald Reagan's first Democratic successor in the White House by looking at the Clinton scandals as a branded event.

The Clinton Scandals

A Branded Event

The Legacy of the 1992 Bush Campaign

Following Ronald Reagan's departure, George H.W. Bush was elected using the Conservative brand. He did so by making use of highly visible, emotive issues and by playing the everyman character by claiming to love baseball, pork rinds, and country music and frequently called his opponent a "boutique liberal" and a card-carrying member of the Liberal ACLU.[1]

While Bush gained a term in the White House, his team did not expand upon the Republican brand story. Not only could he not communicate his message in simple English, his lack of the so-called Vision Thing meant that he added nothing to put into the brand story. Instead, he rode Ronald Reagan's coattails into office and did not keep the Reagan brand promise.

As Grover Norquist put it: "Bush 41-the dad, he ran as Reagan. The problem was he did not govern as Reagan."[2] Other conservatives said similar things such as "If Bush the candidate was prepared to fight like a Southern redneck, Bush the president preferred to govern like a Tory paternalist."[3] Bush didn't expand conservative dominance but instead said "I don't think about the word 'mandate' . . . I want to work with Congress to determine the will of the people."[4] This was not the way in which the Conservative movement's brand story or behavior was structured and putting someone like Bush into office on the heels of Ronald Reagan's departure had to be an enormous blow to it.

This Bush administration left little impact on the Conservative brand story's contents and Bush was deemphasized in the short term by the Conservative movement. Bush's failures show the importance of having sales and communicative skills as an occupant of the Oval Office, as well as the importance of authenticity for politicians and movements trying to use a brand strategy. George H.W. Bush was never rhetorically able to convince Conservatives that he was one of them, and when he made a highly visible decision to raise taxes, the point was visibly proven. The one branded initiative that the Bush team undertook was the expulsion of Iraqi invaders from Kuwait that was first sold as Operation Desert Shield and then later as Operation Desert Storm.

His failure to expand on the brand story and increase its number of line extensions haunted him when the economy soured in 1992. Bush simply did not have the Conservative activist audience to turn to and, because of his tax flip-flop and attendant failure to reposition the brand, could not run using the Conservative brand with credibility in 1992. The tax flip-flop was a major problem, and as discussed in the last chapter, they were so displeased with Bush and his attitudes toward their movement by 1992 that "they staged an open rebellion with the candidacies of Pat Buchanan and Ross Perot."[5] He could, in short, no longer use the brand strategy without extensive repositioning because he had broken a key promise.

Many leading Conservatives were less than disappointed by his defeat as we can see in the words of Tom DeLay who said of Bush's defeat: "Oh yeah, man, it was fabulous," given that he appeared to regard another potential Bush term as "four years of misery."[6] No longer forced to defend a man whom they did not really feel was one of them, Conservatives were free to attack the man who had defeated him.

   The Bush campaign's contribution to this effort was its creation of an attack strategy that failed in the short term but in the longer term provided the basis for an eight-year-long branded marketing campaign against that year's winner: Bill Clinton. The attack strategy developed by the Bush team served as the basis of the anti-Clinton campaign for years to come. Many of the seeds planted by it did not really catch fire in the public imagination until well after Mr. Clinton's inauguration. By then, Mr. Bush was back in Texas but some members of his administration, a few conservative organizations, and some media outlets were reaping the fruits of the seeds that his campaign had planted.

   What happened to Bush shows that brands take time to acquire equity and that, unless a political brand is launched far in advance of the event in which it is to be used, its effectiveness will be limited. Once the seeds that the 1992 Bush campaign planted began to germinate, a host of organizations and politicians moved to use it. The Slick Willie[7] campaign, developed during the 1992 campaign as a way to raise doubt about Clinton's personal traits, showed that these were juxtaposed against what this work argues as the core of the Conservative brand.

   The anti-Clinton campaign, I am arguing, developed as much to differentiate a variety of products from each other as it did for political reasons. Though this was the first time that they were not in control of the White House since Reagan had led them into power and there was an incentive of Liberal policies actually being implemented in the new unified government,[8] the Clinton scandals were also about holding the Conservative movement together and, as time wore on, about educating its audiences on a variety of Conservative political products. Branding Slick Willie helped Conservative marketers remind their audiences of how much worse Clinton was than other parts of the Conservative movement and teach them about what new things Conservatism had to offer. Without Slick Willie, Conservatives might have had to deal with their movement's ideological contradictions as noted earlier in this work. Clinton gave them real things to be concerned about as well because his agenda offered the possibility of politically advantaging Democrats[9] and, as a result, quickly ending the Conservative era.

Clinton the Preemptor

The Clinton scandals took place because of his stated desire to move his party rightward in order to increase its electoral viability, and he seemed to be making good on that promise because a lot of the agenda was very much in keeping with the centrist theme.[10] In this he looks a lot like the preemptive leader about which Skowronek (1997) has written. Even worse for Conservatives from a marketing perspective, Clinton targeted many of the sectors in which they had made electoral inroads since the 1960s.[11] Conservatives had good reason to fear that Clinton's shifting of the Democrats to the Right would doom their chances of building a governing majority that would implement their ideas. In short, Clinton's election seemed, on the face of it, to undo the smashing Electoral College victories won by Reagan and Bush, roll back Conservative gains in Congress, and seemed to have put an end to Conservatism's golden era. Worst of all, Conservatives felt that Clinton's victory was not legitimate, but was the product of a third party candidate, the Liberal media's misinformation about the state of the economy, a vengeful special prosecutor who released his final report on Iran-Contra on the Friday before election day, and Bill Clinton's lack of candor about his beliefs.[12]

The Slick Willie branding campaign was a product of a culture of scandal and partisan strife that began during the 1960s and continued through Clinton's time in office.[13] The Watergate scandal began an era in which the extent to which the voters trust government had dropped, and was continued by Vietnam. These events have created a sense among Americans that their government is corrupt and it was into that sense that Conservatives tapped with the Slick Willie brand.

The Clinton scandals were informed by Watergate and Iran-Contra in several interesting ways. First, the "gate" suffix has become commonly used shorthand for scandal as it was in this case. Second, all of these scandals have had multiple congressional investigations.[14] Third, all of them featured an independent counsel and howls from counsel's targets about the scope of their jurisdiction and the politicization of their work.[15] Fourth, subpoenas, extensive requests and searches for documents, and extensive legal fees for the targets are parts of recent scandals. Fifth, these scandals, even when they had a policy focus, all focused on the president's personal traits.[16] They dealt with essentially the same themes, including that of the personal corruption of the president. Sixth, the public agenda and public attention shifted from other business onto the scandal at hand.[17]

Scandal is well suited for use by Conservatives in brand building because it proves the validity of the Conservative's antigovernment message. It is ideally suited for making the kinds of appeals to which babyboomers will respond and has the potential to fill up hours of time and attract attention for media outlets. The scandals that Conservatives emphasize fit their brand story and tend to involve social programs while ignoring problems in areas such as military procurement.

Policy scandals have contributed to the core of the brand that they have built around Liberals and they had had good success branding each of Clinton's three Democratic predecessors as logos for scandal. First, there was the promiscuous John F. Kennedy; second, the crude Lyndon Baines Johnson; and third, the incompetent Jimmy Carter. Doing so has given Conservatives a way to present the public with visual proof of their Liberal brand story, allowed them to position themselves in a way that plays up their virtue as a contrast, and helped avoid any discussion on Watergate.

With what they perceived to be Clinton's illegitimate election and the potentially damaging impact on their movement that a rightward shift by Democrats would have on Conservatives, it is hardly surprising that the Conservatives mounted an anti-Clinton campaign based on his personal traits, as well as on the fellowship between him and the Liberals of the brand story. Turning Clinton into another in a line of scandalous Liberal politicians gave Conservatives a way to maintain relationships with their consumers, prevent the public from understanding and Clinton from promoting those parts of his agenda that they opposed on ideological grounds, and provided a sense of vengeance for those caught up in earlier scandals. It was, in short, a way for Conservatives to continue occupying their ascending market position.

A Sign of the Times

The Clinton scandals show the power that the Conservative brand strategy has to mobilize people, even in an era of peace and prosperity like the 1990s. The United States during the period had no international rival for global dominance and the U.S. economy was thought by the public to be soaring by the middle of Clinton's term.[18] Second, the brand gained power because it fit with a culture rife with consumerism, celebrity culture, individualism, and spectatorship that had America affected by the 1990s.[19] This is the culture in which Conservatives have used the brand strategy to build a mainstream movement and, in the absence of a clear policy crisis, it should not be surprising that they found something else that fit with their core brand story and audience expectations: Clinton's personal traits. Absent the advocacy explosion and the proliferation of new media in general and Conservative media in particular,[20] however, the Clinton scandals probably would not have had the large-scale social resonance that they attained. In this they are an evolutionary step forward from the way in which Conservatives used branding through the 1980s to the way in which they use it in the era of 200-channel cable television and the ubiquity of the World Wide Web. Only in such a stable, prosperous national climate could the Clinton scandals have taken place, but the tranquility of the climate also provided an incentive to brand because without a visible, highly emotive series of events out of which to build a narrative, the Conservatives would not have enjoyed the success that they did.

A Different Kind of Marketing

The Clinton case is worthy of examination because it illustrates the differences between the ways in which Conservatives use branding to promote their ideas, personalities, and organizations while they control the White House versus the ways in which they do so when they do not. There are several differences between the way in which Conservatives use branding to sell their organizations and ideas while in government and the way in which they use these things while in opposition. Through its use the Conservatives were able to (1) help create a partisan shift in institutional arrangements by taking over the House of Representatives for the first time in forty years[21]; (2) make the public more aware of the various Conservative think tanks and interest groups than they once were and, as a result, increase these organizations' viability; (3) make use of the work of a number of anti-Clinton activists to both refine their brand story and disseminate it[22]; and (4) take advantage of new partisan media to spread its gospel to new audiences.

The anti-Clinton campaign shows how Conservative interest groups and partisans use the brand strategy without control of the White House or the presence of a high stimulus public event like a presidential election to attract audiences' attention. The way in which Conservatives worked with the brand strategy during the Clinton years shows how they have become an inside Washington instead of grassroots-based movement but one that has many years worth of established brand equity with which to work. This shows how Conservatives have applied the brand strategy to the techniques of the corporate campaign that has been more commonly used by the Left.[23] The Conservative brand strategy let the movement build momentum, take over Congress, and promote a generally weak product in an effective way in order to make up for the loss of the White House.

The anti-Clinton campaign typifies the way in which Conservatives use branding to make focused appeals to select audiences and switch the aspect of the brand being presented to individual audiences. The Clinton scandals fit the brand strategy as they were turned into a narrative focusing on Clinton's personal traits, as well as a few policy preferences that allowed new events to be quickly folded into it. This narrative was solidly rooted in the archetypal brands that Conservatives have built around themselves and the Democrats, because a logo, essence, and slogan were built around Clinton and these too were rooted in the archetypal Conservative brands, and because this very hot narrative was endlessly repeated through a wide variety of media in order to maximize the core audience's exposure to it.

As is typical of corporate campaigns, the movement roots of Conservatism, which we saw in Chapter 2, and the competitive world of media and interest group marketing, those promoting an issue had a variety of motives for doing so. For interest groups, think tanks, and new Conservative media outlets, promoting these scandals raised their profiles, built their audiences, and improved the bottom line.[24] For Conservative politicians, the incentive was to build their own support and, as we see in the example provided by the Contract with America, develop a single-focused point against which to campaign. For members of the Nixon, Reagan, and Bush administrations, there was a more personal motive: revenge.[25] Especially after 1994, they were typical of the institutional battles that had taken place earlier in the era of divided government.[26]

The Clinton scandals show the benefits that branding bestows on Conservatives in the crowded marketplace of political ideas that has come into being because of the explosion in interest groups, think tanks, and the partisan press.[27] The brand's power has only increased this well because of the celebrity-based political culture that is developing here,[28] as well as the consequences of a media that devotes most of its coverage to public affairs through the use of an infotainment formula.[29] The upshot of these trends has been to produce a political environment in which a brand strategy can give a significant advantage to those making use of one.

As discussed in Chapter 1, the Conservative movement has a long tradition of brand-based marketing. The Clinton scandals were very much informed by this experience because they depended on a hot, focused narrative to hit their audience targets and, as typical of branded Conservative direct mail marketing, played upon the audience's feelings to succeed.[30] In the Slick Willie case, the feelings were distrust of both Clinton personally and Democratic public officials in general.[31] Further, they were a device through which Clinton was extended into the Liberal brand that Conservatives have been building around Democrats for the past forty years. Because the Clinton scandals were brand based, they were durable and able to produce great interest within focused audiences. Because they were a branded event, backed up by focused marketing efforts, it took a long time for the final impeachment stage to take place. Consequently, Conservatives were able to deemphasize these scandals in order to reposition their core brand after their defeat in the 1998 election and in the impeachment effort. Also, the movement's next presidential nominee was able to focus on his own favorable traits and only implicitly raise the branded campaign. Both the Conservative movement in general and George W. Bush specifically moved away from talking about Slick Willie toward talking about their heritage brand: Ronald Reagan.

The narrow nature of the anti-Clinton campaign explains both why it endured and why it failed to build broad public support for Clinton's impeachment. Unlike the earlier scandals of the late twentieth century the Clinton scandals fit the niche, lifestyle orientation that we saw most brand-building activity entails in contemporary America. The Clinton scandals appear to have been targeted at three specific demographic groups: orthodox religious elements, culturally insecure lower class white males, and baby boomers.[32] The earliest phases of the campaign resonated with those who did not like Clinton as governor, those for whom the George H.W. Bush's 1992 marketing campaign about Clinton's personal traits had resonated, the Conservative policy networks that would suffer setbacks if Clinton's agenda was implemented, Conservative activists whose businesses would suffer if Clinton successfully shifted the Democratic Party rightward, and ardent Bush backers of whom many had lost high prestige jobs with Clinton's election. The early Slick Willie campaign recycled accusations made by his home-state political opponents because such material was easy to get, because it fit with the personal-attribute marketing that the Bush team had done, and because much of it fit within the core Conservative brand story about Liberals.[33]

The brand strategy helped Conservatives prove to their audiences that Clinton really was an unreformed 1960s Liberal as they had claimed in 1992. The brand story focused almost entirely on Clinton's personal traits of which two in particular stood out: his womanizing and his inability to tell the truth. These two issues are ideally suited for the brand strategy because they tap into the morality and 1960s' aspects of the brands that Conservatives have built around liberals. Clinton's opponents developed a brand around his personal traits but they were traits that fit squarely within the brands Conservatives had spent the last several decades building about Liberals. Clinton's dishonesty fit squarely within the line of thinking among Conservatives that suggested that if Clinton told the public the truth that he was a Liberal politician, and if he would govern as a Liberal then he would never have won the 1992 election.

Just as would eventually be done to Al Gore ("He invented the Internet") and John Kerry ("He voted for it before he voted against it"), a Clinton quote was used to encapsulate the essence of the brand that Conservatives were building around him and to prove its validity. This quote, taken from a flippant answer about youthful marijuana use, "I tried it but I never inhaled" came to sum up the Slick Willie brand during its early period much as his direct denial about his affair with Monica Lewinsky, "I didn't have sex with that woman—Ms. Lewinsky" later encapsulated its essence and proved its validity.

Slick Willie became the embodiment of all that was wrong with Democratic Liberals at the present time and in the past. Clinton's efforts to associate himself with the legacy of John F. Kennedy played right into the Conservatives' hands because they had built a successful movement in opposition to these kinds of Liberal programs and because public knowledge of Kennedy's womanizing seemed to underscore the message that Clinton could not be trusted. The Slick Willie campaign shows branding's worth in a politics that is generally conducted in a niche-media environment. The brand strategy lets the marketer focus only on those aspects of the brand to which the audience is most likely to respond strongly.

The use of the brand strategy and the fellowship built between the Slick Willie and archetypal Conservative brand, as well as its promotion through niche interest group and Conservative friendly media campaigns meant that the Conservative audience understood what was generally wrong with Clinton and cared deeply about it. The rest of the population, which was not on the receiving end of these brand-based marketing and media campaigns, saw a series of not very serious isolated events. This difference in perception explains why those exposed to the brand story were ardent impeachment supporters while nobody else was. This is why the campaign endured for so long yet failed to build broad public support for the Clinton impeachment.

The Slick Willie brand was pitched at the mature, baby-boomer and generation X audiences. One of the places in which we can see this is in the amount of heat placed in the brand because such a message appeals to the baby-boom audience.[34] Most of the campaign's issues had something to do with the 1960s, a decade that is irrelevant to younger generations but one about which boomers and matures care deeply. As Smith and Clurman show, the Vietnam War created divisions in baby-boom attitudes from the 1960s until the time Clinton took office.[35] As we have seen, the 1960s form much of the basis upon which the archetypal Conservative brands are built. Conservatives built fellowship between Clinton's personal traits, life story, and that decade in order to place him within the movement's core brand stories. The Slick Willie brand was pitched to generation X because its aspect that focused on Clinton's dishonesty fit with this generation's worldview that political institutions and politics are corrupt.[36] Thus, the brand was pitched at the three biggest age groups within the electorate.

Polling results dealing with Clinton's personal attributes show that the campaign successfully built a negative brand essence about him with a large segment of the electorate. For example, a 2006 *Wall Street Journal/NBC News Poll* found that 27% of respondents thought very favorably about Clinton while 21% thought otherwise[37] A similar poll, in 2001, found 18% very favorable and 31% unfavorable,[38] thus showing that the Slick Willie brand still has power. One of the upshots of which is that there is little possibility that Clinton could soon serve as a heritage brand for the Moderate wing of the Democratic Party in the same way that Ronald Reagan does for the Conservatives. If the goal of the campaign was to do that—block Clinton's agenda and build audiences for a plethora of Conservative producers—then the Slick Willie campaign was a huge success.

The Clinton Scandals and the Conservative Brand Strategy

The Clinton scandals represented the state-of-the-art use of the Conservative brand story in their day. They remain a textbook example of the way in which Conservative organizations pursue the brand strategy to market their products. These scandals are of interest in this book because they are a good case study of the way in which ideological media, interest groups, and think tanks use the brand strategy to sell their products to their desired audience segments and, by doing so, stay in business and gain influence.

The Clinton scandals are a classic example of the way in which an entire category can be grown because, through these events, each Conservative producer was able to differentiate themselves while building the overall market for the Conservative product.[39] These efforts offered the additional possibility that Clinton's policy proposals could be blocked and, maybe, that Clinton might be removed from office. The Slick Willie brand was a means through which Conservatives could continue building relationships with their audience targets even though they no longer controlled any of the elected institutions of government. It offered a way for the large number of now unemployed Conservatives to find and keep jobs because it offered the potential to grow the overall category and differentiate organizations.

The Slick Willie brand and the marketing campaign that was launched to promote it took advantage of the tools and talent available in a market that required these organizations to differentiate themselves and, in this, it was ideally suited to the Conservative movement's needs at the time. The Clinton scandals offered Conservative producers a chance to introduce themselves to new audiences, reinforce their relationships with extant audiences, and keep the customers fired up at a time when the other guys were running the government. Although some Conservative organizations had been using a brand strategy for years, for others the Clinton scandals offered them a chance to establish their own identity and increase public awareness of that identity by making use of the brand strategy. The brand strategy is of use to these kinds of groups because it lets them build a narrative that can prod people to action. In this, it is the marketing equivalent of what Schier (2000) terms an activation strategy.[40] It is this motivational goal that provides an incentive to produce a hot brand story because people become more active when they feel threatened.[41] Heat is put into a brand as a way to deepen the relationship that the audience feels and their loyalty toward it over time.[42] The Slick

Willie brand was deep because it focused on a single concept, ended up defining the category of American and Conservative politics, was durable, had a somewhat consistent selling proposition, and its communication was very regular.[43] The anti-Clinton campaign shows why these organizations use activation strategies, hot messages, and do so over time in order to build an enduring brand. In Clinton's case, the brand that was built rested on his personal failings because they fit with the brand strategy, because they fit the audience's interests and media coverage formulas, and because they could be repeatedly reiterated.

Branding became particularly important for Conservatives as a slew of new products appeared during the 1990s about which the public needed to learn and which needed to be differentiated from each other.[44] Branding Clinton offered a vehicle through which entrepreneurs could (1) expand ratings, circulation, support, and make dues payments, (2) increase their public profiles in order to teach the public about their products, and (3) develop a dedicated customer base.[45] The goal was not just to impeach Clinton, it was to continue building the movement and promoting its agenda.

The Clinton scandals show how difficult it is to move from a niche to a mass-based campaign. The niche campaign was aimed at the Conservative movement and those swing voters who were likely to support Conservative candidates. The niche campaign was long-running, built the Slick Willie brand, and raised the profiles of many of the organizations associated with it. The mass campaign, while it made the public aware of Clinton's personal foibles, did not do those things nor did it arouse public ardor for Clinton's impeachment or increase popular support for the Conservative movement based on the outcome of the 1998 congressional election and polling data from the period. The difference between the two shows the importance of repetition, multiple distribution channels, and creating a consistent narrative in support of the brand. Conservatives, who were predisposed to like the anti-Clinton message, were exposed to it for years and understood the way in which it fit into the movement's core beliefs the way nobody else did.

There are three reasons why the Clinton impeachment was not salable to a mass audience. First, the Slick Willie brand did not appear in the mainstream press until years after the Conservative audiences had seen it.[46] Thus, there were fewer impressions generated for it and, because it was presented through the press that was not allied with the Conservative movement, the brand story received by the public was much more mediated than the brand story received by Conservatives. In short, the mass audience did not have the same brand awareness of the importance of Clinton's crimes and how those fit into a pattern with Liberals because they had not been educated about these topics for so long and so completely. The number of scandals presented, while a function of the need to differentiate that we saw in Chapter 1, also caused the brand to lose focus and hence lose its power.[47] To Conservatives, impeachment seemed necessary while to everyone else it seemed an illogical overreach.

Second, the mass audience was not as biased against Clinton and toward this message. It required a much higher level of proof for each allegation and this proved to be the bane of the impeachment campaign. Conservatives were likely to believe what was being told in this brand story because, as we saw in Chapter 1, brands are about relationship building as much as they are about immediate selling. Conservative audiences had relationships with these marketers and their brands and, as a result their second subbrands and line extensions built more credibility with their target audiences around the anti-Clinton message than would a general audience.

Third, Conservatives lost the consistency in their message during the fall of 1998 when they began trying to draw a parallel between the Clinton and Watergate scandals as a justification for the looming impeachment vote. Much too late in the game, they suddenly tried to introduce a Nixon/Watergate aspect into the brand that they built around Clinton in order to teach the public how this scandal was just like that one. While Conservative audience segments immediately got the connection between the two, the rest of the public did not understand how Clinton was, in the Conservative brand story, guilty of exactly the same kind of obstruction and perjury as was Nixon. Conservatives failed to convince the public that the Clinton scandals were like the archetypal Watergate scandal because they started to incorporate the latter into the brand story and public image building efforts much too late in order to justify Clinton's impeachment. Had they done so earlier and not seemed to have been politically motivated, thus giving their brand the problem of credentials,[48] the public might have received more exposure to that aspect of the brand story and been more willing to buy into it. Thus, it is obvious from our discussion that Slick Willie was a brand and it is important to understand the story underlying the brand as we now do.

Brand Story and Essence

The Clinton impeachment would not have been possible without Slick Willie, the brand promoted throughout the scandals. The Slick Willie brand contained a narrative built out of Clinton's dishonesty in marriage, in service to his country, in outlining his policy preferences during the 1992 election, and in telling his personal story during that same contest. These latter two points were important to the creation of Slick Willie because the 1992 Clinton campaign had presented its man as a sax playing, barbecue eating, everyman who understood the problems facing average Americans and would implement policies to help.[49] Because the Clinton team had made such good use of the Reagan everyman aspect of the Conservative brand, his election posed a threat to its continuation as a core part of the Conservative brand capable of differentiating the movement from the Democrats and, as a result, it is not surprising that the Slick Willie brand was aimed at demolishing Clinton's everyman aspect by pointing out that his values were not like those of average Americans.

Conservatives had failed to build fellowship during the 1992 election between Clinton and their core Liberal brand in general and its elite aspect in particular, but it appears that they never stopped trying to do so afterward. They did so by sometimes turning Clinton's everyman story about his humble roots into a lurid tale about what is sometimes called "white trash" in the South,[50] noting that he was the product of three elite educational institutions at a time when they were solidly in the hands of the Liberals of the Conservative brand, had received preferential treatment during the Vietnam era, had journeyed to the USSR during the 1960s, and that he had protested the Vietnam War while overseas. As time went on, Conservatives also noted that Clinton loved high-end products and snazzy vacation spots, as well as hung out with other members of the American Liberal elite, and as the impeachment gained steam Conservatives began referring to him by his full name. Eventually, they built fellowship between Clinton and Ted Kennedy, as was done to John Kerry in 2004. In both cases, the point of doing so was to extend the Liberal brand to place these candidates solidly within it, and in the Clinton case, it was to show what he really was versus what he claimed to be. All of this was intended to resonate with the Conservative audience by extending Clinton into the Liberal brand, launching the Slick Willie brand and, on some level, appears to have been aimed at reducing the chances that the Democrats could credibly run an everyman candidate again soon.

As Democrats often do, Clinton helped his Conservative opponents by showing how his campaign promises had not been kept and, indeed, on one of the ways about which Conservatives and a lot of middle-class voters care deeply, tax cuts, Clinton broke his promise (much as the first George Bush had but the second would not) and by doing so, gave credibility to the Slick Willie brand story. Clinton's first two years in office gave the Conservative brand credibility as well when he nominated two women to be attorney general, both of whom had to withdraw because they had not paid their nannies' taxes. The problem was a double score for the Conservatives because everymen pay their taxes and they do not hire nannies.

The way in which Clinton went about staffing this and other positions introduced a hot button issue that resonates with Conservative voters, affirmative action, into the brand story and his promotion of it helped Conservatives to show that Clinton was not really a "New Democrat" but just another Liberal politician and there was a measure of truth to the accusation that he was trying to revive the Liberals in government. Clinton received no help from the members of his own party in Congress who immediately engaged him in a debate about allowing gays to serve in the military. Clinton's advocacy in favor of a gay's right to serve resonated negatively with a large segment of the public.[51] Clinton's early missteps[52] and decisions gave Conservatives an opportunity to present him personally as dishonest and politically as the Liberal of their brand stories. By the end of 1993, Conservatives had been able to reacquaint the public with their version of the Clinton life story and to using it in the story that would underlie their own Clinton brand: Slick Willie.

Why There Was No Vast Right-Wing Conspiracy

A loose network promoted the Clinton scandals and, for that reason, these scandals bear a relationship to the corporate campaigns of which Manheim has written and the way in which branding is used by entrepreneurs to support their new companies and products. Branding is a useful tool in promoting new products because it can (1) get the consumer interested in the product category being promoted and (2) show the consumer why this particular product is the best in the category.[53] Conservative marketers used the Clinton scandals to build general interest in Conservative politics and their political products specifically. Thus, it took two years for the Slick Willie brand to emerge as a whole.

Clinton was not the target of a single coordinated effort. The "vast right wing conspiracy" of which Hillary Clinton so famously spoke was a typical branded consumer product marketing campaign. Those Conservative entrepreneurs who jumped into the product category bandwagon early on had the most success with it as Ries and Ries explain is often the case with branded campaigns.[54] As is the case in all branding campaigns, later market entrants have to find a way to distinguish themselves.[55] In the Clinton case, this meant finding a unique scandal or a unique aspect of a scandal. It was the need to differentiate, not blind hatred or a partisan conspiracy, that pushed the campaign in so many different directions, and through disunity, gradually reduced the amount of credibility that each and the entire campaign was given by the public.[56] This, in turn, gave the entire campaign the problem of credentials.

The message's early disunity was also a product of the way in which niche marketing works as each producer was trying to fit the anti-Clinton aspect into their brand and, to do so, had to make sure that this was relevant to their target audience. Slick Willie became the dominant brand as (1) it and its many variations appeared prominently during his administration, (2) it captures the brand narrative of the time, and (3) the vast bulk of the Conservative marketers tapped into this essence, story, and brand aspects, and made use of the same examples to prove the validity of what they were saying. One example is provided by Rush Limbaugh's frequent references to Clinton as "Der Slickmeister." Despite the slightly different phrasing, the essence and narrative into which these words tap is very much the Slick Willie brand story and the visual images that it conjures are very much those of the Slick Willie brand.

The entrepreneurial nature of the anti-Clinton campaign is further shown by the shift that took place during the campaign's impeachment phase away from Slick Willie, which by then had serious credential problems, toward the use of Clinton's full name in an obvious effort to build fellowship with Richard Nixon. Further, this was an attempt to educate the public about the seriousness of Clinton's crimes, as well as to show the general public that they were as serious as those committed by Nixon in Watergate as the Conservative audience already believed. Lastly, an equation of Clinton with Nixon was another effort to make sure that the Democrats would not be able to use him as the Conservatives use Reagan as a heritage brand for a successful movement's products.

From a branding standpoint the problem, was that Conservatives tried to establish this fellowship too late in the game to teach the audience about it in the same way that years of activity had already done in the Conservative audience.

The competing points of emphasis in the early Clinton campaign show that it was not an organized conspiracy but was a differentiated branded marketing campaign. A conspiracy would have produced a single logo, slogan, brand story, and essence and a few aspects of Clinton about which it spoke. Those would have been held steady, reiterated, and gradually incorporated wholesale into the Conservative brand story instead. The number of scandals and the too numerous points of emphasis about the brand story were equivalent to the problem of too many line extensions.[57] By having so many different parts of the brand story in the public discourse at once, the value of the overall branding exercise became diluted. This dilution was a direct result of the producers' need to differentiate themselves from each other or, if not doing so, to find an aspect of a Clinton scandal that would let them use a "me too" strategy in the way that Ries and Trout argue can be done.[58] An organized effort would not have faced the competitive pressures requiring differentiation and could have developed a single brand story, logo, and essence, would have kept the vast bulk of the business generated by the scandals in the hands of the extant producers, and would not have been in the interest of the new entrants.

This was not a conspiracy, the same needs to target, differentiate, and educate the public about the brand that exists in all sorts of consumer marketing existed in this case. Some stressed the military, others stressed the moral, others stressed rights claims, and others emphasized policy choices. What was constant was that all agreed that Clinton was too clever for his own good and played fast and loose with the truth when it served him to do so. Consistency is one of the keys to brand building because it helps the public understand what the brand stands for.[59] And, in this case, there was no message consistency.

The anti-Clinton campaign was very effective in terms of reinforcing brand loyalty among Conservatives and in attracting some new recruits for their causes. The more one consumed Conservative media, participated in Conservative-oriented interest groups, and was affiliated with one of the relevant religious denominations, then the more likely one was to believe in the scandal message.[60] Each Clinton scandal broke in niche media aimed at Conservative audiences but the better quality ones moved into the mainstream press and audience. The niche campaign successfully kept the attention of its most attentive public and its backers tried to expand it one niche at a time. The problem was that this campaign eventually reached an audience resistance level that reduced its chances of removing Clinton from office but made its perpetuation profitable. The marketing model at work is outlined below[61] and its organization in great part explains why the scandals unfolded as they did:

Step I	Republican Party, Conservative activists, or interest groups promote story to
Step II	Conservative media. This produces
Step III	A trickle of corporate media coverage and this leads to
Step IV	More Conservative entrepreneurs attempting to fit their niche products into the scandal of the moment. This in turn generates
Step V	More media coverage in the corporate and Conservative media and talk radio.

This, in turn, generates

Step VI	A large number of impressions (the number of times that an idea is presented in the media and the average receptor hears it) of a negative nature about Clinton and these build
Step VII	The brand (with the subsidiary logos of Slick Willie/William Jefferson Clinton as a counter to Nixon) among targeted constituencies.

An example of this is provided by the Troopergate scandal. It was promoted by Little Rock activists,[62] and was prominently reported in the Conservative media by the *American Spectator*,[63] made its way onto Conservative talk radio, and quickly entered the mainstream media.[64] Because it was wildly successful in building awareness about Clinton and the magazine that first published the story, as is true for all producers the first market entrant has more advantages and those who came later had to find a way to differentiate themselves from the current occupants. Like a lot of the material out of which the Slick Willie brand was created, this one had a serious credential problem because the Troopers allegedly had ulterior motives in raising the issue.[65] Thus, those audiences that were predisposed to dislike Clinton bought into this story while the rest of the public either did not pay any heed or adopted a discounted version of it.

This, in a nutshell, was the core problem with the Slick Willie brand. The anti-Clinton message being sold to Conservatives was, by the time of the impeachment, serving only to reinforce brand loyalty not expanding market share. It very much resembles the marketing problems facing high-technology marketers of which Moore (1991) has written because, although the Conservatives were able to convince their core audiences that Slick Willie's crimes were a hot product, they could not convince anyone else of this proposition. The segment-by-segment strategy that Moore argues can lead to market dominance,[66] failed in this case because they were never able to find the single highly identifiable theme to which the public would respond and, as a result, failed to cross the chasm from niche player to market ownership.[67]

Role of New Media

We can see the importance of the brand strategy generally and the Slick Willie brand in particular in educating Conservative audiences about the rapidly burgeoning partisan media that Conservatives built during the period. Because the Conservative movement has always felt excluded from the mainstream, it has always made an effort to develop its own media and intellectual capital-generating institutions.[68] Two innovations: the World Wide Web and talk radio made it possible for these institutions to reach bigger audiences and the Slick Willie brand and the scandals on which it rested was the vehicle through which Conservatives did so. While all sorts of Conservative producers and politicians made use of these technologies and the Slick Willie brand to increase their audiences and bottom lines, perhaps no part of the Conservative movement made out better over the long term through the use of these branded scandals than did the Conservative media.[69] The Clinton scandals were not only about politics but also about building brand loyalty and establishing positions for new Conservative products.

Talk radio and the Internet were key tools through which the Slick Willie brand was promoted as (1) Conservatives dominated the talk radio category in terms of hosts and outlets, (2) both tapped into a large, previously underserved market for Conservative political products because they were readily available in the places in which Conservatives lived, and (3) both, as does direct mail, allowed the Conservatives to get their message out efficiently without mediation of the mainstream media and were very important in building the Conservative movement.[70] These opened new markets for Conservatives that were well suited to their branding technique. As Hunter[71] shows, direct marketers feel it is very important to have a devil in their appeals. Bill Clinton served as that devil and the Slick Willie brand that was built had a powerful enough logo and deep enough equity to keep the Conservative issue networks activated.

Talk radio was particularly important in spreading the Slick Willie brand story, and this was particularly true of the Rush Limbaugh program. Limbaugh's program was aired in a number of very small markets in which Conservatives happen to reside in large numbers.[72] Limbaugh, in short, found a bigger market for Conservative political products. Other Conservative producers bought time on the Limbaugh show to reach this audience and made use of the Slick Willie brand to rapidly teach this new audience about their products. Talk radio could simply distribute the product more quickly than could the prior Conservative marketing medium: direct mail.[73] Limbaugh, in effect, developed a better distribution system for the brand. Like the groups that bought ad time on his program, Limbaugh loved to point out the inconsistencies in Clinton's campaign and his behavior in office, as well as to reiterate the brand stories that Conservatives had built around Liberals since the 1960s.[74] This made their ads a natural fit on his show and with his audience.

Limbaugh's success attracted others who had the problems noted above. As a result, this limited the consistency of the message because they had to figure out how to differentiate or tag along, which, as noted earlier, is a typical problem for later entrants into a category. The niche nature of these producers meant that all of them were emphasizing slightly different aspects of the Slick Willie brand even though, to the untrained ear, this sounded like a single disciplined message. In reality each producer pointed out the problem with Slick Willie to which the target audience would respond. The consequences of this competitive but conservative new media system were (1) a shifting scandal subject, (2) a lack of a clear scandal narrative until just before the impeachment process began in earnest, (3) a constant conversation among Conservatives about Bill Clinton's corruption that was invisible to the rest of the nation, and (4) a stronger imperative to use the brand strategy. In such a highly visible, competitive environment, Conservatives were not able to take the years to focus the Slick Willie brand that they had had to build their own. This, in part, explains why there was never a single effort to target Clinton and, why, when Conservatives had to present a serious, substantive, single charge against Clinton, they could not, but it also shows the brand's power in building and sustaining political organizations.

The power that the Slick Willie brand had in promoting new Conservative products produced more Conservative products. For example, the Weekly Standard, National Empowerment Television, and GOPTV were all launched during the Clinton administration.[75] The Slick Willie brand energized the Conservative publishing business, brought it new readers, and produced a large number of new titles. Among the many titles published were *The Final Days: The Last Desperate Abuses of Power by the Clinton White House* by the late Barbara Olsen (who had earlier authored a study of Hillary Clinton entitled *Hell To Pay: The Unfolding Story of Hillary Clinton*), Edward Timperlake's *Year of the Rat: How Bill Clinton Compromised U.S. Security for Chinese Cash,* and R. Emmett Tyrell's *Boy Clinton: The Political Biography.*[76] By the end of Clinton's term, Conservatives had established a number of organizations, captured a congressional majority, and built an independent mechanism through which they could communicate with their audiences. In this sense, the scandals should be considered a big success.

In order to teach the public about their brand and the products being promoted by it, Conservative interest groups and think-tank leaders used new media to present the specific aspect of the Slick Willie brand, the unique aspect of the scandals or, in some cases, new scandals to their audience targets. The aspects of the Slick Willie brand that the producer chose to emphasize appear to act more to differentiate one Conservative organization from another, in the way that Trout and Rivkin (2000) suggest, than to damage Clinton politically. The result of this being that the constant buzz that developed around the brand deepened loyalty to it among Conservatives; the producers failed to convince members of other audience segments to buy into the branded product being sold.

As noted in the earliest portion of this work, the Slick Willie brand was aimed at baby boomers, X-ers, and matures.[77] It should not come as a surprise that the brand was most widely distributed in the media noted above and that its brand story had contents and a feel to which its three kinds of target audiences would respond, especially baby boomers who are highly moralistic and respond to such messages.[78] We can see how the 1960s' archetypal Conservative brand aspect was included within the Slick Willie brand in the following chart:

Clinton Scandals and Subtexts

SCANDAL	SUBTEXT
Extra-Marital Affairs	Free Love Movement
Oxford Student Protests	Vietnam War
Moscow Visit/ Chinese Campaign Donations	Communism
Arlington Cemetery Sales	Patriotism
Clinton's African American Child	Civil Rights Movement
Whitewater	Ordinary Corruption
Travelgate/Filegate	Elitism/Ordinary Corruption
Katherine Willie/Juanita Broaderick/ Paula Jones	Feminism
Monica Lewinsky	Watergate/Feminism/ Traditional Values

On the left column are the specific scandals and on the right are the 1960s-based issue categories into which each falls. It is logical to assume that Conservatives built the Slick Willie brand to appeal mostly to boomers because, at the time, boomers made up a very big share of the population and, as a result, the political marketplace.[79] Because these are issues that are highly visible and emotive, perfect for use in a brand-building campaign and as an archetypal aspect of the core Conservative brand, the 1960s are something that the audience is used to hearing and deeply caring about.

Branding Slick Willie in this way was a logical way for Conservatives to reinforce brand loyalty and maintain relationships that had been built over years with their consumers while the movement was temporarily out of the White House during the 1990s. Even if a coherent narrative never developed, the niche branding campaign was very successful as an exercise in organization building. The Republican Party raised money, blocked Clinton's proposals, won control of both Houses of Congress and, in part, used the Slick Willie brand to sell its 2000 candidate. Second, a number of new media producers used the Slick Willie brand to build audience awareness of and market share for their products. Third, Conservative interest groups and think tanks used specific aspects of the Slick Willie brand to do the same. Their early efforts were aided by the fact that Democrats controlled Congress and the White House, thus putting them in a position to implement their "liberal" agenda, as well as to soon pack the Supreme Court.

Later, Clinton's failure to keep his visible promises and his work with a number of highly charged social issues gave the branding campaign momentum because it showed the audience that what was being said about Clinton was, in fact, true. The Slick Willie branding campaign gained further momentum because it fit the large number of cable television channels that had come online during the 1990s that needed to fill endless programming hours.[80] It was a story with a lot of heat, in which each player could choose one aspect to focus on, and just as did Conservative media entrepreneurs, could differentiate themselves by doing so. The bulk of these channels appear to have followed the infotainment formula of which Bennett (2003) has written. One of the other aspects of their coverage formula that furthered the Clinton scandals was an emphasis on social scandals that seems to have focused mostly on crime and sex.[81] The Clinton scandals worked for these outlets because what they came to be about fit their apparent coverage formulas. The need among the Conservative movement to differentiate its products from one another meant that there would always be new angles of old scandals to be analyzed and new scandals to talk about.

How and Why This Lasted So Long

Why the Slick Willie campaign lasted for so long with so little fact behind it is a testimony to the advantage that the brand strategy has bestowed upon Conservatives. Even though the Clinton administration might have been doing a good substantive job, its performance on the highly visible, emotive matters upon which Conservatives have launched their brand strategy was not good. Clinton broke promises, tapped into the minority side of a variety of cultural issues, and, given the security that surrounds the President, was easily shown to not be an everyman, a problem that his early communicative stumbles exacerbated.

Clinton's highly visible errors were enough to enable Conservative marketers to show that there was considerable validity to their brand promises. In the end, it did not achieve Clinton's removal from office because it was too difficult to create enough line extensions out of personal failings to attract a majority of public support for impeachment. Also, it did not do so because, as noted elsewhere, his removal would not have been as good for business as this was a crisis that could be promoted on an ongoing basis. An affair with an intern was exactly the kind of thing that most people could understand, see (especially because of the endless replays of a Clinton-Lewinsky hug on television), and about which most people held strong feelings.[82] By focusing on these kinds of highly visible, emotive issues, Conservatives launched a somewhat successful branding campaign against Clinton, albeit one with little substance until the Lewinsky scandal emerged, behind it. Clinton, in contrast, never built an enduring positive brand around himself and this is why the Conservatives were able to brand him in this way, without discussing the policies that Clinton did brand. Also, it means that the public perceives Clinton as not having the core values that either the branded George W. Bush or Ronald Reagan are widely believed to have had.

Before closing our examination of Clinton, I shall briefly run through the evolution of the campaign from its early days to its conclusion shortly after Bill Clinton left the White House. My points in doing so are to illustrate the ways in which Conservatives build and distribute their brands. As noted in the beginning of the chapter, Americans met the traits that would become Slick Willie during 1992. These traits were Clinton as a draft-dodger of questionable patriotism. They did so by raising questions about his involvement in antiwar rallies, his visits to Moscow, and by producing a letter that Clinton had written to an ROTC officer in Arkansas that quoted him as saying that he "loathed" the military. This latter point was used to buttress Bush's assertions that Clinton was a man of questionable integrity as it showed him backing out of an earlier commitment to serve. Fourth, the Bush campaign began the process of building fellowship between Slick Willie and the 1960s and tax and expenditure aspects of the archetypal Conservative brand. There was no need for Bush to discuss Clinton's reputation as a womanizer because that had been thoroughly discussed during the primaries. It was Clinton's own errors early in his term that gave validity to these assertions. Clinton, through his appointments, through the battles he had waged with Congress, and through his change of heart on tax cuts had revealed himself to be another in the long line of Liberals as presented in the Conservative brand story.

The Slick parts of Clinton's character were reinforced during the early years of his administration, as was noted above, because of Clinton's appointments policy (which brought up the affirmative action, feminism, and gay rights issues), and the fight that his administration got into with the Senate over the military's policy on dealing with homosexual soldiers. Further evidence for this was provided by the sex education advice that his female African American Surgeon General could not stop giving out, by Clinton's repeated attendance at African American church services on Sundays, by the gays and lesbians that he nominated to high government positions, and by the scandals that some his appointees got themselves into that were garden variety stuff in post-Watergate Washington.[83] Even though the scandals that took place in the early Clinton years were over policy and appointments just as those during the Reagan and Bush administrations had been,[84] the brand strategy dictated that they be put to a different use—that of showing the Conservative audience that the Liberals had once again taken over.

The early anti-Clinton campaign relied on a great deal of buzz and viral marketing, the bulk of which took place outside the view of the mainstream media. Early in the decade, the buzz was generated in Conservative media and marketing appeals. For example, Viguerie and Franke show that Conservatives made a concerted effort to get their anti-Clinton narrative out in the talk radio format.[85] The early campaign was promoted by a series of ideologically driven individuals working for think tanks and law firms, as well as by long-standing Clinton opponents in Little Rock.[86] While this campaign produced a lot of buzz among Conservatives, it produced little interest within the general public. The biggest substantive accomplishment that the anti-Clinton network had achieved prior to the 1994 election was the appointment of Robert Fiske by the Attorney General to investigate the Whitewater scandal (in January 1994) but this too produced disquiet among Conservatives when Fiske cleared Clinton of wrongdoing in mid-1994, and the disquiet was probably in part produced because Fiske, as Klein notes, had been appointed at Clinton's request.[87]

It was Clinton's reauthorization of the Independent Counsel statute that enabled a three-judge panel in Washington to appoint Kenneth Starr as Independent Council[88] and the scandal marketing campaign to begin again. While the Whitewater scandal was substantively incomprehensible, it came with an interesting cast of characters, and one benefit of the complicated substance was that it would take years to get to the bottom of it and this, in turn, gave Conservatives years to promote their Slick Willie brand. Whitewater was a superior marketing vehicle because it offered an emotive scandal with some highly visible events and a lot of dead time during which Conservatives could fill in the blanks in the story for their audience.[89] It was superior when compared with the other scandals that could have been used because the latter were either of little consequence, had even less relevance to Clinton in office, were too inside the beltway for popular consumption, or had no relationship to the core Conservative and Slick Willie brand story. The numerous gate scandals were useful for keeping the core audience activated and consuming Conservative products, but it was Whitewater that seemed to offer the best vehicle through which to support the brand. Its problem was that, outside of those Conservative audiences that followed every nuance, the story was difficult to understand by audiences that were periodically exposed to parts of the Slick Willie brand story.

Happily for Conservative marketers, something that fit the brand strategy's focus on highly visible, emotive events was looming on the horizon: a sex scandal. Not only did the subject fit the brand strategy and bear out the Slick Willie brand promises, it did so with great visuals. If Starr was in some ways "his own worst enemy"[90] and not personally of great value to the campaign, the topic was ideal because it resonated with a number of Conservative audiences,[91] proved the Slick Willie brand promise to have been correct, and demolished Clinton's own credibility. In addition, the story had broken just in time for the 1998 midterm elections for which it could serve as the basis of a Conservative coordinated contrast campaign focused on Slick Willie.

The problems with the Lewinsky scandal were the problems of credentials, too many line extensions, and of being a generally poor product.[92] Social Conservatives cared deeply about and responded emotively to this but it had no resonance with most other audiences and, in fact, turned Clinton into a sympathetic figure. This was in part because Clinton's team had been polling throughout the period and was more responsive to public opinion.[93] The 1998 coordinated campaign was, as a result, a flop.

The Conservatives' second mistake, aside from actually trying to run a coordinated campaign around the impeachment, was to try to build fellowship between Clinton and Nixon only a couple of months before the election. Doing so undercut whatever equity that remained in the Slick Willie brand and set up a comparison between the crimes of Watergate and those of Clinton that, unlike what Conservatives had hoped, pointed out how disproportionate their actions in this matter had been when compared with what had been done a generation earlier. The effort that Conservatives made was to try to build fellowship between Clinton and Nixon. Building fellowship between Clinton and Nixon was an obvious attempt to make the public aware of the connection that Conservatives saw between the offenses that Clinton was accused of in the proposed articles of impeachment and the archetypal Watergate scandal. Doing so made the Slick Willie brand, its story, and its promise irrelevant at exactly the time when the public was paying attention to the campaign in big numbers and had before it an example, Monica Lewinsky, which seemed to prove the Conservative brand promise. By switching from a brand with which it worked for years to one aspect of a negative icon with which it only worked for a couple of months (and for that reason it cannot be called a brand), the Conservatives lost any hope of persuading the public. The general audience that had followed the campaign only sporadically during Clinton's time in office had no idea why he and his crimes were like Nixon's, although the campaign's Conservative audience targets did. But, had the Slick Willie brand story been stuck with, the Lewinsky scandal would have proven that Clinton was a bad guy and that would have lessened the chance that he would ever become a useful figure on the campaign trail and in the national conversation about public policy ever again.

Clinton became something of a martyr to Democrats: Conservatives lost seats in that year's House races, and two Speakers of the House within short succession when it turned out that they were doing in their own offices just what Clinton had in the Oval Office and in the process undermining the chance that this episode could be used as part of a future branded campaign because it made Conservatives look hypocritical.[94] The fact that Conservatives were engaged in the same kinds of immoral activity as was Clinton, in some case while they were impeaching him, called the validity of their brand story about being the party of morality and everymen into direct question. The entire affair ended so badly that the Conservatives moved to reposition their overall brand by nominating a man for the presidency in 2000 who could play the Reagan role, George W. Bush, then having him run a campaign based largely on his favorable personal traits. This is further proof of the brand's power because, even after mounting a politically damaging campaign, just two years later, Conservatives were able to reposition themselves to win both the White House and retain control of the House of Representatives that had become so unpopular during the impeachment.[95]

The Final Daze

The Clinton scandals needed a happier ending than a defeat in a Senate trial in order to justify their existence, restore the public's faith in Conservatives, prevent Bill Clinton from becoming a heritage brand, and potentially allow these scandals to someday be used in a future marketing campaign. An acquittal after a Senate trial obviously did nothing to accomplish these things. A final scandal, to reiterate the campaign's overall themes, left a lasting impression of Clinton that fit with the brand story and provided a highly visible, emotive example of George W. Bush making good on his brand promise to clean up.

Conservatives found three vehicles through which to create a lasting negative impression of Clinton. They were (1) the gifts received by or allegedly taken by the Clintons from the White House on their way out of town, (2) the numerous pardons issued by Clinton during the same period, and (3) the alleged vandalism that took place in the White House just prior to the transfer of power.[96] Waldman (2004) discusses these events but does not put them into the context of the differentiation portion of a branding campaign as I am arguing was actually the case. Consistent with the brand strategy, the Conservatives spoke about specific objects that the Clintons had supposedly taken with them that supposedly appeared on E-Bay within a few days, pointed to a couple of pardons (Mark Rich and the New Square Elders), and mentioned that Slick Willie's staff had gone so far as to remove the letter W from all the computer keyboards in the White House in addition to leaving insulting graffiti and links to pornographic Web sites on White House computers.

Typical of the rest of the way in which Conservative branding campaigns work, there was a grain of truth to some of the accusations. But that truth was removed from its context and then shaped into a highly emotive set of accusations (and in this case with the highly visible symbol of the White House to boot). As was typical of the way in which Conservative brands are built, each was introduced to a few niche audiences, then gradually made its way into the mainstream media, but it is among Conservatives that these assertions became articles of faith. In addition to perpetuating the negative essence around Clinton, this effort's goal was to allow the Bush administration to begin creating a buffer zone between itself and the Clinton administration, as well as to reiterate the themes of the 2000 election campaign without discussing the events that had put Bush in the White House. In the world of the marketers and their consumers, Bill Clinton left town in the same shady way as he had entered it. This set of scandals could now be used to remind people of the overall impression that they had formed during the period and cement their memories of the Clinton years.

This chapter has examined the Clinton scandals as a whole. The next chapter will examine the Contract with America because it exemplifies the way in which Conservatives used branding and contrast techniques to establish favorable positions for their candidates and political products in order to win elections. The Contract is the second part of the Clinton scandal campaign because it clearly differentiated the House Republicans from Slick Willie.

Single Best Example of the Conservative Brand Strategy

The impact of the Conservative branding has been significantly amplified by the emphasis that the movement has placed on the use of positioning and contrast marketing techniques when promoting their brands.[1] They have achieved the maximum impact from this combination when they juxtaposed the Conservative brand versus the ones that are built around their opponents. The result is that the brand strategy produces choices between the good, Conservative product and the bad things that will come from public support for the Liberal product. Conservative congressional candidates have done so through coordinated campaigns in every midterm election since 1992. In 1994, they used the branded Contract with America; in 1998, they ran with the Clinton impeachment as well as Slick Willie brands, and, in 2002, with a single issue of Iraq as part of the Broader War on Terror. In all of these cases,

Conservatives built highly emotive comparisons that have been part of the reason why they have won these contests.[2] These comparisons stress the downsides of their opponents and the negative brands that Conservatives have built around them at least as much as they say anything good about Conservatism. Doing this means that Conservative candidates for office do not have to spell out their full agenda or the exact contents of their policy proposals unless they want to. The target audience is, as a result, much more aware of what is wrong with the Democratic candidate than it is aware of what is right with the Conservative candidate. In keeping with the brand strategy, the contrasts developed fit within the brand story built around an individual candidate, issue or are a line extension of the archetypal Conservative brand.

The use of contrast and differentiation techniques allow Conservatives to amplify the branding's effect as it allows Conservatives to present themselves in the most flattering and their opponents in the least flattering light possible. The contrast technique is an important means through which Conservatives differentiate themselves, their movement, and its ideas from their opponents. As a result, the use of contrast techniques in support of the brand strategy helps Conservatives develop a clear brand identity for themselves. The contrast marketing technique is another way in which the frame and the brand work together. Simply put, the frame is the contrast and the brand is the vehicle through which the contrast is made. This chapter opens with a brief examination of the branded contrast technique; presents the single best example of the way in which Conservatives have used the brand strategy and contrast techniques to win elections: the 1994 Contract with America; and it then concludes by looking at the way in which these techniques have subsequently been used by George W. Bush.

Why Conservatives Use Both?

Conservatives use contrast techniques in conjunction with the brand strategy because doing so positions Conservatives on the right side and Democrats on the wrong side of an issue as far as their audience goes, paper over the disputes within the movement in favor of a focus on the flaws of their opponents, allow them to clearly define their opponents but not themselves, argue that disaster will surely follow if their idea or candidate is not chosen, present Democrats and Liberals as being un-American, and present themselves as the party of innovation while depicting the Democrats as the defenders of the failed status quo. At the same time, contrast marketing is one of the ways in which differentiation can be accomplished, a key aspect of brand building.[3] Conservatives are, as a result, presented as united, patriotic, innovative, populist defenders of American culture while Democrats are presented as being opposed to all of these things. Conservatives use contrast and positioning techniques in a way that has led the Democrats to defend failed or outdated elements of the New Deal and to refight the most controversial battles of the 1960s about which Conservatives care deeply.[4] All of which provides a second example of the way in which branding and framing are brought together through the use of the contrast technique. The contrast technique has allowed Conservatives to frame the public's perception of their movement and its brand in a very favorable way while, at the same time, building an unfavorable impression of the Democrats. Overall, this contributes to the public's favorability ratings of both parties, of the institutions of government, and of the policies being both marketed and implemented by the government. For example, NES feeling thermometers show that the Conservatives' average score was 62 and 60 in the two Reagan campaign years, rose again to 61 in 1988 when George H.W. Bush squared off against Michael Dukakis, and reached this number in 1994 and again in 2004.[5] Further, the two biggest differences (11 points) in thermometer scores between Liberals and Conservatives took place in 1994, showing the power of the branded, contrasted Contract with America.[6]

The contrast technique fits with the brand strategy because it usually deals with the same themes with which the brands work and, like the brands, leaves some audience room to interpret the message. It works with emotion, but emotion alone would not cause somebody to make a purchasing decision, but when paired with information showing the ways in which two products differ, it can help clarify choices.[7] The contrast technique fits the reactionary, outsider, and insurgent mentalities extant within the Conservative movement and, unsurprisingly, Conservatives have made their best use of it when trying to capture control of an institution from the Democrats or to change an institutionalized Democratic policy. Contrast techniques accentuate the impact of the brand strategy because both are devoted to firing up the audience, increasing its size, and sharpening the difference between the Conservative product and others to the point that, for the target audience, Conservatism becomes its only logical choice.

It Works Best Under Specific Conditions

Conservatives regularly use the contrast technique in support of their brand strategy in a few specific circumstances. First, it is used to support their brand when challenging Democratic incumbents or when running in open seat races. Second, it is used to build support for Conservative ideas when they are under consideration for adoption as public policies. This is the point at which the technique is used to play up the wonderful things that will come from their ideas vis-à-vis the failed, almost always Liberal, status quo or the surefire disaster that will come if ideas fail to become law. A case in point is the way in which Conservatives made good use of contrast techniques and a coordinated campaign around a single issue; in this case, the Iraq line extension to the War on Terror brand. It was used to convince the public that (1) Conservatives would do a better job than Democrats in providing national security, (2) invading Iraq was both related to the War on Terror and a good way to make the nation safer, and (3) the choice facing the public was one between the invasion and an all but certain terrorist attack in the United States using weapons of mass destruction.

Third, they are used to frame Conservatives' branded proposals and candidates in an effort to shape the way in which the public perceives political developments and the media covers them. Fourth, it is used to shift media coverage, policy debates, and public concern away from issues that might prove politically damaging to them onto more politically beneficial issues. Fifth, it is used to favorably position the Conservative and to negatively position the Democratic branded product's issues and individuals within the minds of the voters. Overall, Conservatives use contrast techniques with the brand strategy in order to show voters that they are average Americans themselves while their opponents are not.[8]

Political contrast techniques appear to work well in only a few specific circumstances that appear to dovetail with the way in which Conservatives use them. First, they work when they are part of a campaign intended to reinforce brand loyalty. For example, the 2004 Bush campaign claimed that the Iraq War had been launched to promote freedom in Iraq because, by doing so, it could tap into American socialization patterns and the emphasis on liberty that is part of the archetypal Conservative brand. A second example is provided by the way in which all sorts of Conservative political entrepreneurs have claimed to support "family" and "traditional" values. Given that this is true, then, what kind of values do their opponents support? Contrast techniques as used above let Conservatives differentiate themselves from their opponents and position themselves favorably and their opponents unfavorably, as well as help build a frame within which their brands can maximize their impact.

Third, it is used with the everyman and tax cuts as economic policy aspects of the archetypal Conservative brand to present them as populist defenders of the public good. Doing so lets Conservatives credibly argue that the New Deal was a mistake, has outlived its usefulness, or that the Democrats have become the tools of Liberal special interest groups.

Fourth, it is used when Conservatives are trying to teach the public about events, policies, and candidates that have some prior recognition and this, in turn, is usually done to extend the core Conservative brand to cover these new product lines. At a minimum, calling one candidate a Conservative in contrast to their dangerous Liberal opponent simply explains to people which candidate belongs to which movement.

Fifth, it is used in conjunction with the repositioning of familiar candidates and policies. For example, the 2004 Bush campaign did so when it repositioned W as a strong leader and then created the Senator Flip-Flop brand around its opponent in order to create a clear contrast in leadership and personal styles.[9]

Sixth, it is used to delegitimatize their opponents and the institutions controlled by their opponents, and this is generally followed by a rebranding campaign once Conservatives gain control of said institution.[10] Doing so helps conservatives reinforce the contrasts that they worked with during the campaign, show the public that the Conservative brand promise has been kept, and, as a result, mark an attempt to build loyalty for the Conservative movement's brand. Three examples are provided by the Reagan rebranding of the Executive Branch during the 1980s, the rebranding of the House of Representatives in 1995, and the rebranding of the George W. Bush administration in 2001. Reagan emphasized the symbols of state, the House Freshman emphasized the Contract and a number of institutional reforms, and the Bush team stressed their dress code as well as work routines to create the visible, emotive material out of which the brand strategy is built. All three campaigns had made use of contrast techniques and the branding during the prior election. As a result, the public was aware that the Conservative entering office was inheriting the mess against which they would run and, as a result, it is likely that the new officeholder will get more of a grace period. In turn, the new officeholder is given opportunities to show improvement in highly visible settings as is consistent with the demands of the brand strategy.

Contrast techniques can provide focusing events and, as a result, the new officeholder can also get a chance to implement less popular or less publicized parts of their agenda while the audience is paying attention to the higher-profile event. Conservative candidates who use the brand strategy and contrast techniques are not usually as specifically defined as are other candidates upon entering office; as a result, they have a freer hand in making policy than do candidates who do not make use of these techniques.

Contrast techniques have not aided the brand strategy when Conservatives have not been able to convince the public that the problem of which they are speaking is serious or that there is the best solution to the problem in question. For example, George W. Bush might have believed promoting a major change in Social Security policy was a good way to spend whatever political capital he had won in 2004. However, he was wrong. First, it is not clear that there actually is a major problem with the Social Security system. Second, even if there is, the crisis it could produce clearly won't happen soon. Third, Bush never was able to overcome the numerous other policy entrepreneurs presenting their own plans as the solution to this problem; thus, he failed to give his audience the binary choice in which branded contrasts work best: the happy conservative future versus the disaster that would surely come from any other choice. The public was not presented with the choice of buying the Bush product or facing ruin, as had been the case in 2002 with the Iraq campaign; thus, when selling Social Security reform, Bush was positioned as are most producers in a crowded marketplace because he had failed to show how his product was the best. Thus, it was his failure to execute the contrast and create the frame into which the brand that caused this failure could be placed.

We now turn from a general examination of the way in which Conservatives have used contrast techniques with the brand strategy to one of the best examples of the technique's use: the 1994 Contract with America. This case is very important because it is the point at which Conservatives began using coordinated campaigns centered on a single branded issue along with the contrast techniques in congressional midterm elections. Subsequent Conservatives have mimicked this campaign to varying degrees of success, as we have already seen, but because the Contract campaign was the first and one of the most successful, it merits considerable examination.

Contract 101: Where It Came From and How It Worked

In 1994 something happened in America that had not happened in forty years: Republicans won control of the House of Representatives. This section argues that Conservatives were able to do so directly as a result of the combination of a coordinated campaign, extensive use of the brand strategy, as well as contrast techniques. The result was that, rather than running as individuals, these Conservatives ran as a block much as candidates in the Westminster model do.

The Contract was the brainchild of Newt Gingrich, who had created a network of candidates, financiers, public relations consultants, and policy activists to shape, fund, sell, and run on a platform capable of putting Conservatives in charge of the House of Representatives and, as a result, give them great influence over the revenue choices made by the federal government. The Contract campaign took advantage of the conditions being created by the Slick Willie campaign.[11] In both cases, Conservative activists were employing the brand strategy, but, in this case, the specific goals of the exercise was to win a majority in the House, show that brand promises were kept, and then build Conservative brand loyalty for generations to come.

Let us examine the techniques that Gingrich and his associates used to promote the Contract and to build support, as well as the number of ways in which the public could become involved with it.[12] While the Gingrich group was looking for supporters as was the Slick Willie campaign, it was also looking to recruit and train people to participate in its activities. Gingrich built a network that introduced people to GOPAC and its affiliated leadership institute, to produce and distribute a college course available at no cost to any institution willing to host it, television programming associated with the course, and highly developed networks–one of fundraisers and one of activists.[13] Gingrich was well suited to make use of contrast techniques in conjunction with the brand strategy because he knew how to attract public and press attention, knew where he wanted to take the Republican Party, and because he had an organization through which he could do so on his own.[14] In short, he had inherited an organization that he built into something that looks a lot like a multilevel marketing company, two examples of which are Amway and Mary Kay Cosmetics, through which he recruited salespeople and built a distribution network for his brand.

Sabato and Simpson note the importance of contrast and positioning techniques through their examination of language's use in the GOPAC manual.[15] This manual shows that Conservatives used contrast techniques to amplify the brand strategy's impact, deepen relationships with their audiences, and win elections. This could be done by

1 achieving a significant increase in turnout
2 creating a positive vision that arouses support
3 delegitimating the opposition
4 creating a civil war within the opposition
5 increasing the scale of resources
6 applying cutting-edge technology.[16]

While the overall goal appears to have been to increase Conservative and decrease Democratic market share, the first four points are particularly relevant to the brand strategy given that what they really touch on is the importance of building a narrative that defines both sides as well as impacts turnout on both sides. Points five and six fit with the brand strategy indirectly because they touch on the need to create and use new marketing channels in order to distribute their brands.[17]

These techniques have become the stock in trade of the Republican brand strategy. They are effective for numerous reasons. First, the brand strategy can increase turnout by increasing the audience's emotional pitch by giving the audience a sense that the next election is the most important and that their vote could be the one that tips the balance of power.

Second, they can be used to build buzz and build a bandwagon effect around their candidates. These techniques can mobilize the core audiences as well as those with weaker affiliations who are in agreement but passive, persuadable, or both. Conservatives use contrast techniques to accentuate public perception of their brands in the way that all product marketers do when trying to lure customers away from a rival brand about which the target has weak or fading loyalty.[18] For example, Pepsi has targeted consumers for years by running blind taste tests in order to show consumers that Pepsi actually tastes better than Coke.[19]

Third, the brand strategy and the contrast techniques employed with it can split the rival brand's audience, thus, allowing Conservatives to win with electoral pluralities and narrow majorities as appears to have happened in recent years.

Fourth, the brand strategy and contrast techniques were more effective from the Contract period onward because Gingrich made an effort to find new distribution channels and, as a result, targeted more focused as well as better performing audience segments.[20]

Fifth, it takes money to create and distribute brands, as well as to figure out who the target audience exactly is. Money's impact was accentuated in this case because Gingrich took advantage of a technological innovation: C-SPAN, on which he cheaply promoted the movement, the contrasted brand story that formed the basis of the Contract, and the personalities that would implement it.[21] The Contract campaign being far from exceptional was simply the best example of the way in which Conservatives have used brands and found unique ways to distribute their branded products during their rise to power. One of the key tools that Gingrich used to amplify the power of the brand, which the Bush team has subsequently used, is to present it and the one that they have built around Democrats in a way that delegitimates the Democratic Party, the political institutions in which Democrats have a majority, policies for which the Democrats have received public credit, and social movements affiliated with Democrats.[22] The contrast created between brands has gone a long way toward changing the nation's balance of power and the support both parties enjoy with the voters. This is in part because, once they have delegitimated the Democrats, Conservatives usually stage high-profile events in highly emotive settings as demanded by the brand strategy in order to show how they have kept promises. When they do so, they are really repositioning or relaunching the damaged brand that they have just acquired.[23] Normally, this has involved producing beneficiaries of new policies or of highlighting the reforms Conservatives have made once in power.

Conservatives have delegitimated two Democratic presidents (Clinton and Carter), two Democratic speakers of the House (O'Neil and Foley), the entire federal government minus the military (especially agencies such as the education, energy, and commerce departments that obviously do not serve the needs of Republican constituencies), and a cornucopia of policies with which they disagree. Sometimes their policy objections have been political and sometimes their opposition has centered on philosophical questions.

One example of both rationales is found in Conservative opposition to AmeriCorps. Conservatives politically opposed it as a form of "coerced voluntarism," to quote Newt Gingrich.[24] There was also a more principled case to be made about AmeriCorps and the power of government that fit within the archetypal Conservative brand story. Gingrich made this point at a joint appearance in New Hampshire with President Clinton:

> But I have two concerns that I think are a different direction philosophically. One is that I believe . . . we want to have less Washington-based bureaucracy and fewer decisions made in Washington. And we want to strengthen the private charities.[25]

Gingrich first worked with the smaller government aspect of the archetypal Conservative brand then moved onto an extension of it that has developed in social policy matters in recent years: the idea of having charities does if followed done by the government.

After noting that several members of Congress were working on bills that would provide tax credits in return for service, thus inoculating himself against charges that he had complaints but no plan of his own, Gingrich presented AmeriCorps through the fiscal responsibility aspect of the archetypal Conservative brand:

> I would just suggest that when you sit down and look at what it takes to balance the budget over seven years or 10 years, it's hard. And if you're setting priorities about which programs to keep and which not, you can have a legitimate, honest debate about how many things you can afford to do in Washington and how many things you need to get back home to New Hampshire or you need to ask the private sector.[26]

In this case, we see how the Conservatives use contrast techniques with their archetypal brand to strengthen their present argument. In this case, Gingrich was attempting to torpedo a program (AmeriCorps) that was one of the signature aspects of Clinton's agenda and, in order to do so without debating the program on its merits, he presented it through the lens of specific aspects of the archetypal Conservative brand story.

These were exactly the kinds of branded contrast campaigns that Gingrich ran during the decade and a half that he was using C-Span as part of his majority-building strategy.[27] In a nutshell, Gingrich and his fellow Conservative Opportunity Society members in the House would make speeches about themselves and their ideas, as well as about the failures of the Democrats on a daily basis after the House had finished its regular business for the day.[28] Doing this allowed these Conservatives to get their brand story about Democrats out to their target audience on the cheap and, by doing so, work to increase the audience's interest as well as attachment to them.

Their work shows that, in order to attract attention and differentiate their user from the competition, the contrasts have to be emotive. For example, one of the most famous examples of the way in which Gingrich and his associates used their C-Span activities to do so involved a skirmish over the anti-Communist credentials of a Democratic member of Congress that escalated to the point that Gingrich goaded the then speaker, Tip O'Neil, into making remarks that later had to be taken down and removed from the congressional record. The entire episode stemmed from a Gingrich exercise to position the Democrats as soft on Communism in order to differentiate their position from that of the Conservatives on the issue.[29]

The quote project featured members of Congress reading favorable quotes about Communist regimes into the congressional record and then noting how the realities of life under communism had not lived up to this sweet rhetoric.[30] The net effect was, of course, to show the truth of the brand story that Conservatives in Congress had been building about the Democratic majority and of the one Conservatives have been nationally building about Liberals for the last forty years. The most notable portion of the exercise was the above-noted incident.[31]

After taking on O'Neil, Gingrich and his fellow Conservative Opportunity Society members continued to pound away at all aspects of Democratic rule and contrasted it with what they would do if put into office. Their next big success came with the resignation of Speaker Jim Wright who, in his valedictory remarks, clearly showed that he had little understanding of exactly what the Conservatives were up to. What Gingrich was fostering in the House was part of a plan and not just "mindless cannibalism" as departing Speaker Jim Wright put it in his departure speech.[32]

Gingrich's plan employed the brand and strategy because it tied the Democrats to the Liberal aspect of the archetypal Conservative brand, then went on to develop favorable contrasts and create favorable positioning vis-à-vis the Democrats. Once these Republicans gained a majority in the House, we can see why they would try to do the same to the Democratic president. Rather than attacking Clinton on personality or with obscure scandals as the Slick Willie campaign was doing, Gingrich took on the brand essence that this campaign had been building around Clinton and developed a point of Contrast for the Republicans: the Contract with America.

The Contract: A Branded Contrast Campaign

The 1994 Conservative takeover of the House of Representatives is the single best example of the way in which Conservatives have used branding along with contrast techniques to position themselves favorably and the Democrats unfavorably, and to win congressional elections.[33] Further, the 1994 election is important because it sets the pattern of Conservatives employing this kind of campaign to sell their political products. To this point, Conservatives have bundled these techniques in the 1998 and 2002 elections, in addition to their use in 1994. As noted above, the Contract campaign tapped into the efforts of the Slick Willie campaign and would not have been possible without the mistakes of that administration or of the Democratic majority in the House. Absent these failures, errors, and scandals, the Contract would not have worked as it did because it would not have had the visible, visceral issues with which the brand strategy works best and around which clear contrasts can be created.

The Contract was not Gingrich's first effort to use the branded contrast strategy to win a House majority. Gingrich had tried the branded coordinated campaign previously. Most notably he used it in 1980 to get Republicans to commit to five goals that were called either a "Capitol Compact" or a "solemn covenant"[34] that Conservative Steven Stockmeyer called a "dress rehearsal" for the Contract campaign and noted that the idea had been Gingrich's.[35] Because the Compact was launched in 1980, it competed with the Reagan campaign and, as we have seen above, Conservative legislative candidates have not made a similar mistake since 1994.

Gingrich's efforts to link his congressional movement with the archetypal brand stories that the movement had built around itself and around Liberals really only made headway with Clinton's election in 1992 because that event gave Gingrich a highly visible figure about whom most Americans held strong feelings against whom he could campaign and, because, by that time, years of building a negative brand essence around House Democrats had taken hold with the voters.

The Contract exemplified the branded contrast technique in a number of ways. First, it created a line extension between this campaign and the archetypal Conservative brands by depicting Clinton as a Liberal of questionable moral values. As a result, relatively unknown Conservative congressional candidates were able to tap into a brand story that had been built years before they appeared on the political scene. Second, the Contract campaign came with low-entry barriers and little cost because it was building on a campaign that had been running on the national stage since 1992 and that focused on the idea that Clinton was dishonest. Third, the president is usually a central focus of congressional midterm elections; the Contract had a central point to its brand story that tapped into broader stories from its inception. The contrast between Conservatives and Slick Willie highlighted the difference between the various failings, prevarications, and controversies of the first Clinton administration and what Conservatives were promising for the future of the Congress.

Fourth, the Contract tapped into the populist themes with which Conservatives frequently work. The Contract cast the Conservatives as the defenders and restorers of popular representation, American values, and the American creed while Democrats were presented as being dishonest and not like average Americans.[36] Theirs was a party that was more interested in defending its own interests, those of its narrow constituencies, and a big government than they were in protecting the rights of average people.

Fifth, the Contract fits the brand strategy because Conservatives went to great lengths to make the public aware of it, including its publication at the RNC's expense in TV Guide.[37] Unlike the Democrats who made promises at election time only to break them, these Conservatives were contractually binding themselves to keep their word. As part of the populist aspect of the brand, these Conservatives stressed the fact that they had not spent their adult lives in Congress, claimed that they favored term limits, and stressed that they had had some kind of career prior to running for public office.

Republicans were pledging to keep their word if elected and the proof of the promise was that they had signed their names to a contract. Doing so was a clear attempt to highlight those things that most upset the voters about the Clinton administration, linked Clinton with increasingly unpopular congressional Democrats, and offered Republicans as an alternative to the latter and as the vehicle through which to send a message to the former. As Dick Armey told a reporter in 2006, the Republican victory in 2004 resulted from two scandals in the House of Representatives (bank and post office), Clinton's failure to keep his promise to pass a national health insurance bill, and a contrast that the "coherent plan of action" provided by the Contract.[38] In short, Conservatives were saying that Bill Clinton had not kept his word, that Democrats had failed and been dishonest in Congress, and that neither was interested in the kind of real reform that the Contract promised.

The upshot was a contrast between the honest, contractually obligated Conservatives and the values-challenged Liberals. The Contract was effective because it juxtaposed a positive message with a negative one. As Gingrich ally Vin Weber noted, "Ultimately there has to be a positive set of issues that attract people to the Republican Party, issues for which they feel confident voting for."[39] It was the Contract, which contained the Conservative brand story about its own movement juxtaposed against that of the Liberals and Clinton, that helped the Conservatives gain power but it would be their implementation of it that made sure that they stayed in power.[40]

A Series of Subbrands

The Contract with America worked because it established a visible contrast between the Conservative congressional candidates and their Democratic opponents, as well as between Bill Clinton and the Conservatives.[41] As is frequently the case with branded campaigns, what was actually in the product did not matter as much to the public as what the brand story was made out to be.[42] Thus, for congressional Democrats and Clinton, the problem was that to oppose the Conservatives on these issues was, by definition, to be on the minority side of the question and that, in turn, introduced the archetypal Conservative brand story into the equation.

The Contract made use of a sub-branding strategy and, as Ries and Ries explain, "sub-branding is an inside out branding strategy that tries to push the core brand in new directions."[43] Each of the initiatives was branded in a way that favorably positioned Conservatives as representatives of the common good and traditional values without getting into the specifics of their contents because much of what was in the bills was not exactly as the subbrand name indicated.[44] Gingrich was also careful to exclude controversial social issues in order to make the Contract brand story as clear as it could be.[45] As we can see below, the initiatives generally focused on some aspects of the archetypal Conservative brand story[46]:

Table 5.1 The Ten Items of the Contract with America

The Fiscal Responsibility Act
The Taking Back Our Streets Act
The Personal Responsibility Act
The Family Reinforcement Act
The American Dream Restoration Act
The National Security Restoration Act
The Senior Citizens Fairness Act
The Job Creation And Wage Enhancement Act

The Common Sense Legal Reform Act
The Citizen Legislature Act

Should the Democrats wander into opposing specific aspects of the proposals, Conservatives could breezily rattle off the brand names; thus, as is common in branded politics, making the audience feel well informed about the Contract when, as noted above, they know little about it.[47] The branding of the issues was an exercise in positioning and differentiation. Thus, when the Democrats opposed these proposals the way was clear for the introduction of the archetypal Conservative brand aspects that presents Conservatives as populist defenders of traditional values versus the inside the beltway Liberals ever eager to defend narrow lifestyle constituencies. The Contract allowed the Gingrich conservatives to tap not only into the current Slick Willie campaign but also into three decades of brand building.

The way in which the document was signed by three hundred sixty-seven out of three hundred seventy Republican congressional candidates at a ceremony on the West Front of the Capitol[48] in front of the spot where presidential inaugurals have been held since Ronald Reagan's first inaugural, replete with patriotic bunting and flags, provided exactly the kind of visuals that the brand strategy requires to be successful. The visuals sent a message that, once elected, Conservatives would be patriotic populists protecting traditional values, unlike the congressional Liberals whom they would replace and Slick Willie whom they would oppose. It only worked because the Democrats called attention to it and, as a result, generated press coverage for its signing ceremony that Gingrich advisor Tony Blankley termed "manna from heaven."[49]

The proof that Republicans understood that one of the key parts of the branded contrast was Slick Willie is clear from Drew's quotation from Representative Jim Nussle that Clinton's opposition to the Contract "just amazed us. Clinton fell into the trap—he legitimated the Contract."[50] The signing ceremony was the equivalent of a product demonstration aimed at giving the public a sense of what it would be like to have a Conservative Congress for the first time in forty years and was also, as a result, an exercise in building brand awareness, recognition, and loyalty. Through the signing ceremony, Conservatives were able to show the public their brand and the contrast between it and the Liberals.

In office, Gingrich and his team showed the public that it was doing as it said it would, the net result of which was to favorably repackage the House of Representatives once it was under Conservative control, much as, we see later in this chapter, the George W. Bush team did with the White House in 2001.[51] First, they allowed the children of the members being sworn in to sit on the House floor during opening day ceremony; children are a sign of hope and the future as well as the kind of emotive visual with which the brand strategy works best.[52] Second, new members of Congress who had interesting resumes, attractive personas, or did not fit the stereotype of the white, male Republican were given plenty of media play and, in some cases, leadership positions.[53] Third, a number of substantive changes in the House's administration, including term limits on the speaker and committee chairs, a financial audit by a private company instead of the General Accounting Office, and the application of all civilian work rules to the House, were all given great emphasis.[54] Fourth, the first day of the new Congress lasted for fourteen hours twenty-four minutes with Gingrich proclaiming it from the speaker's chair "one of the most productive sessions for any single day in House history."[55] All of these moves were in keeping with the brand strategy because all were highly visible and all helped to show that the Conservatives were keeping their promises in office unlike what Slick Willie had done.

The Contract itself had been the campaign's centerpiece and, once in office, the Conservatives moved quickly to implement it. First, they established a hundred-day time limit for its passage in homage to the first hundred days of the FDR administration and, given the emphasis that Ronald Reagan had placed on FDR during his administration, this was also a way to work the growing Reagan brand into the message. The hundred-day deadline ensured that the Democrats would not have time to organize against the Conservative proposals.[56] The hundred days provided a focusing deadline for the Contract and, at the end of it, the public would know if the Conservatives had passed it or not. Having done so, Gingrich made a great show of pointing out the accomplishment in television interviews and with an address to the nation.[57] The speech, as Drew notes, was produced with the assistance of Reaganites Michael Deaver and Kenneth Duberstein.[58]

Second, the new members of Congress spoke about the Contract frequently, thus generating more impressions for and public awareness of both the contract and the fact that, once elected, Conservatives were actively working on it. Third, the new Congress invited talk radio hosts to the Hill in order to increase public awareness of its passage.[59] Additionally, talk radio allowed the brand story to be distributed in full minus the scrutiny about its specifics that might come from appearances in the print or electronic media that were not part of the Conservative media as has been done since the Reagan years.

Fourth, Conservatives made a point of making all of their policy choices relate to the Contact in some way during their first few months in office. Fifth, each time one of the Contract's branded initiatives was passed, Speaker Gingrich took out his laminated copy of the Contract, then punched a hole across the item that had just passed the House. Doing this showed the public that another item had been crossed off the list just as Conservatives had promised would happen during the Fall campaign.

Sixth, the Contract's passage that had begun with the high-profile event of inauguration day closed with a high-profile event celebrating its passage. The event was held on the Capitol Grounds and because of it the circus came to town. The public was treated to the sight of the elephant that is the Republican logo parading around the East Front of the Capitol during the week of April 8, 1994. These techniques let the Conservatives show the public that they were not like Slick Willie and, as a result, the Contract typifies the way in which Conservatives have used the brand strategy to take over an institution, as well as to contrast themselves and establish favorable positions versus the Democrats.

The Contract was an ideal device through which the Conservatives could execute the brand strategy and take over the Congress because it was built on years of brand-building activity, because it used brand names for its policies instead of specifics, and because, as noted above, it moved through a well-constructed narrative from the first to the last of the hundred days, all through which Speaker Gingrich made sure that the country knew how things were going. Additionally, the Contract brand was sold with the kinds of visual imagery and packaging, in addition to verbiage, upon which a successful brand relies.[60]

The Contract was a big success because its brand contained a narrative that allowed Conservatives to differentiate themselves from the former Democratic majority and from Slick Willie, as well as because through its implementation, Conservatives made sure that the public knew that they were keeping their word. As Frank Luntz noted, the point to the Contract was to show that Republicans could do more than talk, they could get things done.[61] Further, it offered the chance for another election win in 1996 as one congressional aide noted by saying that

> the Contract is a political document for 1996. . . . If the Freshmen do everything
> the Contract says they'll be in excellent shape for 1996 and we can add to our major-

ity in Congress. But if compromise the Contract to pass laws, we lose support.[62]

The high-profile events promoting it ensured that the public was well aware of these things. The way in which the Contract was implemented showed the public that the promises made in the Fall had been kept and that this, in turn, offered the possibility for future electoral success.[63] Brands have to keep their promises, as happened in this case.

The Contract brand was effectively sold because of the differentiation and contrast techniques that were used with it. One of the key elements of that was the way in which Gingrich's team built a vocabulary that both built their brand and created favorable contrasts that were effective because they repositioned the Conservatives, the Congress, and the Democrats in the way that Ries and Trout (2001) suggest is possible.[64] This language could clearly differentiate the two parties in a way that could counteract the best efforts of what Gingrich saw as a hostile press.[65] Gingrich saw language as a key means to make sure that the GOPAC message was distributed to the audience.[66] The need to slice through the press to reach an audience is commonly found among corporate marketers. Not surprisingly, Gingrich behaved as do those marketers and language was a key part of his strategy. Eddie Mahe, explaining the importance of positioning in building Gingrich's argument, said "because you have to relate ideas in the context of the audience that you're talking to and usually in the language or a simile that they can relate to."[67]

The Contract was an ideal device through which the Conservatives could execute the brand strategy and take over the Congress because it was built on years of brand-building activity, because it let them avoid specific policy proposals in favor of the emotive, visual style and, as a result, avoid angering specific constituencies. The Contract was a big success because it was the centerpiece of a clearly constructed brand narrative that moved from a beginning phase during which Congress was in the clutches of corrupt Democrats, through a campaign phase during which a set of reforms were promised, to an ultimate phase during which reforms were passed and honor restored to Congress. The Contract had a brand story that started with a crisis but concluded happily in a way that fit nicely into a broader brand story that Conservatives had been building for decades. The Contract also shows in a nutshell the difference between the way branded and nonbranded politics work. Simply, consider the amount of attention that the Republican takeover of the House attracted in 1994 in comparison to the amount of attention that the same year's Republican takeover of the Senate attracted.

Thus, the Conservatives in general and Gingrich in particular under-stood the importance of language and narrative in political brand building. A GOPAC memo to members illustrates the point because it notes that Republicans should always try to make use of "Optimistic Governing Words" and "Contrasting Words."[68] The former helped to give people something to support while the latter, applied to an opponent, unfavorably differenti-ated them.[69] Conservatives have repeatedly used both kinds of words to set up the contrasts and brand stories that they wanted and have, as a result, enjoyed great success when playing the positioning game. An example of such dif-ferentiation is provided by the 2004 Bush campaign that went so far as to have a television advertisement entitled "Optimism versus Pessimism" that presented Bush as an optimist interested in creating new jobs at the same time that it depicted Senator Kerry as a nattering nabob of negativism to steal a phrase from Pat Buchanan. In short, the idea is to build a brand narrative and essence that shows the public how Conservatives are heroes and Democrats are villains.

Just as they were given a document that explained what language should be used, the candidates that Gingrich recruited were also given a manual that explained how to use contrast marketing.[70] The manual encouraged Republicans to build the kinds of contrasts about which we have spoken at length in this chapter. We can see how this combination of positive and negative words can be used to draw an effective contrast. By looking at the above lists, we can see how common such words are in the rhetoric of the Conservative move-ment from the Contract period through the present. Gingrich and com-pany's efforts to rebrand the House and build loyalty among the voters did well until they engaged in a high-profile budget battle against the Clinton administration during the fall of 1995.[71]

Despite the failure in the budget battle, Gingrich used these techniques to change the partisan alignment of the House in a lasting way and to pio-neer a style of midterm, coordinated campaign that Conservatives again used in 1998 and 2002. The Gingrich case shows how contrast and position-ing techniques can be used to magnify the brand's power. While building the Contract with America as a set of branded initiatives was fine in and of itself, its chances of success were greatly enhanced because the organization build-ing and media promotion of the Contract juxtaposed against the dishonest Liberals in Congress fired up the Conservative faithful. The subsequent

Bush campaigns have relied on a great deal of the same kinds of branded contrasts that Newt Gingrich used to win a House majority, as well as the Reagan heritage brand to win two elections. What Ronald Reagan and his team had begun in Conservative politics, Newt Gingrich took to a level that continues to be used by Conservative candidates to the present day.

Using the Playbook: George W. Bush 2000

The strategies that Gingrich brought into national politics during the Contract campaign have never truly left the national stage even though Gingrich himself is no longer visible on it. In recent years, the branded strategy, along with contrast technique were used by two Bush campaigns and Bush in office. In the first case, Bush presented himself as the person most capable of restoring honor to the White House, of reuniting the nation, and of bringing dignity back to the White House. All of which was a fancy way of saying that George W. Bush was not Bill Clinton nor was he the House Republicans. The first Bush campaign used these themes most effectively in order to draw a contrast between its candidate, the incumbent, and because of the fact that his challenger had been Clinton's Vice President. Just as Gingrich had in the House, President Bush during his campaign focused on the dysfunctional personalities and institutional corruption in the Clinton White House. The Bush camp used the Gingrich playbook, in part, to win the 2000 election, to place its man within the core Conservative brand story, and to show the public that its man was different from Clinton and was keeping his campaign promises.

Just as Gingrich had done with the House as noted above, the new Bush administration worked to change the public's perception of an institution that had been subject to years of branded attack by Conservatives. Relaunching a damaged brand that has recently been acquired is commonly done in the world of consumer marketing. First, like Gingrich's, Bush's team now accentuated the positive about the institution instead of the negative. Second, like Gingrich, the Bush team tried to clearly draw a line between its tenure in office and Slick Willie's. Third, like Gingrich's, Bush made a highly visible effort to clean up an institution that had been labeled as corrupt during the Fall campaign. Both had made allegations of mismanagement as part of their campaigns for office and both took steps to show the public that those institutional flaws were being cleaned up. In both cases, allegations of serious mismanagement and corruption were lodged, investigations initiated, and major changes were announced. During the 2000 election cycle, the Bush campaign promised to clean up the moral sewer of the Clinton White House as is clear from Bush's 2000 speech to the RNC:

> That background may lack the polish of Washington. Then again, I don't have a lot of things that come with Washington. I don't have enemies to fight. I have no stake in the bitter arguments of the last few years. I want to change the tone of Washington to one of civility and respect. . . . So when I put my hand on the Bible, I will swear to not only uphold the laws of our land, I will swear to uphold the honor and dignity of the office to which I have been elected, so help me God.[72]

Bush distanced himself in this way from partisan bickering, at the same time that he drew a contrast between a putative Bush administration and Slick Willie's White House that in the Conservative brand story had become a combination House of Ill Repute, fraternity house, and Democratic fundraising machine. By promising to restore honor, dignity, and integrity, the Bush team was drawing contrasts between itself and all of the major Washington players.

One of the ways that the administration showed that its assertions about Slick Willie were valid was through the leaking of stories of White House vandalism and through the story that Air Force One had been looted by the departing Clintonites on Inauguration Day. The assertions were emotive and focused on highly visible institutions as demanded by the brand strategy. Allegedly, pornographic materials had been left, the letter W had been removed from all computer keyboards in the White House, and the plane that had carried the Clintons came back minus china, bedsheets, silverware, and champagne glasses.[73] The White House and Air Force One are highly visible symbols of the presidency so it is clear why an administration using a brand strategy to differentiate itself from its predecessor would pick these two symbols to make its closing point about Clinton.

That the allegations were subsequently proven to be completely unfounded, negligible or explainable by other events[74] misses the way in which the Bush team used them to prove that its brand promise from the Fall was being kept, as well as to reinforce the Slick Willie brand one last time. These allegations not only infuriated the Conservative base and provided visual proof that Slick Willie was as had been advertised during the prior eight years but also provided Bush with an opportunity to show the country that he was not a wild-eyed partisan. Consider the understated way in which Bush responded to a question about these issues and what should be done about them:

> It's time now to move forward. It's time to focus our attention on what's possible and how to get children educated (author's note the word educated appears in a direct quote from Bush).[75]

Answering in this way showed that Bush himself was a man of civility who was interested in dealing with the substance of running the government just as he had promised he would be during the previous autumn's campaign.

At the same time, people in the Republican Party continued to provide the media with accounts of the damage that they found, in order to accentuate both brand stories being promoted. For example, consider the CNN story that outlined the pranks based on comments from Republican sources that included the letter removal tampering with phone lines,[76] signs making fun of the malapropisms that have come to be known as Bushisms, graffiti, and disheveled work space.[77] The contrast between Slick Willie and the new Bush administration was reinforced as the source told CNN that White House Chief of Staff Andy Card had told his staff "to focus on the business of governing and not on these alleged pranks."[78] Thus, we can see how these leaks cemented the Conservative brand stories about both administrations while allowing Bush, as Gingrich had done, to begin the process of talking up the White House under his administration while showing the public in a highly visible way that it was keeping its brand promises.

A second way in which the Bush team contrasted itself from its predecessors in order to accomplish the above-noted goals was by talking a good deal about the corporate management model that it planned to use to run the White House.[79] Doing so was smart given that Conservatives had long complained about the atmosphere in the Clinton White House. The contrast between management styles fit into the core Conservative brand story because it presented its administration as serious, respectful, and run in the efficient style of the corporation, while it presented the Clinton administration's employees as being "not expected to be properly attired and that in fact they dressed in a manner that did not accord the office of the president the respect it deserves."[80] The legacy of the 1960s fed into this because the Bush administration argued that the dress code signaled the reinstatement of "order and discipline."[81] The net effect is to create the contrast between Liberals and Conservatives with which Conservatives have worked for four decades, to show that brand promises were being kept, and to reiterate the brand stories that the Bush team had built about its man during the campaign and the Conservatives had built around Clinton during the past eight years.

The emphasis on easily understood, highly visual contrasts is exactly the same playbook that Newt Gingrich and the House Republicans followed during their initial months on Capitol Hill as has the Conservative movement during its rise to power in the United States since the 1960s in order to make the public aware of and loyal to its brand. This chapter has examined the way in which the branded contrast technique blossomed during the 1990s and given but one example of the way in which Conservative candidates continue to use it. Our next chapter looks at the way in which Conservatives created a brand that gave them wide latitude to do as they wished within a given policy area. The case that we look at is the War on Terror and, specifically, the way in which it was used to sell the public on an invasion of Iraq.

How Conservatives Brand Their Policy Proposals

We have seen the ways in which Conservatives have branded themselves and their opponents, build their movement, and sell their candidates. This chapter considers how Conservatives brand their policy proposals in office and does so by looking at the way in which the Bush team developed a branded response to the events of September 11, 2001, called the War on Terror, and built this brand in a way that it could be extended to justify a different kind of American foreign policy in general, and the invasion of Iraq in particular.[1]

Doing so enabled the Bush team to move off of selling difficult domestic policy changes or Slick Willie on to dealing with the highly visual, deeply emotional crisis at hand. Dealing with the crisis offered the administration a selling opportunity in which its dramatic changes in foreign policy could be peddled. The Iraq issue was on the Bush administration's radar screen from its earliest days in office.[2] After 9/11, the Bush team moved quickly to place its ideas for transforming American foreign policy into a brand story that justified them, as well as the invasion of Afghanistan and the tightening of domestic laws. It did so, as we saw in Chapter 1, by intentionally defining its response in the broadest terms possible.

This case shows how the Conservative brand strategy and the relationships that it has created can pay off. It does so by allowing Bush, as it does all Conservatives, to quickly take advantage of opportunities as they present themselves. The Bush team built a brand out of 9/11, a brand that focused broadly on the issue of terrorism and justified a global battle against it—instead of focusing more closely on 9/11, Al Qaeda, and Osama bin Laden. That broader brand is, of course, the War on Terror and its creation allowed the Bush team to promote its broader foreign policy goals, advantage the executive vis-à-vis the Congress, and increase the sense of legitimacy it enjoyed with the American public.[3] It was most effective because it enabled the Bush team to tap into the anti-Communism, strong leader aspects that had been built into the Conservative brand from its beginning.[4] One of the places this is visible is that, just as Ronald Reagan talked about the evil empire, so has George Bush spoken of the evil one or an entire axis of evil.

While the administration's direct response to 9/11 included the Afghan War and the package of domestic security legislation that was passed quickly by Congress in the aftermath, the War on Terror brand gave the administration latitude to pursue a more unilateralist foreign policy, changes to privacy rights, a justification for continued Cold War-level military spending, and the foundation upon which a justification for the invasion of Iraq could be built.[5] Branding their response to 9/11 as the War on Terror was a tool to claim the political capital, agenda control, and moral high ground to silence critics, implement policy, and win elections.[6] This brand's creation also enabled the administration to silence questioners about the whereabouts of the Al Qaeda leader or its failure to capture him in order to contest the next elections on a more favorable ground.[7]

Had the administration simply focused either on responding to 9/11 via the use of international institutions or on the source of the problem (Al Qaeda, Osama bin Laden, and its bases in Afghanistan), it is difficult to say if it would have won the next two elections. But presumably, Bush's public and congressional approval levels would have dropped back to their pre-9/11 levels more quickly. It was only when another kind of disaster, Hurricane Katrina, contradicted the strong leadership aspect that Bush had used the War on Terror to build around himself that Democrats, the public, and the media really began to examine indepth what had been done in its name during the previous five years and that Bush's job approval rating numbers began a decline from which they have not recovered.[8] Branding the War on Terror allowed the administration to pursue a niche marketing strategy and adjust its points of emphasis as circumstances dictated while appearing to govern in the consistent style that was very much an aspect of brand W in 2000. Instead, the War on Terror brand made this weakest of presidents one of the strongest in the nation's history.[9]

Striking While the Iron Is Hot or 9/11 as a Marketing Opportunity

The 9/11 events gave the Bush team an opportunity to promote foreign policy proposals that were on its agenda but not on the nation's priority list when it came into office.[10] The Bush team, as its 2000 campaign documents show, had spoken at length to niche audiences about its desired foreign policy changes. It has been suggested that Bush was supposedly heard discussing the political benefits from doing so even before being elected.[11] The reason for this was that, in 2000, the American public was not paying much attention to foreign policy; few had ever heard of Osama bin Laden and most thought that the Iraq situation was, at least, stabilized by the 1991 Gulf War. In short, the same happy conditions that had encouraged the creation of the Slick Willie brand continued and, were the Bush administration to gain public support for its proposals, something would have to happen to show the American public that all was not right with the world, otherwise Bush would be left to spend four years bringing the nation together and serving as a "reformer with results" as brand W had promised. That something happened, in the media capital of the world and on live television, on a beautiful September morning in 2001. The administration quickly responded by building a broadbrand story that allowed it to take advantage of these events to sell its agenda, rather than simply to fight Al Qaeda.

Branding its response, the War on Terror gave the administration a tool through which it could emphasize specific aspects of its agenda as circumstances dictated and allowed. The ability to switch brand aspects became most useful after Osama Bin Laden's escape from the Battle of Tora Bora in December 2001. While the battle was raging, the administration spoke confidently of his imminent capture or death, yet, at its end, he was nowhere to be found. This embarrassment put the lie to Bush's statement that bin Laden could neither run nor hide, and it could have presented Bush, who had won election under a cloud in 2000, with a gigantic credibility problem in 2004 and a political problem for the party's congressional candidates in 2002. The brand strategy allowed Conservatives to respond to 9/11 in a way that let them tap into their Cold War-brand aspects, as well as to switch the subject away from either their failures on 9/11 or the sluggish economy. It then, as it has throughout its use by their movement, gave Conservatives an ability to discuss issues of their choosing in a way that taps into the psychological needs of their audiences while shaping a favorable political climate. It was the use of the brand strategy that enabled the administration to gain significant control over the public agenda and to occupy a politically advantageous position.[12]

As long as Bush could credibly say that he was a "war president," questions regarding the 2000 election, the impact of his policies on average people, the nation's weak economy, and alternative responses to 9/11 would receive little public attention.[13] The broader-brand story helped the Bush team keep questions of responsibility for the massive security failure that took place on September 11 off the agenda. For example, as Jamieson and Waldman note, when comparisons between 9/11 and Pearl Harbor came up, the administration moved quickly to shut these down by directing attention toward its War on Terror-brand story.[14] Some Conservative interest groups and media commentators tried to build a narrative that placed blame for 9/11 on Slick Willie's shoulders. The administration implied that Clinton shared responsibility for these events and blamed Clinton, as well as 9/11 for a recession to which it had the solution: tax cuts.

The administration built the War on Terror brand to reward its friends and to justify its policy proposals. The most famous example of both points was the Conservative Project for a New American Century (PNAC) that wanted to invade Iraq and to launch a second century of American empire.[15] The War on Terror brand enabled the administration to move off of the hunt for Al Qaeda in order to sell other parts of its agenda and to avoid constant questioning about how that difficult search was coming. This ability was of particular value in light of the failure to capture bin Laden during or after the Battle of Tora Bora. The Bush team, from early January 2002 until the War on Terror brand-coordinated congressional midterm election campaign was rolled out, spent a great deal of time talking about the probability that a second wave of attacks was inevitable, developed and repeatedly manipulated a terror alert system to reemphasize the domestic threat aspect of the brand story (one famous incident involved the Homeland Security Secretary urging the public to stock up on water, food, duct tape, and plastic sheeting in preparation for a chemical attack).[16] Ridge's response to his critics in this incident shows the extent to which the administration was employing brand-building techniques to sell the War on Terror brand. In this case, Ridge said his department had worked for the last eight months, even using focus groups, to find the best ways to prepare the public in the event of terrorist attacks.

The administration took advantage of the domestic security elements of its broader-brand story when it touted the arrest of Jose Padilla who the administration alleged of planning to build and detonate a dirty bomb in the United States.[17] It also played up the breakup of two Al Qaeda cells, one in Buffalo, New York[18] and one in Detroit, Michigan[19] as validation of the domestic threat aspect of the War on Terror brand story. These successes were also useful in proving the validity of the strong leader aspect of brand W, showing that Conservatives really were strong on national security issues and putting them in position to avoid difficult questions, as well as to win the next elections.

The brand's power in public policy is shown by the strong public, political, and media support that the Bush team built for its Iraq line extension to the War on Terror brand.[20] The broad way in which the War on Terror brand was established ensured that lots of line extensions could be placed into it. One of the ways in which Iraq was placed into it was through a fellowship-building campaign premised on shadowy meetings between Iraqi intelligence agents and 9/11 mastermind Mohammed Atta as proof of Iraqi involvement in these attacks.[21] Such relationships were not as clear in real life as in the brand story but this, as we saw in Chapter 1, is one of the ways in which brands serve as quick learning tools. As long as there was no visible proof to the contrary, the administration could get away with using its War on Terror brand.

When the Bush team built its brand story, most Americans knew that the 9/11 hijackers were Middle Eastern and that allusions were made to that region in the letters accompanying the subsequent anthrax attacks. That almost all of the hijackers were Saudis, that the Iraqi Baathist Party and its leader Saddam Hussein enjoyed mutually hostile relations with bin Laden and his movement, and that the source of the anthrax attacks was most likely domestic were all stories for another day and were drowned out by the War on Terror brand. To justify its Iraq invasion, the administration created fellowship between that country and Osama, and between terrorist attacks and the weapons of mass destruction (WMD) that Iraq surely possessed. In short, it told Americans that Iraq had either been involved in the 9/11 attacks or certainly would be in the next one. In this way the brand strategy was used to build public support for a foreign policy called preemption.

The effort to build fellowship between Iraq and 9/11 was so successful that, just prior to the invasion of Iraq, about 70 percent of the public believed that the administration's assertions about a link between the two was accurate.[22] This fellowship was built by having administration officials other than Bush and friendly Conservatives juxtapose the two. As a result, the administration could later claim with some credibility that its man had never made the claims that created it. The administration implied a relationship in a brand story that had been built out of highly selective, incorrect, and falsified intelligence.[23] In response to charges that its rationale for going to war had been flawed, the Bush team immediately tried to shift the rationale for invading Iraq from one based on the preemption of an attack on the United States to one that touched on the branded archetypes that resonate with Americans: bringing freedom to the oppressed.[24]

The Iraq invasion was included in the War on Terror brand almost from the moment that the 9/11 attacks happened.[25] The 9/11 attacks provided the justification for an Iraq invasion and the brand strategy gave the Bush team a vehicle through which they could promote it. The Iraq aspect was incorporated into the War on Terror brand story and moved from a niche to a mass market product as outlined below.

The brand story told Americans a tale about a relationship between a past terrorist attack and a future one, of a relationship between Iraq and Al Qaeda, and of the use of weapons of mass destruction shared between the two—a threat that tapped into the marketing done by Conservatives since 1964 but most particularly since the Reagan years. The brand story's truth was made real to the public through implication, through a public relations campaign in support of the brand, and by tying events dealing with Iraq (such as the president's speech to the United Nations in New York about WMD) to the events of 9/11.[26] The administration provided proof for its assertions by playing up evidence that supported its position and playing down or discrediting information that called its assertions into question or blurred their clarity.[27]

Fellowship was also achieved through the use of the same word "evil," when Saddam and Osama were publicly discussed. Working together, these evil ones would doubtlessly attack the United States. The use of the term evil to describe these American adversaries allowed the administration to favorably position the United States against these opponents and, as we will see, to reiterate the contrasts that were drawn during the Cold War. The result of the latter would be to place the current conflict into the anti-Communist, strong national defense aspect of the archetypal Conservative brand: that of fighting an evil empire as we will also see in this chapter. In light of this, it is not surprising that, faced with the same dire brand story that justified massive militarization for half a century, Americans responded in favor of military action designed to prevent another terrorist attack. The Iraq War was a difficult sell "unless you judiciously avoided the facts."[28] As we saw at the outset, this is one of the things that the brand strategy does for Conservatives, it gives them a tool through which they can present stories instead of facts and produce feelings instead of analysis from the audience.

Once it became clear that the assertions made in this case were wrong, the Bush team employed the brand strategy as Conservatives do to switch aspects from protecting Americans to promoting freedom, part of the Reagan heritage and Conservative archetypal brands as noted earlier. The latter was an easier point to make using the brand strategy because there were all sorts of highly visible, highly emotive events that could be used to promote the brand and prove that its promises were being kept. An example of which is provided by the numerous photos of Iraqis holding up their blue thumbs to prove that they had voted.[29]

While the failure to keep the original brand promises hurt Bush's reputation among a lot of Americans, it did not seem to make any difference to his core audience because his 2004 campaign would very much play up another aspect of the War on Terror to win their votes. Over time, it caused the administration to deemphasize the Iraq and military aspects of the War on Terror brand to stress the ideological nature of the battle in favor of a much more amorphous title "The Global Struggle against Extremism."[30] This shift offered the Bush administration a way to continue using a damaged brand, and the ideological nature of the conflict gave it a way to explain why the conflict has not and is not likely to be won soon, making it just like the Cold War.

Studying the War on Terror brand is of great use because it shows how the brand strategy allows Conservatives to incorporate divergent policies into a single brand, past brand-building efforts facilitate new brands being built, and one way in which a brand can be damaged or killed. This was a wildly successful brand because it made a weak president strong, sold a number of controversial policies, silenced critics, and allowed the administration to avoid responsibility for its numerous failures. In addition, it was wildly successful because it formed one of the key aspects of the brand that got George W. Bush reelected in 2004 and the Conservatives a majority in Congress in 2002.

The 9/11 Initial Response

On September 10, 2001, the Bush administration was marketing a branded initiative to the American public: Social Security reform. The public was interested in the issue; the Bush administration had a plan that would not be discussed again until 2005. The events of 9/11 changed the nature of the issues about which most Americans worried. Suddenly, people stopped worrying about a secure retirement and started worrying about a secure daily homecoming. The nation was plunged into a period of mourning, introspection, and anger from which it took until at least the aftermath of Hurricane Katrina to fully emerge.

This national and personal tragedy provided a significant opportunity for the politically weak Bush administration and for Conservative policy entrepreneurs. Consistent with John Kingdon's argument in *Agendas, Alternatives, and Public Policy,* the events of September 11, 2001 served as a focusing event that opened a policy window for the administration to accomplish its foreign policy goals.[31] The Bush team seemed aware enough of the opportunity and the importance of building a brand broad to allow its agenda items to appear to be related to the 9/11 events. First, it was obvious to those in the national security community that 9/11 had been perpetrated by Al Qaeda about whom most Americans had known little or nothing prior. This presented the Bush administration and Conservative policy entrepreneurs with a brand-building opportunity because the organization could be made to appear as whatever the administration claimed it to be. The same was true of the Taliban and the nuances of Afghan politics. Widespread ignorance is one of the situations in which public relations techniques, including branding, are ideally suited. Thus, the Bush administration found itself facing an audience that wanted its problems solved but did not fully understand which of the available products would do the best job. This gave the administration a chance to use the brand strategy to both appear to be doing so and to implement its own agenda.

Bush's speech of September 20, 2001, is but one example of the way in which the administration began presenting the brand story that would become the War on Terror brand and the justification for the broader War on Terror. In this speech he presented his audience with a simile, as is consistent with the brand strategy by arguing that Al Qaeda was "to terror what the mafia is to crime."[32] Given that genre's popularity, this was something that educated the audience quickly. One of the most popular genres of American film focuses on the mafia, thus making it something about which most Americans are familiar. Bush noted that Al Qaeda's goal was not monetary as is the mafia's but ideological and involved "remaking the world— and imposing its radical beliefs on people everywhere."[33]

Bush introduced bin Laden as the organization's leader and began building the broader War on Terror brand by saying it was linked to many other organizations in different countries: "There are thousands of these terrorists in more than 60 countries."[34] After outlining the broad band story, Bush introduced its first product, an Afghan invasion, by noting that the country had served as a terrorists training group for the organization. Once trained, these terrorist were "sent back to their homes or sent to hide in countries around the world to plot evil and destruction."[35] By doing this, Bush showed the public that disaster could happen if no action were taken.

He then tapped into the Cold War aspect of the Conservative brand by calling the organization and its leader evil and radical, as well as when he claimed, much as Conservatives had claimed during the Contract with America campaign, that the opponent was against "freedom.[36]"

Thus was the War on Terror brand launched with several aspects of the core Conservative brand within it. Freedom is an aspect that has been contained in the Conservative brand since at least the Reagan years and this freedom aspect is generally juxtaposed against a threat in order to narrow the audience's choices. In this case, the Bush team used the brand strategy to promote its domestic and international policy shifts. We can see that the War on Terror brand was launched with several traits of the archetypal Conservative brand within and that the techniques that were used to sell it were very much in keeping with those used in recent decades to sell Conservative political products. Without a visible problem it is not clear that the brand strategy works as well because the number and consequences of the consumer's choices are not as constrained. In this case, the Bush brand narrative presented the public with a tale about America taking on evil extremists in order to make itself safe, very much in genre of the Cold War and in the everyman or commonsense aspects of the Conservative brand story.

While Bush never tried to establish blame within the U.S. government for the 9/11 events and initially fought efforts to establish an independent commission to look into the matter, other Conservatives tried to blame Slick Willie for them possibly because doing so would have provided proof that that campaign had been justified. Bush as president had a set of imperatives that did not include things monetary; thus, he and his team focused on building a part of the narrative around the War on Terror that could be used to differentiate him from Slick Willie, which could enhance his position vis-à-vis Congress and the voters and be recycled during 2004: that of Bush as a strong leader. This was done by arguing that Bush's response had been stronger than Clinton's, and that its visible strength proved that Bush was a better leader than was Slick Willie. Beginning the brand story with 9/11 allowed the Bush team to avoid dealing with anything that went before, to avoid dealing with the blame game and stop the Pearl Harbor narrative as we saw above. The brand strategy let the administration talk about its agenda instead of events over which it would never have control.

Bush's remarks that "Our response involves far more than instant retaliation and isolated strikes"[37] shows the way in which the Slick Willie contrast was implicitly built into the brand from the outset. Bush prepared the public for the idea that this was going to be a war that had the potential to last for years and, by doing so, lower expectations about quick successes, as well as set the stage for years of military spending by and policy initiation from the White House. He made this clear by saying that "Americans should not expect one battle, but a lengthy campaign, unlike any other we have ever seen."[38] He further lowered expectations for a quick success by saying: "It may include dramatic strikes, visible on TV, and covert operations, secret even in success."[39] His brand story included the notion that the effort would take on a variety of forms that would end well by saying, "We will starve terrorists of funding, turn them one against another, drive them from place to place, until there is no refuge or no rest."[40] Building the brand story in this way let Bush set the stage for the promotion of his foreign policy agenda and his administration's desire to make the workings of government less open to public scrutiny and, in the process, make the public's understanding of what the president does daily more a function of narrative than reality.

The early phase of the brand-building campaign saw the administration working to present Americans with the same kind of favorably positioned binary choices that as Conservatives had presented them with during the Contract with America and Reagan administration campaigns. As was true in these early campaigns, the choice was between adopting the Conservative solution to the problem and a calamity; in this case, more terrorism. Bush gave the rest of the world the same kind of binary choice and gave Americans a binary metric upon which they could easily divide up the world by saying "Every nation, in every region, now has a decision to make. Either you are with us, or you are with the terrorists."[41]

This is exactly the way in which Ronald Reagan initially fought the Cold War as president and is consistent with the Conservative, us and them, worldview that has been part of the movement since its inception. Thus, the brand story told Americans that they were attacked by evil people who would surely strike again and that, as was true in the case of the Reagan Cold War branding, Americans had to choose on which side they were going to be. The old world of us versus them that had died with the end of the U.S.S.R. in 1992 was back, and along with it came easily drawn contrasts, the strong versus weak brand aspects that Conservatism has about itself and the Liberals, as well as an easy justification for the full range of administration policy proposals. The use of the brand strategy gave the Bush administration more latitude, more power, and an ability to tap into several generations of previous Conservative marketing.

Branded Domestic Changes: The Patriot Act and Department of Homeland Security

Having neatly divided the world into good and evil, the War on Terror brand was next built by showing that the threat was clear and present, as well as that the steps being taken by the Bush administration were making the nation safer. Domestically, 9/11 produced immediate policy outputs in two areas: the centralization of the U.S. intelligence and law enforcement services into something called the Department of Homeland Security and the Passage of the U.S.A. Patriot Act. Rather than discuss the minutiae of public policy, the administration created a brand story and worked to place each of its proposals within it. Thus, Bush could prove that his initiatives were making America safer, and if there were specific problems with any of them, the blame for that would fall outside the brand story, in a lower visibility environment and away from the White House.[42]

The package of domestic policy reforms that became law after 9/11 was known as the Patriot Act that was signed into law on October 26, 2001[43] just forty-five days after the 9/11 attacks had taken place. This is lightening speed in the U.S. legislative process. The act was a key part of the broader War of Terror brand because it showed that the administration's assertions about the prevalence of terrorists in the country was accurate and that Bush was committed to doing something about them. Bush sold the legislation as a key means through which the War on Terror could be fought and the homeland protected when he said "This legislation is essential not only to pursuing and punishing terrorists, but also preventing more atrocities in the hands of the evil ones."[44] Bush worked the highly emotive terrorist and evil terms into the point but never spelled out how the Act itself was going to make Americans safer. The Act mattered less for its substantive impact and more for the fact that its passage was a highly visible event capable of making Americans see that Bush was protecting them and making them feel better about having him at the nation's helm.

Fighting the Evil Ones: Whomever They Happen to Be

Having established the War on Terror as being another conflict in the mode of the Cold War, the administration gained an opportunity to implement many aspects of its distinctive foreign policy agenda, much of which appears to have been developed by administration officials while they worked in think tanks during the Clinton years. Many of these people thought that an invasion of Iraq was justifiable given that country's recent history with biochemical weapons and its desire to acquire nuclear weapons, as well as out of their broader desire to transform the orientation of American foreign policy.

Even before Bush had gotten into office, members of his team had expressed considerable interest in creating a much different kind of foreign policy than the United States had pursued since at least the end of the Cold War and really since the beginning of World War II. The members of the Project for A New American Century (PNAC) were especially interested in creating a more unilateralist, more nationalistic foreign policy.[45] It is not surprising that the administration moved to sell an invasion of Iraq as part of the War on Terror brand, given that many of these PNAC veterans were now serving in it and that other members of this Bush administration had been in the George H.W. Bush administration during the first Gulf War.

The PNAC had been promoting its version of American foreign policy since the mid-1990s and had even written an open letter to the president in support of its goals. The letter employed the verbiage that the Bush team would eventually incorporate into the War on Terror brand to justify its invasion of Iraq. After noting their belief that Clinton's Iraq policy was not working, the letter foreshadowed the arguments that would be made during the run-up to war by saying "we may soon face a threat in the Middle East more serious than any we have known since the end of the Cold War."[46] The letter urged Clinton to use an upcoming high-profile event, the State of the Union, to "chart a clear and determined course for meeting this threat."[47] The goals of which would be to "secure the interests of the United States and our friends around the world" and to accomplish this by "the removal of Saddam Hussein's regime from power."[48] The letter moved on to suggest that the withdrawal of U.N. inspectors raised the uncertainty level of the threat facing the United States and that, as a result, the United States should act to achieve regime change in Iraq and, by so doing, deal with the threats posed by that regime.[49]

Much of the argument for the unilateralist foreign policy that the administration eventually pursued through the War on Terror brand was laid out in this letter when it said "Given the magnitude of the threat, the current policy, which depends for its success upon the steadfastness of our coalition partners and upon the cooperation of Saddam Hussein, is dangerously inadequate." The solution to the possibility that Iraq "will be able to use or threaten to use weapons of mass destruction" was, of course, "in the near term, a willingness to undertake military action as diplomacy is clearly failing. In the long term, it means removing Saddam Hussein and his regime from power. That now needs to become the aim of American foreign policy."[50] Without the events of 9/11, it is not clear that the Bush administration would have been in a position to even consider such an effort given its weak political position.

The letter suggested that Clinton should make Saddam's removal a centerpiece of U.S. foreign policy as the Bush administration would when it asked Clinton to "turn your administration's attention to implementing a strategy for removing Saddam's regime from power."[51] The strategy would include "a full complement of diplomatic, political and military efforts[52]" based on the idea that even though undertaking this effort would be hard and risky "we believe the dangers of failing to do so are far greater[53]," much as the administration would argue during the run-up to and the aftermath of the Iraq War when its rationale for launching the war proved to have been fallacious. As the Bush administration would, the letter argued that the United States did not need any further UN authorization for actions up to and including military measures "to protect our vital interests in the Gulf."[54] As marketers like to do, the letter closed with a call to action that included a binary choice when it urged decisive action to promote U.S. national security interests in contrast to "a course of weakness and drift, we put our interests and our future at risk."[55] These points of emphasis appeared in the Iraq War line extension to the War on Terror brand, were a major theme in the Conservative congressional-coordinated contrast campaign of 2002, and was a major part of the strong leader aspect of brand W in 2004.

We can see why the Bush administration was eager to invade Iraq and why it built the Iraq line extension into the War on Terror brand by examining a list of its signatories who held positions in the George W. Bush administration as follows[56]:

Elliott Abrams	*First Term:* special assistant to the president and senior director on the National Security Council for Near East and North African Affairs. *Second Term:* Deputy National Security Adviser.
Richard L. Armitage	*First Term:* Deputy Secretary of State.
John Bolton	Undersecretary of State for Arms Control and International Security. U.S. ambassador to the UN .
Paula Dobriansky	Under Secretary of State for Global Affairs, both terms.
Francis Fukuyama	President's Council on Bioethics. 2001–5.
Zalmay Khalilzad	Special envoy to Afghanistan after the fall of the Taliban. Special envoy to Iraq during the U.S.-led occupation of Iraq. U.S. ambassador to Afghanistan U.S. Ambassador to Iraq.
William Kristol	Consultant on Second Inaugural Address.
Richard Perle	Served on the Defense Policy Board Advisory Committee from 1987 to 2004. He was Chairman of the Board 2001 to 2003.

Peter W. Rodman	Assistant Secretary of Defense for International Affairs.
Donald Rumsfeld	Defense Secretary.
William Schneider, Jr.	Chairman of the Defense Science Board.
Paul Wolfowitz	*First Term:* Deputy Defense Secretary. *Second Term:* World Bank president.
Robert B. Zoellick	*First Term:* U.S. Trade Representative. *Second Term:* U.S. Deputy Secretary of State until July, 2006.

Only five signatories did not end up with some position in or affiliation with the administration and many of those who ended up in such positions appear to have been able to directly influence the way in which foreign policy was made and implemented. This is especially true of the Secretary of Defense and the Deputy Secretary of Defense but is not meant to suggest that everyone on this list favored everything that has been done by the administration during its time in office.

As think tanks do,[57] the PNAC marketed its policy proposals with the overall theme that a need existed for a U.S. foreign policy that was generally more muscular and more nationalistic. One of the examples of this is an article entitled *Cowering Superpower* written by Project for the New American Century Middle East Initiative Project Director Reul Marc Gerect that appeared in the *Weekly Standard* on July 30, 2001, and in one of its closing paragraphs said ominously that "the Taliban chieftain Mullah Omar ought to discover that dead Americans mean cruise missiles coming through his bedroom window and cluster bombs all over his front line troops."[58] Many students of U.S. foreign policy saw events in Afghanistan prior to 9/11 as a serious problem, so it is not surprising that the PNAC was producing articles about it during the time period. What is of interest is that it was working on Iraq at the same time. The marketing problem was that, outside Conservative circles, the PNAC worldview attracted little attention or support because, without a crisis, selling its militaristic philosophy would indeed be difficult. It was 9/11 that provided the agenda shift necessary for PNAC's plans to be put into place and, given how many PNAC members were in the administration, it is not surprising that the brand built in response to 9/11 contained PNAC's themes and policy prescriptions.

The War on Terror brand and its story accomplished just that through extensive implication and via direct repetition of the claims by Bush's underlings but seldom by Bush himself about WMD.[59] Primarily this was accomplished by having an administration official remind the public about what had happened in New York followed by a mention of bin Laden and Saddam Hussein in the same context and sentence whenever possible, followed by an assertion that it was possible that one would help the other to attack the United States. The second way in which fellowship between Iraq and Al Qaeda was put into the brand story was through the assertion that they had cooperated to plan the 9/11 attacks.

As is typical of Conservative marketing campaigns, this aspect was planted in the core audience for Conservative products during the fall of 2001 by repeated suggestion in the press that Iraqi intelligence agents had met with 9/11 ringleader Mohammed Atta or that various Al Qaeda members had been hosted by the Iraqi government. The third way in which this was done was to suggest a link between the two evil ones in the subsequent anthrax attacks that were delivered by post in October 2001.[60] The *Wall Street Journal,* on October 18, editorialized that the anthrax's likely source was Saddam and the paper's thoughts were echoed by PNAC member and guest columnist James Woolsey.[61] As Rothschild goes on to note and a search of the *Weekly Standard,* a Conservative newspaper edited by William Kristol who had signed the PNAC Iraq letter, Web site shows, the magazine's October 1 cover featured a wanted poster displaying the faces of bin Laden and Hussein next to each other.[62] As they generally do, Conservatives in government seized these Conservative press and think-tank positions to justify their policy preferences and the brand story being built in support of their preferences. One way in which this was done was by having government figures discuss a variety of scenarios for a second Al Qaeda attack, but this time weapons of mass destruction would be employed. Thus, the conditions under which an invasion of Iraq could become part of the brand built in response to the 9/11 attacks was present from the beginning. Simply, the brand strategy gave the voters the choice of either supporting Bush or waiting to see if they or their loved ones would be killed in a nuclear or biochemical attack.

Conservative audiences were predisposed to favor the Iraq invasion because, as noted above, some of Bush's 2000 campaign materials contained references to it but the campaign spoke to no other audiences about it. Thus, when the chance to invade Iraq presented itself after 9/11, the core Conservative audience saw such an invasion as proof that the administration was keeping its campaign promises. During the fall of 2001, the administration focused on its successful campaign to drive the Taliban from Afghanistan when selling the War on Terror brand publicly. The message that was distributed to Conservatives focused on the relationship between Iraq and Al Qaeda as a matter of fact. Throughout the run-up to the war, during the war, and even in the aftermath, the existence of this link was repeated as a justification for the war. Conservatives explained away the failure to find WMD as the result of (1) clever hiding places,[63] (2) Saddam destroyed them just prior to the war's outbreak,[64] or (3) they were moved to a neighboring country just prior to the war's outbreak.[65] The WMD threat gave Conservatives a narrative with which they could incorporate Saddam into the War on Terror brand story.

The broader brand story that was the War on Terror became of great use to the Bush administration almost at once because of the murky way in which the military phase of the Afghan campaign ended and the next section will examine the way in which the Bush brand story changed in response to the fact that bin Laden was not captured. This failure gave the Bush team a marketing problem because it put the lie to a high profile Bush statement but also a marketing opportunity because, as was true in the Slick Willie campaign, it offered the opportunity to add line extensions.

The Battle of Tora Bora and the Axis of Evil: Marketing Problems Abroad

During December 2001, it looked like the Afghan War was about to end very favorably. The Taliban and Osama bin Laden were driven into the high mountains along the Afghan-Pakistani boarder. Bin Laden's quick capture and the end to the threat seemed to be all but assured. For a variety of reasons, this did not happen. The Bush administration solved this seemingly difficult marketing problem in two ways. First, it played up the domestic security aspects of the War on Terror brand and began working with its Iraq line extension by stressing the supposed relationship between Iraq and Al Qaeda. This reduced the amount of negative impressions of Bush and the War on Terror brand that could have been generated by the failure at Tora Bora and created a vehicle through which other goals, such as the PNAC-inspired foreign policy, could be sold by the administration. Thus, it is hardly surprising that the aspects of the War on Terror brand changed in response to this high-profile failure.

The Tora Bora failure produced a political problem for the Bush administration: how to keep the War on Terror going without having to explain to the public how bin Laden escaped from what had been billed as a looming surrender on December 12, 2001, that turned into a failure to find him by December 16, 2001.[66] It would not be clear what had happened to bin Laden for several months. This created a marketing problem because it turned out that, contrary to the president's statement: "If he thinks he can hide from the United States and our allies he will be sorely mistaken,"[67] he could do both. One way that the administration solved this problem was to shift the brand aspect that it was stressing from the hunt for bin Laden toward its broader policy of preemption and the domestic security aspects of the brand. The 2002 State of the Union Address, given just over a month after the end of the Battle of Tora Bora, shows how the administration had started to sell its new foreign policy as part of the War on Terror brand story. The State of the Union is a profile event through which the administration can launch or promote its brands. The 2002 State of the Union contained five paragraphs that put the new foreign policy and the Iraq invasion into the War on Terror brand. Typical of the way in which Bush did this was his statement that "Our second goal is to prevent regimes that sponsor terror from threatening America or our friends and allies with weapons of mass destruction."[68] This line closely resembles the language that was used in PNAC's letter to Bill Clinton and shows how the brand story that was constructed contained the justification for their policy preferences.

Bush drew a link between 9/11 and the way in which his administration's aggressive response to it had modified some nation-state's behavior when he said "Some of these regimes have been pretty quiet since September the 11th. But we know their true nature."[69] After which he outlined the problems that the United States had with North Korea and Iran (two members of the PNAC invasion wish list), before presenting an Iraq that Bush claimed in the highly emotive language of the Conservative brand strategy,

> continues to flaunt its hostility toward America and to support terror. The Iraqi regime has plotted to develop anthrax, and nerve gas, and nuclear weapons for over a decade. This is a regime that has already used poison gas to murder thousands of its own citizens—leaving the bodies of mothers huddled over their dead children. This is a regime that agreed to international inspections—then kicked out the inspectors. This is a regime that has something to hide from the civilized world.[70]

By doing so, he was including the PNAC foreign policy in the War on Terror brand. Bush then tried to introduce a new brand for the PNAC invasion wish list when he said,

> States like these, and their terrorist allies, constitute an axis of evil, arming to threaten the peace of the world (author emphasis). By seeking weapons of mass destruction, these regimes pose a grave and growing danger. They could provide these arms to terrorists, giving them the means to match their hatred. They could attack our allies or attempt to blackmail the United States. In any of these cases, the price of indifference would be catastrophic.[71]

Introducing the "axis of evil" could have helped the administration make its case for its new foreign policy succinctly and place it squarely within the archetypal Conservative brand that has been fighting evil in the world for decades, the problem was that the facts of the matter in each of the nations included were somewhat different than what the administration was claiming them to be.[72]

The axis floundered because it had a credibility problem. For a time, it let the administration promote preemption as part of the War on Terror brand and, in some ways, set the stage for the more specific campaign about Iraq that was to come. Fellowship was built between the two via the employment of the same kinds of implication that would be rolled out later in the year to sell the Iraq War. Note, how—as it would from this point forward—the Bush team used 9/11 to set a context into which other foreign policy issues could be placed and, as a result, make them more comprehensible to the audience. This is something that will be examined in great depth in this and the subsequent chapters. As we have seen, creating binary choices is one of the key means to maximize the brand strategy's effectiveness. Further, the shift in the aspects of the War on Terror brand being emphasized is made more conspicuous by the absence of Osama bin Laden from this speech. Instead of a pursuit of an evil one, the War on Terror brand after Tora Bora came to focus on a fight against an axis of evil that made the case for the foreign policy shift being implemented by the administration.

During the Spring of 2002, the administration emphasized the domestic security aspects of the War on Terror brand in addition to using the axis of evil to sell its foreign policy. This combination kept bin Laden off the public's mind and out of the media. The administration stressed high-profile arrests, manipulated the terror alert system, and played up the security changes that it made at airports in order to show that it was keeping its promise to make Americans safer even while it was suggesting that another terror attack was all but inevitable, thus justifying the Patriot Act and its preemptive foreign policy.

Additionally, by this point, the administration seemed to know that the War on Terror brand had the power to dominate news cycles and shift the agenda in favorable directions. The War on Terror brand had this power because it visually appeared to offer solutions for a problem that most people had seen for themselves that produced strong emotions. Thus, the War on Terror fit the way in which Conservatives have used the brand strategy. The use of the War on Terror brand allowed the Bush team to sell its foreign and domestic policy proposals while reducing the amount of attention paid to stories that had the potential to be politically damaging.

The administration built awareness of the War on Terror brand and used it to shape favorable media and public opinion climates about itself through a number of changes to the nation's terror alert system and missives from the Department of Homeland Security that Americas should buy duct tape, bottled water, and plastic sheeting to protect themselves in case of a chemical attack. These kinds of activities built impressions for the brand story and showed that the promises made in it by the administration were being kept. It faced the eventual problem of either finding bin Laden or, short of that, finding a way to declare victory without having done so or find another way to use the War on Terror brand that was capable of serving its policy and political needs. By the Fall of 2002 and its congressional elections it was clear that the administration had opted for the third course of action.

The 2002 Midterm Elections: War as a Coordinated Campaign

Looking objectively at the upcoming congressional midterm elections during the summer of 2002, a reasonable observer would not have been wrong in concluding that Republicans were going to have some trouble holding its majority on Capitol Hill. The U.S. economy had failed badly, 9/11, a series of anthrax attacks, and bin Laden's escape from Tora Bora had all taken place during 2001. Republicans did well in 2002 through the use of the brand strategy with the same kind of coordinated contrast campaign with which they had done well in 1994 and been badly burned in 1998. The War on Terror brand story in general and its Iraq line extension in particular gave Conservatives a single issue on which they could run as a block that tapped into their archetypal brand story about Liberals and Conservatives on security policy, as well as a mandate to invade Iraq.

The Bush team won its mandate and Conservatives won the 2002 midterm elections because of the War on Terror brand story that they had built from 9/11 onward. This work gave Conservatives the ability to gloss over their failures in fighting the terror war, avoid discussing issues like the economy on which they were badly positioned, and gain a vehicle through which they could market their new proposals. Thus, there was little discussion of responsibility for allowing 9/11 to happen, the administration's efforts to block an independent investigation into the matter, the U.S. economy, the exploding federal debt or any of the other problems that had come to face the nation since the Bush administration came into office nor was there any real discussion of how the administration had gotten into office in the first place. Instead, the election focused on a single issue, Iraq as presented through the War on Terror brand story.

During the summer of 2002, the administration began building fellowship between Saddam and Osama while reiterating the idea that another terrorist attack was surely coming.[73] Although the enemy might still be among us, this was no longer as important as the aspect of the brand that stressed the relationship between Osama and Saddam that would surely produce a WMD-based terrorist attack in the United States. While Osama was not directly mentioned because the Bush administration could not produce him, Al Qaeda could be and was mentioned but this time in close proximity to Saddam. Doing this let the administration link public memories with the brand story that it was selling in order to amplify the brand strategy's emotional impact.

Without the events of 9/11 and the use of the brand strategy to build public support for the administration's response to these events, it is not clear that a justification for an invasion of Iraq for which broad public support existed could have ever been found. As it was, the public discussion of such a policy took place through a branded marketing campaign that appears to have been aimed at keeping Republicans in charge of Congress and at gaining authorization for the Iraq policy that some in the administration had been promoting since the PNAC days. The White House chief of staff, Andrew H. Card, Jr., even said that: "From a marketing point of view," on the rollout this week of the campaign for a war with Iraq, "you don't introduce new products in August."[74] In short, this is because most Americans had been paying attention to other things as summer turned into fall; thus, waiting a few weeks to unveil that year's brand strategy made considerable sense. Card's remarks show the high level of awareness that the administration had about the importance of selling to win elections and selling to change public policy. Both could be accomplished because the brand strategy has always helped Republicans present themselves as being stronger on national security matters than Democrats and it gave them an opportunity to build fellowship between Saddam and Al Qaeda in order to justify an Iraqi invasion. The brand strategy was used in a way that encouraged the public to feel that Iraq had a relationship with Al Qaeda, that only through the election of another Republican Congress and the authorization of another Iraqi invasion could Americans be fully kept safe. The brand strategy, as noted, allowed Conservatives to mute discussion about all other issues in favor of the one on which they were best positioned and on which the brand strategy has given them a clear advantage over the Democrats.

Once the Conservatives got the Fall campaign to center on Iraq, they could then present themselves to the electorate based on a series of highly favorable issues. A focus on a high-profile issue around which to build a branded coordinated campaign has become one of the hallmarks of Conservative congressional politics. In 1994, there was the Contract with America, in 1998 there was the Clinton impeachment, and in 2002 there was the debate over an Iraq War. The Iraq question worked for Conservatives because it differentiated the hawkish Republicans interested in protecting the nation from the ill-defined Democrats.

As they had in the above-noted elections, Conservatives used another branded, coordinated campaign to sell their legislative candidates in 2002. In all of these elections, Conservatives ran as a unified group, worked with a set of branded issues, and used positioning to produce the binary choice of supporting the Conservative proposals or the disaster that would ensue if Democrats were put into power. The difference with this campaign was that it also presented individual Democratic candidates with a difficult binary choice of either voting to give Bush the authority to invade Iraq or find themselves starring in the archetypal brand story that Conservatives have built about Liberals. This is true for the following reasons: (1) the Republican Party ran as a unified group, (2) on a highly visible, highly emotive platform, and (3) the election turned into a national contest on a single theme. Because Conservatives initiated this discussion as a group while Democrats responded as individuals, it is easy to see where the electorate could have gotten the idea that it was Republicans who were protecting them from terror while the Democrats dithered.

One of the centerpieces of the campaign was a joint resolution giving Bush the authority to invade Iraq. It mentioned earlier UN resolutions twelve times on its first few pages in order to establish its credibility and it contained Iraq as the War on Terror element when it said: "Whereas members of Al Qaeda, an organization bearing responsibility for attacks on the United States, its citizens, and interests, including the attacks that occurred on September 11, 2001, are known to be in Iraq"[75] followed up with another of the Iraq line extension's key assertions: "Whereas Iraq continues to aid and harbor other international terrorist organizations, including organizations that threaten the lives and safety of United States citizens."[76] It mentioned the WMD threat and linked it directly to 9/11: "Whereas the attacks on the United States of September 11, 2001, underscored the gravity of the threat posed by the acquisition of weapons of mass destruction by international terrorist organizations"[77] before cementing the link between its three topics by saying: "Whereas Iraq's demonstrated capability and willingness to use weapons of mass destruction, the risk that the current Iraqi regime will either employ those weapons to launch a surprise attack against the United States or its Armed Forces or provide them to international terrorists who would do so."[78] Thus, the point to the resolution was very much the same as the brand story that Conservative policies and politicians would keep the nation safe while the Liberals would not.

We can see the protective rationale in the resolution's wording "and the extreme magnitude of harm that would result to the United States and its citizens from such an attack, combine to justify action by the United States to defend itself."[79] As was the case with this overall campaign, the resolution never says that there was a relationship between Iraq and Al Qaeda but through positioning, and implication, there was no possible other conclusion that the public could have drawn from it.

The resolution incorporates much of the message that would make up the fellowship campaign that placed Iraq and Al Qaeda on the same side against the United States in the global War on Terror. In its closing section, the Joint Resolution reemphasizes the points that Iraq and Al Qaeda were on the same side and that a U.S. invasion would be totally in self-defense:

2) acting pursuant to this joint resolution is consistent with the United States and other countries continuing to take the necessary actions against international terrorist and terrorist organizations, including those nations, organizations, or per-

sons who planned, authorized, committed or aided the terrorist attacks that occurred on September 11, 2001.[80]

Through this resolution, the War on Terror was legally and conversationally expanded into a war against Iraq. This was a war that was totally about the United States defending itself, not trying to build an empire as the detractors of former PNAC members serving in the administration claimed. Again 9/11 was used to set the context in which the administration implied and suggested that a relationship between those events and its two targets existed. This paragraph also showed how the Conservatives put the terms "Iraq," "Al Qaeda," and "9/11" near each other to visually emphasize the brand story. This is exactly the story and visuals that would be presented by the Conservatives from the fall of 2002 through the aftermath of the invasion.

It is little wonder that most Americans thought, by the start of the war, that some kind of relationship existed between Saddam and Osama. The War on Terror brand story had been telling them implicitly and explicitly for months that this was so, and the Bush administration had appeared to have kept its promises in fighting the Afghan War and in making the nation safer so it was plausible to believe that they were being honest once more. The remainder of the resolution takes the relationship between Iraq and Al Qaeda as a fact rather than an assertion. The Joint Resolution gave credentials to the brand story because it could be and was repeatedly referred to legitimate whatever action the administration opted to take in Iraq without saying during the campaign season exactly what that was going to be.

The resolution's passage gave Republican candidates something to which they could point in order to show that they were supporters of the president, the War on Terror, and increasing the nation's safety, as well as to show that it was Conservatives who were keeping their promise to provide a strong defense. Democrats who opposed the resolution in effect defined themselves as being Liberal in the sense provided by the Conservative brand and, in this case, could expect to have their patriotism questioned. A famous example of this latter point occurred in a Georgia Senatorial race in which Saxby Chambliss defeated the incumbent Max Cleland by pointing out his opposition to the creation of a Department of Homeland Security until worker protections in it were increased and by running a television ad that showed Cleland with Saddam Hussein and Osama bin Laden.[81]

It was the brand strategy that allowed Conservatives to overcome their problems in 2002, create support for a new kind of foreign policy and, as it became clear that the rationale upon which the first test of that new policy was undertaken was fallacious, has protected them from suffering political damage. Like the rally on the Capitol steps or the release of the Starr Report, this congressional resolution served as the public kickoff to that Fall's branded coordinated campaign. By the time that the resolution was working its way toward final congressional passage, Bush focused his attention solely on the new product being sold by the War on Terror brand: invading Iraq in order to remove Saddam from power. For example, his statement at the very public signing ceremony for the resolution, delved into the history of Iraqi violations of UN resolutions, the brutality of the Iraqi regime and Iraq's suspected WMD program but not what Al Qaeda had done. The events of 9/11/01 were only mentioned in the close of the remarks but in a way that it related to the branded product being sold clear:

> In the events of September the 11th, we resolved as a nation to oppose every threat from any source that could bring sudden tragedy to the American people. This nation will not live at the mercy of any foreign power or plot. Confronting grave dangers is the surest path to peace and security. This is the expectation of the American people, and the decision of their elected representatives. (George W. Bush remarks at signing of J.Res 114).[82]

Bush never mentions exactly who was behind the 9/11 events but, given that his remarks were made at a bill-signing ceremony giving him the authority to invade Iraq, the implication that Iraq was somehow involved was clear to the audience. That this resolution could establish a factually inaccurate relationship in the public's mind and knock a series of controversial domestic issues off of the agenda and out of the public mind shows the power that the brand strategy can have, especially when augmented by contrast marketing and a coordinated congressional campaign. The brand strategy produced expanded powers for Bush, a policy coup for PNAC, and an electoral vote for congressional Conservatives even though the president's party generally loses seats in midterm elections.

Marketing the Iraq Product Using the War on Terror Brand

The resolution passed with a month to go until Election Day and this gave Conservatives a valuable tool to be used to win. Many of them did so by being a good bit less subtle about the supposed relationship between Saddam and

Al Qaeda than the White House had been. Doubtlessly, the most noted example of the way in which these two events were packaged for an election year was an ad run in a Georgia Senate race by Republican challenger Saxby Chambliss, but this was not an isolated case. It was the focal point of the Conservative branded contrast campaign.[83]

This is exactly the way in which branded politics works. Rather than focus on substantive security issues, the Conservatives were able to generate a contrast based on a highly visible, highly emotive single event that could be explained by their brand stories; in this case, this meant that a resolution was debated while substantive conditions extant at the time were ignored. The overall effect was to nationalize the election around security questions in a way that favored the Conservatives and allowed them to reiterate their core brand stories about themselves and their Liberal opponents. The 2002 midterm was a rerun of the 1994 and 1998 midterms because the brand stories promoted in both focused on contemporary issues but also on that which Conservatives have been building for a generation to show that they are on the side of average Americans while the Liberals are not.

The major difference between these earlier coordinated campaigns and 2002 was that this one was run against two branded individuals and dealt with foreign policy matters instead of domestic politics or personal traits. The fellowship built between Saddam, Al Qaeda, and 9/11 became the way in which Republicans contrasted themselves versus Democrats. By adding the Iraq line extension to the War on Terror brand, Conservatives found a way to keep it alive and keep the election competition on favorable terrain.

An example of this is provided by Bush's speech in Cincinnati that went much further in drawing the link between the three than Conservatives had done to this point before a national audience. Bush could do so because admission policies to Bush events at the time assured that the audience would be composed of Conservatives who had already seen how this extension fit into the War on Terror brand line and because of the event's lower profile. Bush outlined the history of the Saddam regime, the United States' dealings with it, and its past ownership of WMD then closed by using 9/11 to set the context for his proposals and of putting Iraq near to that event in order to build fellowship between them:

> The attacks of September the 11th showed our country that vast oceans no longer protect us from danger. Before that tragic date, we had only hints of al Qaeda's plans and designs. Today in Iraq, we see a threat whose outlines are far more clearly defined, and whose consequences could be far more deadly. Saddam

Hussein's actions have put us on notice, and there is no refuge from our responsibilities.[84]

Again we see Iraq being brought into the War on Terror brand. The Cincinnati speech added a new twist that would eventually come back to haunt the Bush administration, because in it Bush asserted that Iraq was trying acquire nuclear weapons for eventual use against the United States. Bush drew a clear line that put nuclear devices in the hands of terrorists courtesy of the Iraqis or had the Iraqi dictator delivering the bomb personally. Both were of course "evil" to place them within the archetypal Conservative brand.[85]

The nuclear threat, which has dominated American thoughts and feelings since 1945,[86] became a core aspect of the Iraq line extension and the War on Terror brand. It was eventually used as a major part of Secretary Powell's speech that made the case for war before the UN and Bush made mention of it during his 2002 State of the Union Address. Given a choice between discussing stolen elections, corporate excess, economic recession or nuclear nightmares, we can see why the Bush administration and the Republican congressional candidates opted for the latter. Moreover, the threat of nuclear holocaust made a much better argument for administration's foreign policy shift.

During the debate leading to the passage of the congressional Resolution, the administration began pressing its case to the UN and in the process presenting the president to the American public as a world leader. In order to subtly maximize the link between 9/11 and Iraq in the public mind, Mr. Bush made an appearance at the UN on September 12, 2002. Bush clearly linked the two events emotively and in time. Bush drew the implicit link of the brand story linking Iraq and Al Qaeda when he said: "Above all, our principles and our security are challenged today by outlaw groups and regimes that accept no law of morality and have no limit to their violent ambitions."[87] He then used the 9/11 attacks to prove his point and to produce an emotive response from his audience when he said "In the attacks on America a year ago, we saw the destructive intentions of our enemies."[88] Bush employed these events to justify his domestic and foreign policies when he said "This threat hides within many nations, including my own. In cells and camps, terrorists are plotting further destruction, and building new bases for their war against civilization."[89]

Instead of a narrow war against a single organization, Bush transformed the conflict before the UN into a battle to save civilization. Doing so allowed him to move on to selling the Iraq line extension as he did by saying: "And our greatest fear is that terrorists will find a shortcut to their mad ambitions when an outlaw regime supplies them with the technologies to kill on a massive scale."[90] Having worked in the nuclear nightmare aspect of the brand, Bush closed by arguing that his proposal for Iraq was in keeping with the organization's traditions when he said "In one place—in one regime— we find all these dangers, in their most lethal and aggressive forms, exactly the kind of aggressive threat the United Nations was born to confront."[91] That place was, of course, Iraq. Aside from an opening reference to success in Afghanistan, the UN speech made no reference to Al Qaeda, progress in the War on Terror, or Bin Laden. In its closing paragraph it linked together all of the themes with which the administration had worked into the War on Terror brand: the new foreign policy, the protection of the homeland, and the strong national defense aspect of the Conservative brand. In the end, it left the audience with the same kind of binary choice that Conservatives have been using the brand story to create for the last several decades. In this case the choice was between a miserable, dangerous Iraq capable of destabilizing the region and the world:

> If we fail to act in the face of danger, the people of Iraq will continue to live in brutal submission. The regime will have new power to bully and dominate and conquer its neighbors, condemning the Middle East to more years of bloodshed and fear. The regime will remain unstable—the region will remain unstable, with little hope of freedom, and isolated from the progress of our times. With every step the Iraqi regime takes toward gaining and deploying the most terrible weapons, our own options to confront that regime will narrow. And if an emboldened regime were to supply these weapons to terrorist allies, then the attacks of September the 11th would be a prelude to far greater horrors.[92]

The same implication and position that was used to include the Iraq product in the War on Terror brand was on display as was the emphasis on high-profile, emotive events that the brand strategy requires to succeed, as it always is when Conservatives employ the brand strategy and its emphasis on high-profile, emotive events to sell their policy objectives. In this case, the public's recollections of the 9/11 events were employed to create a choice between more of the same and the Conservative policies and politicians who could make sure that these bad things never came to pass.

While such a branded appeal had considerable resonance with average American citizens who were not well versed in foreign affairs, it did not have nearly the same kind of success within the global community of nations.

Old allies like Canada and France were reluctant to support an invasion and hopes for a UN resolution authorizing action faded during the autumn. Conservatives dealt with these problems by launching a buzz campaign based on the brand strategy.

This is because the buzz was highly focused on two entities about which Conservatives hold strong feelings that are part of their archetypal brand story: the UN and Europeans in general but the French in particular. There was little discussion of the facts of this case instead, there were highly emotive arguments made about French culture or the ineffectiveness of the UN. Other countries about whom Conservatives did not hold strong feelings, like Canada and Germany, were not subjected to the same kind of attacks as were the French and the UN because doing so would not have tapped into the audience's feelings. The French, for example, were the target of a Google bomb that asked if one meant "French military defeats" after searching for French military victories and a variety of sites sprang up during the winter and early spring of 2003 that listed the wars in which France had fought and strained to show how they had not clearly won many of them.[93] While this particular site was not written by a U.S. Conservative, it shows the extent to which a buzz marketing campaign had been able to shape a more hostile public opinion toward France in a short time.

U.S. Secretary of Defense Donald Rumsfeld coined the phrase "Old Europe" as part of the effort to reassure the U.S. public that the world was not totally alienated from the cause and to show that the assertions being made about the relative strength of the United States versus the weakness of Europe were valid. In the course of doing so, Rumsfeld said "But you look at vast numbers of other countries in Europe, they're not with France and Germany . . . they're with the US." "You're thinking of Europe as Germany and France. I don't," he said. "I think that's old Europe."[94] "Old Europe," the French, and the long-standing hobgoblin of the Conservative brand story, the UN,[95] would not join the fight in Iraq but their opposition could be used to show Americans that their government was acting strongly and directly confronting the threat facing the nation.

While the public may have been upset about the administration's inability to recruit coalition partners in as large a number as had the first Bush administration, the administration worked to develop a branded product that would provide cover for this shortcoming: the coalition of the willing. Creating this brand was an obvious effort to give Americans a sense that they had more allies and were receiving more contributions from these allies than actually was the case.[96] Its credibility was established by pointing out its four biggest members: the British, Spanish, Italians, and Poles. This exercise enabled the administration to counter charges that it was going it alone in Iraq. One way in which the public could be reassured about that and proof produced for the administration's assertions that a coalition existed was through frequent mentions of the term coalition, "coalition forces," and references to highly emotive examples of sacrifices made by individual soldiers in order to build the public impression that a large international coalition like the one that fought the first Gulf War was working away in Afghanistan. The administration did not want to explain exactly what contributions were being made by coalition members and, when pressed on the issue, would fall back on the highly emotive brand strategy consistent examples outlined above. By the start of the war, the American public had been told that the country had willing partners who were in Iraq to fight the threat posed by a looming Iraqi-Al Qaeda operation using WMD in the United States.

War at Last: The Coalition of the Willing Launches Operation Iraqi Freedom

On March 20, 2003, forces composed of troops mostly from the United States, United Kingdom, and Australia invaded Iraq.[97] The operation was branded in a way that stressed Saddam's regimes' attributes but omitted the link to Al Qaeda or the WMD threat upon which it had been sold in the United States. The so-called Operation Iraqi Freedom took place in four phases. First, the United States attempted to knock Saddam out of power in one fell swoop via a decapitation act that was shown repeatedly on U.S. television on March 19. In the early phase of the war, a new phrase, "embedded journalists," entered the lexicon and the public was prepared for a long slog to Baghdad. Second was the launch of the actual war followed by Shock and Awe, Friday both of which were presented in highly visible ways to the American public. The administration had put a lot of thought into its strategy for selling the war at home and a key part of its strategy was to "embed six hundred journalists with the military"[98] in order to show the war and presumably the military's successes in it on live television.[99] Showing the American public the military's scripted version of the war was a way to build up support for it and to silence critics. Both events let the public see for itself that brand W was keeping its promises and had the salutary effect of proving to the Iraqis that Saddam was being removed. These events were later used to prove the validity of subsequent assertions made by the administration to reposition the Iraq line extension following the failure to find WMD.

In the popular mind and as a media event, the Iraq War came to an end with the televised fall of a Saddam statue in downtown Baghdad in mid-April.[100] A high-profile photo op was staged off San Diego on May 1, 2003 that featured President Bush landing a U.S. Naval aircraft that he had copiloted onto the deck of the USS Abraham Lincoln. This was followed by the president giving a speech to a cheering crowd of sailors beneath a red, white, and blue banner that had "Mission Accomplished" printed across it. Having such a high-profile ending is typical in branded Conservative campaigns. On May 1, 2003, it looked like the Bush administration had successfully avoided answering questions about anything other than a highly stylized version of the War on Terror, had achieved significant foreign and domestic policy victories, and had helped establish unified party government. The War on Terror brand itself seemed poised to live on for many years and, at the time, the Iraq War looked like an example of the Bush administration keeping the brand promises that it had made in the wake of 9/11 and in the 2002 coordinated congressional campaign.

Reality Differs From the Brand Story

If the United States had a parliamentary democracy, George W. Bush would have dropped the writ on May 2, 2003 and won an election shortly afterward. The war was won, the mission was accomplished, Bush's approval ratings were high, and more quick triumphs against Al Qaeda and its axis-of-evil allies seemed to be assured. The aftermath of the Iraq War is a lesson in how a political brand can be damaged or killed by a failure to keep the promises that it initially made.

Just after the war ended, the administration rebranded the nation that it had just conquered. The Americans were now running "the New Iraq." This is exactly the same thing that Conservatives did after taking over the House and W's return to the White House after the Clinton years. The U.S. media had begun referring to the nation of Iraq as the "New Iraq." Much of the press coverage from the "New Iraq" focused on the suffering of the Iraqi people under the Hussein regime or of the potential for democracy in Iraq to burst into full flower because of that nation's experience with it prior to the Hussein regime. The initial reports of violence and unrest in the nation were met dismissively by U.S. officials who argued that such things were a normal part of the collapse of any repressive regime.

All seemed to be ending well but nothing could have been further from the truth. Instead of a reconstruction after an accomplished mission, the U.S. military quickly found itself locked in a low-intensity conflict that continues to the present. As a result, the promises made during the runup to the war that the Iraqi people would greet the Americans as liberators and that U.S. troops would come home quickly were not kept.

The second promise that was not kept was that there were no large stores of WMD ever found in Iraq after the war. This meant that the brand promise of a WMD attack in the United States using weapons of Iraqi origin was equally false. This failure had some administration apologists claiming that even one vial of mustard gas found was enough to justify the earlier WMD claims in order to try to show that the original promise had been kept but such claims were so patently ridiculous that few people believed them.

The third promise that was not kept was that of finding a large number of Al Qaeda cells in Iraq. Instead, what the Bush administration was eventually forced to admit was that there was no relationship between the two protagonists around which it had built the brand story for the Iraq War. The net result of these three broken brand promises has been to kill the War on Terror as a brand through which the Bush administration can sell its foreign policy goals to the public. As was noted in the beginning of this chapter, the Bush team has even gone so far as to limit the extent to which it uses that term. It now favors the nonbranded, very bureaucratic term "the Global Struggle against Extremism."

The War on Terror brand was effectively killed because the administration built fellowship between the events of 9/11 and the Iraq line extension that did not exist in reality. The fruits of doing so were that, in the short term, Conservatives were able to change the nation's policy direction, win two elections and, for some, settle old scores. These are not small accomplishments and they illustrate the brand strategy's power. Conservatives, because of the additional line extension, will not be able to use the War on Terror brand for a long period of time because the contradiction between the story sold to include the line extension and its reality was great enough to undermine the entire brand's credibility.

Setting the Stage for the Campaign

Bush was able to win reelection in part due to the broader War on Terror brand that had been built during the prior three years. At the time of this writing in 2006, it appears that the War on Terror brand has been so damaged by its association with the Iraq War that it is being phased out. In product marketing parlance, this is an exercise in stock keeping unit (sku) rationalization. It makes sense to phase out the War on Terror because: (1) years have passed and Osama bin Laden is still nowhere to be seen, (2) there have been major terrorist incidents in Madrid and London since the Iraq invasion, so Al Qaeda might not be as devastated as it seemed when Mr. Bush gleefully read off the overwhelming percentage of its leaders that had been killed since 2001, (3) the Iraq War itself has moved from smashing military victory into a low-intensity conflict in which it is difficult to state credibly that the United States is clearly winning, (4) polls show that the public has clearly grown tired of the Iraq War, feels that it did not make the country safer and, as a result, Mr. Bush's personal favorability ratings have dropped. When a product is damaging the overall line, companies do things like sku rationalization. Thus, it makes sense from that perspective to end the War on Terror even if both the Iraq War and the global struggle against extremism continue.

The War on Terror brand was damaged by the failure to keep its brand promises. Instead of fighting a war against Al Qaeda in Iraq, Americans found themselves involved in nation building. Instead of trying and convicting terror suspects, Americans found themselves learning about a network of secret prisons around the globe, rendition flights, and prisoners held without charge or trial. Although the administration was able to shift emphasis within its Iraq brand story to one of freedom being on the march, the ways in which the United States has dealt with terror suspects and Iraqis do not appear to be grateful for the continued U.S. presence in their country means that the lie has been put to this aspect of the Bush brand story too. The use of the War on Terror brand let the administration win elections, implement public policies, and invade other nations but it has been significantly damaged, if not killed outright, as a result of this failure to keep promises. This failure eventually not only damaged the brand but has also come back to hurt the administration that created it.

The Branded Presidency

The response to 9/11 and the Iraq War were worth presenting in depth because they typify the way in which the White House, Congress, and Conservative activists employed branded initiatives during this administration. These two related cases are worth looking at because there is actually nothing unusual about them. The Bush team developed a branded policy initiative in each case then marketed through the large number of channels that Conservatives now have at their disposal. The Bush team did the same thing in education policy via the No Child Left Behind Act, in medical insurance via the Medicare Modernization Act, in fiscal policy through the Tax Fairness and Tax Relief plans, as well as the checks that were mailed to Americans in order to show that the brand promise was being kept after these Acts passed into law, and in retirement programs via the initiative to strengthen the Social Security that Bush promoted during his early second term and in a wide variety of other policy initiatives. In all of these cases, a brand story, essence, and logo were developed. Bush himself often stumped for the plans and the Conservative message distribution system helped to promote them. In several of these cases, either the public did not actually know what was in the plans or focused on the favorable aspects of them that were contained in the brand stories. The next chapter will look in great depth at the 2004 Bush campaign because it shows how a branded political campaign fully works.

One could very much argue that Bush is both the product and epitome of a branded politics. Those branding techniques that allowed him to rise to the presidency were also, the next chapter will argue, in large part responsible for his reelection in 2004. The next chapter will look at the way in which the Bush reelection campaign took advantage of the brands that it and other Conservatives had built over the last forty years or so, as well as the marketing techniques that the movement has perfected over the same period to transform what appeared to be a very difficult electoral situation into a definitive victory.

Reelect Me Because
At Least I Am Not John Kerry

Bush 2004

The next three chapters show that the 2004 Bush campaign was the latest in a series of branded political campaigns that have been employed to win elections by Conservatives since 1980. The first chapter examines the broad way in which the Bush team used the brand strategy and covers the period up to the Conventions. The second chapter considers the Conventions and debates as high-profile events to which the target audience pays attention. These events gave the Bush team a chance to build impressions through repetition of its brand story for free and, in the process, educate its chosen audiences about its message. The third chapter analyzes the way in which the Bush brand story was included in the campaign's media efforts right up until the outcome of the election became known.

The Bush campaign is the epitome of the branded politics that has developed in the United States over the past twenty years. The Bush team engaged in—for exactly the same reasons as does their corporate counterparts—direct, targeted, relationship marketing of which we spoke in Chapter 1.[1] The Bush campaign mounted an effort to find the right audience for its products. The Bush campaign made very good use of integrated marketing techniques in order to coordinate its message and relationships.[2] Integrated marketing can best be understood as a wide variety of communicative techniques, including messages and the rest that the media was able to sell products united into a whole.[3] My argument is that one of the key ways for this was the use of a targeted distribution of the Bush brand. As Bush strategist Matthew Dowd noted, the campaign analyzed magazine subscriptions, car ownership or their place of residence, issue positions, and "household habits" in order to figure out partisan affiliations.[4] This is very much in keeping with the use of marketing segmentation tools in order to find the most effective segments and build brand loyalty through relationship building.[5]

The Bush team used these techniques to produce a highly targeted, highly individualized brand[6] that was aimed at only a few groups of people, not the entire electorate.[7] Just as is the case for all sorts of brands, brand W was able to appear in as many things to many people while at the same time serving the deeply held needs of the individuals at which it was pitched.[8] Like other kinds of marketers, the 2004 Bush campaign was able to build a brand and an image of that brand, which was based on the demographic and lifestyle traits of their audience targets.[9] The Bush team was able to do so because it coordinated its message across media. At the same time, improved research tools gave them an ability to understand very narrow audiences to make sure that their message got to those audiences.[10] Just as is the case for all sorts of marketers, the Bush team seems to have used these techniques in order to target the right customers. It used these targeted marketing techniques to build their brand in such a way that it tailored and personalized to the interests of the customer.[11]

The Bush team placed great emphasis on grassroots activity. This is very much in keeping with the idea that marketers cannot only attract a given audience, but also actually begin dialogues with and between their audiences, as well as to answer the audience's needs in a very specific way.[12] In the case of the Bush campaign, the *Washington Post* reported upon campaign manager Ken Mehlman's appointment to head the Republican National Committee that he had "a ravenous appetite for political data on issues such as voting patterns among key demographic blocks"[13] that was used as part of the campaign's Election Day strategy of contacting voters and making sure that they voted. [14] The Bush team pulled this off by building a 7.5 million e-mail address database, making 27 million phone calls, mounting a door-to-door sales operation, and through the use of niche advertising in a variety of relevant outlets like farm and Christian radio.[15] All of this resembles the as we discussed in relationship-building efforts that marketers make, chapter 1. The goal of these efforts was to increase brand loyalty and sales as is clear from Mehlman's remark that one of the things that the Republican Party could do to build a lasting majority was to "deepen the GOP by identifying and turning out Americans who vote for president but who often miss off year elections" even if they agree with the Republicans on the issues.[16] Rather than throwing away the targeted marketing that had been done in support of its brand in the prior election year, the Grand Old Party (GOP) was planning to build on it much in the way that other kinds of product marketers that employ targeted marketing strategies do. As Mehlman's writing shows, the Bush camp was keenly aware of exactly how much work was being done on its behalf by its 1.4 million volunteers and 7.5 million activists, who made 102,000 calls to talk radio shows, wrote 411,989 letters to editors, knocked on 9.1 million doors and made 27.2 million phone calls.[17] The value of these efforts was that they produced word-of-mouth advertising for the brand that cannot be purchased at any price, something that Mehlman noted when he wrote that even though the Democrats outspent the Republicans by more than $100 million, their monetary efforts were overwhelmed by the person-to-person contact that took place on the Bush campaign's behalf.[18]

The Bush campaign shows, as Turow explains, how a targeted marketing campaign can support a political brand just like commercial brands. The 2004 Bush campaign fits into this targeted universe because its campaign appears not to have run a campaign aimed at all Americans but instead focused on increasing turnout within their best performing audiences in the way in which all sorts of corporate marketers have come to do.[19] Bush, like branded media formats, became a package that people in the target audience saw as reflective of their identity while, at the same time, totally repulsing others.[20] In many ways, the strategy that his campaign used made him the president of a collection of lifestyle niches much more than it made him the President of the United States.[21] This is very much in keeping with the consequences of targeted marketing and niche media's impact on American society and the brand strategy's power in modern America.[22] The overall Bush campaign has done exactly like most marketers who have responded to these conditions, because rather than trying to do anything to improve them, the Bush team simply used them to accomplish their own ends by producing a series of targeted messages that enabled a number of different groups to vote for Bush even if they did so for different reasons that resembles other kinds of product marketers.[23] At the root of all of this is the brand because it is the basis upon which the rest of the targeting campaign rests.

The Conservative brand strategy helped the Bush team dispel doubts about their candidate and sow doubts about Kerry. The 2004 election shows the numerous advantages that Conservatives reap from their use of the brand strategy. These include the ability to more easily reposition themselves, extend, and build fellowship between different politicians and policies, as well as educate the public more quickly about both their own products and their opponents'. The brand strategy has given Conservatives a tool with which they can win even those elections that indicate otherwise. W was a vulnerable incumbent in 2004 because the nation had suffered an economic downturn, two terrorist attacks (9/11 and the anthrax mailings), and fought (and was still fighting) two wars, all in a four-year period. Bush's high profile that promises Osama bin Laden and weapons of mass destruction would be found had been proven wrong. Similarly, measures like the Patriot Act that were enacted in response to 9/11 had proven to be extremely controversial. Still lingering as well was the question of how Mr. Bush had gotten into office at all. It is the use of the brand strategy that enabled the Bush team to overcome these problems and win again.

The brand strategy let the Bush team alter the campaign dynamic by repositioning Bush to emphasize the positive parts of his record, repositioned his personal traits in a more favorable direction, and positioned his opponent as another in a long line of elitist Liberals who had problems telling the truth. It allowed the Bush team to develop a structured narrative that shifted blame for problems onto Democrats, devoted a lot of time to personality, and featured the social issues prominent in the core Conservative brand. In a nutshell, the Bush team applied the brand strategy to itself and its opponent in the way that Conservatives have over the past two decades. The brand strategy augmented by the positioning and contrast techniques that Conservatives developed from the 1980s to 2004 gave the target audience the impression that their only real choice was to reelect George W. Bush.

The Bush campaign typifies the Conservative brand strategy. It does so because it depended on the same use of a highly visible, emotive setting in which appeals were made that were aimed at specific portions of the electorate.[24] It used the brand strategy in the way that Conservatives have used it since the days of Ronald Reagan. Grover Norquist put it in answer to the question of how Bush and Karl Rove had won in 2000, "They ran as Ronald Reagan."[25] This is yet another example of the way in which Reagan has become a heritage brand for Conservatism.

In 2004, Bush did much the same by working with economic, security, cultural, and leadership issues in order to play to its strength and, by doing so, expanded the depth of its support among its traditional audiences while reaching out to three new ones. The Bush team built a narrative that focused on three aspects of their man: a strong leader in a time of war, an everyman of good moral values and conviction, and a man who had cut taxes in order to make the economy grow out of an inherited recession that was exacerbated by the 9/11 attacks. In short, the brand story told people that only Bush would be a better warrior, better economist, and better person as president than would John Kerry. It neither mentioned that Bush had a patrician background that included an Ivy League education nor did it speak of his considerable involvement in his father's political campaigns.[26] It spoke only about those things that would sell brand W to the target audiences and did it in a way that pointed out those things that would prove that brand W had kept its promises and show its authenticity.[27] Because the Bush team had used the brand strategy throughout its first term in office, the campaign had several readily recognizable initiatives; for example, the No Child Left Behind Act and the War on Terror were presented to voters to prove that brand W had kept its promises the first time around and would do so again.

The Bush campaign camp aped Conservative campaigns of the past in an effort to play on the brand loyalty that had already been built in order to increase turnout within its audiences. It continued building Conservative strength among Roman Catholics, started doing the same with Jewish voters, and launched niche campaigns to improve its support among African American and Hispanic voters as we see later. A strategic consequence of this was that the Bush campaign used a lot of viral marketing techniques in its efforts and improved on these techniques that seem to have begun with the contract with America.[28] It was this combination of branding and a structured distribution system aimed at a few specific parts of the electorate that put Mr. Bush back into office in spite of his questionable first term record. This chapter looks at the way in which this accomplishment reflects the power that branding has to shape electoral outcomes.

The Bush campaign used branding, as all Republicans have since the Reagan years, to create favorable contrasts between its brand and the

Democrat, as well as to position it favorably. The contrasts that they used were typical of what Conservatives have done throughout the period and had the effect of positioning Bush as the best person for the job, as well as a man more like the average voter than was his Democratic opponent. The Bush team linked these contrasts to the brand story that it was building around its opponent.

This was particularly true in the contrast it created between W the strong leader fighting the War on Terror versus the senator flip-flop brand that it created around Kerry. The voters could find the narrative that Bush was a strong leader and Kerry a flip-flopper, both because they had seen Bush in action during the War on Terror, albeit presented in accordance with the brand strategy and because of Kerry's own words. Further, Kerry's patrician manner, Boston residence, and numerous gaffes (including a failure to name his supposedly favorite baseball team's best two players correctly), lent credibility to the Bush brand story about him. Kerry's personal traits were ideal fodder for the contrast technique that Conservatives love to use because they created a choice between the aspects of brand W noted above and an indecisive, patrician Liberal for the voters.[29] This is the contrast that Conservatives have worked to create in all of their efforts since 1980. The Bush team, then, used the brand strategies and marketing techniques Conservatives developed over the past twenty years in order to overcome their man's poor record in office and to defeat a formidable Democratic opponent. This is the advantage that Conservatives have gotten from their two-decade use of the brand strategy.

This chapter looks at the way in which the Bush campaign and its allies built its brand. Chapters 8 and 9 deal with the way in which the brand story was presented in a variety of settings and media. This is because branded politics involves much more than media advertising or the length of the campaign. John Kerry's 2006 assertion that he lost because "We had a 13-week general election; they had an eight-week general election. We had the same pot of money. We had to harbor our resources in a different way and we did not have the same freedom"[30] illustrates in detail the ongoing failure among Democrats to grasp the advantages that a brand strategy gives Conservatives. More money would not have solved Kerry's problem, as he had asserted in the same passage, because the narrative that his opponent's campaign was telling had been a long time in the making.

We will see the key role that Conservative pundits and activists played in shaping the repositioned brand W story during these early days and briefly examine the value of the relationship marketing efforts in which the Bush administration engaged during its first term. This is also a case study on how a political brand can be repositioned because this was done to good effect by the campaign and Conservative activists in the period leading up to the fall campaign.

By the time that year's party conventions rolled around, the Bush team had repositioned its brand in a way that played to its strengths, begun the process of branding its opponent, as well as making use of the contrast and positioning techniques noted earlier. We see later how the aspects of brand W that the campaign wanted to use were promoted during the party convention just as other kind of products are promoted through long-form television commercials. Though branding is about narrative, it is also about visuals because, as Karl Rove has been quoted, "you campaign as if America was watching TV with the sound turned down. It's all visuals."[31] While the visuals attract attention, without a well-constructed narrative, the brand strategy does not work nearly as well.

Conventions matter, as we see, because they are infomercials that sell the branded product and are an effective way to reach the product's core audience. They serve as a similar marketing opportunity through which the brand can be sold to the audience target. As the 2004 Bush campaign showed, the debates are not to win substantive arguments, but to generate impressions for the brand through the tremendous media exposure that debates generate.[32]

After looking at the debates, we look at the Bush media strategy and Bush on the stump. Both are key ways through which brand loyalty can be built in a political campaign. Especially on the stump and in television ads, Bush emphasized the everyman aspects of the Conservative brand. By doing so, he was transformed from a man sharing a socioeconomic, educational, and regional background with his opponent, into a bubba who happened to be president. It was because of the brand strategy that the Bush team accomplished all of this.

Viral Marketing and the Bush Campaign

The Bush campaign made good use of mass and niche marketing techniques to distribute its brands. Niche techniques were particularly important to its effort because much of its electoral strategy was to increase the performance of its best electoral segments. The brand strategy let the Bush team alter its message so that Bush made general remarks to large audiences, and much more specific and more emotive statements on narrow issues to niche audiences. The niche brand strategy was supported by extensive new media and viral marketing campaigns. All of this produced the political equivalent of the bricks-and-clicks campaign model that enabled the campaign to speak directly to its best performing segments about one set of issues and more generally to the rest of its targeted segments. It used this bricks-and-clicks model to encourage voluntarism and provided its audience with a personal stake and a sense of ownership in the campaign. Trying to build a sense of ownership of the product is a typical goal of a branded political campaign.[33]

The campaign invited those on its e-mail list to participate in a range of events, including parties and walks for the president, inviting them to campaign appearances and requesting volunteers for other Conservative campaigns.[34] Additionally, these e-mails were highly personalized and localized in contrast to the more anonymous general e-mails sent out by the Kerry camp. The Bush team regularly sent e-mails to those on its list from its campaign manager, nationally known Republicans, the president and vice president, and members of their families. The e-mails addressed the recipient by name, outlined their theme, and closed with a call to some kind of action as is typical in branded advertising campaigns. Using electronic communication in this way is a method to attract more repeat business for consumer products and its goal in the Bush campaign was doubtlessly to attract more attention to brand W.[35] The net effect is to establish a relationship between the producer and the customer and the brand is a key part of this because its best use can be considered the ability to build loyalty and, as a result, increase the amount of profit or, in this case, the number of votes that the producer earns over time.[36] It is direct marketing that can do this job very efficiently because it combines the knowledge of who is buying the product in terms of lifestyle group, psychological needs, and demographic profile with a number of relationship-building tools in order to build something resembling a conversation with the prospects.[37] One of the most efficient ways in which this could be accomplished was to "build connections with individuals by linking the door-to-door salesperson's ability to relate to individual customers with the computer's ability to come up with more information about the customer than ever before."[38] The goal was to use these tools to "overlay the buying experience with qualities that reflected the special customer's characteristics and lifestyles and linked them to the product or service."[39] This is very much in keeping with the Bush team's 2004 bricks-and-clicks model and, as we have seen, the brand is central to its execution. Further, it is also in keeping with the argument being made herein about the way in which Conservatives have built their brand because the overall goal of these programs was to generate repeat purchases or, for our purposes, multiple votes for Conservative candidates.[40]

The bricks-and-clicks model became another tool through which the Bush team distributed its brand story intact without observation by or interference from the mainstream media.[41] Another way that the Bush Web presence distributed the brand intact was through its hosting of hours of video of less than newsworthy events promoting the brand that the viewer could watch on demand. While most voters and members of the media might not have found this video to have been of great interest, it appears to have been another effort through which the Bush camp could dig deeper into its best performing segments. The Bush team used video much in the way that other kinds of marketers have to reach those parts of the audience with which they most wish to communicate.[42]

Increasing involvement and building brand loyalty were the tools through which turnout could be built and, ideally, word-of-mouth advertising (with the personal endorsements implied by that) could take place. The Bush team spent a lot of time making sure that it knew who its supporters were and how to find them on what was sure to be a tight Election Day. The Bush team's get-out-the-vote effort was based on person-to-person marketing efforts so much so that the campaign had spent two years studying what had increased turnout in prior years.[43] The Bush team's efforts in this area were akin to a door-to-door sales strategy. Such a strategy is particularly effective when its target either has been referred by an extant customer or has shown some interest in the product.[44] True to form, those contacted by this operation were so because they had attended a Bush event or because they had been referred by a Bush supporter.[45] This is very similar to the way in which timeshare vacation homes and high-end vacuum cleaners are sold. The campaign used its live events to gather information for its get-out-the-vote drive and volunteers to staff it, as well as the events leading up to it like phone-a-thons in order to increase turnout for Bush.[46] The Bush team's bricks-and-clicks model allowed it to make good use of the social institutions, like churches, in which its targeted segments were most active and to use members of those institutions to spread its message cheaply and, in the process of doing so, lend their own credibility to it. The Bush bricks-and-clicks model differed from past

Conservative push-marketing efforts[47] because this campaign encouraged people to participate in the campaign.

It appears Conservatives have used viral marketing techniques since the 1990s; the difference in this case is that the Bush team worked to create a sense of ownership and involvement among the voters in the way that targeted appeals now do.[48] Viral marketing is defined as a strategy that "encourages individuals to pass on a marketing message to others, creating the potential for exponential growth in the message's exposure and influence."[49] Hotmail is, as Wilson notes, a commercial example of a successful viral campaign.[50] Viral marketing has six principles: giving away something of value, doing so in a way that requires little effort, the size of which can be adjusted to fit the size of the audience, "exploits common motivations and behaviors," uses existing communications networks, and builds on other resources.[51] The Bush campaign offered its audience valuable information and access to events at which its candidate, the president, would appear. All one had to do to be invited was to sign up in advance by providing a little contact and demographic information. Distributing the valuable information was little work for the campaign, especially given the valuable contact and marketing information it was getting in return. Campaigns are used to scaling the size of their efforts, the brand strategy depends on exploiting what its targets do and think, and Conservatives have been using other social networks to distribute their brands for years as we saw earlier. Speaking again of Mr. Mehlman, Fineman notes his devotion to "viral marketing' in which word-of-mouth, talk radio, and chatter on web-based communities supplement the air war."[52] The bricks-and-clicks model that the Bush team developed for 2004 was very much a viral campaign, was a key vehicle through which the brand story was distributed intact, and provided the campaign with hot prospects that it could contact to either volunteer to recruit others, participate in its get-out-the-vote operation or simply ask to vote on Election Day. Bush campaign manager Ken Mehlman justified the activity in terms of product marketing and keeping the campaign's story consistent across media and noted that these techniques were being used to market all sorts of products.[53]

The Bush team had begun working on its viral marketing campaign very early on during its first term in office. It had cemented the relationship through constant communication filled with "Rove-isms," event invitations, and other memorabilia.[54] This is very much in keeping what was described in the opening portion of this chapter regarding relationship marketing and its importance to brand building. Unlike corporate marketers, the Bush campaign probably didn't try to drive away their worst performing demographic segments but they probably didn't spend much energy trying to attract or keep audiences from these segments.[55] Those from better performing segments could be turned into billboards for Bush much in the way other companies have turned their core consumers into billboards for their products.[56] Viral marketing is of use to politicians for the same reason that it is of use to companies: it can get the brand out quickly and generate a lot of buzz about the brand.[57] This, in turn, can attract more customers to the brand and increase its popularity.[58]

The Bush team did not just market to these segments during the campaign; it worked to build relationships with them throughout its first term, such as the one that it worked to build with Jewish voters.[59] These efforts were the foundation of 2004's viral campaign and it was through the viral campaign, extensive use of the Amway model, and the bricks-and-clicks strategy to present its brand intact to the audience, to encourage audience ownership of it, and to encourage the audience to evangelize on behalf of brand W. As the *Washington Post* noted on the day after the election, the viral technique meant that much of the social values aspect of brand W was not discussed in the bigger cities or mainstream media because the people living in those places or working in those institutions never saw the materials that emphasized it.[60] As noted earlier, this is consistent with the ways in which Conservatives have used alternative media throughout the movement's lifetime. As described by University of Akron political scientist John Green, one mailing carried the headline "George W. Bush shares your values. Marriage. Life. Faith."[61] The mailer contained an image of a traditional family in front of a church.[62] In addition to personalizing the brand, direct mail and other viral techniques let the Bush campaign work with a hotter message than it could have used in the mainstream media. A hotter message in a more visible medium could have caused a loss of votes in Moderate voter segments, given the Kerry campaign had an opportunity to rebut the point, and opened the message to analysis and muddying by journalists. Viral techniques let the Bush administration present very specific aspects of its brand story to focused audiences without being lectured to about ethics and questions about intellectual merit by outsiders. The Bush viral techniques distributed its brand intact; much like Conservative activists and media had distributed the Slick Willie brand six years earlier. In both cases, Conservatives were educated about the issue and called to action. In the Bush case, they were also invited to volunteer and spread the message to their friends. It would have taken a lot of campaign stops, ad buys, and free media coverage on the part of the Kerry campaign to overcome the advantages that the bricks-and-clicks model bestowed on the Bush team.

The Bush Slogan, Logo, Narrative, and Contrasts

Aside from viral marketing, the Bush campaign placed more emphasis on its logo, print fonts, and color schemes than have many other recent presidential campaigns. This emphasis is consistent with a brand strategy. As is the way in which the Bush team used and presented their logo as a visual representation of their brand is consistent with the way in which most marketers do in order to build brand identity. The logo included the letter W, usually had the American flag colors in the background, and sometimes came with a slogan in order to present specific aspects of the brand to individual audiences without diluting the brand's overall recognition. The targeted audience segments were the audiences that traditionally compose the Conservative movement. Some segments received W logos that came with slogans that emphasized an aspect of the brand that meshed with the audience's interests. Consistent with the way in which visuals are used to build brand identity, the Bush Web site on the day after the election had a front page that featured the W logo, "Still the President," and a smiling George W. Bush with fireworks going off behind him juxtaposed it. From beginning to end, the Bush team used its logo to communicate important information about its brand.

The Bush campaign built on an aspect of the Conservative brand that has been successful with its targets in all of the cases examined in this book, that of Conservatives defending the country. In this case, Bush was defending the country against the terrorists and the bad values of the Liberals. While the terrorists were a line extension, they fit nicely into the aspect of the Conservative brand that stressed the movement's commitment to a strong defense as we saw in Chapter 6. It was, after all, Ronald Reagan who spoke of the original evil ones: the Soviet Union. As we have seen, Conservatives have spent decades branding Liberals as being responsible for a panoply of national problems and using those problems to justify Conservative public policies. The Liberal brand has appeared in Conservative presidential and congressional campaigns since, at least, 1980. Kerry was presented as a captive of Liberals in Congress. These congressional Liberals were presented much in the way that Ronald Reagan and Newt Gingrich had done years earlier. Even though, as a member of the party that was a minority in both Houses of Congress, there was no chance of Kerry's or his Liberal friends seeing their proposals become law, the point to introducing the Liberal brand was to encourage an emotive reaction from the Conservative base, not to educate them about the nuances of legislative life.

The W campaign theme and slogan evolved gradually but the points of emphasis in the W and senator flip-flop brands remained constant. The evolution in themes was consistent with the creation of a brand narrative because this happens gradually. The campaign began by talking about how the country was "Safer, Stronger, Better" and ended by arguing that "Freedom is on the March." Each of these themes focused on an aspect of brand W that could then be used to set up contrasts between the mess Bush inherited and the one that would likely be created should Kerry be elected. The overall effect was the creation of a contrast between a positive brand W and a negative senator flip-flop. The net effect was to present the target audience with a choice between the positive offered by brand W and the negative offered by Democrats. These themes explained that Bush had inherited a mess from Clinton, reminded people why they voted for Conservatives at all, and showed that Bush had done a good job in the first term. They did so by creating a contrast between Bush's successes, what had gone on before, and what would surely come after, as well as a specific contrast that amplified the strong leader versus flip-flopper brand stories. The net result was to position Bush and the Conservatives as being better leaders on the issues that their core audience cares most about: defense, economics, and personal traits. Their point was to create a sense among the voters that George Bush was a good guy who shared their attitudes and values, had done a good job on defense, done a good job on the economy, and would do so again in the second term. John Kerry, in contrast, was presented as being not strong enough to be president, aligned with the Liberals on economic and social issues, not at all like the voters, and generally not as good of a choice for the White House as was W. It was the brand strategy that allowed the Bush team to accomplish all of this quickly and in a way that did not raise too many questions about their man.

The Bush team made good use of the family values brand.[63] The family values brand dates back at least twenty years and is a kind of Conservative postmaterialism.[64] It can be applied to a range of political products that cover the spectrum from bad television to gay marriage. Family values in 2004 dealt mostly with issues of marriage, life, and contraception. Presenting the voters with these aspects of the family values brand paid big dividends because Bush held his voters from 2000 and attracted new ones "through an elaborate targeting plan on TV and radio and in the mail—of luring inconsistent voters to the polls who already were inclined to support him."[65] It was the family values brand and its abortion line extension that most appealed to this audience based on the exit poll result from Bush voters, 61 percent of who thought abortion should be illegal "in all or most cases."[66] Of these voters 70 percent were married, half went to church at least weekly, 20 percent said that they went more than once a week, and a third described themselves as born-again Christians.[67] The percentage of Kerry voters who self-identified as members of these categories was much lower.[68] While these figures show the importance of targeted marketing campaigns generally, they also show the advantage that the brand strategy gives to Conservatives. In this case, the brand strategy let the Bush team contest the election on far more favorable terms than the nation's economic and security environment indicated would be the case. Instead of a campaign based around a discussion of substantive issues and logical analysis, the brand strategy allowed the Bush team to conduct the election on the more emotive playing field on which Conservatives have been winning for years. The next section looks at the way in which the Bush team attempted to find new audiences for the Conservatives brands by focusing on increasing its support among audiences normally associated with the Democrats: Hispanics, Catholics, Jews, and African Americans.[69]

Outreach to New Constituencies

The 2004 Bush campaign incorporated the morality and values aspects of the Conservative brand into its campaign in order to score points with the religious segments in which it was already successful, as well as to reach out to the three new segments: Hispanics Jews, and Catholics. The Bush team sought to link its targeting of Catholics and Hispanics to moral issues and its targeting of Jewish voters to its support for Israel. The latter is clear from a piece written by former New York Mayor Ed Koch that argued that W had a much better record on the issue than that of his father before arguing that, of all presidents, it was W who had done the most to ensure Israel's security.[70] The power of this appeal is its ability to hit voters with an issue about which they care and with an appeal made by a source that they trust. Koch dealt with Bush's problematic lineage on this issue, noted the good work he had done on the issue, and closed by emphasizing the strong leadership aspect of brand W and senator flip-flop contrast by arguing that Bush's devotion to the U.S.-Israeli relationship was not something he would give up to gain political favor at home or abroad while the same could probably not be said about Kerry.[71] This appeal shows the importance of consistency in branded politics. Even though this appeal was targeted at a relatively small audience, it contained the aspects of the brand that the campaign was promoting and focused on a set of issues that fit with the campaign's brand story and on which it had some chance to hit some of its audience targets.

The brand strategy helps Conservatives expand into new audience segments, as it did with Jewish voters in 2004, because it helps them become known quickly and because it allows them to incorporate narrow issues into their overall brand emphasis. The idea that Bush would do a better job than Kerry would on Israel policy could be believed because this audience knew a bit about and was hearing plenty from Bush through his War on Terror brand story but, unless one lived in Massachusetts, Kerry's record on Israeli security issues was really known only in the way in which it was being presented by his opponents.[72]

The Bush team acted aggressively in its courtship of Hispanic voters as it had in 2000. The Bush team made the same value appeals to its Hispanic targets as it did to its English language audience. For example, Bush's campaign closed with a contrast spot entitled "Tus Opciones" (Your Options) and it contained several exact translations of its English language ads in Spanish.[73] In short, the Hispanic outreach was done in accordance with the brand strategy because the same points were made using the same techniques and visual images (for the most part) that were used to court other voters. The only real difference seems to have been that the brand strategy was executed in a different language.

Bush targeted Catholics as well, and this can be considered as an extension of the campaign's effort to target Hispanics, the vast majority of whom are Catholics, while Republicans have done so around life and reproductive rights issues since the 1970s. George Bush was unusually positioned to take advantage of the spilt among Catholics on such issues given that his opponent was a practicing Catholic. Bush was so keen on winning Catholic votes that he visited the pope in the Vatican while on a European swing, much as Ronald Reagan had once done.[74] A poll by John Green found that the only group of Catholics that Bush was winning a clear majority in the summer of 2001 was the most traditional segment.[75] The Bush team was trying, as it was with other segments, to win enough to tip the election and it used viral marketing techniques and spoke primarily about the branded social issues with which Conservatives regularly work, especially life issues. Abortion was simply a way for Conservative political marketers to gain the attention of the Catholic voter because it summed up "other cultural grievances"[76] and because Catholics could "overlook" Conservative positions on those that differed from church teachings.[77] Thus, by following the same branded strategy that has been followed with other religious, interest, and demographic communities, the Bush campaign was able to focus on topics that advantaged it with some segments of Kerry's own religious faith.

The campaign again tried to expand its share of the female vote, as it had during 2000.[78] This time it had aimed specifically to attract suburban and unmarried women through an emphasis on security issues.[79] Bush had an advantage in marketing to women that he did not have in 2000, when that campaign had mounted a similar effort[80] because he had appointed a large number of them to positions in his campaign and administration and, as a result, was well positioned to show that the W stands for Women brand promise had been kept and neutralize charges that, because of some of the social policy implemented by the administration, it was not sympathetic to women's issues. We can see this in a quotation from one of Bush's sisters at a campaign event as she highlighted Bush's family and female advisors and explained that Bush was very good on women's issues because "He's surrounded by strong women."[81] The W stands for Women effort had the typical Bush visuals with the slogan "W Stands for Women" written under it. Again, the young single female demographic has not traditionally been one in which Republicans have done well but, in a tight election, only a few more votes might be necessary to win. The campaign held targeted events to hit the segment that regularly featured these walking, talking embodiments of the brand promise. This focused campaign stayed away from the issue on which Bush was most vulnerable, abortion, in favor of an emphasis on the issues that it felt its above-noted targets would be receptive to. Barbara Bush noted that women have a stake in every issue facing the country, then provided a laundry list of examples ranging from the economy through education and health care to national security.[82] After encouraging the target audience to expand its focus, the campaign told the brand story of how W stood for women because women had benefited from the administration's tax cuts, job training, and marriage initiatives among others.[83] One of the key aspects of the brand story overall was that Bush was a wartime president for the same reasons as was true for the general audience. The Iraq and Afghan conflicts were presented as W's effort to promote the liberation of women[84] as were the large number of women serving in leadership positions in the administration.[85] Bush's mother played up her son's personal traits and made mention of his consistency by saying "You can be sure when he tells you something today, he won't be telling another person something else tomorrow."[86] She closed her presentation with a call to action based upon Bush's personal traits, urging people to "get out and do your best" because her son was "a good man."[87] Like many of the Bush events, this one employed the viral marketing model because it was both a rally and an organizing opportunity. Those in attendance saw the brand promise kept and were asked to evangelize in their own communities.

The Marketing Problem: A Weak Record in Key Areas

The way in which the 2004 Bush campaign used branding to favorably influence the strategic climate shows both the power of branding and its potential uses by incumbents who have a mediocre-to-poor record in office. By 2004, economic conditions by many measures were worse than when Bush became president—the nation had suffered a major terrorist attack and fought two wars that seemed to have no end in sight. One could see parallels between Mr. Bush's situation in 2004 and that of another U.S. president in 1980: Jimmy Carter. Unlike Carter, Bush was the beneficiary of a branded politics that would see his way clear to a second term. That Bush was able to eek out a victory as an incumbent with this record shows the power that branding has to shape campaigns in ways that favor those candidates and movements who make consistent use out of it. The brand story that the Bush team built about itself tapped into the extant Conservative brand story and presented a narrative of the past four years that was general and favorable for its candidate, while it placed the blame for all problems that had happened during the period elsewhere in the way that we saw in the Chapter 6.[88] Consider the case of steel tariffs in which the costs of the policy were borne by the society generally and was relatively small while the benefits were large, highly visible, and concentrated.[89] This is exactly the way in which the brand strategy has been used by Conservatives during the past three decades as we have seen throughout this work. It was the Bush team's use of it in 2004 that allowed it to win what, at the beginning of the year, seemed to be an unlikely victory at best.

Economic questions should have been a big problem for the Bush team because they had made visible claims about the number of jobs that their policies could be expected to create during the 2000 election; yet the new job figures never matched these, and employment is a highly visible measure. We can see branding's power to shape public perceptions by looking at the way in which people thought about the economy. Kerry voters, who had probably been exposed to less of the Bush brand story, felt economic issues were much more important than did the people in Bush's target audience. A postelection Harris Poll found that 36 percent of Kerry voters thought that the economy was the most important issue facing the country, whereas only 7 percent of Bush voters believed this to be the case.[90] An *LA Times* exit poll found that 48 percent of Kerry voters said that the economy was their driving force while only 18 percent of Bush voters said so. Bush's brand stories provided his audience with a four-part alternative explanation to Kerry's assertion that Bush had caused these problems.[91] First, the recession began on Clinton's watch and was his fault. Second, 9/11 and two wars have caused our economic problems. Third, things are not nearly as bad as people think, are actually getting better, and for this we have the Bush tax policy to thank. Fourth, as a congressional Liberal, John Kerry would raise taxes faster than frat boys drink beer at keg parties if given the chance. In short, the Bush team's story amounted to this: Liberals caused our nation's economic problems, 9/11 added to them, and we solved them by cutting taxes. This story line excused the failures of the Bush administration, worked with the Conservative tax cuts as economic policy brand, and let the Bush team discuss how their man differed from the Liberals while building an extension between Kerry and the Liberals.

One of the first things that happened in order to put this explanation into play was for administration officials to try to change the public's awareness of the recession's start date to the end of the Clinton administration. They did so by arguing that the economy shrunk during the third quarter of 2000, on Clinton's watch.[92] These presentations failed to note that the economy had expanded during the subsequent quarter.[93] The Clinton recession was further established by technical changes in some official economic reports that moved the start date to the third quarter to give the concept more credibility.[94] Doing this let the Bush team speak of the "Clinton recession" as an established fact, which it was not but, by doing so, they could introduce the ideas that Bush had cleaned up an economic mess through the Conservative brand for economy policy "tax cuts" and that only Liberals could possibly oppose such measures. Conservatives had tried, during the Reagan administration to do exactly the same kind of thing by speaking of a Carter recession in order to explain away a poor economy.[95] In both cases, Conservatives sought to show that they had inherited a mess from Liberals that they cleaned up through the most important aspect of the Conservative brand story in economic policy: tax cuts. Some observers felt that Conservatives were working to create the perception of a Clinton recession from the moment that Bush won the 2000 election and a Media Matters for America poll showed that these efforts had borne fruit, as over 60 percent of respondents to one poll expressed agreement with the idea.[96]

The Clinton recession brand was built in the usual way and it was presented most often at important times on the electoral calendar. Media Matters for America further found that the Clinton recession was referred to more during the period leading up to the 2002 election than at any other time.[97] The report provided an example from CNN that shows the Bush team's argument that it had "inherited a recession" through Bush's mentions of it on two out of five days.[98]

Once the Clinton recession was established in government documents, Conservative activists could begin marketing it and the Conservative press could begin writing about it to both reassure the faithful and attempt to sway the mainstream media's coverage of economic conditions. Consistent with the argument made in the above-noted report was a Newsmax.com piece entitled "Clinton Recession: 'Bill' Comes Due for 8 Years of Corruption" by Charles R. Smith that appeared on March 21, 2001 and asserted that Clinton's economic success was really a product of low energy prices and that as soon as those rose, the economy slowed.[99] The piece argued that prices had risen only because the Clinton administration had secretly used "OPEC oil diplomacy to supply Russia increased oil profits" through a scheme that involved Iraqi oil, the UN and Russian suppliers.[100] These price increases, along with Clinton's environmental policies, led over time to a rearmed Saddam Hussein and a national recession.[101] The piece concluded by asserting that the "liberal media's" attacks on Bush for the recession were misplaced and that these attacks should have been directed at Clinton.[102] This piece was but one more example of the way in which having an independent media gives Conservatives an opportunity to distribute their brand stories intact.

The Clinton recession brand story was built through the use of another favorite Conservative rhetorical strategy: that of causing confusion about an issue. This is clearly the case in a *National Review* piece written by Donald Luskin that appeared on May 5, 2004, that presented significant data to argue in support of the changed recession date, quoted seemingly independent experts to make its point, and drew an artificial equivalence between the federal economists who set the date for the recession's start and other economists.[103] All of this provided a source that Conservative citizens could use to buttress their belief that the recession was Clinton's fault and, as a result, justify their decision to have voted for Bush in 2000 and to vote for him again in 2004.

The third rhetorical strategy that Conservatives often use to build their brand stories is one of building equivalence between their actions and those of the Democrats. This is especially the case when it appears that what the Conservatives are doing in a given area is somewhat less than ethical. In short, Conservatives defend their own actions by pointing to the things that Liberals have done in the past. The above-noted Luskin piece did just this by claiming that "liberals" had never really worried about this organization's "official dates," and as proof of the point it cited a magazine by economist Paul Krugman that shifted some of the credit for the economic boom that took place during the Reagan years to events that took place while Reagan was not in office to diminish his record in that area.[104] It noted that "liberals" were not happy with the National Bureau of Economic Research's decision and cited a prominent one, New York Times columnist and economist Paul Krugman as a case in point.[105] It closed citing the above-noted poll numbers as proof of the recession that was Clinton's fault, and then switched to an economic measure, to argue that growth was now taking place.[106] Shifting the date on the recession and identifying it with a predecessor that Conservatives generally believed to be unethical was one way to make sure that Bush was covered on the economic issue with his base, and that the campaign had, at a minimum, a fig leaf to cover its culpability in the nation's difficult economic situations.

Having blamed Clinton for the recession, the Bush team could present the Conservative brand for economic policy, tax cuts, as having provided the solution. The core Conservative brand story has always emphasized that taxes are too high, the 2000 Bush campaign had been no exception, and once it was able to argue that the tax cuts had solved a recession, the Bush campaign was able to claim a success for its economic policy as Reagan had done. The Bush campaign built a fellowship between its specific changes in tax policy and the tax cut aspect of the Conservative brand story then did, as Conservatives have done since Reagan, worked to present that as the root cause of economic prosperity. The Bush team employed the rationale that Conservatives have employed throughout their use of the brand strategy to justify these policies. Simply, across-the-board tax cuts (1) give everyone more money, (2) give the wealthy more investment capital, and (3) produce economy prosperity as a result. Minus the Clinton recession, Bush would have had a difficult time justifying his tax policies as constituting anything other than a cash grab by his partisans and would have been faced with the prospect of trying to explain why the highly visible economic number about which most Americans care, employment, had fallen on his watch.

The tax cuts were important for a second reason: they enabled the campaign to show that its brand promises from 2000 had been kept and, as a result, were a way to reinforce the positive personal traits of the brand aspect. Bush had stated that he would cut taxes, in his inaugural with a recitation of the traditional Conservative brand story on the issue as was the case when he said "And we will reduce taxes, to recover the momentum of our economy and reward the effort and enterprise of working Americans."[107] Once in office, the White House issued a document entitled "The President's Agenda for Tax Relief," in its executive summary, which put into official documents the tax cut brand story:

> Over the past several months, the economy has slowed dramatically. President Bush's tax cut will give the economy a timely second wind by placing more money in the hands of consumers and entrepreneurs. President Bush also understands that, over the long run, wealth is created by hard-working, risk-taking individuals, not government programs. Countries with low taxes, limited regulation, and open trade grow faster, create more jobs, and enjoy higher standards of living than countries with bigger, more centralized governments and higher taxes. The United States has led the way in economic performance over the last century because America is a freer country. If people are given the freedom to create, they do. If people are given a stake in the outcome, they succeed.[108]

By talking about the tax cuts in its brand story, the Bush team was able to show that it had kept its campaign promises in contrast to their slick predecessor and their overly ambitious challenger, as well as to claim that Conservative economic policy had worked again, and gained an ability to work with one of the core aspects of the Conservative brand.

While the brand name "Clinton Recession" was not widely used during the general election, its essence was incorporated into the overall tax cuts as an economic policy aspect of the Bush brand story. One example is provided by a Bush answer to a query in a debate about spending and the national debt during the second presidential debate:

> We have a deficit because this country went into a recession. You might remember the stock market started to decline dramatically six months before I came to office, and then the bubble of the 1990s popped. And that cost us revenue.[109]

As the brand strategy requires, Bush referenced a highly visible, emotive event to prove his point and gave his audience a vivid visual to bolster his words, as well as to undermine any claim that his predecessor might have had to creating real economic prosperity. He used the Clinton recession brand to show that he had solved the problem:

> I think if you raise taxes during a recession, you head to depression. I come from the school of thought that says when people have more money in their pocket during (sic poor) economic times, it increases demand or investment. Small businesses begin to grow, and jobs are added. We found out today that over the past 13 months, we've added 1.9 million new jobs.[110]

His answer again fits the brand strategy because it uses improvement in a highly visible measure to show that his tax policies have caused economic improvement. He restated the claim about inheriting a recession when rebutting Kerry's answer to the above:

> But let me talk back about where we've been. The stock market was declining six months prior to my arrival. It was the largest stock market correction—one of the largest in history, which foretold a recession.[111]

He did not give his audience a sense of whether the improvement that had taken place after his tax cuts were in effect had been better or worse than what would have taken place had those policies not been put into place as is consistent with the use of a brand strategy. As the brand strategy demands, he gave his audience a good sense of the highly visible benefits that his policy had provided to them:

> Because we cut taxes on everybody—remember, we ran up the child credit by $1,000, we reduced the marriage penalty, we created a 10 percent bracket, everybody who pays taxes got relief—the recession was one of the shortest in our nation's

history.[112]

Using the brand strategy to create the Clinton recession was a way in which the Bush team protected itself from the wrath of an angry electorate. As Conservatives always do when trying to defend their tax policies, Bush argued that his were fair because everybody got one. As Bush himself said during the debates "And plus, we cut taxes for everybody. Everybody got tax relief, so that they get out of the recession."[113] This, in turn, played into the populist aspect of the Conservative brand because it positioned Bush as arguing for giving more money to everyone.

The Bush campaign's basic tax cut pitch included allusions to tax cuts as the solution to the Clinton recession, as a way to reinforce W's credentials with a largely Conservative audience used to the core antitax brand story and as a way to reinforce the contrasting personal traits aspects of the brand stories being built around W and Senator Kerry.

If the assertion that Mr. Bush had inherited a recession that he cleaned up through the promotion of fair tax cuts was not the right fit for some parts of the audience, team Bush had another aspect to the Clinton recession story that it wanted to sell, namely that the 9/11 attacks were actually to blame for the economic downturn and, given that the nation was at war and concerned with issues of basic security, the fact that it was doing as well as it was should be considered something of a minor miracle caused by the combination of Mr. Bush's personal traits and his tax policies. The combination of an inherited recession that deepened further after a terrorist attack allowed the Bush team to shift blame for it away from itself and discuss these issues within the Conservative narrative. A clear example of this is the text for one of the Bush kickoff ads "Safer, Stronger" that alludes to the Clinton recession then referenced 9/11 by saying "A day of tragedy. A test for all Americans" before moving on to argue that under Bush the country was "Safer, stronger" and closing with the tag line of "President Bush. Steady leadership in times of change."[114] Notice how the recession is moved to absolve Bush from responsibility. At the same time, 9/11 is introduced as a tragedy, not as a preventable debate, and a discussion of Mr. Bush's leadership style is begun. In short, Mr. Bush inherited a mess, had to deal with a random tragedy, and cleaned it all up through his steady leadership. This ad works with three out of four of the brand W aspects emphasized in 2004: personal traits, tax cuts as economic policy, and the War on Terror. It also worked because its inclusion of 9/11 imagery caused controversy that, in turn, generated a lot of free media for and buzz about this aspect of brand W.[115] It would be difficult to imagine a more favorable brand story than that upon which to run a reelection campaign in such circumstances.

The War in Iraq Is Part of the War on Terror

The Bush team's second hurdle to winning reelection was the ongoing conflict in Iraq. The military had won an easy victory in the spring of 2003, Mr. Bush had participated in an infomercial that used the USS *Abraham Lincoln* as a prop (itself an allusion to one of the Conservative archetypes of which we spoke in Chapter 1) on which was placed a banner saying "Mission Accomplished" behind Mr. Bush's head while he spoke to an adoring naval audience off San Diego. All seemed to have ended well and the Bush team appeared to have a clear victory with which it could market itself in 2004 but, by that spring it was clear that the United States was actually bogged down in a guerrilla war that seemed to have no end in sight, the weapons of mass destruction on which the war had been sold had not been found, and the administration had taken to justifying its policies in terms of the other benefits that it could bring to Iraq-like freedom and democracy. The Bush team dealt with its substantive failures in Iraq by stressing the value of the conflict in the broader War on Terror branded product, by speaking generalities and only making vague promises, and by working with issues and images that would produce emotional rather than analytical responses from the audience.

The 2004 Bush campaign built a brand story that resembled the ten major points of a memo allegedly written by Frank Luntz. This memo was, in essence, a justification for the Bush War on Terror and the new unilateralist foreign policy that the administration had implemented. It was very similar to the brand story the Republican congressional candidates had employed as part of their successful coordinated campaign to gain seats during the 2002 midterms.

In short, the memo entitled "Communicating the Principles of Prevention and Protection" encouraged Republicans to (1) use 9/11 as background, (2) talk about homeland security first, (3) talk about what is being protected, (4) sell the broader War on Terror story and Iraq's role in it and make the case for being on offense, (5) explain that this was a war against radical ideologues not against a religion (6) it is better to fight abroad than in the U.S., (7) present terrorism as a product of a dysfunctional culture, (8) point out that Republicans were leading a fight to preserve our freedom and security, (9) mention Saddam a lot, and (10) support the troops.[116] In such a fashion did the Bush campaign, as had the Bush administration, as had Republican congressional candidates in 2002 speak about 9/11 and everything after. Consistent with this work's earlier argument about Ronald Reagan serving as a heritage brand for Conservatism, the memo alludes to Reagan in several places and makes several references to the Cold War as a paradigm for understanding the current situation.[117] It is a typical brand story.[118] In the case of the War on Terror brand and its use by the Conservatives in 2002 and 2004, the goal was to provide the public with a brand story that satisfied their psychological needs in order to win elections and justify changes in public policy: this is exactly the way in which Conservatives have been using the brand strategy throughout their lifetime.

Two of the biggest advantages that the brand strategy gives to Conservatives is the ability to build fellowship between issues and policies, even if they are unrelated in reality, and the ability to create a durable public impression that Conservative politicians and policies are working to solve a given problem, even if in reality they are not. By using the strategy in its reelection effort that had been used to sell the original policy and to win an early election, the Bush team was (1) able to tap into the brand equity built by these earlier campaigns, (2) avoid discussing the problems in Iraq and the failure to find weapons of mass destruction on which the original conflict had been based, (3) raise the issue of Bush's leadership traits, especially during the period just after 9/11, and (4) create a contrast between those and the flip-flop brand that the campaign was building around Kerry. Again we see the use of contrast and positioning techniques to enhance the power of the brand. Such a strategy gave Democratic congressional candidates fits in 2002 and would do the same to the Kerry campaign in 2004.

Personal Attributes

Having developed explanations of economic and security conditions that improved the standing of their brand, Bush's team moved on to develop a strong personal trait aspect to their brand and to build a brand around Kerry that was solely about personal attributes. In Bush's case this was done, as it had been throughout the first campaign and administration, by using Ronald Reagan as a model as noted earlier as well as Bush's faith commitment and, to a lesser extent, his family commitment. The brand that was built around Kerry was, based on his personal traits, Senate voting record, affiliation with congressional Liberals, and marriage to a wealthy Austrian heir. This brand can best be termed the senator flip-flop brand. Its net effect was to position Kerry before the core audience as being unlike them and too weak to act as president in a time of war.[119] This first appeared during the convention, important because this is an event that can generate a large number of impressions. The other event that can generate a lot of impressions for a brand is the three candidate debates. Because the Conservatives employ a brand strategy, their approach to these events is somewhat different from the approach taken by the Democrats. For Conservatives, these events are brand-building activities while, for Democrats, they are intellectual exercises to be won. What matters for branded Conservatives is not the public's or media's overnight impressions of which candidate won the debate. What matters for branded Conservatives is how many times and in how many ways the target segments can be exposed to the brand. George W. Bush's campaign took these two opportunities to teach the public about brand W and its line of political products. The next chapter examines the way in which the Bush team got its brand story out to the target audience through these events.

Conventions and Debates

Reposition and Build Brand Awareness

As was mentioned in the close of Chapter 7, branded Conservatives use their conventions and debates in a different way than do Democrats. While the press, academics, and public see these as intellectual exercises, for branded Conservatives they are extremely important opportunities through which brand awareness and loyalty can be built. The point to a convention is not to educate, it is to teach people about the brand. The point to a debate is to reinforce the brand story that had been presented during the primaries, through the convention, and on the daily stump. Both are ideal vehicles through which audiences can be repelled or attracted to the brand and through which buzz can be built for the brand.[1] Thus, while opinion polls and most pundits revealed that the popular opinion came down on the side of a Kerry victory in all three debates, this missed the point that Bush had worked his brand story, promises, aspects, and branded products into as many of his answers as he possibly could and did a good job of staying within the overall themes with which his campaign had chosen to work. The only flaw in Bush's debate performance was that he did not look as much like the strong leader aspect of the brand as he could have. This chapter examines the way in which the Bush campaign employed its convention and the presidential debates to build awareness of and loyalty toward its brand within its target segments.[2] The way in which the Bush team used its convention is in keeping with the way in which other kinds of marketers work to build brand loyalty, lure back old customers, and reach some new ones. This chapter first examines the way in which the Bush campaign promoted its overall brand before moving on to a case study of the way in which Bush promoted one brand aspect, the War on Terror brand, in its second half.

Conventions are an effective tool through which brand awareness can be built because they are multiple day events. They are so because they receive a variety of kinds of free media coverage, giving the campaign the opportunity to present very specific and very general aspects of its brand depending on the medium of coverage and audience segment pursued. They are so because they give general election voters who may not have voted in the primary, who may have supported a candidate defeated in the primary or who are members of the incumbent president's party to be educated about the brand that the campaign will promote during the general election campaign. They are so because they provide an opportunity to reinforce brand loyalty among core audience by reminding them what is wonderful about the branded product and, by laying out a favorable narrative to pique the interests of people who fall into the desired segment but have not yet purchased the product. This fourth point was particularly important in 2004, given the considerable emphasis that the Bush campaign placed on viral marketing techniques and other segmentation techniques.

Conventions: A Summer Infomercial

Political conventions are not what they once were. Candidates win the nomination in the primaries, platform fights are rare, and the composition of the ticket in recent years has been made public prior to the event's start. In light of this, and their use of the brand strategy, we should not be surprised that Conservatives have turned the Republican National Convention (RNC) into an infomercial. This is a logical thing to have done given that conventions have become tightly structured events because of the changes noted above and the proliferation of television,[3] the result of which is to transform them into ideal products through which the public can be educated about the branded products that the party is selling. The infomercial can be well defined as "audiovisual ads that displayed the attributes of a product in a program ranging in duration from several minutes to half an hour" and their logical extension is home shopping channels.[4] The infomercial is very much a direct response marketing technique.[5] The Bush team's approach was very much in keeping with the direct response approach. This is because in corporate direct response marketing "the focus was on reaching out—signaling—to a particular population with certain categories"[6] or, in other words, to focus on specific audience segments.[7] This is exactly the strategy that the Bush team used in 2004 and two of the key vehicles that it used to do so were debates and conventions. Network television only devotes a couple of hours of coverage per day to these events because they are so scripted, which is more time than the average consumer product marketer gets in a week to sell their products. While the audience share as a whole is down for conventions, it is not clear that it is so among those who could be persuaded to vote for a candidate after several days' exposure to the Conservative branded products as presented through the infomercial format. In the commercial world, the infomercial has been one of a number of a variety of marketing forms that has been eating away at the traditional advertising business and it should not be surprising that a campaign that was focused only on attracting a few segments would attempt to use such a tool to do so.[8]

The convention as infomercial model works when it is tightly scripted, when the party has an awareness of what its brands are and which aspects of them are to be focused upon, when the party takes all aspects of its convention to be part of its branding strategy, and when what is spoken of at the convention is followed-up upon at once before the target audience. The brand can also be useful, as the Bush team showed in 2004, when trying to counter the message that the other party sent out at its convention. My argument is that the 2004 Bush convention fits two specific forms of the infomercial: the demo and the documercial.[9] The former features the product in a starring role, can sometime have an audience, has product demonstrators who speak to the camera, and is designed to show exactly how the product works.[10] Branded Conservative nominees speak at their conventions because doing so offers them a chance to prove the brand story's validity. In short, the nominee can, after several days of testimonials from supporters and endorsement by experts emphasizing various aspects of the brand, stand up to show that they are exactly as promised. It is for this reason that the nominee speaks at the convention.

The second technique that the 2004 RNC made use of was the documercial technique.[11] A documercial looks like a documentary because it borrows many of the techniques used to produce documentaries and, like a television news magazine is usually based on factual events.[12] Both techniques can educate the target segments about the brand. In branded politics, the convention is simply another form of infomercial. During this infomercial, Conservatives have used the documercial technique to build fellowship between their branded candidates and policies, as well as to extend their product line to include new ones. One of the most important video moments at the 2004 convention was the video tribute to Ronald Reagan because it again exposed the audience to the heritage brand, but also because it built fellowship between it and George W. Bush.

The documercial was one of the key vehicles through which the personal traits and War on Terror aspects of brand W were presented to the audience. For example, on the day that he was nominated, a documercial, "There She Stands," was screened and a speech filled with 9/11 references followed from New York Governor Pataki.[13] Pataki noted the acts of generosity of people from the battleground states of Iowa, Pennsylvania, and Oregon during that period.[14] This was both a pitch for votes in those places but also could have been an effort to remind Americans what their troops were now fighting for overseas as we saw has been part of the War on Terror brand story all along.

The 2004 RNC used direct marketing to motivate their branded products. This is a logical technique to be used by a campaign looking to get people involved as was the 2004 Bush campaign. Direct marketing is essentially the bricks-and-clicks model that was presented in the previous chapter. Conservatives, who pioneered the use of direct mail,[15] are well acquainted with this kind of marketing because it involves making direct-to-consumer sales.[16] The infomercial is a televised form of direct marketing.[17] The focus of contemporary direct marketing is to reach out to specific audiences.[18]

As is the case with other kinds of infomercials, conventions let the candidates and parties teach the public about their branded products directly through mass media. This is another advantage that Conservatives reap from using the brand strategy because the message that they send out over these unmediated airways will have a narrative with only a few aspects, be very coherent, and hit people on an emotive level. The convention provides the Conservatives with an opportunity to remind people of why they should be excited about the party and its candidate or, if they have drifted away from it, why they should come back, or if they are undecided, why they should begin choosing the Conservative brand. While the Democrats appear to use many of the same techniques at their conventions, the brand strategy amplifies their effectiveness for Conservatives.

The overall objective of the 2004 Republican infomercial was the education of the public about those aspects of brand W about which the party wanted to speak while introducing the public to a very different side of Senator Kerry than the one that his campaign had been selling to the nation for the past several months. That the convention's point was the sale of brand W is clear from the press release that announced its schedule included the campaign's major theme as is shown in the following passage from it that said that those appearing at the convention

> "are a testament to the strong leadership of President George W. Bush and the support for his vision of a safer world and a more hopeful America," said Bill Harris, CEO of the 2004 Republican National Convention."[19]

The personal traits aspect of brand W is right in this release and its content points to the idea that all of the program choices made during the convention were made to support brand W and its product line.

The 2004 convention built on the Clinton recession and War on Terror brand but was also the point at which brand W, which had been repositioned during the spring, was rolled out. Rolling out the repositioned brand meshes with the historical uses of the brand strategy by Conservatives. This is so because the convention is a high-profile event and, because the 2004 RNC took place blocks from the site of the 9/11 attacks, it was a highly emotive site. As we have seen throughout this work, these are two of the key ways in which Conservatives have implemented the brand strategy. Thus, the convention functions as one of the signature events through which specific audiences can be taught about the Conservative brand just as specific television programs can be used to teach an audience about a network's overall programming.[20] This can serve to signal an audience that it should or should not be interested in a given product as we saw in Chapter 1.[21] Even though

Bush had been battered by bad news all through the spring of 2004 and a Democratic primary process that focused on the administration's failures, the convention gave the campaign an opportunity to reposition the brand and enhance Bush's chances of winning again. As Kevin Chappell noted, the goal of the convention was "to show Bush's more personable side."[22] Even if the Conservatives spoke about domestic issues, they could, as we saw in the last chapter, do so in a way that played to the strengths of the Bush team and the core Conservative brands.

The physical setting assured that no matter what was spoken of, 9/11 as a justification for the War on Terror brand and the strong leader aspects of brand W would be on constant visual display. The physical setting of the convention itself becomes part of the infomercial. New York had been chosen to host the convention in January 2003[23] after the 9/11 attacks had happened, but before the Iraq War had been launched so that the Bush team knew that the physical location would either give it proof that the War on Terror brand promise had been kept or further evidence for the need to keep a strong leader in office depending on the outcome of the Iraq conflict. That 9/11 was a major part of the infomercial's theme is also clear given that this was one of the latest party conventions ever held and one of the big reasons for the delay was to time it to coincide with the third anniversary of the 9/11 attacks. Putting a convention in a city that the party had no chance to carry in November and in a state in which their chances were marginally better only makes sense when we look at that choice in marketing terms. New York City gave the Republican Party a physical setting and the concomitant visuals that backed up the products being promoted inside the convention hall. When the party leaders spoke about their branded response to 9/11, "The War on Terror," the physical location in which they were speaking elicited feelings in the audience that could serve to validate the speaker's points.

Conventions are an important vehicle through which brands can be built, repositioned, and disseminated to different audiences. As the Bush team showed in 2004, Conservatives use their brand strategy to build fellowship between the core brands about Democrats and the challenger of the moment. The brand strategy lets Conservatives emphasize specific aspects of their candidate as the Bush team did by stressing both the War on Terror brand, Bush's leadership traits as a consequence of that, and his softer personality traits. The softer aspects of the brand were stressed as well by the appearance of moderate Republicans in prime time to either provide testimonials for or endorsements of W, as well as an emphasis on consensus social issues. As was true of the entire brand W campaign, the constituencies in which it was attempting to expand its vote total were well represented. The infomercial communicated that this brand was visibly interested in these communities' business. Finally, a message was sent that, because of the War on Terror and Bush's leadership traits, it would be okay to switch parties this time. These kinds of emotive appeals are used to sell all sorts of products including politicians.[24] In a hotly contested election either of these last two appeals had the potential to turn the tide.

As is true of all infomercials, the way in which the convention was organized, located, the constituencies that appeared at it, and the themes with which it worked, all taught the audience about the brand. The convention's four themes dovetailed with the aspects of the repositioned brand W that the campaign was emphasizing. The first day was entitled "A Nation of Courage," and it dealt primarily with the events of 9/11 as part of the broader War on Terror branded product, as well as with Bush's leadership during that crisis.[25] Entitled "People of Compassion,"[26] the second day's theme was an effort to show that the promises made by brand W during the 2000 election of compassionate Conservatism had been kept and to imply that the brand promise would be kept once more. A homage to the core Conservative brand story and American cultural belief about the nation's economic present and future entitled "A Land of Opportunity" took the stage on the third day.[27] The final day shared a title with the overall Bush campaign theme, "A Safer World, A Stronger America."[28] This theme united the overall infomercial message into a coherent whole and transmitted the brand story intact on the night when conventions generally attract their largest audiences. The use of these four distinct themes and days allowed the Bush campaign and the RNC to present the public with their overall branded products in terms of their various aspects, promises, and the overall story that would be stressed during the spring to the first Tuesday in November. These four themes allowed the RNC to employ the infomercial and direct marketing techniques of which we spoke above to favorably position and sell brand W.

Even though the Republican convention had four themes of the day, the brand story was that of the core Conservatism and fit with what George W. Bush had said in 2000 and done in office. Through their summer infomercial, Conservatives were able to launch a number of positioning initiatives based on cultural issues such as patriotism and religious values. These initiatives fit with the Conservative and Bush brand stories. Each day opened with a flag presentation from a patriotic group appropriate to the day's theme. On National Security Day, it was Boy Scouts and Explorers from the local area and the NYPD did the chore that evening, on Tuesday three veterans groups did it, on Wednesday it was done by the FDNY, and on Thursday it was done by the Port Authority Color Guard.[29] All of these groups had been directly affected by 9/11 and were in the targets being courted by the campaign. The presence of the Boy Scouts could also be seen as a nod to social Conservatives (Boy Scouts versus Dale). Thus, the War on Terror, core Conservative aspect on patriotism, and social issues were built into all of the convention in order to constantly tell the brand story.

Since at least 1988, Conservatives have used the Pledge of Allegiance to communicate the patriotic aspect of their brand and establish a favorable contrast with Liberals as they did in 2004. In another effort to communicate the brand story and signal interest, the pledge leaders either lived in swing states or were in one of the constituencies in which the campaign was trying to expand its audience share. To reiterate the patriotism aspect and positioning, the national anthem was sung at each session. Of the five anthems, two were sung by African American Christian acts, a third was sung by Christian singer Gracie Rosenberger whose inspirational personal story fit the session's theme, a fourth was sung by a country act whose music combines gospel and popular elements, and a fifth was sung by a teen from a swing state.[30] Three of the acts hailed from Tennessee and four had significant female membership. Having women perform in highly visible roles at the convention was yet another way to show that the W stands for Women brand promise was being kept, as well as because, in some way each of them embodied an aspect of brand W.

Eager to transmit its brand to the religious and reiterate the contrast between the faiths of the Conservative brand versus the secular Liberal brand, each session opened with a prayer called the invocation and closed with one called a benediction. The list of those who led prayers at the RNC shows that the campaign (1) made sure that its image was one of religious inclusion to position itself on the side of the majority, (2) communicate with its core Christian audience, and (3) reach out to the Jewish, Catholic, and Hispanic audiences. Three of the ten prayer leaders were female, two were Hispanic, and two were African American. There was one Mormon, one Jew, and one Greek Orthodox leader, as well as four Protestants, and two Catholics. Thus, is shown how the brand strategy can communicate with audiences on a descriptive as well as an emotive basis.

Patriotism and Religion Are Great But How About Some Fun?

Conservatives have had a high degree of success attracting young people to their party and of finding ways to signal specific audiences of their interest in them. This has been accomplished in a number of ways, not the least of which was by recruiting celebrities to build some cool around their brand. At the 2004 RNC, this was accomplished through the appearances of popular athletes, actors, and musicians. While some sang, some spoke, and some just appeared, the effect of their presence was to provide celebrity endorsements to brand W.

The convention featured appearances by athletes who also represented a variety of demographic, regional, and cultural constituencies, thus all could promote specific aspects of brand W or promote the overall brand to specific audiences. There were three Olympians; a former football player turned television analyst and an active player, as well as the wife of another current player who was herself in television. Actors were highly visible at the RNC. Two prominent appearances were made on the first evening by Angie Harmon and Ron Silver. Silver's appearance shows how celebrity appearances can be used to push a specific aspect of the brand. He fit into the theme of the night, touched on a core aspect of the brand, and was pitched at two of the campaign's outreach audiences. His testimonial was heavy on the War on Terror brand and Bush's leadership trait, as well as the "switch this one time" pitch being made. Silver described himself in interviews during the Convention period as "a 9/11 Republican."[31] He said that the War on Terror was so important that he would vote for Bush even though there were a number of issues on which he did not agree with him.[32] Such an endorsement was a boon for Bush given Silver's Hollywood and Democratic roots. His testimonial was that of a consumer who had switched products and whose words fit with the aspects of the brand that was being promoted. This rationale emphasized on the War on Terror brand, hinted to the undecided that it would be okay to switch this once, and went a long way toward repositioning the brand.

This convention presented a large number of musicians who fit into the Christian, Gospel, country and western, Hispanic, and rock genres; the audiences for which overlapped those at brand W. Like the prayer and pledge leaders, as well as the anthem singers, the musicians represented a diverse collection of styles and appealed to a wide variety of regional and demographic audiences. The musicians all added something to the program. For example, Brooks and Dunn sang their song "Only in America" at the end of the session themed "A Land of Opportunity." The act and their song enhanced the evening's theme and played into the contrasting aspects of the optimistic W versus pessimistic Kerry that the campaign was establishing. Another example of this was provided by country singer Darryl Worley who sang about family and the relative fighting overseas but was not asked to deliver either his "Have You Forgotten?" or "I Miss My Friend" emotional paeans to the troops in Iraq and Afghanistan,[33] in the middle of an evening that dealt mostly with 9/11-related events and the broader War on Terror brand story. In such ways was music employed to transmit the Bush brand story.

The RNC featured appearances by contest winners who appealed to the taste of the youth and African American audiences. One won an essay contest sponsored by MTV and the other was the reigning Miss America. Both presented speeches that fit with the convention's themes. As was the case with all of the celebrities at the convention, these two contest winners and celebrities gave the Bush brand more cool, signaled interest on brand W's behalf to nontraditional audiences, and provided user testimonials. These appearances let us see how specific aspects of brand W were being presented to specific audiences and how the campaign made use of members of these audiences to testify on behalf of its product.

Political Testimonials: The Heavyweights Weigh In

Like all infomercials, the RNC taught the public about its brand through the use of expert testimonials and endorsements. This is very much in keeping with the infomercial model that we saw above. Testimonials from politicians give the brand story more credibility than they would have if only based on the marketer's efforts, and are another opportunity to generate impressions for the current, as well as heritage brand stories. Testimonials amplify the overall impact of the brand strategy. The testimonials presented at this convention reiterated the repositioned aspects of brand W and built fellowship between Bush and the core conservative brand story, as well as between Bush and the Reagan heritage brand in order to fit the first Bush administration and this candidacy into the overall branded product line. In addition to generating impressions for the brand story, these testimonials reiterated the contrasts and positioning that the campaign was working to establish between its brand and the one it was building around Kerry.

George W. Bush: Fellowship with Lincoln or Reagan?

One of the ways that these testimonials emphasized Bush's leadership skills was to try to build fellowship between him and the Reagan heritage brand, as well as between these two and two Conservative icons: Winston Churchill and Abraham Lincoln. The rationale for their doing so was explained in Chapter 1 in the section on archetypal branding. Speaker Hastert's remarks are typical of the way in which this fellowship was built in 2004 as he noted that like Lincoln and Reagan, Bush believed in "the American Dream," "the power of freedom," and the Republican Party before noting that Bush, like these other two leaders, had a "hopeful vision."[34] Hastert's construction touches on the leadership aspects of Bush, the optimistic Bush versus pessimistic Kerry aspects of the campaign's two brands, then fits Bush into the core Conservative brand through references to Reagan and Lincoln, both of whom fought wars to save the nation. Conservatives regularly build fellowship between their core brand and the current brands in an effort to present the public with a seamless product line as is consistent with the arguments noted in Chapter 1. The second purpose of their fellowship building effort was to show that George W. Bush was akin to these figures from the Conservative archetypal heritage brand while John Kerry was not. Doing so allows Conservatives to fight the same election battle that they have been fighting since at least 1980.

It is the same as an infomercial marketer explaining to his audience how the product being promoted is a wonderful product whereas the one compared to is a product of inferior quality. This is plain in the way in which Hastert presented Bush as another strong leader in the branded Conservative line. Hastert then contrasted him with senator flip-flop. He did so by saying that like Lincoln and Reagan, Bush was willing to gain global respect by possessing "the courage to stand for America."[35] It was in this way that Bush shared "the Lincoln and the Reagan vision."[36] Having showed how Bush fit within the overall Conservative brand on leadership and patriotism issues, Hastert amplified on the brand story about Bush by presenting the senator flip-flop brand through the same "he's voted for it and he's voted against it"[37] aspect upon which the entire thing rested. Hastert closed with a call to action, which told the audience that Bush was like the Conservative heritage brand and its other historical archetype; Hastert first noted that Kerry was "weak on the war and wrong on taxes"; he then argued that Bush was a "strong leader"; he restated his points about the vision Bush shared with Lincoln and Reagan, which was also "the American vision."[38]

One of the heroes of 9/11, New York Mayor Rudy Giuliani, did the same by linking Bush specifically with Lincoln, then arguing that the Republican Party's "great contribution is to expand freedom in our own land and all over the world."[39] Having built fellowship between Lincoln and Bush, he moved to incorporate another great wartime leader, Winston Churchill, with the Reagan of the heritage brand, noting how critics had scorned their vision, and then placed them directly in line with Bush by saying that like him they were forward-looking optimists.[40] These remarks are an obvious effort to blunt charges that Bush was a stubborn ideologue. Instead, these remarks built fellowship between him and two Conservative leaders who had stood against totalitarianism, as well as who shared the optimism and strong leadership traits being emphasized about W.

Senator Elizabeth Dole built the same kind of fellowship as noted earlier and worked on the contrast between the Bush and Kerry leadership aspects, as well as the broader differences between the Conservative and Liberal brands, when she said that Lincoln's party "has not wandered in a desert of disbelief or uncertainty."[41] Instead, under Bush leadership it was "guided by a moral compass," in an obvious reference to the Liberal brand in general and that of the moment: Senator flip-flop that was followed up by the assertion that the party felt that "character was king,"[42] which also happens to be part of the title of a book about Ronald Reagan by Peggy Noonan. Dole argued that Reagan himself had embodied this and, in a clear attempt to play up the strong leader and Cold War aspects of the Conservative brand mentioned that he "called an empire evil" before arguing that he won that long-standing conflict.[43] All of which was a way to remind Conservatives why they liked Reagan, what the party stood for, and how John Kerry was simply another Liberal. Mitt Romney provided a product for comparison much as sometimes happens in infomercials by building a fellowship between W and Reagan while doing the same between Ted Kennedy and John Kerry by saying that if people thought Reagan was wrong and Kennedy right during the 1980s, then they should vote for Kerry.[44] In addition to a negative testimonial, Romney's fellowship building effort was a clear attempt to remind the target audience about the men who had driven them away from the Democrats and toward the Conservatives, as well as the Reagan heritage.

The brand strategy gives Conservatives the ability to quickly create line extensions in the brands that it is building around itself and its opponents, and build fellowship between the branded initiatives it has recently launched and those sitting at its core. In 2004 it allowed them to claim that George W. Bush was not an ideologue; he was a great leader in the style of Lincoln and Reagan while John Kerry was simply another weak kneed Liberal. This, in turn, allowed the Conservatives to create a very favorable contrast between the solid leader aspect of brand W and the flip-flop aspect of the brand that it was creating around Kerry.

Solid Leader Versus Flip-Flopper

The leadership aspect of both brands went to the core brand story that the Bush campaign was trying to tell and through its successful establishment the War on Terror brand could be used in an offensive, as opposed to defensive, way. Simply, leadership mattered because of terrorism's fanatical practitioners and the Bush campaign worked to show that its man was fit to fight that enemy while Kerry was not. This was one of the points to the earlier-noted fellowship building activity and was a way to show that Bush's stubbornness was a good thing. Rudy Giuliani noted that as a strong leader Bush would hold his ground in the face of public opinion while Kerry's record indicated that he would not.[45] Since he had lived through 9/11 and worked directly with Bush in its wake, he was well suited to provide a personal testimony about him and to raise the leadership aspects in order to promote the strong leader aspects of brand W.

Romney, the testifier best acquainted with Kerry, made the link between the War on Terror and leadership aspects of both brands explicit by noting that despite Kerry's claims to holding a consistent position on the War on Terror his voting record indicated otherwise because "he voted no on Desert Storm in 1991" but "yes on Desert Shield," he voted against troop funding after just having voted for it, and he opposed the war all through 2004 "but says he'd vote yes today."[46] Having outlined these distinctions, Romney drew a contrast between Kerry's leadership that "comes in 57 varieties"[47] versus "the decisive president who stands his ground," that was and would continue to be George W. Bush.[48] Romney's overall point was to show the strong leader aspect of W while presenting Kerry as somebody who is too weak to be the president. He used Kerry's voting record against him to prove that point and, in an obvious attempt to show that Kerry was not an everyman, noted Kerry's marriage to a wealthy heiress.

Another testimonial from a person who had intimate knowledge of the competing product, the former Democratic governor of Georgia drew the same contrasts and worked with the same brand aspects by saying that Bush would "grab terrorists by the throat" while Kerry would give them "a yes-no-maybe bowl of mush" that would confuse allies and "encourage our enemies."[49] As a Democrat, Zell Miller was in a unique position to provide a testimonial telling people that Bush was a better leader and that it would be okay to vote for Bush just this once. This example typifies the use to which Conservatives put the brand strategy. Instead of having to debate Kerry on their substantive products, they had moved the debate into a more visual, more emotive realm and could blunt Kerry's factually based complaints.

Vice President Cheney was well situated to provide a testimonial for the repositioned brand W. He first reiterated the contrast between W and senator flip-flop by expanding it beyond the War on Terror brand by arguing that Kerry had "a habit of indecision" that was "part of a pattern."[50] Cheney listed two of the administration's branded initiatives, the Patriot Act and the No Child Left Behind Act, as things on which Kerry had flip-flopped before turning Kerry's argument about economic inequality on its head by saying that Kerry saw two countries and that "America sees two John Kerrys" in a seeming attempt to reiterate the flip-flop brand.[51] Cheney provided examples from a variety of areas to call Kerry's leadership traits and personal credibility into question as Conservatives did to their opponents in 2000 and 1992. Cheney presented the leadership and personal attribute aspects of brand W, mentioning that Bush was "a man our nation has come to know"[52] whom Cheney had seen face difficult choices and "make those decisions with the wisdom and humility Americans expect in their president."[53] The Bush that Cheney was promoting was an everyman, not the elite that the Democrats were arguing that he was. Like a Boy Scout, Bush was "a person of loyalty and kindness"[54] who "brings out these qualities around him." Unlike senator flip-flop, the Bush of which Cheney was speaking was "a man of great personal strength."[55] Cheney also worked to show the audience that Bush was a real compassionate Conservative by saying that he was "a man with a heart for the weak, and the vulnerable, and the afflicted."[56]

This was a restatement of the 2000 brand story, the everyman aspect that has been in every conservative campaign brand since the Reagan years, and a clear statement of the repositioned brand's leadership aspect. Cheney's testimonial synthesized the 2000 Bush brand story, the current one, and the archetypal Conservative brand story into a whole. Cheney was able to do this effectively only because of the work done by the earlier speakers to reposition brand W, as well as to teach the public about Kerry's flip-floppy Liberalism. The best example of this early work was provided in Giuliani's speech in which he used Kerry's words that he had voted for war appropriations before voting against them in a way that made clear the contrast being drawn by the event as a whole. [57]

This description, devoid of context but always with the assertion that "he voted for it before he voted against it" became the core aspect of the flip-flop brand. When linked with the War on Terror brand, it showed why voters should not choose Kerry, and allowed Conservatives to introduce their heritage brand, as well as the security aspect of the overall Conservative brand and the contrasts regularly used with each to the campaign. Even though 9/11 happened when Bush was in office, there were no WMD found in Iraq, and bin Laden was still in hiding, the brand strategy allowed Conservatives to shift the campaign away from these specifics onto more emotive, more visual matters and to wage the same electoral campaign that they have been waging since the Reagan years.

The Softer Side of Bush

Conservatives, in addition to discussing Bush's leadership traits, had to reposition their candidates in order to minimize the public's perceptions that he was an ideologue unwilling to admit to making errors. This repositioning was accomplished in part by stressing aspects of Bush's personal traits other than leadership. This, in turn, was accomplished via the presentation of testimonials from moderate Republican leaders, who hailed mostly from the Midwest and Northeast, and were not overtly associated with the Christian right. The way in which the television networks have reduced their coverage of the conventions facilitated this strategy because these more moderate speakers could be put on for the large prime-time audiences while more Conservative faces could appear at other times. The repositioning was further accomplished by the presentation of testimonials from Bush's family members.

The net effect was to reposition Bush's rigidity as firm leadership in the face of crisis and to humanize the person about whom the public had heard so many negative things in recent years. One of the most important testimo-

nials came from Senator McCain, who had been the subject of public spec-
ulation as a potential Kerry running mate and could lend his own credibility to Bush on military affairs and by doing so blunt the Vietnam aspect of
Kerry's message, as well as to provide Bush with a set of moderate Republican
credentials. McCain talked about his relationships with Democratic moderates, invoked Democratic icon Franklin Roosevelt, made an appeal for unity,
and softly emphasized the War on Terror brand and the leadership aspects
of brand W by saying, in a nutshell, that it was okay for Americans to discuss their differences but should remember that they were "comrades in a
war against a real enemy"[58] and should be heartened by knowing that the
only thing equal to U.S. "military superiority of our ideals and our uncon-
querable love for them."[59] This is not the hotter message that was presented
by Conservative politicians and Conservative press. This was an effort to
reposition brand W in a way to make it more acceptable to a slightly more
moderate audience.

Another way in which brand W was repositioned, as well as pitched to
its new target audiences, was through an emphasis on diversity. These audiences were pitched as they would be throughout the campaign with an
emphasis on the mainstream aspects of brand W, stress on cultural issues, and
the American dream. There were nine Hispanics on the podium at one time
or another, at least two speeches by African Americans and a number of
other appearances, and at least one Jewish politician who appeared in speaking roles. One of their better pitchmen was Governor Arnold Schwarzenegger
who argued to immigrants that joining the Conservative Party was good
because Conservatives shared their values because: As he put it in a pitch to
recent immigrants, they were welcome in the party because "Republicans admire
your ambition," "encourage your dreams," and "believe in your future."[60]
Arnold began educating the audience about the Reagan heritage brand by
using one of its core aspects: American revival in an effort to build fellowship between Reagan and W with this audience by using an old Reagan line
"America is back."[61] In this case it was back from "the attack on our homeland" and in an obvious reference to the Clinton/September 11 recession,
the country had returned from "the attack on our economy. . . . the attack
on our way of life."[62] All this was attributable to Bush's "perseverance, character and leadership."[63] This speech linked the Cold War with the War on
Terror brand and linked Bush directly to the Reagan heritage brand. The net
effect of all of these appearances was to show these new audiences that the

Bush campaign had interest in them, as well as to take the edge off of the more anti-immigrant sentiments that are popular with some Conservatives.

Bush's family contributed to the repositioning through their speeches, and the convention featured a documercial about George H.W. Bush, who had become something of an icon for decency during the Slick Willie campaign. Bush's daughters spoke in a way that made extensive reference to humor, popular culture, and images of a happy family. By having them speak in this way, younger voters and family values voters could be courted, an offset to the strong leader aspect was provided, and Bush was repositioned back to being an everyman instead of an ideologue. They did so by saying that having George and Laura as parents gave them "a special appreciation for how blessed we are to live in this great country."[64] The Bush of which they were speaking was not the hard man but was a typical parent who read to his kids, drove them around, made sandwiches, and attended youth sports events.[65] This is clear emphasis of the everyman, patriotism, and family values aspects of the Conservative brand.

Laura, Bush's wife, presented a soft justification for her husband's foreign policy. She humanized the Iraq conflict first by mentioning service members' parental obligations and second by noting that her husband had agonized over foreign policy questions in order to show that W was a human, not an ideologue, and to blunt assertions that the Iraq War had been planned long before Bush took office. Her speech softly worked in the strong leadership and flip-flop brand aspects:

> People ask me all the time whether George has changed. He's a little grayer. And of course, he's learned and grown, as we all have. But he's still the same person I met at a backyard barbecue in Midland, Texas, and married three months later. (APPLAUSE) And you've come to know many of the same things that I know about him. He'll always tell you what he really thinks. You can count on him, especially in a crisis. His friends don't change and neither do his values.[66]

She moved on to close with both the strong leader and the softer side of Bush aspects of brand W when she said:

> George and I grew up in West Texas, where the sky seems endless and so do the possibilities. He brings that optimism, that sense of purpose, that certainty that a better day is before us to his job every day. And with your help, he'll do so for four more years. These are times that require an especially strong and determined leader. And I'm proud that my husband is that kind of leader.[67]

These lines softly summed up the optimism versus pessimism, the strong leader versus senator flip-flop contrast built into the brand stories without using the harsh rhetoric that many of the campaign's ads, speeches, and Conservative supporters would use to make the same point. After all of the endorsements from moderate Republicans and personal testimonials from family members, brand W was a good bit softer and more moderate than it was at the beginning of the infomercial.

Bush: A Product Demonstration

As noted earlier in this chapter, the 2004 Bush campaign appears to have made extensive use of the demo format of infomercial at its convention. One portion of this format is, as it was noted, showing the ways in which the product works. Political speeches are like an automobile test drive, tour of a time share, or home demonstration of a high-end vacuum cleaner. Thus, they offer a chance to show what the candidate is like and, in the process of doing so, provide an opportunity for the candidate to educate the audience about the brand once more. Candidate speeches are a key means through which the public can be shown that brand promises have been kept and the brand story told through the prior four days is truthful. Bush's remarks closely matched the brand story presented during the week, as well as that that would be presented during the remainder of the campaign.

Bush worked with the Clinton recession and War on Terror brands in a consistent way. He tried to shift blame for the period's problems by claiming that "none of us could have envisioned"[68] them, then took credit for good things by saying "we have seen a shaken economy rise to its feet"[69] before summing up his accomplishments in a manner consistent with the safer, stronger, better brand story and television advertisement script:

> Since 2001, Americans have been given hills to climb and found the strength to climb them. . . We will build a safer world and a more hopeful America—and nothing will hold us back.[70]

Consistent with the story being told by the convention, Bush worked to soften himself by mentioning his family, and then reiterated the fellowship building efforts that had been made on his behalf by mentioning Reagan. In order to show that the first Bush administration kept its promises, he made mention of three of its branded products: the No Child Left Behind Act, the Medicare Modernization and Reform Act, and its tax cuts as economic policy brand.

When Bush spoke of national security policy, he did so by mirroring the ad script for the commercial "Solemn Duty." Bush did so by saying that the "most solemn duty of the American president is to protect the American people."[71] He followed that up by referring to the impact of electing senator flip-flop by saying, "If America shows uncertainty or weakness in this decade, the world will drift toward tragedy."[72] He then reiterated the repositioned brand W; the brand promises made in 2000, and put those into the core Conservative brand story by saying:

> I am running for president with a clear and positive plan to build a safer world and a more hopeful America. I am running with a compassionate conservative philosophy: that government should help people improve their lives, not try to run their lives. (APPLAUSE) I believe this nation wants steady, consistent, principled leadership—and that is why, with your help, we will win this election.[73]

This passage again lays out the contrast between leadership aspects of both brands, as well as the risk versus safety aspect with which the media advertising would come to work, and the contrasting aspects of optimism versus pessimism.

After rolling out the "Freedom is on the March" theme, Bush reiterated the branded domestic initiatives that he had mentioned earlier in order to show that brand promises had been kept, to reiterate the brand contrasts being used in this campaign, and to signal his interest to the Hispanic audience because many of his examples specifically dealt with members of this community. The section reiterated the optimism aspect of the brand and mimicked the media advertising to come when Bush said, "To build a more hopeful America, we must help our children reach as far as their vision and character can take them."[74] Bush's speech presented, as the fall campaign ads would, the election as a binary choice in which "My opponent's policies are dramatically different from ours."[75] To prove that he was on their side while Kerry was not, Bush talked about Kerry's votes against the tax cuts, his flip-flops on education reform, and his opposition to the Medicare and legal reforms that are core Conservative agenda items.[76] He continually worked with the strong leader versus flip-flopper brand aspect contrast through the use of the culture war issues to which Conservative audiences consistently respond.[77] Bush talked about their issues as part of his overall plan for strengthening families. Brands define issues and individuals in specific ways and, as a result, items that contradict the brand story are left out by their promoters. It falls to their opponents to point them out and this is something that Democrats have done a poor job of during the past several electoral cycles.

Bush worked with the War on Terror brand, then built fellowship with the Afghan and Iraq wars much in the way that Conservatives had in 2002 and when building the War on Terror brand. His points were in keeping with the ten-point strategy memo mentioned in the prior chapter:

> So we have fought the terrorists across the Earth, not for pride—not for power, but because the lives of our citizens are at stake. Our strategy is clear. We have tripled funding for homeland security and trained half a million first responders because, we are determined to protect our homeland. We are transforming our military and reforming and strengthening our intelligence services. We are staying on the offensive—striking terrorists abroad—so we do not have to face them here at home. (APPLAUSE) And we are working to advance liberty in the broader Middle East, because freedom will bring a future of hope and the peace we all want. And we will prevail.[78]

Doing this let Bush take advantage of all of the branded marketing that his party and administration had already done. He veered from the original brand story to argue that Iraq was a more preemptive response but was sure to work Saddam in twice in his answer as the memo advised:

> We knew Saddam Hussein's record of aggression and support for terror. We knew his long history of pursuing, even using, weapons of mass destruction. And we know that September the 11th requires our country to think differently. We must, and we will, confront threats to America before it is too late. (APPLAUSE) BUSH: "In Saddam Hussein, we saw a threat.." . . . AUDIENCE: U-S-A. U-S-A. U-S-A.[79]

Again we see the use of audience participation to reinforce the branded message. In the same passage, Bush later used Saddam again and noted that Democrats, including his opponent, had supported giving him the ability to use force, thus making Kerry out to be either dishonest or a flip-flopper.[80] Bush reinforced the importance of the leadership aspect of brand W by saying:

> And I faced the kind of decision that comes only to the Oval Office—a decision no president would ask for, but must be prepared to make: Do I forget the lessons of September 11th and take the word of a madman, or do I take action to defend our country? Faced with that choice, I will defend America every time.[81]

In these ways, Bush reinforced the idea that he was a strong leader with support abroad defending the nation, worked in the softer aspects of the brand and the flip-flop aspect of the brand being built around Kerry.

During Bush's recitation of the senator flip-flop voting record, the convention audience again participated in order to amplify the brand story. In this case the audience booed Kerry's Iraq funding vote and chanted "flip-flop, flip-flop, flip-flop" in response to Bush's presentation of it.[82] Bush closed by reciting the softer side of Bush attributes of the W brand story in order to close with good feelings about him after such a tough speech and to reiterate his everyman credentials. He closed by echoing Laura Bush's question about how he had changed by saying "One thing that I have learned about the presidency is that whatever shortcomings you have, people are going to notice them-and whatever strengths you have-you're going to need them."[83] The speech fit nicely with the story that had been told during the four-day long infomercial. Bush, speaking as the branded product, spoke on his own behalf and showed that the promises others had made about him were true and that he would work as advertised.

This infomercial gave people a good sense of what the brand being promoted was all about, what the product was, and why it was better than its competitors. The brand strategy advantages Conservatives because it allows them to make the most of the fact that American political conventions have become infomercials. An infomercial format is ideally suited to selling brands and branded products. It lets Conservatives quickly make their audience aware of new line extensions, make specific appeals to focused constituencies and remind the audience why it liked the product in the first place. The Bush convention was successful because it moved the polls as we can see in a *USA Today* Gallup Poll taken just after the convention, which showed that the audience had gotten most of the messages about Brand W and senator flip-flop, so much so that Bush's lead shot from two to seven points over Kerry by the time the convention ended.[84] The brand story presented at the convention made the public supportive of Bush's credentials on the terrorism issue because his lead on the issue increased by seventeen points during the month in which it aired.[85] The convention was successful because it encouraged voters to rethink their opinions of Bush.[86] This shows the advantage that the brand strategy gives to Conservatives. By emphasizing favorable aspects of the Conservative branded policy products and W personally, the Bush campaign gained more of an advantage from its convention than Senator Kerry gained from the Democratic National Convention (DNC).

Bush got more of a bounce out of the RNC than Kerry got out of the DNC because Bush used aspects of his brand story before, during, and after it in all of the campaign's communicative efforts. John Kerry, who had the beginnings of a brand and a brand story when his campaign rolled out "The Real Deal" brand failed to put such effort into brand building and suffered as a result. The Conservatives used their convention to launch their fall marketing campaign while the Democrats used theirs to launch a fall political campaign. In subsequent weeks, Kerry went around the country talking to group after group in different ways and teaching the public about his myriad nuanced issue positions while Bush simply stuck to the story about brand W that had been presented to the country at the RNC.

After seeing the branded product on television, consumers in the key markets who would decide if its infomercial had been a success or not got a first-hand look at its product at once when Bush hit the road in three swing states.[87] The campaign press release that outlined the postconvention schedule emphasized the Opportunity Society and hopeful aspects of brand W entitled "Bush-Cheney '04 Announces Post Convention 'Opportunity Tour.'"[88] This release worked in the brand W's current theme as it noted that Bush was traveling to "rally support for his plan for a safer world and more hopeful America."[89] The overall brand promise was worked in when explaining that the campaign team would be going along "spreading the President's vision of a safer world and a more hopeful America."[90]

Much as the convention had been a branded infomercial, the subsequent tour was an equally branded event. Every day it worked on some aspect of brand W that had been presented at the convention. Particularly at the weekend, Bush's team used branded events to get their message home. On the Saturday of the tour, "the President will highlight 'Opportunity Zones'[91] while on Sunday the President will launch a 'Jobs and Opportunity' tour"[92] in West Virginia, and visited Poplar Bluffs, Missouri to discuss small business.[93] The first lady worked with a specific aspect of brand W as she attended a "W stands for Women"[94] event in Lewiston, Maine on the Friday of this tour. The other niche audience that was targeted for follow-up on this tour was veterans. As the press release noted, "There will also be events across the country featuring heroic veterans supporting the President, including former Marine Corps Commandant Gen. P.X. Kelley and multiple Medal of Honor recipients."[95] The branded follow-up tour repeated the brand story that had been told the prior week and let people see the branded product for themselves. We now turn to the second mass opportunity to get the branded product out to the audience: the presidential debate. This section shows the extent to which branded politics is scripted politics.

Debates: A Second Major Marketing Opportunity

Conservatives use presidential debates to build brand awareness. Instead of trying to win the argument, Conservatives simply generate impressions for their brands by repeatedly emphasizing the aspects that the campaign is promoting.[96] The Bush team appears to have done just this in the presidential debates in 2004.[97] This section examines the way in which this was done and the extent to which Bush stayed on the points outlined in the memo to sell the public on the administration's version of the truth about the War on Terror by examining the extensive use that Bush made of the points noted at the end of Chapter 7. They are again:

1 use 9/11 as background,
2 talk about homeland security first,
3 talk about what is being protected,
4 sell the broader War on Terror story and Iraq's role in it and make the case for being on offense,
5 explain that this is a war against radical ideologues not against a religion
6 it is better to fight abroad than in the United States,
7 present terrorism as a product of a dysfunctional culture,
8 point out that Republicans were leading a fight to preserve our freedom and security,
9 mention Saddam a lot, and
10 support the troops

By doing so, he was able to emphasize the strong leader aspect of his brand and the flip-flop aspect of the brand his campaign was building around Kerry, as well as to justify his administration's security policies. I have placed the memo point that corresponds to the point that Mr. Bush is making in the statement. The first debate is examined in great depth because it is directly related to foreign policy issues. There is little point to presenting all of the foreign policy answers provided in the second and third debates. The only difference between the contents of these latter debates was that Bush adjusted his answers to fit within the patriotic/isolationist aspects of the core Conservative brand story and to incorporate a recent Kerry statement about a "global test" into his answers in order to emphasize that Bush was the strong leader and Kerry the flip-flopper of the brand stories.[98]

Bush worked with the aspects of brand W that the campaign was promoting; he repeated them frequently and worked his brand story into every possible response. Consider how well he follows the script in the first debate's opening question: One example of this is provided in his response to the debate's opening question in which he stays right on the script:

> "September the 11th changed how America must look at the world. (Memo point 1) And since that day, our nation has been on a multi-pronged strategy to keep our country safer. (Memo point 2) We pursued Al Qaida wherever Al Qaida tries to hide. Seventy-five percent of known Al Qaida leaders have been brought to justice. The rest of them know we're after them. (Memo point 4) We've upheld the doctrine that said if you harbor a terrorist, you're equally as guilty as the terrorist. (Memo point 4) And the Taliban are no longer in power. Ten million people have registered to vote in Afghanistan in the upcoming presidential election. (Memo point 4) In Iraq, we saw a threat, and we realized that after September the 11th, we must take threats seriously, before they fully materialize. (Memo point 6) Saddam Hussein now sits in a prison cell. (Memo point 9) America and the world are safer for it. We continue to pursue our policy of disrupting those who proliferate weapons of mass destruction. (Memo point 8) Libya has disarmed. The A.Q. Khan network has been brought to justice. And, as well, we're pursuing a strategy of freedom around the world, because I understand free nations will reject terror. Free nations will answer the hopes and aspirations of their people. Free nations will help us achieve the peace we all want" (Memo point 8).[99]

Bush worked six of the ten points into this single answer as he would do again and again during the debates. This is the way in which a brand strategy is executed in a presidential debate. The point to the exercise is to tell and retell the brand story so that the audience knows what it is and how it feels about it. In short, the standard idea of who won or lost the debate is irrelevant because Conservatives use debates to promote their brand story. What matters is how they look, how many times they can repeat their brand story, and how people feel about them after they have done so.

Bush consistently repeated the memo's points throughout each debate. His answer to a question of what the chances were of another attack in case of a Kerry victory shows how he worked current events and the themes of his campaign ads into his responses to show the audience how the entire brand story fit together across all kinds of media:

> This nation of ours has got a solemn duty to defeat this ideology of hate. (Memo Points 5 and 7) And that's what they are. This is a group of killers who will not only kill here, but kill children in Russia, that'll attack unmercifully in Iraq, hoping to shake our will. (Memo Point 4) We have a duty to defeat this enemy. We have a duty to protect our children and grandchildren. (Memo Points 2 and 3)

The best way to defeat them is to never waver, to be strong, to use every asset at our disposal, to constantly stay on the offensive and, at the same time, spread liberty. (Memo Points 2 and 8) And that's what people are seeing now is happening in Afghanistan. (Memo Points 4 and 8) Ten million citizens have registered to vote. It's a phenomenal statistic. They're given a chance to be free, and they will show up at the polls. Forty-one percent of those 10 million are women. In Iraq, no doubt about it, it's tough. It's hard work. It's incredibly hard. You know why? Because an enemy realizes the stakes. The enemy understands a free Iraq will be a major defeat in their ideology of hatred. That's why they're fighting so vociferously. (Memo Points 4, 5, and 7) They showed up in Afghanistan when they were there, because they tried to beat us and they didn't. And they're showing up in Iraq for the same reason. They're trying to defeat us. (Memo Points 4, 5, 6, and 7) And if we lose our will, we lose. But if we remain strong and resolute, we will defeat this enemy.[100]

Bush worked seven of the memo points and one of his ad themes into this answer. He made reference to statistics in order to show that progress was being made but provided no source for these numbers. There is, as Donald Rumsfeld once noted,[101] no way to definitely know how much progress is being made in that conflict. Another way in which Bush used numbers was to present voting registration figures for Afghan women as proof that their treatment had markedly improved in that country as a result of the government that came into being after the American invasion. As other marketers do, the Bush team used numbers to show that brand promises were being kept.

We can see how Bush moved to build fellowship between 9/11 and Saddam Hussein, as well as to introduce the senator flip-flop brand into the story when he rebutted Kerry's assertion that the Iraq War had diverted resources away from the Al Qaeda war:

My opponent looked at the same intelligence I looked at and declared in 2002 that Saddam Hussein was a grave threat. (Memo Points 9 and 2) He also said in December of 2003 that anyone who doubts that the world is safer without Saddam Hussein does not have the judgment to be president. (Memo Point 9) I agree with him. The world is better off without Saddam Hussein. (Memo Point 9) I was hoping diplomacy would work. I understand the serious consequences of committing our troops into harm's way. (Memo Point 10) It's the hardest decision a president makes. So I went to the United Nations. I didn't need anybody to tell me to go to the United Nations. I decided to go there myself. And I went there hoping that, once and for all, the free world would act in concert to get Saddam Hussein to listen to our demands. (Memo Point 9) They passed the resolution that said, "Disclose, disarm, or face serious consequences." I believe, when an international body speaks, it must mean what it says. Saddam Hussein had no intention of disarming. Why should he? He had 16 other resolutions and nothing took

place. As a matter of fact, my opponent talks about inspectors. The facts are that
he was systematically deceiving the inspectors. (Memo Point 9) That wasn't going
to work. That's kind of a pre-September 10th mentality, (Memo Point 1) the
hope that somehow resolutions and failed inspections would make this world a more
peaceful place. He was hoping we'd turn away. But there was fortunately others
beside himself who believed that we ought to take action. (Memo Points 3 and 8).
We did. The world is safer without Saddam Hussein. (Memo Point 9)[102]

This answer only worked in four of the ten points, yet it also contained
the repositioned brand W and flip-flop brands. Even better, it questioned Kerry's
motives for his position switch, much in the way that Conservatives have done
to Democrats since at least 1992 in order to indirectly challenge their
integrity. Bush again made an assertion that could not be verified or disputed
by the average viewer: that U.S. senators receive exactly the same intelligence briefings as does the president. There was no way for the bulk of the
audience to know if this assertion was or was not true. This is where Bush's
personal traits helped him sell the brand story to his target audiences. Because
they liked him and trusted him, they would take these reasonable sounding
assertions on faith and, as a result, they would see Senator Kerry as a flip-
flopper. Kerry had no reasonable way to defend himself against the flip-flop
brand story, once Bush had framed it using unverifiable assertions to do so.
Here again, we see the important way that framing and branding work
together and why Lakoff's (2004) argument about the importance of setting the frame is so crucial in branded politics.

Bush worked in the same answer to moderator Jim Leher's "What about
Senator Kerry's point, the comparison he drew between the priorities of
going after Osama bin Laden and going after Saddam Hussein?" by saying:

We're facing a group of folks who have such hatred in their heart (Memo Point
7), they'll strike anywhere, with any means. And that's why it's essential that we
have strong alliances, and we do. That's why it's essential that we make sure that
we keep weapons of mass destruction out of the hands of people like Al Qaeda,
which we are. (Memo Points 1, 2, 6 and 8). But to say that there's only one
focus on the war on terror doesn't really understand the nature of the war on terror. (Memo Points 4, 6, and 8) Of course we're after Saddam Hussein (Point 9)—
I mean bin Laden. He's isolated. Seventy-five percent of his people have been brought
to justice. The killer—the mastermind of the September 11th attacks (Memo
Point 1), Khalid Sheik Mohammed, is in prison. We're making progress. But the
front on this war is more than just one place. The Philippines—we've got help—
we're helping them there to bring—to bring Al Qaida affiliates to justice there.
(Memo Point 4) And, of course, Iraq is a central part in the war on terror. (Memo
Points 4 and 6) That's why Zarqawi and his people are trying to fight us. Their

hope is that we grow weary and we leave. The biggest disaster that could happen is that we not succeed in Iraq. We will succeed. We've got a plan to do so. And the main reason we'll succeed is because the Iraqis want to be free. (Memo Point 8) I had the honor of visiting with Prime Minister Allawi. He's a strong, courageous leader. He believes in the freedom of the Iraqi people. (Memo Point 8) He doesn't want U.S. leadership, however, to send mixed signals, to not stand with the Iraqi people. He believes, like I believe, that the Iraqis are ready to fight for their own freedom. They just need the help to be trained. There will be elections in January. We're spending reconstruction money. And our alliance is strong. That's the plan for victory. And when Iraq is free, America will be more secure." (Memo Point 8)[103]

In this answer, Bush worked in six of the ten points. He reiterated the War on Terror brand story, visibly showed people that progress was being made abroad, foreign leaders were onboard, and that Al Qaeda leaders were being captured. The net effect was to show that past brand promises had been kept and would be so again. He even closed with an exit strategy that fit within the archetypes upon which the entire Conservative brand strategy relies. While light on verifiable facts, this answer was long on items that are capable of producing an emotive response from the audience because it was solidly grounded in archetypes toward which they were favorably predisposed.

Kerry's attempt to frame Bush as untrustworthy and, by doing so, call the personal and leadership aspects of brand W into question wonderfully illustrates the advantage that Conservatives get from the brand strategy. While Kerry could assert that Bush had misled Congress and the public into Iraq, he could not clearly prove it and, by the time he had made these assertions, Conservatives had already spent years building the War on Terror and W brands. All his effort accomplished was to let Bush reiterate a variety of brand stories:

BUSH: "My opponent just said something amazing. He said Osama bin Laden uses the invasion of Iraq as an excuse to spread hatred for America. (Memo Points 1, 4, and 6) Osama bin Laden isn't going to determine how we defend ourselves. (Memo Point 2) Osama bin Laden doesn't get to decide. The American people decide (Memo Point 3). . . I don't think he misled you when he said that, you know, anyone who doubted whether the world was better off without Saddam Hussein (Memo Point 9) in power didn't have the judgment to be president. I don't think he was misleading. I think what is misleading is to say you can lead and succeed in Iraq if you keep changing your positions on this war. And he has. As the politics change, his positions change. And that's not how a commander in chief acts."[104]

Bush again made six of the memo's points. He did so by recasting a question that could have blown up the personal attributes aspect of his brand in a way that turned it into another advertisement for those attributes, his campaign's brand story and that of the Conservative movement.

Bush's next answer dipped into the Reagan playbook to use a frame that personalized the brand narrative. He did so by opening his discussion of the fellowship built between two current wars with a discussion of a meeting that he had had with the family of a U.S. soldier who had been killed in action:

> I told her after we prayed and teared up and laughed some, that I thought her husband's sacrifice was noble and worthy, because I understand the stakes of this war on terror. I understand that we must find Al Qaeda wherever they hide. (Memo Points 1 and 4) We must deal with threats before they fully materialize—and Saddam Hussein was a threat—(Memo Point 6), and that we must spread liberty because in the long run, the way to defeat hatred (Memo Point 7) and tyranny and oppression is to spread freedom. (Memo Point 8) Missy understood that. That's what she told me her husband understood. So you say, was it worth it? Every life is precious. That's what distinguishes us from the enemy. Everybody matters. But I think it's worth it, Jim. I think it's worth it, because I think—I know in the long term a free Iraq, a free Afghanistan (Memo Point 4 and 8), will set such a powerful example in a part of the world that's desperate for freedom. It will help change the world, that we can look back and say, we did our duty.[105]

Bush again put six of the memo's points into the answer. This branded pitch closed with the core aspect of duty and patriotism of the larger Conservative brand.

In his next answer, Bush presented the fact that elections were held as proof that a democracy was being built and that his brand promise to promote freedom was being kept.[106] He accomplished this by framing his response in a way that produced the kind of binary choice with which the brand strategy best works, in this case the idea that Islam prevented Iraqis from being democratic citizens:

> I believe that 25 million people, the vast majority, long to have elections. I reject this notion—and I'm suggesting my opponent isn't—I reject the notion that some say that if you're Muslim you can't free, you don't desire freedom. I disagree, strongly disagree with that. (Memo Points 5 and 8)[107]

By framing the issue as a binary choice, then inserting his brand story into the frame, Bush was able to avoid having a serious discussion about how a democracy could be built in a former totalitarian state. By presenting the question above as a matter of religious toleration, rather than of nation building, Bush transformed the question from a technical one to the kind of emotive question with which the brand strategy works best.

Kerry's assertion that the Iraq War had lured terrorists into the nation to fight the United States simply opened the door for Bush to reiterate the War on Terror and strong leader aspects of brand W:

> The reason why Prime Minister Allawi said they're coming across the border is because he recognizes that this is a central part of the war on terror. (Memo Point 4) They're fighting us because they're fighting freedom. (Memo Point 8). They understand that a free Afghanistan or a free Iraq will be a major defeat for them. (Memo Point 8) And those are the stakes. And that's why it is essential we not leave. That's why it's essential we hold the line. That's why it's essential we win. And we will. Under my leadership we're going to win this war in Iraq. (Memo Point 3)[108]

Far from showing that the administration's policy was a failure in Iraq, by the time Bush finished reciting his brand stories and three memo points to the target audience, he now could be seen as having made the wise choices that a strong leader must make. He did exactly the same in response to a query about another preemptive war:

> But the enemy attacked us, Jim (Memo Point 1), and I have a solemn duty to protect the American people, to do everything I can to protect us. (Memo Points 2 and 3) I think that by speaking clearly and doing what we say and not sending mixed messages, it is less likely we'll ever have to use troops. But a president must always be willing to use troops. It must—as a last resort. I was hopeful diplomacy would work in Iraq. It was falling apart. There was no doubt in my mind that Saddam Hussein was hoping that the world would turn a blind eye. (Memo Point 9) And if he had been in power, in other words, if we would have said, "Let the inspectors work, or let's, you know, hope to talk him out. Maybe an 18th resolution would work," he would have been stronger and tougher, and the world would have been a lot worse off. There's just no doubt in my mind we would rue the day, had Saddam Hussein been in power. (Memo Point 9) So we use diplomacy every chance we get, believe me. And I would hope to never have to use force. But by speaking clearly and sending messages that we mean what we say, we've affected the world in a positive way. (Memo Point 8) Look at Libya. Libya was a threat. Libya is now peacefully dismantling its weapons programs. Libya understood that America and others will enforce doctrine and that the world is better for it. (Memo Points 2, 3, and 4) So to answer your question, I would hope we never have to. I think by acting firmly and decisively, it will mean it is less likely we have to use force.[109]

This response literally included the title of a Bush ad, "Solemn Duty," included six memo points, and let Bush talk in highly emotive terms about being attacked by an enemy without mentioning which enemy he meant as had been done in 2002. This answer allowed Bush to reiterate the War on Terror brand and the strong leader aspect of brand W, as well as to provide the audience with an example, Libyan disarmament, that proved that the administration's policies worked and that it kept its promises. As is usually the case in branded politics, the truth of the Libyan disarmament claim was more complicated but brands work because they provide informational shortcuts and the American public knew next to nothing about this issue, thus, Bush's assertions seemed credible because brand W had strongly developed his personal credibility.

When Kerry made a fact-based assertion that the administration's strategy at Tora Bora had failed and questioned Bush's assertions about the Iraq War, Bush responded by presenting the War on Terror brand story just as he had during 2002. Instead of a substantive rebuttal of Kerry's points, Bush provided the emotive responses with which branded politicians prefer to work. The only difference in this case was that Bush first acknowledged who exactly had attacked the United States on 9/11, then immediately moved on to the brand story that fit the question:

> First of all, of course I know Osama bin Laden attacked us. (Memo Point 1) I know that. And secondly, to think that another round of resolutions would have caused Saddam Hussein to disarm, disclose, is ludicrous, in my judgment. (Memo Point 9) It just shows a significant difference of opinion. We tried diplomacy. We did our best. He was hoping to turn a blind eye. And, yes, he would have been stronger had we not dealt with him. He had the capability of making weapons, and he would have made weapons. (Memo Point 9)[110]

Bush simply discounted Kerry's assertion then placed Osama and Saddam next to each other just as had been done to build fellowship between Iraq and the War on Terror. Again, this allowed Bush to tap into years of branded marketing in order to minimize the impact of Kerry's fact-based assertions.

While the public and media perception was that Bush lost these debates, they were hugely successful in terms of building brand awareness. Bush had done a good job of staying focused, of working within the brand stories, and of applying them to every possible circumstance. What he had not done well in the first debate was visually appear to be the man of the brand story. Despite this, Bush had sold his brands as the campaign had constructed them and prevented Kerry from using fact-based frames to discredit them. While Kerry had won more often on the facts of the matter, these are often not as important in the era of branded politics as the feelings about the matter that develop within the audience. On that score, Bush and his campaign did a masterful job.

Bush did much the same thing in the second debate as he had in the first to the same popular and press reaction that he had received the first time: John Kerry won the debates. The Bush team was successful because it stuck to the brands that it had developed for the campaign and for the policies with which they had been associated during Bush's time in office. Unlike Kerry, Bush did not try to drown his audience in facts but, instead used facts to produce the emotive response that the campaign desired from the audience and to make the audience more familiar with and excited about the various aspects of brand Bush than they had been prior to the fall campaign. Brand W had its story and, through the debates, W stuck to it.

The major differences between the second debate and the first was that Bush added to the War on Terror brand story, a statement about scandal in the UN Oil for Food program that had become a staple of the Conservative media's take on Iraq by saying:

> "So I tried diplomacy, went to the United Nations. But as we learned in the same report I quoted, Saddam Hussein was gaming the oil-for-food program to get rid of sanctions. (Memo Point 9) He was trying to get rid of sanctions for a reason. He wanted to restart his weapons programs." (Memo Point 4) We all thought there was weapons there, Robin. My opponent thought there was weapons there. That's why he called him a grave threat."[111]

This passage worked in the flip-flop brand and presented the core Conservative audience with a narrative with which they were already somewhat familiar. Bush's other foreign policy answer similarly moved more into the core Conservative brand story about the strength of the movement's commitment to national defense and contrasted it with that of Kerry and his fellow congressional Liberals:

> "You remember the last debate?
> My opponent said that America must pass a global test before we used force to protect ourselves. That's the kind of mindset that says sanctions were working. That's the kind of mindset that said, 'Let's keep it at the United Nations and hope things go well.'
> Saddam Hussein was a threat because he could have given weapons of mass destruction to terrorist enemies. (Memo Points 1, 2, 4, and 8) Sanctions were not working. The United Nations was not effective at removing Saddam Hussein." (Memo Point 9)[112]

Like his "I voted for it before I voted against it" statement that was decontextualized and used to provide credibility for the Bush brand story, his global test comment would become the title of a Bush TV ad. We can see the way in which a grain of truth existed in what Bush was saying by examining what Kerry actually said that evening:

SENATOR KERRY: "The President always has the right and always has had the
right for preemptive strike. That was a great doctrine throughout the Cold War,
and it was always one of the things we argued about with respect to arms control. No President, through all of American history, has ever ceded, and nor
would I, the right to preempt in any way necessary to protect the United States
of America. But if and when you do it, Jim, you've got to do in a way that passes
the test, that passes the global test, where your countrymen, your people understand fully why you're doing what you're doing and you can prove to the world
that you did it for legitimate reasons."

"Here we have our own Secretary of State who's had to apologize to the world
for the presentation he made to the United Nations. I mean, we can remember
when President Kennedy, in the Cuban missile crisis, sent his Secretary of State
to Paris to meet with de Gaulle, and in the middle of the discussion to tell them
about the missiles in Cuba, he said, here, let me show you the photos. And de Gaulle
waved them off, and said, "No, no, no, no. The word of the President of the United
States is good enough for me." How many leaders in the world today would
respond to us as a result of what we've done in that way?"

"So what is at test here is the credibility of the United States of America and
how we lead the world. Well, Iran and Iraq are now more—Iran and North Korea
are now more dangerous. Now, whether preemption is ultimately what has to happen, I don't know yet. But I'll tell you this, as President, I'll never take my eye
off that ball. I've been fighting for proliferation the entire time—anti-prolifera-
tion the entire time I've been in the Congress. And we've watched this President
actually turn away from some of the treaties that were on the table. You don't help
yourself with other nations when you turn away from the Global Warming Treaty,
for instance, or when you refuse to deal at length with the United Nations. You
have to earn that respect. And I think we have a lot of earning back to do."[113]

Bush seized on Kerry's phrase "global test" to immediately establish a
contrast between himself and his challenger by selling the doctrine of
preemption:

PRESIDENT BUSH: "Let me—I'm not exactly sure what you mean, passes the
global test. You take preemptive action if you pass a global test? My attitude is you
take preemptive action in order to protect the American people, that you act in
order to make this country secure"[114].

The Bush team, including Bush himself, moved immediately to seize on a
highly selective aspect of its opponent's statements to prove its points about
both. This is roughly the same technique that was applied to Al Gore and
his supposed claim to have invented the Internet in 2000.

Bush's response to a question about what he had done to improve homeland security shows the way in which branded politics works to encourage
emotive responses and to consider small parts, rather than the entire issue

(as Thomas Frank has noted). After linking Kerry with "tax and spend liberals" who are a staple of the Conservative brand story, Bush returned to the War on Terror brand story, then provided specific examples to show how brand promises had been kept:

> "I don't think we want to get to how he's going to pay for all these promises. It's like a huge tax gap. Anyway, that's for another debate. My administration has tripled the amount of money we're spending on homeland security to $30 billion a year. (Memo Point 2) My administration worked with the Congress to create the Department of Homeland Security so we could better coordinate our borders and ports. (Memo Points 2 and 3) We've got 1,000 extra border patrol on the southern border; want 1,000 on the northern border. We're modernizing our borders. (Memo Point 3) We spent $3.1 billion for fire, and police $3.1 billion. We're doing our duty to provide the funding. But the best way to protect this homeland is to stay on the offense. (Memo Points 3 and 6) You know, we have to be right 100 percent of the time. And the enemy only has to be right once to hurt us. (Memo Point 8) There's a lot of good people working hard. And by the way, we've also changed the culture of the FBI to have counterterrorism as its number one priority. We're communicating better. We're going to reform our intelligence services to make sure that we get the best intelligence possible. The Patriot Act is vital—is vital that the Congress renew the Patriot Act which enables our law enforcement to disrupt terror cells. But again, I repeat to my fellow citizens, the best way to protection is to stay on the offense." (Memo Point 6)[115]

Bush provided an answer consistent with the brand strategy because the highly visible numbers and the branded Patriot Act produced an answer capable of producing emotion but not factual analysis of the Act and its consequences for public policy.

Bush showed the extent to which a brand strategy is a strategy based on feelings and emotions, in his response to a question about the value differences that existed between him and his opponent. Bush took this opportunity to present Kerry as one of the congressional Liberals and as senator flip-flop to boot before moving onto selling the strong leader aspect of brand W:

> I admire the fact that he served for 20 years in the Senate. Although I'm not so sure I admire the record. I won't hold it against him that he went to Yale. There's nothing wrong with that. My concerns about the senator is that, in the course of this campaign, I've been listening very carefully to what he says, and he changes positions on the war in Iraq. He changes positions on something as fundamental as what you believe in your core, in your heart of hearts, is right in Iraq. You cannot lead if you send mixed messages. Mixed messages send the wrong signals to our troops. (Memo Point 10) Mixed messages send the wrong signals to our allies. Mixed messages send the wrong signals to the Iraqi citizens. And that's my

biggest concern about my opponent. I admire his service. But I just know how
this world works, and that in the councils of government, there must be certainty
from the U.S. president. Of course, we change tactics when we need to, but we
never change our beliefs, the strategic beliefs that are necessary to protect this country in the world." (Memo Point 2)[116]

Even if he was substantively wrong, Bush argued that the fact that he was
certain made his leadership style superior to that of his challenger and, thus,
made him better equipped to lead the nation in its current wartime circumstances. When pushed by Kerry that being firm but wrong was no virtue, Bush
responded in a manner consistent with the brand strategy and its emphasis
on visual images designed to produce emotive responses:

Well, I think—listen, I fully agree that one should shift tactics, and we will, in Iraq.
Our commanders have got all the flexibility to do what is necessary to succeed.
But what I won't do is change my core values because of politics or because of
pressure. And it is one of the things I've learned in the White House, is that
there's enormous pressure on the president, and he cannot wilt under that pressure. Otherwise, the world won't be better off.[117]

While Bush personally would not flip-flop, his answer specifically said that
it was okay if the commanders in the field did so but the key point in this
answer was selling the personal traits aspect of brand W.

Bush's closing statement was typical of the brand strategy's emphasis
on the production of emotive responses:

If America shows uncertainty or weakness in this decade, the world will drift
toward tragedy. (Memo Point 1) That's not going to happen, so long as I'm
your president. The next four years we will continue to strengthen our homeland
defenses. (Memo Point 2) We will strengthen our intelligence-gathering services. We will reform our military. The military will be an all-volunteer army. We
will continue to stay on the offense. We will fight the terrorists around the world
so we do not have to face them here at home. (Memo Point 6) We'll continue
to build our alliances. I'll never turn over America's national security needs to leaders of other countries (Memo Point 8), as we continue to build those alliances.
And we'll continue to spread freedom. (Memo Point 8) I believe in the transformational power of liberty. I believe that the free Iraq is in this nation's interests.
(Memo Point 8) I believe a free Afghanistan is in this nation's interest. (Memo
Point 8) And I believe both a free Afghanistan and a free Iraq will serve as a powerful example for millions who plead in silence for liberty in the broader Middle
East. We've done a lot of hard work together over the last three and a half years.
We've been challenged, and we've risen to those challenges. We've climbed the
mighty mountain. I see the valley below, and it's a valley of peace. By being stead-
fast and resolute and strong, by keeping our word, by supporting our troops

(Memo Point 10), we can achieve the peace we all want. I appreciate your listening tonight. I ask for your vote. And may God continue to bless our great land.[118]

Bush's rhetoric in this paragraph would fit nicely into a religious service, spoke directly to his Conservative constituents in both style and substance, contained four of the memo points, reiterated brand stories current and past, worked with his current stump and media strategies, showed how old brand promises had been kept, and gave the audience some new things to go on.

Just as had happened after the first debate, the public and media consensus was that Kerry had won the next two and, again, such analysis missed the role that debates play in the branded political strategy. This chapter has shown how the Bush team used the debates, as it used its convention: not to educate the public about substance, but to reposition and build awareness of their brand. Branded politics involves building the architecture to support the brand that promotes the product not educating the public about the facts of any matter. This is one of the key explanations for why Democrats seem to always, in retrospect, nominate weak candidates. The problem lies not with the candidates or the issues on which Democrats choose to run; the problem appears to lie in the way in which Democrats fail to make as good a use of the brand strategy as Republicans make of it.

Brands in Other Channels

This chapter looks at the ways in which the Bush team presented its brand through electronic and print media,[1] as well as on the stump. In doing so, it examines how brand aspects are kept constant across marketing channels and briefly looks at the way in which the brand strategy equips independent groups to latch onto a campaign's brand narrative. Like the debates and convention, media advertising gives branded politicians another channel through which the public can be taught about the brand and the political product it is supporting while stump speeches let people see the candidate for themselves in order to evaluate if the brand promises are being kept and, as we saw in the last chapter, were used in this election to cement relationships with potential voters. The point to this exercise is to examine the extent to which the Bush team kept its brand story constant across forums and, as a result, examine the extent to which it built public awareness of it. The brand presented through the media was very consistent and featured four aspects: (1) the War on Terror, (2) Bush as a strong leader, (3) tax cuts as a solution to the 9/11 or Clinton recession, and (4) Bush's softer personal traits. The Bush message, as it had throughout the campaign, built line extensions between Kerry and the Liberal brand built by Conservatives, presented Kerry as a flip-flopper, and therefore too weak to be president and worked, as Conservatives do, to show people that John Kerry was an elite unlike everyman Bush.

The War on Terror

The War on Terror brand was the key part of the Bush media strategy because, through its use, W's leadership aspects were stressed, the creation of senator Flip-flop was facilitated, the last four years' policy decisions could be justified, and the nation's poor economic performance could be explained away. The War on Terror brand appeared in a variety of Bush ads and contexts. The net effect of this was to create an overall image of Bush as a strong leader in tough times positioned against a weak-kneed opponent. An emphasis on leadership is a key way to build the brand because it is the "most powerful way to differentiate a brand."[2] This is because leadership is

> the most direct way to establish the credentials of a brand and the credentials are the collateral that you put up to guarantee the performance of your brand. Also, when you have leadership credentials, your prospect is likely to believe almost anything that you say about your brand because you're the leader.[3]

The War on Terror was, as was shown in the prior chapter, a key theme of the early Bush ad "Safer, Stronger" that focused on Bush's leadership traits as well as the Clinton recession and 9/11's impact on American life.[4] The brand strategy let the Bush team create a contrast between its candidate and Kerry, as we can see in the ad "Weapons." In this ad, a narrator told us "As our troops defend America in the War on Terror, they must have what it takes to win," then mentioned a list of Cold War weapons systems against which he had voted before asserting that "Kerry even voted against body armor for our troops on the front line of the War on Terror."[5] These votes were used to show that John Kerry's record on national security issues was, in the ad's words, "troubling."[6] This ad builds on the "he voted before it before he voted against it" aspect of the senator flip-flop brand to present Kerry as not favoring a strong defense because of his votes on weapons systems that were designed to fight in a conflict very different in nature from the one in which the United States found itself in 2004. They presented his voting record without context. The War on Terror referenced in this ad and Kerry's voting record on it have much more to do with a brand story developed than with any real-world engagement.

The War on Terror brand was also used to build fellowship between Kerry and the Liberals of the larger Conservative-brand narrative. This is quite clear in the ad "Patriot Act" that opened with a mention of Bush's signing of the Patriot Act in order to show how the leadership and War on Terror aspects of brand W had been all about promises kept before highlighting Kerry's flip-flops by pointing out one of the security areas about which the audience cares deeply: "He voted for the Patriot Act, but pressured by fellow Liberals, he's changed his position."[7] This one sentence worked in the senator flip-flop aspect and began building a fellowship between Kerry and the Liberals. It closed by working to undermine Kerry's integrity by accusing him of "Playing politics with national security,"[8] a smart move given the personal traits aspect of brand W. It implied that Kerry was blindly ambitious yet too weak or unwilling to do what was necessary to win the War on Terror, unlike W. This spot likened the War on Terror to a battle against drug dealers and criminals in order to bring the contrasting brand aspects that it was promoting even closer to home for the audience.

The aspects of both brands that created the strong leader versus flip-flop contrast were repeatedly established by juxtaposing Kerry's voting record against a specific action that Bush had taken to fight the War on Terror. Kerry was branded as senator flip-flop by an emphasis on his Senate voting record on defense that included votes from the War on Terror era but, as we saw above, stretched back to the Cold War era. How exactly a war against terrorists on the ground would be conducted via the use of traditional military equipment is the kind of fact-based question that the use of brand strategy discourages the audience from considering. Kerry's voting record on unrelated defense issues was important because it offered visible proof that the senator flip-flop brand and the fellowship that the Bush team was building between him and the "liberals" of the core Conservative brand system were valid.[9] This, in turn, allowed the Bush team to tap into a long-running narrative in the brand stories that Conservatives had built for themselves and the Liberals in which Conservatives are for a strong national defense based on their support for huge defense budgets while Liberals, who have generally voted to fund defense at a lower level, have, as a result, shown a willingness to leave the nation undefended. One of the most prominent examples of this is provided by the battles that the Reagan administration had waged against a Congress controlled by Democrats at a time when more Americans were becoming more receptive to the Conservative message. The Bush team's presentation let it tap into the Reagan heritage brand in support of their candidate at the same time that it was able to build fellowship between Kerry and Reagan's Liberal opponents in Congress. The assertions being made by the Bush campaign were credible because W, like Reagan, favored a robust national defense as measured through bigger budgets and confrontation, while Kerry, like his fellow Liberals, favored a morally vacuous America dependent on the whims of foreigners to protect itself from harm. It was credible because it used Kerry's own words to make the point. This line of argument turned Kerry into a Liberal and a weak leader at the same time that it built fellowship between Bush and the Reagan heritage brand. Bush, like Reagan, would keep America safe while Kerry, like all Liberals, would leave it defenseless.

As had been the case at the convention, the flip-flop brand was created through repeated references to a single vote on a single bill, as well as Kerry's own statements that made the Bush team's assertions credible. We can see this in the ad "Troops=Fog of War," that opened with a voice-over emphasizing the importance of a well-armed military, then placed Kerry's vote into a favorable context for the Bush camp by saying that funding the troops was very important, then pointing out that Kerry voted for the war in Iraq, then voted against funding for the troops in order to reiterate the weak leader, flip-flop aspects of the brand being built around Kerry.[10] Kerry's fault was that he had failed to develop a countermessage to what Bush was putting forth.[11] The ad provided a dramatization of Kerry's voting record, first on body armor then on health care and combat pay increases for troops that featured a Senate clerk calling Kerry's name, a voice-over that said no, in response to mentions about body armor, higher pay for combat troops, and better health care for reservists. Making the audience aware of Kerry's votes on health care and pay was one way through which the Bush team worked to reduce the visibility of its man's own problematic record of support for the funding for current and past service personnel. The ad then used Kerry's own damning words "I actually did vote for the $87 billion before I voted against it,"[12] against him in order to validate Bush's closing assertion made orally and graphically that Kerry was "Wrong on defense"[13] and, by implication, that W was right on it.

Kerry had changed his votes on some areas for reasons to do with the way in which senate amending rules are written and contents of specific amendments to the body armor bill.[14] While Kerry tried to explain this, he did so in a way that sometimes gave credibility to what the Bush team was saying as he had done in the first place to answer a heckler at a West Virginia campaign event.[15] The other way in which the Bush camp worked to create the senator flip-flop brand was to present any vote against a defense bill that came up after 2002, as proof that Kerry was against a strong national defense, indecisive, dishonest, or all three. This contrast of the steady, ethical Bush versus the vacillating, liberal, dishonest Kerry formed the basis of the brand built around both candidates and with which, as we have seen throughout this work, Conservatives have been working for years. Some or all of these aspects appeared in the Bush national security and War on Terror ads.

While Bush may have flip-flopped in office as much as Kerry had in the Senate,[16] his campaign used the brand strategy to build a narrative based on a few Kerry votes and statements that it both repeated and linked to as many Kerry policy choices as it could. For example, in the ads that we have seen so far, issues were raised about Kerry's willingness to vote for military appropriation and domestic security measures but no mention was made for the rationale behind these requests by the candidate whose administration had made them nor was there a single explanation ever provided about the rationale for the War, Iraq's involvement in 9/11 or a number of other domestic and foreign policy issues.[17] Through the use of the brand strategy, the Bush team was able to put the focus on a couple of highly emotive Kerry votes. Kerry, in contrast, faced the problems that Democrats have faced since 1980 when facing branded Conservatives because he could not get the media to consistently focus on them. The Bush team could reach its audience with its message because of years of brand building activity. The brand that Bush built around Kerry defined him on security matters in a way that Kerry was not able to do to Bush because it tapped into years of Conservative brand building efforts.

The brand strategy used by the Bush team let it focus on narrow but emotive issues and isolated legislative votes as the brand strategy has let Conservatives do for the last two decades, while avoiding the larger issues.[18] Branding helped the Bush team present its actions since 9/11 as a piece called the War on Terror, avoid any serious culpability for the fact that 9/11 had happened at all, limited the damage to its candidate by the failure to find WMD in Iraq and Osama bin Laden anywhere. Building the brand narrative let the Bush team put the emphasis on specific aspects of both candidates and parties throughout the campaign. As a result, it became a contest between the Conservative brand and the Liberal brand that Conservatives have built about Democrats as much as it did between the specific brand aspects built by the Bush and Kerry campaigns.

In this campaign, the brand strategy let the Bush team turn the election into a contest between a strong leader and a vacillator, rather than one between an incompetent ideologue versus a man who had spent a lifetime competently serving his country. A spot entitled "100 Days,"[19] presented Americans with the impact Kerry's flip-flopping would almost immediately have on them. This was an introversion of a standard kind of ad run by challengers that encourage people to consider what life would be like if they changed horses. "100 Days" built a fellowship between Kerry and the tax-and-spend Liberals by noting the he would increase government spending, and to pay for that "raise taxes by at least $900 billion,"[20] and make Americans less safe because he would "Weaken the Patriot Act used to arrest terrorists and protect America."[21] In short, Kerry would raise taxes, increase spending, yet make the average voter less safe. In a clear effort to tap into the antipathy that exists toward the UN within the Conservative movement and brand story, Kerry, the ad states, "wanted to delay defending America until the United Nations approved."[22] This was an ad that Bush's economic and security audiences could love. It presents proof for the brand story that W had made the nation safer and had cut taxes at the same time that it suggested that Kerry would undo these things if elected. The effect was to show the audience that clear, important differences existed between the two candidates in a highly visible, emotive way that the brand strategy does. Because Kerry never offered the kind of succinct narrative that a brand can provide, it becomes clear why so many Americans believed the Bush team's assertions about their and Kerry's likely actions on security matters.

In addition to Kerry's voting record, the Bush team developed an aspect of the flip-flop brand based around the ideas that Kerry would change his mind when he could make it up at all and, even when he could, would change it again to score political points. Kerry was a prime target because of his Senate voting record, the institution's proclivity to analyze issues in depth, and his campaign's inability to stick to a single message in contrast to the Bush brand strategy. The Bush team's brand story worked, his campaign team argued because people believed it as "the popular perception is true."[23] Regarding Bush's "principles" on taxes and "confronting overseas threats" while Kerry's "maneuvering on Iraq and other issues"[24] caused doubts about his willingness to "stand steady for core beliefs."[25] In short, the Bush team branded itself and its opponent in a way that took advantage of extant public perceptions of their candidate, as well as the fact that the public was not well acquainted with Kerry and that his campaign was not built upon the decades of branding as was the Bush campaign.

Interestingly, the Kerry campaign was aware of the way in which the Bush team was building and repeating the flip-flop narrative from the earliest point of the campaign and even an awareness of how something similar had been done to Al Gore four years earlier regarding his ability to tell the truth yet "then as now blame the media for accepting and promoting a caricature."[26] This promotion of a caricature worked because it was, in reality, the promotion of a brand story, and the Democrats' response to it shows their ongoing failure to appreciate the brand strategy's impact on their electoral fortunes since 1964.

The attack on Kerry's ability to make up his mind and his honesty has been part of the GOP branding and positioning strategy toward Democrats for years. The senator flip-flop brand was effective because it was rooted in the Slick Willie and Al Gore as Internet inventor brand narratives from campaigns past.[27] The senator flip-flop brand resonated because it had been built over the life of the campaign and tapped into years worth of Conservative brand building activities. In September, a Pew Center Poll revealed that 53 percent of respondents felt that Kerry "changes his mind too much."[28] This had decreased since the convention infomercial but 62 percent of respondents said that the "attribute 'takes a stand'" applies more to Bush than to Kerry and Bush was seen by 57 percent of respondents as more deserving of the phrase "strong leader."[29] The brand that Conservatives were building around Kerry, that tapped into years of Conservative brand-building efforts was, in short, taking hold.

The creation of the flip-flop brand was a key to the Bush media strategy. Many of Bush's television and Internet spots either stated or implied that Kerry did not hold consistent positions. From the earliest, the Bush team worked to teach the audience that Kerry was weak on the truth as is clear in the ad script for "Tell the Truth"[30] in which Kerry is quoted as saying that he was going to do just that.[31] Kerry's claim to truthfulness was that he had not run negative ads in the primaries or early in the general election. The ad then graphically claimed that Kerry had released his first negative ad against Bush on September 3, 2003, then stated that 57 percent of Kerry's spots had "directly attacked the President."[32] It further argued that over 73 percent of the Kerry campaign ad budget had been used to fund such ads.[33] It then noted that Kerry had spent multimillions on negative spots that had been shown almost thirty thousand times.[34] The ad closed by restating Kerry's claim to truthfulness several times[35]and reiterated Kerry's claims to have run positive, not negative ads.[36]

As was done in the case of the body armor vote, Kerry's own words are used against him in this ad with ill-defined statistical data. The net effect was to seemingly show that, like Slick Willie and Al Gore, Kerry is not honest and, like them, will do anything to get ahead in contrast to the steady, honest Bush. An Internet ad, "Unprincipled Chapter One," used similar techniques to question Kerry's honesty and to depict him as a Washington insider. The ad visually opens with Kerry's name being typed into a search engine followed by a Kerry quote to the effect that "special interests and influence peddlers" would be leaving once Kerry came to power.[37] The ad's voice-over emphasized the words, "special interests" which was then typed into a search engine that returned an article from the *Washington Post,* to the effect that Kerry had "taken more special interest money than any other Senator"[38] thus giving the ad's pitch more credibility than if Bush's team alone had made it.

It then cited an amount of $640,000 for "paybacks" based on an Associated Press article that appeared in the *Kansas City Star.*[39] It referenced the Center for Public Integrity while its voice-over said "Brought to you by the special interests." Then it moved onto its punch line in which it directly attacked Kerry's integrity, as well as his ability to tell the truth about his own activities when it accused Kerry of taking large sums from "HMOs, telecoms, drug companies" and moved onto its tag line: "Ka-Ching! Unprincipled."[40] The flip-flop and dishonesty aspects of the Kerry brand were stressed in this case through reliance on independent sources, as well as through the use of a medium with which the audience could identify and probably used itself to do similar research. The Bush team used this ad to put Kerry on the defensive about fundraising but did so only in order to lend credibility to the brand story that it was telling about Kerry, and Conservatives have been telling about Democrats for the last two decades. The beauty of it is that as branding does for Conservatives, it encouraged the audience to look at Kerry's funding and sponsors but in no way encouraged a similar consideration about George W. Bush.

It was not just that Kerry could not make up his mind on foreign policy or had a hard time telling the truth, he also could not figure out what he wanted in domestic policy either. We can see this in a spot entitled "Medicare Hypocrisy"[41] that focused on Kerry's five votes to raise Medicare premiums, and called the passage of one such increase "a day of vindication." It then mentioned his missing 36 out of 38 roll call votes on Medicare in 2003 without mentioning the context of each vote except for one that touched on a Bush long suit, the provision of a drug benefit to seniors.[42] This time the ad applied the flip-flop brand to Medicare premiums.[43] Irrespective of the issue, the Kerry of the Bush brand story consistently voted for things only to change his mind later, thus proving that Kerry was too weak to be president or, even more conspiratorially, knew that if he told the truth to the voters, he would be defeated so like Slick Willie before him, he was waiting until after the election to spring his plans on the voters. Thus, the senator flip-flop brand played into the contrast that Conservatives have built since the Reagan campaigns of their candidates being straight-shooting everymen looking out for the interests of average folks like them versus the Liberals.

The Return of the Liberals

The Tax and Spend Liberals

Building fellowship between Kerry and the Liberal brand that Conservatives have built around Democrats was another important way that the Bush team employed the brand strategy to defeat Kerry. The Bush team built fellowship between Kerry and the Liberal brand via a general association between the two, as well as by linking the two with the tax issue and through the use of a kind of guilt by association to show that Kerry was simply another congressional Liberal seeking to moderate his image in order to win the White House. This brand and its tax aspect were used to differentiate the candidates, then position Bush favorably and Kerry negatively.

Kerry's intention to raise taxes was directly mentioned in a variety of Bush ads (by the author's count it was ten) and many of these also mentioned Kerry's allies in Congress, Liberals in Congress or both. The tax aspect of the Liberal brand was used to put Kerry squarely in the long line of Liberals who wanted to raise as many taxes as they could and the Bush team went to great lengths to show all of the ways in which Kerry would do so and what the impact of these increases would be as all branded Conservatives do.

An example is provided by the ad "Thinking Mom" that shows how the Bush team used the tax brand to try and reach the female-married-with-kids segment.[44] The ad opened with a mother getting groceries as part of a daily routine followed by an announcer claiming that Kerry and congressional Liberals "have voted to raise gas taxes ten times."[45] The ad included the commentary from the mother about the price of gas, a narrator reading a list of tax increases that included Social Security benefits, and 18 votes to increase taxes on "middle class parents" before mentioning an issue about which the target audience would care greatly—the marriage penalty.[46]

The ad closed with the radio voice-over claiming that the total number of tax increases was 350 and ended by restating the point that this was a result of Kerry and his fellow congressional Liberals.[47] The ad is obviously targeted at married women in general and socially Conservative married women in particular because of the way in which it brings taxes around to the idea of the marriage penalty. This ad puts the tax aspect of the Liberal brand into an emotive context with which its targets might identify, used statistics to provide credibility for and to make its points and we see how the brand strategy encourages voters to look at visible, emotive, matters instead of the root causes of problems. Instead of looking at the actual causes of gasoline price hikes, this ad lays them squarely at the feet of the Liberals who love to raise taxes.

A second example of the tax aspect in order to put Kerry squarely within the Liberal brand for this same audience is provided by the ad entitled "Clockwork."[48] This presents essentially the same points minus the female narrator, instead provides a total number of 350 votes to increase taxes or that, over twenty years, averaged out to one tax increase per three weeks.[49] The ad uses numbers to show that Kerry and his friends raise taxes like a clock ticks then moves onto make an implicit assumption that these specific tax increases have had negative effects on the economy without ever providing proof that they have done so. This is because the ad works on the tax cuts as an economy policy aspect of brand W that came straight out of the Reagan playbook when it said "John Kerry and the liberals in Congress on the economy . . . Troubling."[50] The high number of increases seems to provide proof that Liberals like to raise taxes, tax increases slow the economy, and that a vote for Kerry is a vote for Liberals and a vote for Liberals is a vote for tax increases and, by extension, a slow economy.

The idea that Kerry would raise taxes and that these increases would be bad for the economy allowed the Bush team to tap into the core aspects of the Conservative and Liberal brand stories on taxes that they have been using since the 1980s. An example of the way in which the Bush team incorporated these core brand aspects into its ads and the way in which they differentiate and position both parties' candidates is the ad "Economy: Common Sense versus Higher Taxes."[51]

This ad presents Bush and the congressional Republicans as having a "common sense" economic plan.[52] It works with the tax cuts as an economic policy, an idea that Conservatism stands for common sense in a way that has been in the movement's brand story since at least Reagan's mention of it in his Farewell Address.[53] This ad reiterates the same idea and notes all of the benefits that will flow from it. This is the way in which the Conservative branding has encouraged a focus on part of economic policy because taxation is not the only thing that decides if a company will expand or not and, unlike the argument made in this ad, the Bush tax cuts' benefits were skewed toward investors, not small-business people.[54]

Kerry, in contrast, is presented as a Congressional liberal who would enact policies that would increase taxes on small businesses whose owners would eventually pay "higher rates than most multi-national corporations."[55] The net effect of this was to visibly position Bush as an everyman on this topic about which people care so deeply. As noted earlier, Bush's gimmicky checks provided proof that the brand promise of tax cuts for all had been kept and his campaign had produced a highly visible, easily remembered running total of Kerry's votes to increase taxes. The ad implies that lower taxes would give people money for college (grants for which have been slashed in favor of loans since 1980), and that their upshot would be to create more jobs, even though the decline in hiring in the United States might have been caused by other things (e.g., outsourcing and automation). The Bush campaign presented tax cuts as the solution to economic difficulty as Conservatives have regularly done.

The ad argues that Kerry and his Liberal congressional friends generally favor higher taxes, on the targeted segment in particular, so much so that these hardworking everymen would pay more in taxes than the big boys.[56] Again, the alternative explanation that Conservatives quietly but consistently reduced taxes on multinationals to the point that these everymen now pay more, is not brought to the audience's attention. The visible proof of Kerry's illogical love of taxation is, of course, the increases that he and his Liberal friends passed on 900,000 small-business people but the definition of what constitutes a small business is vague as is the norm in branded politics.

Few Americans would have favored closing 900,000 small businesses or the job losses that would have ensued. To use statistics in this way in order to position Bush as favoring common sense and economic growth and Kerry as yet another Liberal built an advantageous contrast, as well as the core Conservative brand aspect of tax cuts as economic policy. Once it had introduced the Conservative and Liberal brand stories on taxation, the Bush team argued that, although Kerry promised that economic conditions would get better on his watch, they would actually decline due to the tax increases that his Liberalism would surely cause.

The ad's full-length version positioned, differentiated, and extended both candidates into the core brands that Conservatives have built about them. We can see this in the full-length version of the same ad that restated the claims of the above ad before closing with the core Conservative brand aspects about taxation and Liberals as it said: "Tax increases would hurt jobs, hurt small business, and hurt our economy" and presented a graphic reading "Liberals in Congress and Kerry's Plan: Higher Taxes, Hurt Our Economy." Given that it had opened by claiming "President Bush and our leaders in Congress have a common sense plan . . . To grow our economy . . . ," we can see how this ad positions both candidates and both parties on these issues.[57] As a result, we can see why those audiences that were predisposed toward voting for Bush would do so, even if they were concerned about the U.S. economy's overall performance because now they had someone to blame other than the administration in office. That earlier Liberal, Slick Willie, had caused the recession that Bush's tax cuts cleaned up, much as Reagan's had cleaned up the Carter recession. Were John Kerry to win the White House, the same downward cycle would doubtlessly repeat itself.

Other Bad Liberal Things

By building fellowship between Kerry and the Liberal brand, the Bush team was able to turn the election into a broader, more emotive contest than a simple battle over its man's record in office would have allowed. This election became a comparison compaign—and the way in which the Conservative movement saw the world and saw its opponents as a result, gave George W. Bush the same strategic advantage that Conservatives have enjoyed over their Democratic rivals for the last 30 years. The Liberals and their bad values appeared justified for a variety of political products, many of them as branded as was the candidate promoting them, in Bush's advertising.

The first example is provided by the ad "Tort Reform,"[58] in which the assertions made by the Bush campaign are buttressed by a testimonial from Dr. Patricia Stephenson claiming that a national healthcare crisis exists. A voice-over then tells us that this is the result of "frivolous lawsuits." Not surprisingly, the ad tells the audience that this frivolity is allowed to continue in our courts because Kerry and his congressional Liberal friends are on the side of trial lawyers and, as result, opposed reforming the legal system on ten occasions. This ad never stated what the impact of these legal reforms would really be or which industries would actually benefit by their enactment and, as we saw earlier in this work, many of those are not nearly as wholesome as are ob/gyns.[59] It simply presented the family audience target with a representative of an industry about which most of them probably held highly favorable feelings in order to make its point.

In a culture in which million-dollar verdicts for burns from coffee cups that spilled have become legends, the Conservative brand story offers the voters a highly visible, emotive solution to these highly visible, emotive problems. The movement's marketing points out how Liberals block the commonsense reforms being proposed by Conservatives and show how the innocent suffer as a result. A second example is provided by the ad "Med Mal" in which a narrator tells us that the "out of control" lawyers with whom John Kerry and the congressional Liberals side, is proven by their ten votes to change the way in which medical malpractice lawsuits, herein termed "medical lawsuit reform."[60] The net effect to the audience, it asserts, is longer waiting lists, the loss of doctors, and the availability of fewer services.[61]

These two spots show how the Conservatives took their overall brand stories about themselves and about Liberals and made them relevant to their current product, as well as that being sold by the Democrats. In the Bush narrative about Kerry and the congressional Liberals, it was as if the 1994 election that gave Republicans control of both houses of Congress had never taken place and that these Liberals still had the chance to pass their agenda wholesale through Congress. This is typical of branded politics because it shows that only the facts matter in-so-far as they are packaged into a coherent story that the public can understand and that supports the product being promoted.

Everyman Rides Again: The Good Guy Versus Not One of Us

While George W. Bush dealt with the issues of economy and Iraq in a way that served his interest, consistent with the marketing literature, he moved off these topics whenever possible. His campaign tried to talk about subjects that would position it both favorably vis-à-vis Kerry, and to fire up its audience as we have seen throughout this work. The Bush team stayed off these difficult issues by placing emphasis on their man's and Kerry's personal traits, as well as the values issues that are very much a part of the core Conservative brand story. Most of Bush's early ads were positive biographical spots, two examples of which are provided by "Lead" and "Safer and Stronger" The former features George and Laura Bush that stressed family, entrepreneurship, education, and Social Security. The ad spoke about Bush's leadership trait when it said that he saw the importance of entrepreneurship. It followed it up with a mention of personal traits by Laura Bush that also contrasted with those of Slick Willie: "strength" and "focus" before she noted that her husband had "the characteristics that these times demand."[62] Laura Bush's line stresses the values theme that resonates with Republicans and created a contrast with Slick Willie's unpredictable behavior and senator flip-flop's uncertain decision-making skills. The President discussed substantive issues in a way that played up the leadership aspects of the brand being built by his campaign by saying that he knew "exactly where I want to lead this country" and that he knew what needed to be done to grow the economy, raise educational standards, and to "fulfill the promise to America's Seniors."[63] After pointing out the leadership aspect of his personal traits, he closed with a set of flourishes to set up the campaign's optimism versus pessimism contrast that came straight from the Reagan playbook. It termed Americans as a "hard working, decent, generous people" and closed with Bush noting that this was the cause of his optimism about the country.[64] This ad was translated into Spanish signaling the onset of what would prove to be a successful outreach to Hispanic voters.

In fact, one of the other opening ads paid homage to the Reagan ad "Morning Again in America."[65] Because Conservatives had spent so much effort on brand building, they could easily swap one candidate for another and one ad for another. This ad was entitled "Safer, Stronger,"[66] and was the opening salvo of the repositioning of brand W that took full flower at the convention. It is also another case of the Conservatives using branding to blunt the fact-based charges made by their opponents. As we saw earlier, this ad made clear that Bush had cleaned up an inherited/terrorist attack-fueled recession before incorporating the Reagan passage when it said that the country was "turning the corner"[67] much as Reagan's media had spoken about America being back in 1984.[68] It used the words "Safer, Stronger," then closed by emphasizing the steadiness of Bush's leadership.[69] This emphasis shows how early in its campaign the Bush team was both repositioning its own brand and presenting its brand about Kerry. A third spot, "Tested," did much as "Safer, Stronger" had done and branded Conservatives have done since Reagan to play up patriotic themes and at the same time place the blame for all problems elsewhere.

The ad entitled "Tested" incorporated the Conservative brand story with its emphasis on "Freedom, faith, families, and sacrifice."[70] These have been the core aspects of the Conservative brand since, at least, 1980 and are the essence of the value-based contrast that they have established with their Liberal brand. As such, their use here represents an attempt to appeal to the core audience for the Conservative message. In the initial Bush foray, we see a candidate who is presenting himself within a specific tradition, as guardian of the country's security and values, and as a strong leader in a difficult time. "Tested" closed with the same emphasis on the steadiness of Bush's leadership traits in difficult times.

The everyman aspect of Bush in 2004 mirrored the same aspect that has been in the Conservative brand since Reagan. In this campaign Bush is projected as an everyman. The everyman persona is important to branded Conservatives, especially to those from patrician backgrounds like George W. Bush, because they help the candidate say to the audience "I am like you," even if this is not actually true. The trick to employing the everyman aspect of the brand is to visibly appear to be like the average voter as Ronald Reagan was able to do. George W. Bush, as he had done in 2000, again played the everyman role to the hilt. In contrast to Kerry, Bush used the everyman aspect of the Conservative brand to present himself as an average guy who cared about the things that average people cared about much as Reagan had. Much was made, for example, about Bush's love for major league baseball, a sport that millions of average people care about. The Bush team used its media efforts, stump speech, convention and debate infomercials and viral efforts to distribute the everyman aspect of W and, by doing so, to place him in a specific Conservative tradition. Simply stated, they showed that W was another average guy pitted against another Liberal who was not like average voters.

Bush on the Stump

As we briefly saw in the last chapter, the brand strategy has not diminished the need for stump speeches. The stump speech is more important in the branded strategy because it lets people see the product firsthand and decide if the brand promises are being kept, can generate free media and impressions for the brand, can recruit volunteers as the Bush team did in 2004, and can serve, as brands do for franchise businesses, to provide local politicians with a ready-made identity. This section looks at three Bush stump speeches, one given just after the DNC, one in October just before the debates, and one at the end of October. The speech evolved as it came to focus on those elements of brand W and senator Flip-flop that were selling well with the voters at any given time, as well as because it "rode the wave" to incorporate newsworthy issues in order to assure press coverage.[71]

The July speech kicked off the campaign's "Heartland of America" tour. It opened by sharpening the differences between the two candidates in terms of taxes, national security, and values:

> There will be big differences in this campaign. They're going to raise your taxes, we're not. I have a clear vision on how to win the war on terror and bring peace to the world. They somehow believe the heart and soul of America can be found in Hollywood. The heart and soul of America is found right here in Springfield, Missouri.[72]

This opening works in the Liberal and War on Terror brands in order to put W's branded products fully into the Conservative line and Kerry's firmly in the Liberal campaign. Bush sold his softer side by mentioning his wife as the best reason for voting for him "perhaps the most important reason of all is so that Laura will be first lady for four more years."[73] Bush used a local example to remind the audience about his position on value-based issues and to show that his 2000 brand promise had been kept:

> I met a fellow named Charlie Graas. He's a volunteer with Stone County food pantry. Let me tell you why I mention him. The strength of America is in the hearts and souls of our citizens, people who are willing to feed the hungry, provide shelter for the homeless, love a neighbor in need. "Charlie, thank you for being an army—a soldier in the army of compassion." [74]

The above has the added impact of playing up Bush's everyman aspect. Having done that, Bush moved onto the central selling proposition of his campaign and core of his brand story:

> Every incumbent who asks for the vote has to answer one question: Why? Why
> should the American people give me the great privilege of serving as your presi-
> dent for four more years? In the past few years, we've been through a lot together.
> We've accomplished a great deal. But there's only one reason to look backward
> at the record, and that is to determine who best will lead the nation forward. I'm
> asking for your vote because so much is at stake: prosperity and peace. We have
> so much more to do to move this country forward. Give me four more years, and
> America will continue to march toward peace and better prosperity. I'm asking
> for four more years to make our country safer, to make the economy stronger,
> to make our future better and brighter for every single citizen. From creating jobs
> to improving schools, from fighting terror to protecting our homeland, we have
> made much progress, and there is more to do.[75]

The pitch is filled with references to the campaign's brand story and came
with a laundry list of accomplishments to show that its 2000 promises had
been kept but also gave the audience a sense of why sending him back to DC
was important. All of which is to say that the brand strategy depends on
repetition in all kinds of media and at all kinds of events in order to be well
executed. As it did throughout the campaign, the Bush message was that the
economy problems that had plagued the country during his administration
were the fault of someone or something other than the administration: "We
have more to do to make America's economy stronger. We've come through
a recession, terrorist attacks, corporate scandals."[76] At the same time, the thing
that was presented as the solution to these problems was the tax cuts as economic policy aspect:

> We gave tax relief to every American who pays taxes. We didn't play favorites
> with the tax code. We didn't try to pick winners or losers. We made sure families
> with children and married couples and small businesses got tax relief. And this time
> the check really was in the mail.[77]

The last point was both a direct swipe at the broken 1992 Clinton promise
and a reminder to them that brand W had kept its promise. Plus, this broad
statement covers all of the portions of the electorate that the Bush team was
trying to attract but, consistent with the brand strategy, avoided discussing
the way in which the specific policy mentioned actually operated. Bush again
gave the tax cuts credit for having solved the nation's economic problems,
only this time, he did it with the highly visible employment statistics that resonate with the audience, then produced three testimonials from two local
people who represented the above-mentioned families with children and
small-business owners to prove his point. Both claimed that the money that
they had received from the tax cuts had been put to good use. Such endorse-

ments by friends and neighbors are an important way to build a connection between the branded product and the average voter.

When Bush moved into national security policy and the War on Terror brand, he did so by making use of the contrast techniques that are a core part of the Conservative marketing playbook. This time Bush contrasted the pre- and post-9/11 worlds in order to make the circumstantial case for invading Iraq that he would make a month later in New York and, at that event, used the disarmament of Libya as proof that his policies were working, declared the Afghan War a success, and showed how women were better off to both prove his point and pitch this audience. He also noted that Pakistan was no longer a transit point for terror and moved on to an explanation of his rationale for the Iraq War that emphasized the strong leadership aspect of brand W:

> After September the 11th, we cannot fail to imagine that a brutal tyrant, who hated America, who had ties to terror, had weapons of mass destruction and might use those weapons or share his deadly capability with terrorists was not a threat. We looked at the intelligence. We saw a threat. Members of the United States Congress from both political parties, including my opponent, looked at the intelligence and they saw a threat. We went to the United Nations, which unanimously demanded a full accounting of Saddam Hussein's weapons programs or face serious consequences. After 12 years of defiance, he refused to comply with the demands of the free world. When he continued to deceive the weapons inspectors, I had a decision to make: to hope for the best and to trust the word of a madman and a tyrant, or remember the lessons of September the 11th and defend our country. Given that choice, I will defend America every time.[78]

This is the same pitch that Bush made at the debates and convention, right down to the tag line "Given that choice, I will defend America every time."[79] He moved on to stress the strong leader aspect of brand W, argued for his foreign policy, then discussed its coalitional nature without mentioning the actual contributions made by U.S. partner states in Iraq as a deflective strategy and saluted the troops. In short, he followed the brand story outlined in the memo that we saw in the previous chapter.

Bush raised the senator flip-flop brand by noting Kerry's vote on the body armor bill. At that point, Bush brought up the senator flip-flop brand as expressed through the vote, listing a bit more of its favorable contents and closing with the kind of positioning point that Conservatives have been making since the Reagan years and which Gingrich perfected in 1994 in selling the Contract with America as he said, "In the Senate, only a handful of what I would call 'out of the mainstream' folks'—that would be 12 senators—voted against that legislation. Two of the 12 are my opponent and his running mate."[80] By positioning Kerry and Edwards as being out of mainstream, Bush could show the voters that they were not like them, thus reinforcing the elitist aspect of the Liberal brand. After the obligatory audience participation in the form of booing, Bush reiterated the campaign's senator flip-flop slogan as he said: "He tried to explain his vote by saying, "I actually did vote for the $87 billion before I voted against it," before moving onto note that Kerry had even flip-flopped about his explanation of his flip-flop as Bush said "He's got a different explanation now. One time he said he was proud he voted against the funding. Then he said the whole thing was a complicated matter."[81] Thus, not only was Kerry a flip-flopper, the Bush brand story positioned him as not being able to understand obvious items such as the troops needing to be properly equipped to work but, as is always the case in branded politics, Bush never pointed out who had committed the troops to Iraq without the proper equipment in the first place.

"Complicated plan" was also the title of a Bush television ad, thus showing how the brand strategy depends on a set of coordinated messages across media to succeed. "There is nothing complicated about supporting our troops in combat."[82] This statement's closing line reinforced the contrast between senator flip-flop and the strong leadership aspect of brand W. Bush finished his speech by reiterating the fellowship that his campaign was building between Kerry and the tax-and-spend Liberals, referenced the reformer with results brand aspect from his 2000 campaign, worked in the ownership society and life brands, and took another page from the 1994 Contract campaign by positioning Kerry as a man of Washington in contrast to brand W's and Conservatism's populist individuality. This speech let Bush practice with the repositioned brand W story before the September infomercial, to reemphasize the brand stories that the campaign was building around Kerry and to present him as simply the latest product from the Liberal brand.

Later in the campaign, Bush's speech changed to feature more direct attacks on Senator Kerry. Bush, for example, stressed the strong leader versus flip-flopper and War on Terror brand stories when he said on October 6, in Wilkes-Barre, that Kerry would lessen the country's strength and the world's safety.[83] He did so by arguing that Iraq:

> is necessary and right and critical to the outcome of the war on terror. If another terror regime were allowed to emerge in Iraq, the terrorists would find a home, a source of funding, vital support. They would correctly conclude that free nations do not have the will to defend themselves."[84]

This is, as we saw earlier, one of the key aspects of the Iraq line extension to the War on Terror brand. Bush used this to position Kerry in a way that shifted the public discussion from Bush's decision to send troops to Iraq to one involving Kerry's Senate voting record.[85] It was, then, hardly coincidental that Bush made these arguments on the day after a report showing that Iraq possessed no WMD when the war was launched, was issued or that it was given only a few days before the presidential debates.[86]

Bush used the brand strategy as Conservatives do to create favorable positions and contrasts but also to shift the media's and public's consideration of an issue onto friendly ground. In this case, he did it by arguing that Kerry's voting record showed that he was weak in his support for the military and weak on his commitment to the War on Terror generally and in the War in Iraq particularly.[87] Doing so was clearly an effort to work with the War on Terror brand but also to place Kerry firmly within the weak-on-defense aspect of its Liberal brand and, by doing so, play up the strong leader aspect of brand W and put it within the core Conservative brand story regarding security. Bush used Kerry's opposition to his Iraq policy as proof of his claims and went further into the weak Liberal aspect of the national security brand when he said:

> Senator Kerry assures us that he's the one to win a war he calls a mistake, an error, and a diversion. But you can't win a war you don't believe in fighting. (Applause.) In Iraq, Senator Kerry has a strategy of retreat; I have a strategy of victory.[88]

This is exactly the way in which Conservatives like to use differentiation and contrast techniques as we have seen throughout the work. As he did during the debates, Bush brought up Kerry's notion of a global test:

> My opponent has also announced the Kerry doctrine, declaring that American actions in the war on terror must pass a "global test." Under this test, America would not be able to act quickly against threats, because we'd be sitting around waiting for our grade from other nations and other leaders. I have a different view: America will always work with allies for security and peace. But the President's job is not to pass a global test; the President's job is to protect the American people.[89]

Bush through this passage has reiterated the leadership contrast around both candidates with which it had been working all fall. Thus, the choice these contrasting brand aspects offered was between an unfettered leader looking out for America and a weak-kneed, retreating, Liberal who was dependent on the rest of the world's approval to defend the country. This is the branded contrast with which the Bush campaign worked throughout 2004 and Conservatives have worked on security matters since 1980.

Bush made this contrast clear that Kerry "approaches the world with a September the 10th mind-set,"[90] linked that to Slick Willie's foreign policy and tried to shift blame for the 9/11 attacks to Clinton by saying "That was the mind-set of the 1990s, while Al Qaeda was planning the attacks on America."[91] Further, strong leader W told his audience "Senator Kerry is proposing policies and doctrines that would weaken America and make the world more dangerous,"[92] and used 9/11 to set the context for the brand story that he was telling. As noted in the prior chapter: "After September the 11th, our object in the war on terror is not to wait for the next attack and respond but to prevent attacks by taking the fight to the enemy."[93] All of this fits the brand aspect about each candidate that the Bush team was promoting and which the Conservative movement has promoted about itself and the Liberals over the last thirty years. Thus, it should not be surprising that Bush kept talking about these same subjects in the same way on all of his travels that day.[94] By pointing to this, Bush generated impressions for his brand and educated the public about why their best choice was his reelection to the White House if they cared about safety from terrorism.

The October speech opened with a reference to average people in the audience, issued the call for volunteers that was part of the viral campaign, as well as the softer side of Bush, before moving onto a reference to the "Safer, Stronger" leadership aspect that had been on display at the convention and in commercials for months.[95] He did so by emphasizing his personal traits, past promises kept, and likely future performance:

> Senator Kerry is proposing policies that would weaken America and make the world more dangerous. As your president, I've worked to make America a more hopeful and more secure place. I've led our country with principle and resolve. And that's how I will lead our nation for four more years.[96]

After showing how he had generally kept his promises and would do so again, he restated the tax cuts as economy policy and solution to the Clinton recession aspects of brand W. He made reference to the economic situation that he had inherited in a way that was consistent with the campaign's media advertising, especially the "Safer, Stronger" ad:

> when I took office in 2001, the bubble of the '90s had burst, our economy was headed into recession. And because of the attacks of September the 11th, nearly a million jobs were lost in three months.[97]

Having established that others had caused the economic mess, Bush presented his tax cuts as their solution and did so by referencing a statistic regarding job creation. Again, because of the way in which branded politics works, there is no mention that many economists argued that this figure represented a significant underperformance by the U.S. economy during that period.[98] This was the argument being made by the campaign's brand story and it was being made consistently in all of the campaign's media.

Bush reiterated the safer, more hopeful aspect of the country under brand W's stewardship. In this speech he spoke more about his domestic policy agenda than he had in the speech above and argued that his ideas were perfectly suited for a country in flux and moved into archetypal branding when he noted that his overall goal was to ensure the American dream's possibility for most citizens.[99] His message on taxes, jobs, lawsuits, and regulation was that of two months ago and the core Conservative brand story. In this case, he directly built fellowship between Kerry and the Liberals on these issues by saying:

> My opponent and I have a very different view on how to grow our economy. . . . Let me start with taxes. I have a record of reducing them. He has a record of raising them. He's voted in the United States Senate to increase taxes 98 times. That's a lot. (LAUGHTER) He voted for higher taxes on Social Security benefits. In 1997, he voted for the formula that helped cause the increase in Medicare premiums. My opponent was against all of our middle class tax relief. He voted instead to squeeze another $2,000 per year from the average middle class family. Now the senator's proposing higher taxes on more than 900,000 small-business owners. He says the tax increase is only for the rich. You've heard that kind of rhetoric before. The rich hire lawyers and accountants for a reason—to stick you with the tab.[100]

This rhetoric mirrors the content of several Bush television ads that are presented elsewhere in this text and is consistent with the contrasting brand stories about taxes with which Republicans like to work. The tax claims fit a brand strategy because they provide the consumer with highly visible, highly emotive points. In the above, Bush showed that Kerry was a serial tax increaser, who would vote to tax popular middle-class entitlements and, in fact, had voted to raises taxes on middle-class people, many of whom were small-business owners before closing with a line calculated to produce an emotive response.

As is typical of branded politics, the full facts of the matter are often a different matter. In this case Bush had made a number of misleading charges,[101] but they could not be visibly and definitively discredited and, as long as that was so, such charges are typical of what is presented in a brand story. Because Conservatives have worked with the tax and Liberal brands for so long they had gained considerable equity and credibility with the audience and, because

Kerry had said that he was going to raise somebody's taxes, it was no problem for the audience to believe that Kerry was what the Bush brand story was claiming he was.

Bush reworked the tort reform brand to include the Democratic association with Washington that was noted above, argued in another homage to the contract with America that Kerry opposed "reform" and more of the brand narrative that Conservatives have built around trial lawyers, a major Democratic donor group, in recent years:

> The senator and I have different views on another threat to our economy—frivolous lawsuits. He's been a part of the Washington crowd that has obstructed legal reform again and again. Meanwhile, all across America unfair lawsuits are hurting small businesses. Lawsuits are driving up health care costs. Lawsuits are threatening OB/GYNs all across our country. Lawsuits are driving good doctors out of practice. (APPLAUSE) We need a president who will stand up to the trial lawyers in Washington, not put one on the ticket. (APPLAUSE)[102]

While the last line was a swipe at Kerry's running mate capable of showing that Kerry really was beholden to them, the passage simply restated the campaign's brand story, albeit in a way that was aimed at tapping into the feelings the audience held for the archetypal Conservative brand. On health care, Bush worked to build fellowship between Kerry and the archetype of the Slick Willie years, Hillary and her health insurance plan in exactly the way that Conservatives had campaigned against it contemporaneously. Conservatives, at the time, noted that people would lose insurance, government would expand, and patient choice would be limited. Bush made exactly these points:

> The senator and I have very different views on health care. . . . He has a different vision. Under his health plan, 8 million Americans would lose the private insurance they get at work and most would end up on a government program. Under his plan, eight out of 10 people who get new insurance will get it from the federal government. My opponent's proposal would be the largest expansion of government-run health care ever. And when government pays the bills, government makes the rules. His plan would put bureaucrats in charge of dictating coverage, which could ration care and limit your choice of doctor. Senator Kerry's proposal would put us on the path to Clinton care. I'll make sure doctors and patients are in charge of the decisions in America's health care.[103]

Given the highly visible, highly emotive way in which Bush weaved his tale, it represents another use of the brand strategy and as such it shared the distortions endemic to branded politics as Bush argued that Kerry would implement "Clinton Care," even though, Kerry had claimed no such thing.[104]

As is typical of branded politicians, Bush claimed that Kerry wanted to spend an additional $2 trillion without mentioning his own plans, before building fellowship between Kerry and the congressional Liberals by presenting his voting record to prove the point, as well as by linking Kerry with an individual whom Conservatives have branded: Ted Kennedy. Bush belittled Kerry's legislative accomplishments but never mentioned that for most of his service he was either a very junior member or in the minority as is common when faced with a legislative opponent by saying "Of the hundreds of bills he submitted, only five became law. One of them was ceremonial"[105] before showing his audience that Kerry's real accomplishment was to be named by the *National Journal* as "the most liberal member of the United States Senate. And when the competition includes Ted Kennedy, that's really saying something."[106] The fellowship building with Kennedy was, as we have seen throughout the work, an effort to present Kerry as a Liberal and, given that the Kennedy brand includes morally questionable and elitist behavior, as being not like average Americans in personality or behavior while the mention of the source was an obvious effort to give the claim stronger credentials than it would have had simply coming from a presidential candidate.

Bush combined the contrasts and brand stories that he was working to create together in the following passage by saying: cemented the fellowship between Kerry's voting record, Kennedy, the hostile Washington brand and the tax brand by saying:

> I'm telling you, I know that bunch. It wasn't easy for my opponent to become the single most liberal member of the Senate. You might even say it was hard work. (APPLAUSE) But he earned that title by voting for higher taxes, more regulation, more junk lawsuits and more government control over your life. (APPLAUSE) My opponent wants to empower government. I want to use government to empower people. My opponent seems to think all the wisdom is found in Washington, D.C. I trust the wisdom of the American people.[107]

This is the brand story that Conservatives used in 1980, used in 1994, and used again in 2004 to brand their opponents of the time as being Liberals who were in no way like average Americans. This is, in short, the brand story out of which Conservatives have built an electoral majority and as this cycle's higher-profile events and "time for choosing" to use Ronald Reagan's words approached, it should not be surprising that Bush made more frequent use of it.

As in the entire campaign, national security policy was the major thrust of this speech. Bush laid out the strong leader versus flip-flop contrasting brand aspects, in this case using the Patriot Act to prove his stories by saying

"Law enforcement intelligence have better tools to stop terrorists thanks to the Patriot Act, which Senator Kerry voted for, but now wants to weaken."[108] In this quote, Bush worked with the senator flip-flop brand but did so by using an issue other than the vote on body armor to show that Kerry was indecisive in general just as the Liberals always are in the Conservative brand story. Following this, Bush rehashed the brand story of the War on Terror and its successes, as well as the justification for the Iraq War that had been rolled out during the early part of the campaign, then moved on to mention the campaign's closing theme "Freedom is on the March" when he said: "America is always more secure when freedom is on the march. And freedom is on the march in Afghanistan and Iraq and elsewhere."[109] This theme summed up the optimism versus pessimism and strong leader versus flip-flop contrasting brand aspects that the campaign had been promoting, as well as to provide a narrative justification of the best defense is a good offense foreign policy that the Bush team had enacted and was incorporated in a big way into its brand story. We can see how Bush linked up the archetypal Liberal brand with the senator flip-flop brand with which his campaign was working when he referenced the presidential debates:

> My opponent agrees with all this except when he doesn't. (LAUGHTER) Last week in our debate, he once again came down firmly on every side of the Iraq war. He stated that Saddam Hussein was a threat and that America had no business removing that threat.[110]

Bush ran through the litany of accusations that we saw above, then summed up their meaning for his audience when he said:

> Now, he's changed his mind. (LAUGHTER) No, he has, in all fairness. But it is a window into his thinking. Over the years, Senator Kerry has looked for every excuse to constrain America's action in the world. These days he praises America's broad coalition in the Gulf War, but in 1991 he criticized those coalition members as, quote, shadow battlefield allies who barely carry a burden. Sounds familiar. At that time he voted against the war. If that coalition didn't pass his global test clearly nothing will.[111]

The Bush team had made a television advertisement that made the same points that Bush made here and, the beauty of both was that they used Kerry's own words to make their points and, as a result, this increased their claims' credibility.

Kerry had made the remark in the presidential debate that was held on September 30 and the Bush campaign seized on it by moving it out of the context in which his prior remarks were made in which Kerry was arguing for a multilateral foreign policy. Karl Rove, upon hearing Kerry, make this statement "exulted"[112] because "he could visualize TV commercials that could be fed to Red State Americans who were suspicious of the United Nations and regarded Kerry as vaguely French."[113] The decontextualized quote suggested that Kerry would wait to defend America until others approved and, given the antipathy toward the UN and some European states (especially France) that is part of the archetypal Conservative brand, we can see why this highly visible quote would produce such an emotive response from Bush's audience targets.

Bush similarly appealed to the core Conservative audience by noting another proposal that would limit American sovereignty: the International Criminal Court and his opposition to the ratification of the treaty that would subject the United States to its jurisdiction. He then tried to resurrect the Coalition of the Willing brand by providing examples of service by Polish, Italian, and British troops, as is consistent with the emotive, visible approach of the brand strategy.[114] This kind of appeal encourages people to think about the sacrifices made by individuals in the war and, as a result, is trying to produce a sympathetic set of feelings within the audience instead of the factual analysis that Kerry's successful recitation of contributions had accomplished earlier in the campaign.

Bush used a common product marketing strategy to point out that almost all of the features of foreign policy that Kerry was promising to bring to office, Bush was already implementing as the "Bush Plan."[115] After flipping some of Kerry's criticism on the Iraq War back at him, Bush asserted that he alone had a plan for victory. He did so by using phraseology that closely mirrored the name of another Bush television ad before again presenting the brand story about the Iraq War first in the kind of terms that resonate with the religious Conservatives when he said: "We're in Iraq because I deeply believe it is necessary and right and critical,"[116] he then noted its importance in winning the Terror War because otherwise, as product marketers do to sharpen the consumer's focus, very bad things would ensue. Given that Kerry was proposing a different Iraq policy, a vote for Kerry could be understood in this narrative to mean a vote for bad things:

> If another terror regime were allowed to emerge in Iraq, the terrorists would find a home, a source of funding, vital support. They would correctly conclude that free nations do not have the will to defend themselves. If Iraq becomes a free society at the heart of the Middle East, an ally in the war on terror, a model of hopeful reform in a region that needs hopeful reform, the terrorists will suffer a

crushing defeat and every free nation will be more secure.[117]

Additionally, reiterating this story was a way to remind people of what their position on it had been the first time that they had heard and was a way of helping them to decide if they like the president enough to go out and vote for him as was consistent with the Bush strategy to dig deeper into its best segments.

He followed this up with endorsements from others; in this case, a Democrat and the leader of the British Labor Party—Senator Joe Lieberman and British Prime Minister Tony Blair. Both had stressed the importance of winning the Iraq War, had placed it within the context of the wider War on Terror brand story and were members of parties with which the Liberals of the Conservative brand story were associated, reiterating the "it's ok to switch because this issue is so important" aspect of the Convention brand story. After mentioning the endorsements, Bush then raised the stakes of the conflict and reiterated the strong leader aspect of brand W: "Iraq is no diversion. It is the place where civilization is taking a decisive stand against chaos and terror. And we must not waver."[118] This set an unfavorable choice between wavering and causing chaos to win out or staying and winning the War on Terror at the same time that it reintroduced senator flip-flop to the discussion. He did so, as had been done throughout the campaign by mentioning Kerry's body armor vote and his overall voting record to play up the weakness aspect of the flip-flop brand:

> Unfortunately, my opponent has been known to waver. His well-chosen words and rationalizations cannot explain why he voted to authorize force against Saddam Hussein and then voted against money for bullets, and vehicles and body armor for the troops on the ground. He tried to clear it all up by saying, I actually did vote for the $87 billion before I voted against it. (LAUGHTER) Now he says he "made a mistake" in how he talked about the war. The mistake here is not what Senator Kerry said; the mistake is what he did in voting against funding for Americans in combat. (APPLAUSE) That is the kind of wavering a nation at war can never afford. As a candidate, my opponent promises to defend America. The problem is that the senator, for two decades, he has built a record of weakness. The record shows he twice led efforts to gut our intelligence service budgets. The record shows he voted against many of the weapons that won the Cold War, and are vital to current military operations. And the record shows he has voted more than 50 times against missile defense systems that would help protect us from the threats of a dangerous world.[119]

In this paragraph Bush tried to point out the difference between loquacity and deeds in order to implant the idea that Kerry was willing to say whatever was popular at the moment in order to get elected. Bush would, of course, do nothing of the sort and he showed this by once again working in reference to his appearance at the World Trade Center just after 9/11: "I have a record in office, as well and all Americans have seen that record. On September the 14th, 2001, I stood in the ruins of the Twin Towers. It's a day I will never forget. There were workers in hard hats yelling at me, "whatever it takes."[120] In this passage, Bush plays up the strong leader aspect of brand W by using a highly visible, highly emotive event to show his audience that what is being said about both candidates is true.

Bush closed his speech with a recitation of his and Senator Kerry's records. The speech closes with an almost exact duplication of the closing campaign television advertisement "The Choice." Given that it takes a large number of impressions to build brand awareness, this is not surprising.[121] First, he presented Kerry as weak on national defense in a way that played up the Clinton role in 9/11, Kerry's voting record and affiliation with the Liberals and the kind of internationalism that is anathema in the Conservative brand story:

> My opponent offers an agenda that is stuck in the thinking and the policies of the past. On national security, he offers the defensive mindset of September the 10th: a global test to replace American leadership, a strategy of retreat in Iraq and a 20-year history of weakness in the United States Senate.[122]

Such an appeal had tremendous potential to move a Conservative voter from a passive to an active stance in support of Bush and to raise the stakes in the election to a contest between a strong and a weak leader on a single issue in order to appeal to a number of other audience segments. Bush wanted to leave his audience with a favorable impression of the branded product being promoted. He did so by first mentioning the strong leader aspect of brand W when he said, "The race for president is a contest for the future, and you know where I stand."[123] This is an obvious contrast to senator flip-flop's leadership style and he worked in the memo, mentioned in the prior chapter, to say "I'm running for president to keep this nation on the offensive against terrorists, with the goal of total victory"[124] and by doing so set up a contrast between the strong leader and flip-flopper-brand aspects.

We can see how the choice set up by this statement between a retreating flip-flopper and a leader that envisions total victory might help clarify an undecided voter's choices and spur the inactive Conservative to become active. His economic pitch included the points that he would "keep this economy moving so every worker has a good job and quality health care and a secure retirement."[125] These are a branded pitch because they play up highly visible, highly emotive policies yet make no mention of how the free trade, free market, less government, and lower tax policies implemented by Conservatives from Reagan and thereafter have placed these things in jeopardy.[126] Bush then worked in the compassionate Conservative brand from 2000 and the prolife aspect of the core Conservative brand when he said that he was running "to make our nation a more compassionate society, where no one is left out, where every life matters."[127] By closing with this, Bush reminded his audience why they were Conservatives and why they had voted for him in 2000.

A comparison of these speeches shows more use of the archetypal Conservative brand and showed Bush much more on offense in the second than in the first. Bush spoke more frequently about the aspects of brand W that his campaign would be presenting at the convention and, unlike in the second speech in which he spoke only of his own brand's aspect in the close, Bush spoke of his own traits throughout the first speech. In both speeches, brand W and the brand that the Bush camp built around Kerry were present but the second speech was much more about educating the audience about all that was wrong with Kerry than it was about noting what was right about Bush. In short, the impact was to put Kerry on defense by making him take on the emotive narrative of the Bush brand story. These two speeches took place at very different points in the campaign and, as a result, it is not a surprise that they stress the same things but in different ways. The second speech was more in keeping with the Bush strategy of digging deeper into its best segments and it used looming crisis and fear to motivate because the election was nigh.

The two speeches contain the same items but their focus is different in each. The similar content is an important part of the brand strategy because only through the repetition of a consistent message presented across marketing channels can a visible political brand be built. Thus, it is equally unsurprising that the branded Bush worked with the same material in his personal appearances, media, and position materials repeatedly. By doing so, the Bush team built and distributed a single brand story that placed its candidate into the archetypal Conservative brand, and built a similar brand narrative that placed Kerry within the archetypal Liberal one.

In branded politics, individual events, debates, and appearances count for little other than a chance to build brand awareness, emphasize specific aspects of the brand and, when possible, show that the promises contained within the brand story have been kept. Stump speeches are a key means through which these goals can be accomplished because they allow the public to see the candidate, hear the message, and because they generate a lot of press coverage in the local market and, especially in a case like this one where the campaign has announced that major statements will be made, can also attract national media coverage. Thus, the stump speech is a key way to reach the local target audience and the national one for very little cost and, given the editing constraints of television, in a way that can get the brand out to the public for free.

Another Side Benefit

The brand story has given Conservatives another advantage that made itself clear in the 2004 election. It made it easy for independent groups to learn about the campaign's brand stories and, as a result, they could adopt a tag-along strategy or concentrate on some aspect of one of the brand stories being promoted by the Bush camp without violating the law regarding coordination. The advantage given by the brand strategy was particularly important in 2004 given the changed campaign finance rules that allowed for unlimited expenditures by so-called "527" groups. The brand strategy allowed the Bush narrative to become clear to other groups, as we can see in the way the Swift Boat Veterans for Truth and the Progress for America's Voter Fund (PFW) were able to independently build media and viral marketing campaigns. The Swift Boat campaign worked both to blow up Kerry's image as a war hero and, more importantly, question his honesty and integrity; two core aspects of the brand that Conservative groups have been building around Democrats since the Slick Willie campaign. The PFW worked mostly with the positive personal traits of George W. Bush. This group hit the target with its viral ad that itself made use of the brand strategy of focusing on highly emotive visible events, "Ashley's Story."

The Brand Works Again: W, Still the President

That George W. Bush was reelected at all is impressive, that he actually won with more than 50 percent of the vote is more so given all the factors that were discussed in the first chapter of this sequence. At the same time that Bush was being reelected, Republicans also picked up four seats in the Senate and the House. By employing a bricks-and-clicks organizational strategy, by targeting specific audiences, and attempting to increase turnout within those rather than trying to compete for every vote, and by focusing their marketing efforts in those areas that were likely to do them the most good, the Bush campaign proved that its strategy worked.

The Bush message worked because it repositioned its brand, then extended it into the archetypal Conservative brand. At the same time, his campaign took advantage of years of Conservative brand building efforts by extending Kerry into the brand that Conservatives have built around Democrats.[128] The brand strategy did not encourage a global examination of Bush's personal story because that would not have served its goal of differentiating him from Senator Kerry in a clear, concise way. Instead, such an examination would have raised more questions than it answered because some of what was being promoted as valuable parts of brand W could take on different means within a different context and because, on a personal level, it is not at all clear that there were very many significant differences in the life stories of the patrician Conservative candidate and the patrician Democratic candidate. The Bush team won because it built another brand quite successfully around Senator Kerry's record, misstatements, and was able to build fellowship between Senator Kerry and some of the classic brands with which Conservatives have worked around Liberals during the last twenty years. The three aspects of the Liberal brand with which the Bush team built fellowship were those of tax and spend, weak on security, and morally questionable. The 2004 election story is the story of brand power and of the way in which a brand strategy can tap into feelings that go beyond current candidates, events, and policies.

The polling data at the time indicates the extent to which the emphasis of certain aspects of brand W and the creation of senator flip-flop helped the Bush campaign. A Gallup Poll showed that 53 percent of respondents were unhappy with the nation's direction, something that does not usually advantage an incumbent seeking reelection.[129] A similar survey taken the week after the election found roughly the same result. When we look at Bush's job approval and likeability ratings for the period, something else emerges. A Fox News/Opinion Dynamics Poll found that Bush was rated favorably by around 47–49 percent of respondents to the four polls that it took during the

10/27–31 period and, in the same polls, his unfavorable rating ranged from 1 to 4 points lower than his favorable rating during the same period.[130] Throughout the month of October, a series of Gallup polls showed that the number of Americans who approved of his job in office ranged from a low of 47 percent on October 9 to a high of 51 percent on October 14 and 22. In the last such poll before the election, Bush had a 48 percent approval to 47 percent disapproval rating. All of these are significantly different from the responses to the question about the direction of the country posed above and, because of that difference, we can see the power that the brand can have in politics.

The exit polling data also show the power of branded messages because, within his targeted audiences, the issues with which George Bush worked are the issues upon which those people voted. We can see that in a series of exit polls. A Pew Research Center Poll found that the two issues that caused people to vote for Bush were moral values and terrorism. Moral values were the number one issue for 27 percent of voters. Of the Bush voters, 44 percent said that this was the number one issue for them while only 7 percent of Kerry voters said it was. Regarding the broad category of terrorism, the term that the Bush team liked to use to discuss its entire foreign policy including the Iraq War, 14 percent of all voters said this was their number one issue and, of those, 24 percent voted for Bush while only 3 percent voted for Kerry. Another way to look at this last point is to examine the difference between the branded terror issue set up by the Bush campaign and the unbranded Iraq issue. Twenty-two percent of voters said that Iraq was the issue that made their voting choice. Interestingly, 34 percent of Kerry voters said this was their number one issue while only 11 percent of Bush voters said that it was. The Bush effort on taxes also yielded a small advantage as 4 percent of Bush voters ranked this as their number one issue. These same polls showed that an overwhelming number of voters (72 percent) felt that there had been a lot more mudslinging in this campaign compared to those in years past.[131]

An *LA Times* exit poll is particularly revealing because it shows the demographic breakdown of the vote. This is of interest given the specific communicative outreach that the Bush campaign did toward Jews, Catholics, Hispanics, and women. Bush won 14 percent of the African American vote (a number up slightly from prior years, but more impressively won 34 percent of the Asian vote and 45 percent of the Hispanic vote. Bush received 57 percent of the vote from married women and, interestingly, 35 percent from single women who had long been thought of as more likely to vote for Democrats because of their position on reproductive rights issues. The Bush team did better in cities (43 percent) than one would expect from a Republican candidate and won the other kinds of residence areas convincingly. The same issue profile that the Princeton researchers found was also apparent in this poll. Bush received most of his support because of his positions on moral issues and the branded war on terrorism. John Kerry's voters made their choice on the economy and on the Iraq War specifically. By these results we can see that Bush's outreach efforts to women and minorities were successful because, at a minimum, they got Bush enough of a share of these audiences to make a difference in the final electoral outcome. The other important point that this poll shows is that the "vote Republican just this one time" pitch that was made at their convention to convince Moderates worked. Not surprisingly, Bush received 82 percent of the Conservative vote and 94 percent of the Republican vote. More interestingly, he received 12 percent of his votes from self-described Democrats and 48 percent from Independents. Senator Kerry, in contrast, received 6 percent of his votes from Republicans while 54 percent of the poll's respondents described themselves as Moderates.[132] We can see, then, that Bush swung just enough Democrats and Moderates, while holding onto his Conservative base, to swing the election. In the end, the polling data show the value of branding in ways that appeal to very focused audience groups, as well as in order to build up a sense of loyalty among the major group being targeted by the campaign.[133]

The 2004 Bush campaign was a textbook example of the way in which branded politics is structured, how it operates, and what its impact can be. As we saw in these three chapters, the Bush team built a narrative and stuck to it across different kinds of media. At a time when the United States was involved in multiple military engagements, faced a mixed economic picture, and had a growing national debt, the single biggest bloc of voters who voted for a single candidate voted for Bush because of his position on morality. The branded strategy allowed Bush to neutralize the economic situation, to succinctly explain his position about Iraq, to negatively introduce his opponent to the public, and to shift the subject onto a series of social policy questions and discussions of his personal traits that had the potential to energize passive Conservatives and to get some undecided voters to dislike Kerry personally enough to vote for Bush. Because of the way in which branded politics works, substantive discussion of issues seldom took place in this campaign outside of the context provided by Bush's brand. Bush's campaign was a textbook example of the way in which the Conservatives have incorporated the brand strategy into their campaigns. When it comes to building brands, Conservatives have been at this for longer, have used it in more situations, and have a deeper heritage upon which they can draw. As a result, it should be no surprise that Conservatives have done so well in American elections in recent decades.

Grassroots Organization and Public Education Campaigns

How the Conservative Brand Strategy Changed American Politics

One of the key ways in which the Conservative movement journeyed from the fringes to the center of American political life was the brand strategy, which has attracted attention and explained the contents of the movement in a way that taps directly into the beliefs held by most Americans. The upshot has been to empower a movement that proposes an economic policy, which is not in the interest of most Americans, by presenting it as being for the good of the whole, laying emphasis on the military aspects of a national security policy, promotion of controversial social issues, and the personal attributes of both parties' candidates. Branding has allowed Conservatives to present their positions on the issues in a way that taps into extant public beliefs and encourages people to look at issues in isolation rather than holistically. It has resulted in placing the Conservative movement at the center of American politics. It has been instrumental in winning elections, building interest groups, bringing media networks under control, and working lasting relationships within the Conservative movement.

The brand strategy has given the Conservatives the advantage of speed, as was noted in this work's early chapters, and this in turn has helped Conservatives to more quickly position and differentiate themselves from their opponents. The advantage of speed extends from policy positions to personality traits to heritage. Through its use, John Kerry, Bill Clinton, Michael Dukakis, Walter Mondale, and Jimmy Carter have all been turned into exactly the same Liberal politician in the brand story, even though in reality there were significant differences between these Democrats.

The brand strategy has come to be of increasing value to Conservatives as the speed of American politics has increased because of the proliferation of media outlets covering it. Improvements in communications technology have allowed these media outlets to cover politics in real time. This change took place at the same time that the number of interest groups and think tanks selling political products has increased and because of the proliferation of public relations techniques in politics during the last fifty years. As Rampton and Stauber show,[1] corporations and Conservative politicians have relied heavily on these techniques to persuade on issues ranging from the first Iraq War to the idea that New York City sludge could be used as fertilizer on croplands. They are smart to do so because these tactics can generate news coverage that can create buzz for and validation of the brand.[2]

As Luntz[3] reports, reliance on corporate marketing techniques began at least as early as the Reagan campaigns and continue to the present. In the case of public policy, the brand strategy has allowed Conservatives to wriggle out of their failures and, in some cases, to flip-flop more easily on their prior positions while ridiculing their opponents for doing the same. Two examples of this are provided by the way in which the Bush administration adjusted the emphasis point of the Iraq aspect of the War on Terror brand once it became clear that no weapons of mass destruction would be found and by the way in which Conservatives, who had cheered their party's use of the filibuster during the Clinton years, began lambasting the Democrats for doing as they had done. In both cases, the brand strategy allowed Conservatives to get their audience to focus on specific visual aspects of each policy, rather than murkier substantive matters because, in both cases, Conservatives had extant narratives into which to place current events. Thus, the brand strategy has given Conservatives a way to quickly put new policies and candidates as well as deviations from old policies into a narrative that provides the appearance of consistency even in cases in which the movement is being nothing of the sort.

The brand has given the Conservatives an ability to look more unified than they in actuality are, as noted earlier.[4] As the brand has helped the Conservatives build relationships with their audience, much of which is rooted in a movement culture as noted earlier, Conservatives gain the ability to shape and quickly define each new Conservative and Democratic innovation as they come along. The consistent use of the brand strategy provides a very plausible explanation for why the Conservatives often seem to have better candidates, run better campaigns, and provide clearer solutions to the nation's problems than the Democrats.

Conservatives have done best with the brand strategy when they have used examples to show the public that they are keeping their promises, as is clear from the following examples. Through the use of the brand strategy, Conservatives have found a means through which they can argue that they are consistent and keep their promises or, alternatively place the blame for not doing so elsewhere. First, Ronald Reagan was able to fudge his failure to submit a balanced budget to Congress in order to offset his administration's tax cuts by blaming the congressional Liberals for the increase in federal debt even though the fact of the matter was more complicated. Second, Conservatives frequently used to "prove" that they have kept their promises through the presentation of statistics that cannot be easily contested or, if capable of being contested, cannot be so in a way that the average American can easily understand as the Bush administration has done by regularly noting the number of Al Qaeda leaders who have been killed or captured since 9/11. As Donald Rumsfeld has pointed out, it is difficult in reality to know how the United States is doing in this conflict.[5]

The failure to keep promises matters when the public can see that such failures have happened, as was the case in the aftermath of Hurricane Katrina. In 2004, one of the key brand aspects on which Bush ran was his strong leadership and ability to manage well in a crisis. In June 2005, slightly under half of those surveyed in an ABC News *Washington Post* poll approved of the job that George W. Bush was doing as president (48 percent). In the aftermath of Hurricane Katrina, the number of people who felt this way fell to 42 percent in September, dropped lower to 39 percent in the month of October, and only reached the 41 percent level again in March of 2006.[6] Bush had, during the Katrina crisis, failed to clearly keep the brand promise of strong leadership made a year earlier. Unlike in the Reagan example, Bush's protestations that the failures were not his alone were overwhelmed by the highly emotive pictures coming from New Orleans and that, in turn, undermined the strongest aspect of brand W.

One of the key reasons why Conservatives have gotten their brand strategy to work well is because they have been able to present the public with so much evidence that their policies and candidates have been successful and, if unable to do so, have been able to reposition the brand away from the problem issue.

The brand strategy has allowed Conservatives to obscure the patrician roots of many of their candidates and the fact that the economic benefits of most of the policies that they propose usually flow toward the upper class as was noted in the chapters dealing with George W. Bush.[7] This has been accomplished by placing great stress on the everyman character that Ronald Reagan injected into the Conservative brand story, as well as by a good dose of positioning that stresses the elite background of Liberals and Democrats while always highlighting the average guy activities of Conservative candidates. The emphasis on personal traits is usually accompanied by the use of social and lifestyle issues to show average people that the Conservatives are more on their side than are the Democrats.[8] Highly visible, highly emotive issues are an effort by these Conservatives to convince average Americans that they are like them and represent their values and interests.[9]

The personal traits, Liberals, and tax cut aspects of the brand strategy have enabled Conservatives to obscure the impacts that their policies are having on average Americans and to discourage them from thinking about what life under the Democratic alternative would be like. While the Democrats also generally nominate patrician candidates, these candidates have usually proposed economic policies that would have a more favorable impact on most Americans than those proposed by the Conservatives.[10] The Conservative complaint, in essence, is that the Democratic patricians have the temerity to act like patricians, that tax increases on any segment of the economy will lead to disaster, and that, because they are Liberals, these Democrats have no idea what would be in the best interest of most Americans. The brand strategy allows Conservatives to focus on such things about which people have strong feelings instead of on the gray substance of policy.

The brand strategy has enabled Conservatives to avoid answering difficult questions about their policies in general and capitalism in particular, as well as about their overall belief in democracy. Conservative policies have weakened the role of the state in protecting the rights of and assuring the well-being of most Americans, and have produced a much less egalitarian society that is significantly dependent on the goodwill of other nations to finance its debt and lifestyle.[11] Peter Singer[12] has argued that Leo Strauss has had a tremendous influence within modern Conservatism and the Bush administration. This is problematic because it is antidemocratic at its core:

> Central to all his writings is the doctrine that there is one kind of truth for the masses and another for the philosophers—that is, for those in the know. Strauss claimed that all of the great philosophers wrote in a kind of code so that the masses could read them in a way that would not disturb the necessary social conventions, while the philosophers could grasp the more radical meaning hidden in their texts.[13]

In short, these elites could use threats to consensus values is a way for elites to mask their true agenda in order to win power and what they need is a vehicle through which they can accomplish that.[14] Some Conservatives have used the brand strategy to do exactly this even though their movement has, as we saw, a very strong populist element at its grassroots.

Conservatives have executed the brand strategy to get people to vote against their own economic interests in exactly the same way that tobacco companies have developed a brand strategy to promote their products to college students. Both the Conservative and tobacco branded marketing campaigns work because they tap into the audience's psychological needs.[15] Conservative elites have used a brand strategy to get their audience targets to support their products that economically have an adverse effect on many of their customers, in exactly the same way as tobacco companies have used it to encourage young people to start using a product that could, in reality, kill them. In both cases, the audience target is repeatedly asked to look at the immediate satisfaction of their needs not the long-term consequences of their choices. In both cases, there is a product cycle through which the targets can be moved as their life situation changes and, as a result, lasting relationships can be built in this way. Thus, the brand strategy has built a loyal audience for the Conservative product among its target audience just as the tobacco companies' brand strategies have done among theirs.

As we saw earlier, the Conservative brand strategy works well with a focus on postmaterialist issues.[16] The brand strategy works both because of the decline of labor unions and because of the transformation of American work from one based on unionized physical labor to one based on intellectual but nonunion tasks.[17] Thus, the brand strategy worked because it came along at exactly the time that the labor union, the social organizing vehicle for prior generations, was in decline. It was augmented by the advocacy explosion's creation of a large number of interest groups.[18] These groups were, as Skocpol[19] has noted, different from the kind of dominant civic association found previously in the United States because they were not the kinds of federated organizations that had local meeting places but were instead run from Washington, DC, and usually require the members to only pay dues than respond to the organizers' calls for participation on an occasional basis.[20] As Singer[21] noted, Strauss' followers, who came to play a more prominent role in the Republican Party during the Bush administration, were fully willing to use such social issues and organizations to advance their cause. The brand strategy is one key means through which they can do so. As Rampton and Stauber showed in *Banana Republicans*,[22] Conservatives aimed both to create new groups that they totally controlled and to infiltrate the leadership structure of extant groups with a leadership of their choosing.[23] Many of these groups are led by people who came out of the Conservative movement and, as a result, these groups act as a distribution channel for the Conservative brands.[24]

Through the use of the brand strategy, Conservatives have been able to build their own media system as we saw. Conservatives control this and, as a result, are able to distribute their brand stories intact or to reiterate specific aspects of their brands. Ways that this are done include daily faxing of talking points to Conservative talk radio hosts[25] in order to play up that day's aspect of the brand story, as well as by the daily meeting at Fox News[26] in which the spin for that day's coverage is determined.[27] These activities generate buzz about and impressions for the brand story while promoting the brand story's version of events and the big story above other issues. For example, consider the amount of attention that was devoted to Bill Clinton's lies about sex versus the limited attention paid to the false impression promoted by the Bush administration that there was some kind of relationship between Iraq and Al Qaeda. The Conservative brand strategy supported by the movement's message distribution system produced this disparity.[28]

Branding works for Conservatives because it places them on the rhetorical offense and reduces Liberal Democrats to defending their New Deal and Great Society achievements. Democrats are much more of an inside the beltway, defensive party than are the insurgent Conservatives.[29] The brand strategy is the major technique that Conservatives have employed against these institutionalized Democratic accomplishments but they have not had as good an effect when dealing with highly visible programs about which Americans feel strongly. Proof of this is provided by the fate of the Bush administration's Social Security Privatization Plan during 2005.

Even though they have not been able to attack these policies with great success, Conservatives have been able to use them as part of their brand story and in terms of positioning themselves as populists fighting the Liberals.[30] It is this populist positioning that has enabled the Conservatives to use the brand strategy to great success. The Liberals who populate the Democratic Party have, in the Conservative brand story about them, lost sight of the interests of average people in favor of the pursuit of the goals of the radical movements of the 1960s. Fairly or not, Conservatives have relentlessly highlighted examples that prove that they are more like them than are the Democrats. Conservatives have done so to both build their movement and their brand.

The brand strategy is effective because Conservatives have focused on value-based questions and because they have a clearly defined set of values and frames about those values with which they regularly work.[31] The Democrats have not done so consistently nor have their issues always been well suited to branding. It is difficult to get people fired up about Social Security Cost of Living Adjustments or the rest of the technical minutiae of public policy. The brand strategy depends on a specific kind of issue in order to work well and Conservatives have made hay with a number of such issues. These kinds of issues let the Conservatives look like the average people that they claim to be and keeps the public from seeing the movement's inherent contradictions.[32]

Values issues and discussions of values fit with the brand strategy because these are emotive questions about which compromise will be difficult or impossible, thus making it possible for Conservatives to use the same brands for years and keeping their audience fired up and consuming Conservative products throughout as is true in the case of abortion.[33] For example, consider the way in which G.W. Bush sold the War on Terror brand as an effort to get "evil doers." This kind of emotive moniker is much more effective in producing reactions from the audience than is the more technocratic "global war against extremism" moniker currently in use by the Pentagon. It is the foundation of the brand strategy in values questions that has enabled the Conservatives to use it to build a movement, build brand loyalty, and gain political power.

Their consistent use of the brand strategy means that Conservatives can either extend their line to include new issues or build a second brand that encapsulates them as was noted in the first chapter. The Bush team inten-

tionally constructed a broad War on Terror brand instead of simply focusing on a response to 9/11.[34] Woodward even goes so far as to claim that no
less than Bush himself was heard to remark that 9/11 was "a great opportunity."[35] September 11 gave the administration an opportunity but the
brand strategy gave it the technique through which it could justify expansion of the federal government's size and power, an invasion of Iraq, and a
campaign issue for use in the next two elections. This is exactly what the brand
strategy gives Conservatives: the ability to fit their current policy proposals
and individuals into an established frame for the audience no matter how tenuous the connection.

The Conservative brand strategy has worked as well because the Democratic
Party is not composed of a unified movement that shares a set of common
values. This is particularly true on economic issues. In fact some would argue
that it has been excessive Democratic moderation on economic policy that
has opened the door for Conservatives to pursue a brand strategy because
their brand strategy is based primarily on social issues, and as long as the
Democratic Party as a whole does differentiate itself on economic policy
matters from Conservatives, it will consistently be faced with Conservatives
making political hay by using the brand strategy. This is the conclusion that
Thomas Frank reaches in *What's the Matter With Kansas?* Frank argues that
the Conservative movement has gained in the number of adherents primarily because Democrats and Liberals have failed to offer a serious alternative
to Conservative economic policy proposals, and the upshot of this is that
American politics primarily occurs regarding those value-based social issues
out of which Conservatives have built their brands. Given that the Democrats
are, by definition, fighting these battles on terms that they did not define and
are usually positioned in a way that leads them to have to defend either the
indefensible or the rights of minority groups, especially unpopular minority
groups like gays, those who do not wish to have students recite the Pledge
of Allegiance in schools, or criminals,[36] the Conservative advantage gained
from this kind of politics becomes clear.

Not surprisingly, fighting such battles has led to a string of Democratic
electoral defeats and to a sense among large segments of the American middle and working classes that it is the Conservatives who actually have their
interests at heart. The Conservatives have used the brand strategy to such
good effect that they have shifted the nation's agenda in a rightward direction. Democratic abdication on things economic has meant that, when they
have been willing to discuss the nation's economic trend, they have only

been willing to do so in a way that is essentially a lighter version of the free market economic policies that Conservatives promote. They have failed to differentiate themselves on economic policy matters and have, as a result, created the conditions under which average Americans find it believable that Conservative tax policy is more beneficial to them. The Conservative brand promise appears to have been kept even in cases where it is not, as was true in the previously noted example of the Bush tax cuts.

This combination of apparent economic populism, security, and the defense of supposedly traditional values contained in their brand have allowed Conservatives to position Democrats and Liberals as not being like or interested in average Americans. They have taken advantage of their opponents' failure to differentiate on the single issue on which they had enjoyed a whopping advantage from the 1930s onward, to shift the debate onto social issues that position each party favorably, and let them reach the working-class white audiences that once voted reliably for Democrats.[37] The Conservative brand strategy would not have worked nearly as well as it has with this key audience absent the Democrats' reiteration of the value of the New Deal regime or, in the years since Reagan, to differentiate their ideas from those of the Conservatives.

What Should Democrats Do?

"The Democratic Party is Toast." So read the headline of a September 2004 *Washington Monthly* article written by one of the key figures of the contemporary Conservative movement—Grover Norquist.[38] They were doomed, he argued, "With Democrats lacking a beachhead in Congress, four more years of Republican governance with President Bush in the White House will badly damage each of the pillars of the Democrat establishment."[39] What he did not count on were four things that led many Americans to conclude that a one party, Conservative state, was not what they wanted: (1) the 2004 election was much more about national security, the personal traits, and strong leadership aspects of brand W than it was about Conservative ideology, as was later demonstrated by Bush's subsequent inability to implement his promised ownership society, (2) the hurricane that put the lie to these aspects of brand W and limited the administration's popularity and political clout, and (3) a series of scandals involving the administration and congres-

sional Republicans, judicial appointments, administration's defense of its
electronic eavesdropping activities, as well as (4) the increasing number of
military and congressional voices led by Rep. John Murtha who began raising questions about the administration's management of and failure to find
an exit strategy from Iraq. While Americans might not like the idea of a one
party state, in no way do these four things give them a reason to do anything
other than vote against the Conservatives.

Conservatives have been able to make good use of the brand story
because their movement began at the grassroots and, as we saw in Chapter
1, the brand strategy has been used by the movement throughout its life. Its
movement roots also mean that there are a lot of people who, because of their
involvement with the movement since its outset, are sincere in their beliefs
about it. Thus, the brand strategy has been used by the grassroots Conservatives
and, later, the Straussians of the Bush administration. A second group of
Conservatives who have furthered the use of the brand strategy to build the
top-down-driven Conservative movement are the wealthy individuals who
have built individual foundations or a network of them like the Koch family, which started a network that was so extensive that it came to be known
as the Kochtopus among Conservatives.[40] Such activities are very consistent with the use of a brand strategy because those at the top frame the discussion and then build and adjust the brand in response to the feedback
given by consumers. In short, a variety of conservatives have used the brand
strategy to accomplish many goals. Given the ever more fractious nature of
the Democratic Party, its more diverse membership, the advantage that
Conservatives have derived from their professional experiences, and ready access
to a deep pool of wealthy philanthropists, it is not clear that the Democrats
could use the brand strategy in exactly the same way or get the same results
as the Conservatives.

The lack of shared values, partisan message distribution system, and
well-funded ideologically sympathetic think tanks further limit the Democrats'
ability to use the brand strategy. The biggest problem with the Democrats
using such a strategy is pointed out in Lakoff's[41] work that notes how
Democrats do not engage in values-driven politics. This failure has meant that
the Democrats have not shown the public exactly of what their core values
are comprised nor have they been able to create fellowship between different issues and candidates or build a consistent narrative about their politics.
The Democrats will not be able to use the brand strategy to good result until

they address this core problem. What they will be more likely to do is to have individual candidates build brands around themselves but not around their entire party, as appears to have been done by Bill Clinton.[42] Because of this, I argue, they will not be able to build the line extensions and fellowship between candidates and issues that we have seen the Conservatives are able to do, especially through their use of the Reagan heritage brand and its numerous aspects.

Conservatives, as we saw, spent a lot of their early years taking over the Republican Party while building alliances with other sympathetic parts of American society.[43] Conservatism uses the brand strategy so well because it spent years figuring itself out. Having a clear set of values and a coherent narrative are so important to the brand strategy and so vital to the Conservative ascendancy that almost all Republican politicians have called themselves Conservatives even if they are not[44] or cover the fact that, as was noted earlier both Bushes did, they are much more like the Liberal elites against whom they are running than they are like the rank-and-file Conservative.

The brand strategy has become more important to promoting Conservatism since Reagan came into office because so much of what it has proposed and enacted, as well as so many of the candidates that it has run for office do not benefit average people and so many of its candidates are not like average people.[45] This has been particularly true during the Bush administrations that have been less populist, more tied to narrow interests, and more supportive of big government once in office than many Conservatives might have believed based on their branding activities. The brand developed about Conservatism and the line extensions that subsequent entrepreneurs calling themselves Conservatives have obscured this fact for most of the Conservative audience at least until after the election. As we have seen, at the end of the G.H.W. Bush administration and apparently at the end of the George W. Bush administrations, Conservatives finally became aware of the reality of the administrations that they had put into office because the highly visible dissonance between the brand promises and the results became too great to ignore.

First, the brand strategy depends on coherent values and a clear narrative. The Democrats could greatly benefit by concentrating on creating these things, and once they did so, could use the brand strategy in the same way that Conservatives are using it to win elections and advance their policy positions, be they Conservative or not. One place where Democrats could start building their brand would be with a focus on economic policy that makes the real impact of Conservative policies obvious in a way that is both emotive and visible in their daily lives. But, in order to do so, the Democrats would have to clarify their party's economic beliefs and which audiences it is targeting. Otherwise it will gain little benefit from the brand strategy's use.

Democrats, to use the brand strategy well, need to figure out what it means to be a Democrat and who qualifies as being one, instead of trying to be everything to everyone. As we saw the Conservatives did this before taking over the Republican Party and by the time Reagan became president, it was clear to most people what constituted their beliefs, how each of their policy proposals related to each other, and which audiences constituted their targets. One cannot say the same of the Democrats, and until it is possible to do so, the Democrats will not be able to use of the brand strategy as it used by the Conservatives. Thus, the Democratic Party should be willing to lose its share of identifiers in the electorate in order to develop a more intense, more productive relationship with fewer but more dedicated constituencies. Conservatives were willing to do so with the Republican Party and, as a result, have been able to build a highly cohesive party that has enjoyed great electoral success during the brand strategy's life.

Conservatives have used the brand to build relationships with their followers, provide some sense of common identity for them, and, in turn, build a much deeper loyalty to the Conservative products than would otherwise be possible.[46] This is one of the reasons why so many non-Conservatives find it difficult to argue with Conservatives. Even when information is presented that would clearly appear to undermine the Conservative worldview, the years of brand building that have been done to instill that worldview in its adherents ensure that information that does not fit the brand stories to which they have been exposed is systematically discarded or sharply discounted. This relationship marketing means that it is easier to launch viral marketing campaigns around the Conservative brands as was done by the 2004 Bush reelection campaign. Years of brand building had created lasting relationships within the Conservative movement that the Bush team was able to tap into in order to sell their candidate.

Second, until the Democrats figure out which audiences constitute the party's core, build relationships with those while purging unwanted audiences and dissenting elected officials, they will not get the same results even if they did use the brand strategy. Thus, the Democrats at present are simply not constructed to use a brand strategy in the same way as are the Republicans.

Individual Democrats could make use of such a strategy, as it can be argued Bill Clinton gradually did as his term went along.[47] Until the Democrats are able to build a more ideologically coherent coalition or, as is more likely to be the case, find an enduring set of issues around which the party's various elements can coalesce for a long period of time as was the case from the 1930s through the late 1960s, the party will have a difficult time using the brand strategy to good effect.

Third, the Democrats need to examine the personal traits of their national level nominees. While their recent candidates have had wonderful resumes, the last one who really understood how to sell himself to average Americans was Bill Clinton.[48] Republicans have experienced their best electoral success when they nominated candidates who had a sales background: George W. Bush and Ronald Reagan. The ability to sell things is very much a part of the job description of a national level candidate in modern America. While Bush and Reagan did not have glittering resumes, they had this ability to sell themselves and were thus able to defeat the Democrats, who had resumes much more substantial than their own. The Democratic infatuation with resumes has allowed Conservatives to visibly show the voters that the Democratic candidate is not like them. Democrats would be wise to recall that most Americans have not finished college never mind an Ivy League one, nor do they have an in-depth grasp of most public issues. They have an understanding of personal traits because those are highly visible and Democrats would be wise to nominate candidates who can, as Conservatives do, appear to share the values and interests of the average American. The last Democrats who have connected with average people over the last two decades were Bill Clinton and Jimmy Carter. Democrats would be wiser to nominate more candidates who had this common touch and interests than to continue nominating the person with the highest IQ or the most glittering resume. While Carter and Clinton were less everymen than members of the elite, so too have been the candidates nominated by Conservatives been equally unlike average people. It was the brand strategy that formed the basis upon which Conservatives could present themselves to the public. Subsequently, it has been the brand strategy built around Reagan that functions in this fashion.

The brand strategy works because the elitism of the Democrats is visible while that of the Conservatives is obscured through the use of the everyman character and the Reagan heritage brand, as well as by the minutiae of legislation and federal rulemaking once in office. The Democrats would be wise to pick a few issues, like specific corporate tax giveaways or specific examples of the way in which Conservative deregulatory policy has hurt consumers, in order to show the public what the overall impact of Conservative policies been.

The Democrats need to regain their understanding of what made their two great icons of the last century icons in the first place. FDR and JFK did not become iconic figures because they were products of elite families and educational institutions. They became iconic figures because they could play the everyman role, because their administrations did things while in office that were obviously in the interest of the majority of the population, and because they were very good at letting the public know exactly what was being done for them. The Democrats need to find candidates who can campaign, govern, and be turned into the archetypes on which brands rest that FDR and JFK were instead of finding candidates who share their resumes and socioeconomic backgrounds. The brand strategy has worked for Conservatives because it is they who have nominated such candidates.

Fourth, the Democrats would have to be willing to make the investments in time, money, institution building, and relationship building that Conservatives have made over the past forty years. While it may take years to produce a payoff, the Conservatives' success shows why such an investment is worth making. Part of the reason why Conservatives are able to use the brand strategy so well is because of their roots as a social movement and the length of time that it took for them to take over the Republican Party as was noted in Chapter 2, particularly as shown through the work of Schoenwald and McGirr (both 2001). Should they wish to use the brand strategy to good effect, the Democrats must be willing to do the same. The investment of time lies in building the initial brand, and to this point Democrats have flirted with the concept of branding but have always done so within the context of the public part of an election campaign during which time is always tight. The Democratic branding effort should begin long before that and last well after that if it is to reach the level of success that has been achieved by Conservatives. As a part of this, the Democrats should be willing to try and fail. As we saw earlier, Newt Gingrich failed to launch the Contract with America on a number of occasions, but the one time that it worked, the Conservatives won a House majority. In short, it took Conservatives a long time to build the core brand story (one could argue it took all the way from 1965 until 1980), but once they did it, they have been able to fit their new products into it and this, in turn, helps to sell those faster and more effectively than the Democrats can hope to at present. The upshot of the disparity in use of the brand strategy is simply this: Democrats have to reinvent the wheel every four years while the Republicans simply have to change the tire.

Fifth, Democrats would be wise to stress populist values-based issues as Lakoff suggested. Ceding economic issues and only visibly appearing to defend the rights of minorities are not keys to building an electoral majority. The public is not passionate in its defense of abortion or affirmative action in part because these things are not under clear threat. Second, many of the issues on which Democrats have taken clear stands run squarely into the question of the rights of the society versus those of the individual[49] and it has been the Democrats who have put themselves in the position of telling focused, motivated constituencies that their rights must be limited in order for the society to progress. The solution for the economic issue is obvious. In the social issue question, Democrats could try to build a core brand story that shows people how they are better off as a result of these policies. Failing that, they could try to build the same kind of brand around Conservatives that Conservatives have built around the Democrats. Edsall and Edsall, writing fourteen years ago, argued that what the Democrats need to do is to persuade the public of their rectitude in pursuing their race policies while at the same time passing along as many of the costs of their race policies to natural Republican constituencies.[50] They also argued, during the late 1980s, that this was the real problem with the race and rights policies Democrats pursued. It is still something that they could do but until the Democrats do so, as Edsall and Edsall noted then and remains true, the "top-down conservative coalition will remain dominant in presidential politics"[51] and, it can be added that the brand strategy will continue to be successful.

Sixth, the Democrats would be wise to stop trying to win the intellectual argument in favor of repeating their points in order to make sure the audience was familiar with them. The case of John Kerry's 2004 campaign is a good one in point because, while Kerry had a number of policy positions on issues about which Americans cared passionately, he did not build a narrative out of them nor did he repeat them in exactly the same form over and over. While the Conservative message is not intellectually deep or particularly nuanced, it is consistent, clear, visual, and emotive. The brand strategy works for Conservatives because they work with issues that are well suited to it, because Conservatives have put much effort into building it, and because they do not see its use or the use of other consumer marketing techniques as being beneath them.

The Conservative brand strategy works because Conservatives have found issues and personalities with which they can build relationships with their audiences in order to build a sense of relationship with them and sense of brand loyalty within them.[52] Conservative politics is, as Lakoff suggests, very much an emotive activity and one that fits well with the brand strategy. Personalization ensures that politics will be an emotive, rather than an analytical exercise. Conservative audiences feel connected to the issues being presented by Conservative movement leaders and feel that these issues are more a reflection of their identity and this builds both a stronger sense of loyalty to the movement, a sense of ownership of it, and a deeper activist pool from which the movement can draw.[53] The brand strategy has worked for Conservatives because it has built an enduring relationship between movement leaders and followers.

Seventh, the Democrats would be wise to build a message distribution that is fully under their control in order to make sure that their brands reach the public intact. Currently, the bulk of the electorate receives the Democratic message in a mediated form because Democrats are dependent on the media to distribute it and much of this media is in the hands of and reflects the interests of a few large corporations. It is unlikely that these institutions will be willing to serve in the advocacy position for Democrats that most Conservatives assume them to be. The Democrats' ability to use the media as a message distribution system has been hindered by an effective Conservative whining campaign about Liberal media bias.[54] In such an environment, Democrats would be wise to build their own message distribution system. There are numerous signs that something like this is beginning to happen.

Eighth, the Democrats would be wise to run coordinated issue campaigns in the same way as Conservatives have run them since the Contract with America period. Doing so is one means through which Conservatives have gained maximum benefit from their use of the brand strategy. While this has not always built an electoral majority, it has always reinforced brand loyalty and identity within the target audience. The brand is most effective when it gains a large number of impressions; the coordinated campaign accomplishes just this for Conservatives. By having candidates for all levels of federal office talk about the same issue in the same way, the Conservatives build a consistent story that becomes magnified in effect when we consider that the brand story that is used in any one of these coordinated campaigns fits with the much bigger overall Conservative brand story. There is a single brand supporting a single product that can be sold more quickly because it functions like a line extension. This is the advantage that brand-based coordinated campaigning has given to Conservatives. Democrats would be wise to follow it.

What Branding Is Doing to American Democracy

The brand strategy is reflective of a number of changes that have taken place in the United States since the end of World War II, but it has had several consequences itself for American politics. First, Conservatism has become central not peripheral in American politics. Second, this has shifted the nation's politics to the Right. Third, the brand strategy has ended the Democratic Party's majority status in the nation. Fourth, the brand strategy has ended the dominance of New Deal Liberalism in a way that would not have seemed possible to an observer at Kennedy's inaugural in 1960. This, in turn, has changed the kind of Democrat who wins the party's presidential nomination from the kind of innovative initiator of policy ideas that Franklin Roosevelt, Jack Kennedy, and Lyndon Johnson were to the kind of preemptive leader[55] that Bill Clinton was. Fifth, Conservatism's ascendancy and the rise of the Straussian neo-Conservative movement have advantaged the wealthy and major corporations at the expense of most Americans. This is clear in the changes in income distribution, the decline in federal benefits to various constituencies, the decline in public sector capacity to deal with disasters like hurricanes, and the ongoing efforts to transfer the costs of old age and illness from the public onto individuals.

The brand strategy has brought electoral success to Conservatives through financial reward to their favored constituencies and a very different kind of life for most Americans than those of them watching JFK take the oath of office in 1960 would have believed to be in the offing forty years on. Sixth, the brand strategy works because of America's cultural transformation from a civic to a consumerist ethos.[56] Seventh, the brand strategy works because it fits American culture.[57]

The brand strategy works because it is an ideal way to take advantage of the cultural and technical shifts outlined above. Just as is the case in so many aspects of life, the brand strategy is asking Americans to buy into stories that are cleverly packaged and repeatedly presented in order to get them to buy something. Through consistent repositioning, Conservatives have managed to stress those aspects of their movement that fit their electoral and marketing needs of the moment. One of the biggest reasons why they can do so is that the messages with which they work stress the everyman aspect of whatever they are promoting, issues that can generate a strong response among the audience targets and issues that can be fitted into the core Conservative brand as line extensions. Candidates who cannot play the everyman role well and issues that cannot be presented as above will have little chance to succeed for as long as the brand strategy dominates.

Our politics will continue to be more about looking at a highly structured aspect of and stories about issues than they will be about looking globally at issues for as long as the cultural conditions that exist remain. Problems will go unsolved as those who have specific knowledge of the issue area in question will realize, but for the vast majority of the public who have only a cursory knowledge of any given subject area, the problems that have been pointed out in the brand story will have been solved by the evidence presented that shows that the branded product has solved the problem. In the case of substantive policy questions like the current slow speed health insurance crisis, there will be no action taken by either party until the crisis is so obvious that it can be ignored no longer. Short of that, the slow decline in quality of service received by citizens from and the capacity of government to deal with national problems will continue its gradual dissipation.

The success of the Conservative brand strategy means that there will be little chance of much fact-based debate taking place as a matter of course in our politics anymore. The brand strategy has built a relationship between Conservative movement leaders and members in a way that reduces the impact of all but the most visual, emotive counterarguments. Thus, when Americans do care about politics, they will do so in a way that leads them to question each other's motives; hardly a healthy situation. This is due to the fact that the brand story helps to familiarize us with a product, and as long as the product appears to be keeping its promises, we are likely to believe the brand story. The success of the brand strategy means that there is little chance of building public consensus in the United States moving forward. Consensus is equally not the environmental condition under which branded politics works best either. Through niche marketed brands, the broad consensus that exists in this country is turned into a fractious disunity that has the potential to make sure that those Americans who are utterly turned off by politics will always be on edge about some looming crisis within it. Conservatives use the brand strategy to keep power and implement policy, not to build the nation's civic culture or sense of social connection. It is favorable personal traits, hot messages, and highly focused narratives that make the brand strategy work, and that is the way in which Conservatives use it to rationally achieve their goal of winning elections.

What Americans Can Do About Branded Politics

While the previous section admittedly paints a bleak picture of the brand strategy's impact on American politics and political culture, Americans are not without means to deal with the brand strategy. One of the key things that Americans could do to deal with the branded politics confronting them would be to adopt one of the key elements through other kinds of branded products that have been forced to change: grassroots organization and public education campaigns. The brand works in politics, as it does in all aspects of consumer life, because it is a short cut that saves people time. One of the first things that could ideally be done to counteract the brand strategy would be to convince people that their participation in politics was desirable, that they would be listened to, and that political leaders would act to deal with the serious problems being raised by them.

The second thing that could help would be if people became convinced that their obligations of citizenship extended far beyond voting. That is to say that one of the key things that individual citizens can do to counteract the brand strategy is to do as smart consumers always do before making a major purchase: research the products that are being pitched through the brand strategy. The brand strategy only works because of the general lack of education about the public life of the nation within the population. Education is one key way through which the Conservative brands can be counteracted just as is the case when all kinds of products are sold to the public. Generally, the more that people research, the less likely it is that they will be talked into a purchasing decision by a brand story.

Another way in which the impact of the brand strategy could be reduced would be by having the nation's press and electronic media devote more time, space, and depth to public affairs than they do at present. While there are serious media operations that do devote a great deal of their effort to doing these things, too much of the media covers stories of socially questionable importance, such as individual tales about crime or one type or another of infotainment.[58] Given that the American media is all about profit-driven infotainment, the chance of the national networks doing this is remote. One possible solution for this problem would be to encourage the Federal Communications Commission to begin regulating program content as it has steadfastly refused to do for all but obscene content in recent years. Finally, the real key to counteracting the brand strategy is for the citizens to come to reject it by becoming more involved in their own communities.[59]

Notes

Chapter 1

1. Something Zyman and Miller, 2000, explain on pp. 58–61.

2. Rampton and Stauber, 2003, pp. 33–34.

3. Zyman, 2000, pp. 67–69.

4. Schiewger and Adami, in Newman, 1999b, pp. 347–364. The early portion of this work provides a rationale for branded politics while the latter portion examines the role of the nonverbal in political brand building.

5. For a discussion of the way in which Conservatism As a social movement: see McGirr, 2001, and for a discussion of the way that it took over the Republican Party, see Schoenwald, 2001.

6. Ries and Ries, 2002, p. 48.

7.   Newman, 1999a, p. 93. I became aware of this fine book very late in the creation of this manuscript. I have tried to incorporate as much of it as possible in the short time that I had to do so. In a nutshell, its argument is about brand images in mass politics while mine is about the way in which Conservatives specifically have used branding to build a very successful niche-based social movement. It appears to focus on candidates in general and Bill Clinton in particular while I am looking at Conservatives as a branded social movement who gained control of the Republican Party and have since tried to attract a few audiences while building deep loyalty within them. I have attributed relevant points in this book where appropriate.

8.   Turow, 1997, p. 91.

9.   Ibid., pp. 31–36, looks at this in media and eventually argues that these trends have been accelerated throughout the society because of media.

10.   His point is in relation to advertisers' desire to get more specific about consumer behavior and the research launched to support this and can be found on p. 55.

11.   Ibid., pp. 55–56.

12.   Ibid., p. 105.

13.   Both quotes ibid., p. 91.

14.   Ibid.

15.   Ibid., p. 105.

16.   Ibid., pp. 92–93.

17.   For an argument about how individuals, especially celebrities, use branding, see Klein, 2000, pp. 45–46.

18.   Interview with Ken Mehlman *PBS's Frontline: The Archetect.* http://www.pbs.org/wgbh/pages/frontline/shows/architect/interviews/mehlman.html, link last visited June 2, 2006.

19.   Turow, 1997, p. 103.

20.   See Ibid., pp. 40–46, for one such analysis that is very much in keeping with this line of argument.

21.   Ibid., pp. 125–160, Turow does a very nice job of outlining the way in which direct niche marketing works.

22.   Ibid., p. 136.

23.   Ibid., p. 134.

24.   Ibid., p. 130.

25.   Ibid., pp. 136–137.

26.   Ibid., p. 91.

27.   See Klein, 2000, pp. 20–26 for a similar discussion of branding and lifestyle marketing.

28.   Turow, 1997, pp. 184–200.

29.   Ibid.

30.   Something that ibid explains in the case of a panoply of product marketers.

31.   Moore and Slater, 2003, pp. 257–258.

32.   Turow, 1997, p. 129.

33.   Ibid., p. 146.

34.   Ibid.

35.   Ibid, p. 145.

36.   For a detailed examination of the way candidate images are crafted using other communicative techniques, see Newman, 1999a, pp. 87–98.

37.   Turow, 1997, p. 92.

38.   For a parallel analysis of the impact of consumer marketing techniques on American political life, please see Bennett, 1996.

39.   Viguerie and Franke, 2004, pp. 94–95.

40.   Ibid.

41.   Ibid.

42.   Ibid., pp. 95–96.

43.   Klein, 2000, pp. 15–16.

44.   Smith and Clurman, 1997, p. 282.

45.   Klein, 2000, pp. 8–9.

46.   Zyman, 2000, pp. 83–84.

47.   Trout and Rivkin, 2000, p. 77.

48.   Something noted by Newman on p. 262 in Newman, 1999b. This is the second work of which I became aware very late in the writing process and I have tried to incorporate its many arguments as much as possible in the short time that I have had to do so.

49.   See particularly Ries and Ries, 2002, pp. 99 and 109 for more about how Volvo has built its brand and Newman, 1999a, p. 44 for an example of how this fits with segmented audience appeals in politics.

50.   Trout and Rivkin, 2000, pp. 95–98.

51.   For an in-depth analysis of the politics surrounding the Nike brand, see Klein, 2000.

52.   Ries and Ries, 2002, pp. 84–85 discuss the law of shape in depth.

53.   Zyman and Miller, 2000, p. 83.

54.   Ries and Ries, 2002, p. 164.

55.   Ibid., pp. 109–110.

56.   Ibid., pp. 105–108.

57.   Newman, 1999a, p. 44 uses this example to explain market segmentation.

58.   Trout and Rivkin, 2000, pp. 23–24.

59.   Ries and Ries, 2002, pp. 105–107.

60.   Viguerie and Franke, 2004, pp. 95–96.

61.   Turow, 1997, p. 56 discusses this in terms of media companies. His other argument about a claim of efficient separation is less relevant to this argument.

62.   See ibid., pp. 18–23 for a history of the brand as a mass market tool and pp. 157–183 for a discussion of its use as a target marketing tool.

63.   Zyman, 2000, p. 64 shows that this is generally important in contemporary consumer marketing.

64.   As Zyman and Miller, 2000, p. 150 note, speed is very important in teaching people about the facts of a situation.

65.   Ibid., p. 134 points out the importance of doing so in any PR campaign supporting a brand.

66.   McGirr (2001) and Schoenwald (2001) provide significant insight into the rise of Conservatism from a historical point of view while Diamond, 1995, does so from a sociological point of view and Viguerie and Franke, 2004, do so from the perspective of movement Conservatives.

67.   For a complimentary analysis of branding's impact on politics from a global perspective, see Klein, 2000.

68.   One example of which is provided by Newman's analysis 1999a.

69.   Wolin, 1989, pp. 180–192.

70.   For a book-length treatment of this transformation, see Newman, 1999a. This specific point comes from p. 146.

71.   Ibid., pp. 45–46 shows the opposing viewpoint.

72.   Bellah et al., 1985, Putnam, 2000, and Turow, 1997.

73.   See Zyman and Miller, 2000, for a discussion of the way in which branding is really a conversation.

74.   Ries and Ries, 2002, p. x.

75.   Ibid.

76.   Mark and Pearson, 2001, p. 206.

77.   Trout and Rivkin, 2000, especially pp. 2–35.

78.   Ibid., p. 13 and Zyman, 2000, pp. 67–84.

79.   Turow, 1997, presents a book-length discussion of the rise of tailored, lifestyle marketing that includes these techniques and their impact on American media and culture.

80.   Zyman, 2000, pp. 126–127 discusses the reasons why product marketers would be wise to behave as do politicians in this area.

81.   Zyman, 2000, p. 80 shows the importance of this in image building while Zyman and Miller, 2000, note the importance of consistency in communicating the brand on p. 41.

82.   Ries and Ries, 2002, pp. 84–85.

83. See Zyman, 2000, p. 82 and Newman, 1999a, pp. 93–94 for a specific discussion of candidate image making in a mass media age and Turow, 1997, pp. 157–181 for a discussion of target marketing and the brand in modern America.

84. As Newman, 1999a, pp. 45–46 argues.

85. See ibid., pp. 89–91 for an examination of emotion's role in political marketing.

86. Postman, 1986, Cohen, 2003, and Newman, 1999a, pp. 37–38.

87. Zyman, 2000, pp. 101–102.

88. For a good history of presidential advertising, see Jamieson, *Packaging the Presidency*, 1996.

89. Ries and Ries, 2002, p. xii.

90. As Newman, 1999a, notes on pp. 92, 93.

91. Ibid., p. 93.

92. Newman, 1999a, pp. 91–92 shows the extent to which corporate marketers mount campaigns to ensure this.

93. Ries and Ries, 2002, p. 191.

94. Ibid., pp. 191–195 and Zyman and Miller, 2000, pp. 108–109.

95. Ries and Ries, 2002, pp. ix, 156, Zyman, 2000, pp. 87–89, Newman, 1999a, pp. 91–92, and Turow, 1997, p. 31.

96. Zyman, 2000, pp. 87–89.

97. Ries and Ries, 2002, pp. 191–195.

98. Ibid., pp. 39–43.

99. Something that Anthony Downs wrote about in the context of political parties seeking to align themselves with the center of the electorate in 1957's *Economic Theory of Democracy*.

100. Ibid., p. 89.

101. For a slightly different take, see Klein, 2000, pp. 7–12.

102. Bennett, W. Lance, "The UnCivic Culture: Communication, Identity, and the Rise of Lifestyle Politics." Ithiel de Sola Pool Lecture, American Political Science Association, published in P.S.: Political Science and Politics, Vol. 31 (December 1998), pp. 41–61.

103. See Turow, 1997.

104. See Trout and Rivkin, 2000.

105. This is called building fellowship as Ries and Ries, 2002, explain on pp. 56–60.

106. Travis, 2000, p. 17.

107. Ibid.

108. Ibid., p. 18.

109. Mark and Pearson, 2001, p. 1. This is a point also made by Klein, 2000, p. 116.

110. Ibid.

111.   Ibid., pp. 5–6.

112.   Ibid., p. 9.

113.   Ibid., p. 11.

114.   Ibid., p. 140.

115.   Ibid., p. 17.

116.   Ibid., pp. 17–18.

117.   Turow, 1997, entire but as far as branding role in such a society goes pp. 91–93.

118.   Mark and Pearson, 2001, p. 44.

119.   Ibid.

120.   Zyman, 2000, pp. 67–69 and 76–83.

121.   Travis, 2000, p. 4 and this is also something of which Newman, 1999a writes on pp. 88–91 regarding politics specifically.

122.   Zyman, 2001, p. 71 notes that not all audiences will share a response to the same stimulus.

123.   Travis, 2000, p. 7.

124.   As Newman, 1999a notes on p. 119.

125.   Travis, 2000, p. 9.

126.   Ibid., p. 11.

127.   Ibid.

128.   McConnell, Huba, and Kawasaki, 2003.

129.   Travis, 2000, p. 11.

130.   Newman, 1999a, pp. 89–91 nicely outlines the importance of emotion in selling products and politicians.

131.   Sabato and Simpson, 1996, examine indepth without naming a variety of common multilevel marketing techniques that were used to build support for GOPAC, Newt Gingrich, and the Contract. For an in-depth examination of viral marketing's use in the 2004 election, please see The Multilevel Marketing of the President by MATT BAI, *New York Times Magazine* http://www.nytimes.com/2004/04/25/magazine/25GROUNDWAR.html (published: April 25, 2004) article last visited October 9, 2006.

132.   Travis, 2000, p. 12.

133.   Ibid., p. 21.

134.   Bennett, 2003, pp. 99 and 140–141.

135.   Ries and Ries, 2002, show the importance of keeping a focused brand throughout their work.

136.   Czerniawski and Maloney, 1999, p. 57.

137.   Ibid.

138.   For a discussion of value's use in political marketing and a good background on the subject, see Butler and Collins in Newman, 1999a, pp. 55–67 but especially pp. 64–70.

139.   Karl Rove Address to the CPAC Convention. February 17, 2005 Federal News Service Transcript.

140.   Ibid.

141.   Ibid.

142.   Ibid.

143.   Ibid.

144.   Lakoff, 2004, pp. 20–34.

145.   http://www.msnbc.msn.com/id/6485241/, link last visited June 1, 2006.

146.   Trout and Rivkin, 2000, for an examination of the way in which branded individuals help to build brands.

147.   Interview with Grover Norquist. *Frontline: The Archetect.* www.pbs.org, link last visited June 1, 2006.

148.   See Newman, 1999a, pp. 49–68 for an examination of the impact of technology on political marketing and see Rampton and Stauber, 2004, pp. 47–100 for a discussion of the variety of ways in which Conservatives have built a message distribution system in different channels.

149.   For an examination of the changing nature of the media system, see West's the Fall of the Media Establishment.

150.   Newman, 1999a, pp. 25–26.

151.   http://www.umich.edu/~nes/nesguide/toptable/tab3_2.htm first accessed October 13, 2005 and last accessed October 9, 2006

152.   See Butler and Collins in Newman, 1999a, p. 59 for an argument about line extensions in politics.

153.   An interesting study of this regarding think tanks is Ricci, 1993.

154.   For an in-depth discussion of the modern political party and its uses in the United States, see Aldrich, 1995.

155.   Ibid., pp. 276–296.

156.   As we saw Newman, 1999a, does on pp. 37–38.

157.   Zyman, 2000, pp. 76–78 examines the way in which these three things fit together to produce a strong brand image and give the consumer a reason to purchase one product over another.

158.   Ibid., pp. 126–128.

159.   See Schnur, in Newman, 1999b, pp. 143–148 for a discussion of audience targeting and message development.

160.   Especially on pp. 7–9 but also throughout the work.

161.   Robert Salisbury, "An Exchange Theory of Interest Groups", *Midwest Journal of Political Science*, Volume 13 #1(February 1969) pp.1–32, and Newman, 1999a, p. 39.

162.   Ibid.

163.   Ibid., p. 23.

164.   Ibid., p. 208.

165.   Ibid., p. 218.

166.   Moore and Slater, 2003, pp. 291, 313, 315.

167.   Woodward, 2002, p. 122.

168.   Ibid.

169.   Moore and Slater, 2003, p. 227 discuss Rove's relationship with the tobacco industry in Texas and its impact on the Bush Administration's policy choices. Lakoff, on pp. 31–32, examines the political value to be gotten from passing this initiative because it defunded Texas trial lawyers who give to Democrats.

170.   Ibid.

171.   Waldman, 2004, pp. 205.

172.   And in that sense, it can be argued, it resembles Key's empty echo chamber argument from 1960's *Public Opinion and American Democracy*.

173.   Key, 1963 *Public Opinion and Democracy*.

174.   Newman, 1999a, pp. 39–42.

175.   Zyman, 2000, pp. 57–62 and 85–87 discusses this problem and Coke's solution to it. Newman, 2001, pp. 99–101 uses it as an analogy to explain the Clinton failure on healthcare.

176.   George Lakoff, *Don't Think Of an Elephant!*, p. 22.

177.   Ibid.

178.   Ibid.

179.   Zyman, 2000, p. 40 shows the importance of this in brand building and positioning.

180.   A point that Lakoff, writing a year in advance of Katrina, made on p. 29 when writing about tax cuts' impact on government capacity.

181.   Lakoff, 2004, notes the way in which the pro-life movement's goals are highly specific and structured on pp. 84–85.

182.   http://www.whitehouse.gov/news/releases/2004/04/20040401-3.html, link last visited June 1, 2006.

183.   For a complementary analysis of the Bush–Reagan relationship and how that is aimed at the Conservative base see "How Bush Went Back to the 1970's" by John B. Judis, Ruy Teixeira, and Marisa Katz, *New Republic*, November 15, 2004.

184.   See Waldman, 2004, pp. 208–216 for a discussion of the goals of the policy and rhetoric supporting what I argue is a brand promoting it.

185.   Tim Wise, *Reagan, Race and Remembrance Reflections on the American Divide Black Commentator*, http://www.blackcommentator.com/94/94_wise_reagan_pf.html, link last visited June 2006.

186.   Something that marketers must take into consideration in order to be successful as Newman, 1999a shows on p. 43.

187.   Thomas Frank, 2004, p. 123.

188.   Ibid., pp. 128, 136.

189.   Ibid., p. 124.

190.   Ibid., p. 125.

191.   Ibid., p. 162.

192.   See Czerniawski and Maloney, 1999, and Newman, 1999a, for an in-depth examination of these topics.

193.   "Matures" as Smith and Culman, 1997, term them.

194.   Ibid.

195.   Ibid.

196.   Jamieson and Waldman, 2003, pp. 143–146.

197.   Mark and Pearson, 2001, pp. 35–36 and see Teixeira and Rodgers, 2000, pp. 37–38 for a discussion of post-materialism in the United States.

198.   Ries and Trout, 2001, p. 2, and for one argument about the way in which positioning works in political marketing campaigns generally see Barnes, pp. 413–415 in Newman (ed.), 1999.

199.   Zyman and Miller, 2000, pp. 77–79 note the importance and benefits that flow from such differentiation.

200.   Indeed many of the econometric models at that year's American Political Science Association Meeting predicted an easy Gore win, something that the author saw in person and Moore and Slater, 2003, note.

201.   Waldman, 2004, pp. 1–4 details Bush's personal attributes and their relationship with Reagan while Moore and Slater, 2003, examine the role that Karl Rove played in shaping brand W throughout their work.

202.   As Newman, 1999, pp. 99–101 in the case of the Clinton healthcare case.

203.   Ries and Ries, 2002, pp. 49–55.

204.   Ibid. and Ries and Trout, 2001.

205.   Newman, 1999, p. 92.

206.   See Manheim, 2001, for an in-depth discussion of corporate campaigns.

Chapter 2

1. For a useful discussion of technological changes and their impact on politics, see Newman, 1999, pp. 46–68.

2. McGirr, 2001, pp. 12–15.

3. See Butler and Collins, pp. 55–56 for a critique of the limits of the political science approach to political marketing in Newman (ed.), 1999b.

4. Nimmo pp. 84–85 in Newman (ed.), 1999b.

5. Ibid. quotes Ellul, 1965, p. 11 on this point.

6. Ibid.

7. For a good description of the period, see Schoenwald, 2001, pp. 1–34.

8. Schoenwald, 2001, pp. 5–6.

9. Ibid., pp. 9–13.

10. See Lowi (1996) Schoenwald (2001), and McGirr (2001) for three thorough examinations of the history of modern Conservatism. Also of note is Balz and Brownstein (1996) that provides an advanced examination of the movement's history as well as its operation through the Contract with America period that is complimentary to much of the historical events of the period covered in this book.

11. Schoenwald, 2001, p. 4.

12. Nancy Reagan as quoted in Rentschler, 2000, p. 6.

13. Viguerie and Franke, 2004, p. 84.

14. Lowi, 1996, pp. 194–197 discusses Reagan's impact as Conservative leader.

15. Johnson, 1991, p. 165 discusses Reagan's admiration for Coolidge.

16. 2001, see especially pp. 251–265.

17. Ibid., pp. 6–7.

18. Ibid., pp. 6–7.

19. Ibid., pp. 10–13.

20. Diamond, 1995, provides a useful history of Conservatism from a sociological perspective in general and this point in particular.

21. Ibid.

22. Schoenwald, 2001, goes into great detail about this phenomenon.

23. See Schoenwald, 2001, and Hunter, 1992.

24. Schoenwald, 2001.

25. 2004 Bonus Books.

26. Most notably Lowi, 1996, on pp. 113–218, does a very thorough job of outlining these different strains, their contradictions, and the way in which Reagan has held them all together.

27.   Lowi, 1996, p. 236.

28.   Ibid.

29.   Schoenwald, 2001, pp. 4–13 and 256–258.

30.   Berry, 1999, especially pp. 87–118. His description of the costs and benefits of Richard Viguerie's activities on p. 95 is particularly enlightening.

31.   Edelman, 1988, especially pp. 1–12 and 66–89.

32.   Schoenwald, 2001, pp. 264–265 nicely summarizes his point about the conflict between the Republican Eastern establishment and the Conservative movement while McGirr's entire study focuses on the role that regionalism played in building Conservatism as a social movement.

33.   McGirr, 2001, pp. 13–19 and 215–216.

34.   Schoenwald, 2001, pp. 7 and 60–61.

35.   McGirr, 2001, pp. 134–135 notes the role that specific industries played in the Goldwater campaign.

36.   These themes and the role that they played in shaping the Conservative movement are examined throughout McGirr's and Schoenwald's work.

37.   See Schoenwald, 2001, p. 138.

38.   Cohen, 2003. While the most relevant portion of the work for this is the last portion, the entire work is a useful examination of the role that the values of consumerism and techniques of consumer marketing played in recent American history.

39.   Ibid., p. 396.

40.   Ibid., p. 409.

41.   Klein, 2000 pp. 21–61.

42.   See Rampton and Stauber, 1995 and 2002, for two book-length discussions of the expanding role that the public relations industry has come to play in American politics.

43.   Putnam, 2000, especially pp. 1–64 and 216–247.

44.   Rampton and Stauber, *Toxic Sludge is Good for You: Lies, Damn Lies and the Public Relations Industry*, 1995.

45.   Ibid., p. 14.

46.   Ibid., p. 24 and for a book-length treatment of Bernays see Larry Tye's work *The Father of Spin: Edward Bernays and the Birth of Public Relations*, 1998.

47.   Ibid., p. 24.

48.   Ibid., p. 162.

49.   For example, Moore and Slater, 2003, pp. 165 and 223–227 show that Karl Rove served in such a capacity for the Phillip Morris Company. For an in-depth discussion of branding and PR campaigns, see Zyman, 2000, pp. 129–152.

50.   Zyman and Miller, 2000, p. 135.

51.   Ibid., p. 135.

52.   Ibid., p. 140

53.   Ibid., p. 137.

54.   Ibid., p. 143.

55.   Just as ibid., pp. 144–148.

56.   Cohen, 2003, p. 408.

57.   See also James Twitchell's, 2003, book *Branded Nation* that looks at the prolif-
       eration of branding techniques throughout American life but fails to delve deeply
       into the way that political branding operates

58.   Krugman, 1994, especially chapter 1, and Ginsburg *and Shefter* 1999, pp. 86–92.

59.   Ibid.

60.   Ibid., Johnson, 1991, p. 97 and Ginsburg and Shefter, 1999, pp. 94–100.

61.   Schoenwald, 2001, pp. 4–5 and 14–29.

62.   Edsall and Edsall, 1992, pp. 1–29 and 116–136.

63.   Ginsburg and Shefter, 1999, pp. 112–115.

64.   For an in-depth discussion of the Cold War's impact on Conservatism, see
       Schoenwald, 2001, pp. 35–61 and McGirr, 2001, pp. 69–70 and 170–176. Page
       176 is particularly useful for a case study of Conservative feelings about the U.N.

65.   McGirr, 2001, pp. 170–176.

66.   Ibid.

67.   Interview with Grover Norquist *PBS's Frontline: The Architect.* http://www.pbs.org/
       wgbh/pages/frontline/shows/architect/interviews/norquist.html, link last vis-
       ited June 1, 2006.

68.   For a thorough history of the 1960s see Isserman and Kazin, 2000, and for the
       way in which this culminated in a mood by the end of the 1970s, see Frank, 2004,
       pp. 138–157.

69.   See Edsall and Edsall, 1992, chapters 6 through 10 for an in-depth analysis of
       these issues and Berry, 1984, p. 33.

70.   Piven and Cloward, 1993, chapters 9 and 10 very much show this point. Edsall
       and Edsall, 1992, and McGirr, 2001, pp. 203–205 and 239–240.

71.   Edsall and Edsall, 1992, chapters 7 and 9 go into great depth about the policy and
       political calculus made by the Reagan camp during the 1980 election and in its imme-
       diate aftermath. This specific point comes from p. 142. McGirr, 2001, pp. 215–216
       nicely summarizes Phillips' argument about the Republican's ability to attract this
       audience.

72.   Ibid.

73.   Ibid.

74.   Berry, 1984, pp. 147–149.

75.   Berry, 1984, p. 91.

76.   Schoenwald, 2001, pp. 256–258 does a nice job of summarizing these movements

and their impact on Conservatism.

77. Lowi, 1996, pp. 76–79.

78. Edsall and Edsall, 1992, p. 69.

79. Schoenwald, 2001, pp. 256–258.

80. Ibid.

81. McGirr, 2001, pp. 225–235.

82. See McGirr, 2001, pp. 217–261 for an analysis of the way in which such social movements influenced the development of the Conservative movement in general and Christian Right in particular and added something to the movement's anti-communist streak.

83. Ibid., pp. 232–235.

84. Ibid. shows this clearly on pp. 225–235.

85. Isserman and Kazin, 2000, pp. 147–186 does a very good job of summarizing this culture's development, spread, and goals.

86. Ibid, pp. 183–186.

87. For a good summary see Schoenwald, 2001, pp. 218 and 251 and for a good examination of Ronald Reagan as a constructed counterweight to this in American political marketing, see Newman, p. 262 in Newman (ed.), 1999b.

88. www.swiftvets.com, link last visited June 1, 2006.

89. See Edsall and Edsall, 1992, pp. 108–109 for further analysis.

90. McGirr, 2001, p. 232.

91. For a complementary view and example of the way in which George W. Bush fits into this, see Waldman, 2004, pp. 12–16. For a thorough examination of many of the topics examined herein relative to the social changes that have taken place in the United States since the 1960s and their impact on the forms of civic association in which Americans engage, see Skocpol, 2003, especially pp. 175–220, but the entire work is useful from the standpoint of understanding how the changes of which she writes sets the stage for the branded politics being presented herein.

92. See Piven and Cloward, 1993, especially pp. 448–449.

93. Lakoff, 2004, pp. 81–88.

94. P.J. O'Rourke "The Shocking Convictions and Astonishing Grabbiness of the Left" in Deaver, 2005, p. 70.

95. See Ries and Ries, 2002, pp. 49–59, 73–81 for the different techniques that can be used to expand the products being promoted by a brand and to expand the number of brands that an individual company can work with.

96. Zyman, 2000, p. 88.

97. See Berry, 1999, pp. 34–60 for a discussion of postmaterialism from the perspective of Liberal interest groups and lobbying.

98. Ibid., pp. 58–59.

99. Ibid.

100. Ibid.

101. Berry, 1999, p. 59.

102. See Diamond, 1995 and 1998, for book-length treatments of these topics.

103. Ibid.

104. Diamond, 1995, pp. 100–103.

105. Ibid., pp. 120 and 123. See also Viguerie and Franke, 2004, pp. 239–244.

106. NRA Endorses George W. Bush for President, Wednesday, October 13, 2004. www.nrapvf.org, link last visited May 20, 2006.

107. Spitzer, 1995, pp. 100–103.

108. Piven and Cloward, 1993, pp. 343–399 describe these economic changes in depth.

109. Berry, 1999, pp. 40–47.

110. See Berry, 1984, pp. 41, 60–61.

111. Edsall and Edsall, 1992, devote chapters to the increasing salience of the tax issue.

112. See Phillips, 1990, for an in-depth examination of the politics of Conservative economic policies through the George H.W. Bush years and 1994 describes the economic sectors that were advantaged by these years in depth.

113. For an example of the uses of class warfare charges, see Waldman, 2004, p. 59.

114. See Johnson, 1991, pp. 34–35.

115. Teixeira, and Rodgers, 2000, especially pp. 23–65. Ginsburg and Shefter, 1999, pp. 115–119 also provides a nice summary of the way in which Conservatives targeted blue collar workers in general and Southerners in particular.

116. Ginsburg and Shefter, 1999, pp. 112–114 provides a nice examination of the politics of the tax issue.

117. An example of this is provided in Waldman, 2004, pp. 211–212.

118. For example, see Edsall and Edsall, 1992 chapter 8, especially p. 168 that examines Conservative economic policy's impact on ratepayers.

119. See Schoenwald, 2001, p. 59 for a discussion of John Kennedy's symbolic role in motivating Conservatives and Newman, 1999a, pp. 103 and 104 for an analysis of Carter's image problems. For a good general history of the 1970's see Feinstein, 2000.

Chapter 3

1. Schoenwald, 2001, p. 256 notes how the neo-Conservatives and religious right especially benefited from the 1980 election. Lowi, 1996, pp. 158–172 does a thorough job of outlining Reagan's foundational role in Conservatism.

2. Ibid., p. 192.

3. Newman, 1999, pp. 24–25.

4. Schoenwald, 2001, p. 203.

5. James Combs, 1993.

6. For data about the actual Reagan popularity versus the impact of the essence of what I term the Reagan Heritage brand, see Waldman, 2004, pp. 3–4.

7. For a concise yet illuminating synopsis, see Schoenwald, 2001, pp. 201–207.

8. See Dallek, 1999, or Combs, 1993, for book-length discussions of this.

9. As was shown in the prior chapter with the Norquist point about the difference between Reagan and Goldwater.

10. Ronald Reagan as quoted in Dallek (1999, p. 27).

11. For a thorough history of Reagan the man and President, see Morris, 1999, and for a history of Reagan plus his early years in the White House, see Dugger, 1983.

12. See Newman (ed.), 1999b, p.262 for a discussion of Reagan's abilities in these areas.

13. See Dallek, 1999, p. 57 for a look at the way in which Reagan consciously worked to appeal to suburban swing voters and Newman, 1999, p. 44 for an example of the use of segmentation in political marketing.

14. As Schoenwald, 2001, shows on pp. 213 and 216.

15. Schoenwald, 2001, discusses the elite nature of Reagan's initial backers on p. 201.

16. See Waldman, 2004, pp. 1–2 and 11–1254 about the way in which George W. Bush has presented himself as just an average guy.

17. Frank, 1994, pp. 89–109 discusses such a phenomenon in the relations between upper and lower class Kansas Conservatives.

18. See Pemberton, 1997, for a discussion of Reagan's Midwest roots and his Western heritage.

19. As quoted in Deaver (ed.), 2005, p. 135.

20. Trout and Rivkin, 2000, p. 115.

21. Dallek, 1999, pp. 26–29.

22. Dallek, 1999, p. 27 shows that Reagan often provided exactly this justification for his partisan switch.

23. Trout and Rivkin, 2000, p. 125 present these commercial applications.

24. Ibid., p. 125.

25. Ibid., pp. 78 and 115.

26. Ibid., p. 115.

27. Carol Moog as quoted in Trout and Rivkin, 2000, p. 116.

28. Ibid.

29. Trout and Rivkin, 2000, p. 116

30. Ibid., p. 116.

31. Ibid., pp. 119–125.

32. http://www.knowledgeboard.com/download/3391/oldfriend.htm, link last visited June 1–10, 2005.

33. http://www.knowledgeboard.com/download/3391/oldfriend.html, link visited as above.

34. http://www.knowledgeboard.com/download/3391/oldfriend.html, link visited as above.

35. http://www.knowledgeboard.com/download/3391/oldfriend.html, link visited as above.

36. Combs, 1993, pp. 25–43 goes into significant detail about the importance of the small town in the Reagan narrative, while Johnson, 1991, p. 45 focuses on the way in which Reagan used it as a selling point or credential and Deaver mentions Reagan's use of it in both of his books. For a book-length treatment of Reagan's history in Illinois, see Wymbs, 1987.

37. Trout and Rivkin, 2000, p. 118 argue that George W. Bush's heritage is that of his family and, to some extent that is true but, as we will see his real heritage is that of Ronald Reagan.

38. http://www.whitehouse.gov/news/releases/2004/06/20040611-2.html, link last visited May 10, 2006.

39. Trout and Rivkin, 2000, pp. 120–121.

40. Ibid., p. 121.

41. See, for example, "Counterattack: Remember Dukakis" by Matthew Cooper, http://www.cnn.com/2004/ALLPOLITICS/02/02/timep.dukakis.tm/ link first visited September 20, 2004 and last visited October 20, 2006.

42. For a good discussion of Reagan's personal traits and political uses, see Schieffer and Gates, 1989, pp. 164–190. For an analysis of several of the traits that make up the Reagan heritage brand and the factual differences between those and the real Reagan that was written in the wake of Reagan's death and funeral, see "The Man, The Myths: Don't Believe Everything That You Hear About Ronald Reagan," http://www.slate.com/id/2102060/ by David Greenberg link first visited July 2, 2004 and last visited October 19, 2006. For a more positive analysis of the traits of what I am calling the Reagan Heritage brand, see "Re-Examining Reagan" by Rebecca Hagelin, http://www.heritage.org/Press/Commentary/ ed112503a.cfm, link first visited August 10, 2004 and last visited October 20, 2006.

43. Cannon, 1991, p. 38.

44. As Deaver, 2001, shows on pp. 51–58, this is because he had refined his message over a number of years by participating in political and corporate town hall events and, as noted above, Newman (1999) argues that this has been very important to creating the image people hold of Reagan.

45. Cannon, 1991, p. 41 has aptly termed this the "everyman" role and Conservatives have used it throughout their use of the brand strategy hence it will be incorporated throughout the rest of this work as such.

46. Cannon, 1991, p. 41.

47. Ibid., pp. 41–42.

48. McGirr, 2001, pp. 23–55 presents this phenomenon in depth.

49. Some observers such as Edsall and Edsall, 1992, pp. 3–31 suggest that the movement has always been top-down driven.

50. http://www.whitehouse.gov/news/releases/2004/06/20040611-2.html, link last visited June 1, 2006.

51. Johnson, 1991, pp. 171–173 for generalities about scandals and pp. 301–365 for Iran-Contra specifically.

52. As Dallek, 1999, pp. 30–60 shows, he had done exactly this while a candidate for and serving as California Governor.

53. See Johnson, 1991, pp. 76–81 for the way in which the events of the 1960s propelled Reagan's early electoral career. See Lowi, 1996, pp. 109–157 for the way in which the Conservative coalition developed during the 1950s and 1960s.

54. Dallek, 1999, pp. 56–58 notes Reagan's ability to do so.

55. Lowi, 1996, pp. 162, 195–196, Pemberton, 1997, p. 47, and Cannon, 1991, pp. 217–218.

56. Lowi, 1996, pp. 158–162.

57. Pemberton, 1997, pp. 4, 73, 105, 204, 209.

58. Dallek, 1999, p. 3 outlines these traits as does Johnson, 1991, pp. 46–51.

59. Pemberton, 1997, pp. 44–45 presents a nice synopsis of Reagan's personal traits and their impact on the Conservative movement's public persona.

60. Deaver (ed.), 2005, p. 162.

61. Mehlman in Ibid., p. 127.

62. See Schieffer's and Gates' 1989 work, p. 324 or Pemberton, 1997, pp. 192–197 for a discussion of the switch

63. Viguerie and Franke, 2004, p. 122.

64. Ibid., p. 124.

65. Ibid., especially pp. 39–97 outlines how Conservatives used direct mail and branding to build a movement, as well as how they aimed at specific audiences and pp. 150–55 for their analysis of the uses of direct mail marketing by liberals.

66. For a good treatment of the way in which George W. Bush campaign tried to package their man as an average guy and the relationship this has with Reagan, see Waldman, 2004, pp. 1–22. For an examination of the 1980 Reagan campaign, see Newman, 1999, pp. 25–26 and 72–74.

67. Cannon, 1991, p. 288.

68.   Susskind, 2004, p. 291.

69.   Waldman, 2004, pp. 12–20 argues that George W. Bush has done just this.

70.   For a discussion of the uses of persona versus Al Gore, see Waldman, 2004, pp. 66–77 and 109–110.

71.   For a discussion of Bush versus Dukakis, see Schieffer and Gates, 1989, pp. 367–374 or Newman, 1999a, pp. 74–75.

72.   "Senate Debates Dismissal," bbc.co.uk, January 26, 1999. http://news.bbc.co.uk/ 1/hi/events/clinton_under_fire/latest_news/262960.stm, link last visited June 1, 2006.

73.   Dallek, 1999, pp. 32–33.

74.   Ibid.

75.   Cannon, 1991, pp. 206–208 for a nice summary of the different ways in which supporters and critics construct the Reagan administration.

76.   For example, Krugman, 1994, shows how this dichotomy works in economic policy.

77.   See Pemberton, 1997, pp. 205–206 for an example of the emphasis that the Reagan team put on building favorable public impressions of their man.

78.   For a good summary of Bush's tax cuts and their impact, see Waldman, 2004, pp. 214–215 and 225–226.

79.   For example, consider the case of David Stockman as presented in Schieffer and Gates, 1989, pp. 141–163.

80.   Peters, 1990, pp. 232–264.

81.   For details of the way in which the Reagan team conducted damage control in this case, see Johnson, 1991, pp. 333–365.

82.   Newman, 1999a, p. 44 uses them as a case study of audience segmentation.

83.   Micklethwait and Wooldridge, 2004, p. 94.

84.   Ibid.

85.   Ibid., p. 94.

86.   See Newman, 1999a, pp. 74–76 for an analysis of the way in which the 1988 Bush campaign in this area.

87.   For a discussion of the marketing strategy of the 1988 Bush campaign, see Newman, 1999a, pp. 26–27 or Jamieson, 1996.

88.   See Schieffer and Gates, 1989, pp. 369–372.

89.   For example, see the home page of the Reagan Legacy Project at http:// www.reaganlegacy.org/about/index.htm, link last visited June 1, 2006.

90.   http://www.reagan.utexas.edu/archives/reference/thingsnamed.html

91.   For a number of examples and a critique of the entire undertaking, see "Honoring the Memory: Trivializing Ronald Reagan," http://www.americanprogress.org/site/ pp.asp?c=biJRJ8OVF&b=88803, link visited June 1, 2006.

92. http://www.reaganlegacy.org/dedications/index.htm, link last visited June 1, 2006.

93. http://www.reaganlegacy.org/projects/index.htm, link last visited June 1, 2006.

94. http://www.yaf.org/ranch/reaganranch.asp, link last visited June 1, 2006.

95. http://www.rememberronaldreagan.com/, link last visited June 1, 2006.

96. http://www.ronaldreaganmemorial.com and http://www.ronaldreaganmemor ial.com/licensees.asp, link last visited June 1, 2006.

97. Trout and Rivkin, 2000, pp. 125–126.

98. http://www.reagansheritage.org/html/briefing_room.shtml, link last visited June 1, 2006.

99. www.margaretthatcher.org, link last visited June 1, 2006.

100. "Reagan, Reagan, Everywhere" by Bill Adair. Article appeared in *The St. Petersburg Times*, September 9, 2000, www. Reaganlegacy.org, link last visited June 1, 2006.

101. "Cows or No Bush's Ranch Works," *The Seattle Times*, August 31, 2005, http://seattletimes.nwsource.com/html/nationworld/2002460551_prairiechapel31. html, link last visited October 8, 2006.

102. Schieffer and Gates, 1989, p. 324.

Chapter 4

1. For an in-depth analysis of the marketing of both candidates in the 1988 election, see Bennett, 1996, pp. 35–40.

2. Interview with Grover Norquist. *PBS's Frontline: The Architect.* {http://www.pbs.org/ wgbh/pages/frontline/shows/architect/interviews/norquist.html}, link last visited June 1, 2006.

3. Micklethwait and Wooldridge, 2004, p. 98.

4. Ibid., p. 99.

5. Viguerie and Franke, 2004, p. 348.

6. Both quotes from Tom DeLay as quoted in Micklethwait and Wooldridge, 2004, pp. 104–105.

7. Bennett, 1996, notes on pp. 69–71.

8. For a discussion of unifed versus divided government and the public policy outputs from both see Mayhew, 1991.

9. Ginsburg and Shefter, 1999, pp. 101–103.

10. Ginsburg and Shefter, 1999, p. 61.

11. Ibid., pp. 57–58.

12.   See, for example, Viguerie and Franke, 2004, p. 348 for one example of such sentiments.

13.   For a thorough examination of Watergate's impact on subsequent Presidents, see Woodward, 2000.

14.   Garment, 1991, pp. 142–169 examines this topic in depth.

15.   Ibid., pp. 83–108 for an in depth examination of this topic.

16.   For an examination of sex as a scandal topic, see ibid., pp. 169–193.

17.   See Ginsburg and Shefter, 1999, *Politics by Other Means,* especially pp. 131–171 or Garment, 1991, pp. 285–303.

18.   For a good description of the period, see Johnson, 2001.

19.   Cohen, 2003; examines the politics of consumerism, Putnam, 2000; looks at the transformation of American civic life, West and Orman, 2003; look at the way in which celebrity culture has changed America; while Bellah et al., 1985, examine the role values play in contemporary America.

20.   Ginsburg and Shefter, 1999, pp. 36–39.

21.   For a useful description of the politics of this era, see Ginsburg and Shefter, 1999, pp. 59–70.

22.   Conason and Lyons, 2001, provide a good case study of the way in which one top- down driven effort, the so-called Arkansas Project, both found and distributed negative information about Clinton as does Brock, 2002, pp. 193–236.

23.   For an in-depth description of the corporate campaign, see Manheim, 2001.

24.   For an in-depth examination of the Clinton scandals on the economic fortunes of Conservatives, see Brock, 2002.

25.   See Garment, 1991, pp. 259–284 for an analysis of the personal costs of these scandals and, particularly, the portion focused on Theodore J. Olsen.

26.   See Ginsburg and Shefter, 1999, pp. 161–171.

27.   For an in-depth description of the advocacy explosion see Berry, 1984, for a look at think tanks and their marketing efforts see Ricci, 1993, and for a look at the Conservative press see Brock, 2004.

28.   West and Orman, 2003, detail celebrity's impact on American politics in general.

29.   Bennett, 2003, pp. 100–104.

30.   See Hunter, 1992, for a discussion on the use of hot buttons in political marketing.

31.   See Garment, 1991, pp. 285–304 for an examination of scandal's impact on public service and those willing to perform it.

32.   See Hunter, 1992, for a discussion of orthodox religious elements; Diamond, 1998, for a thorough examination of the Christian Right's activities during the period; Texeria and Rodgers 2000, for working-class white men; and Smith and Clurman 1997, on Vietnam and the baby boomers.

33.   See Conason and Lyons, 2001, for an in-depth examination of the sources of the anti-Clinton campaign among his Arkansas political opponents.

34.   Smith and Clurman, 1997, p. 54.

35.   Ibid.

36.   Ibid., p.10.

37.   www.pollingreport.com, link last visited June 1, 2006.

38.   Ibid.

39.   Ries and Ries, 2002, pp. 39–43.

40.   Ibid., pp. 7–35.

41.   Ibid.

42.   See Braunstein and Levine, 2000, especially pp. 36–53.

43.   Ibid., pp. 59–65.

44.   Brock, 2004, examines the development of Conservative media.

45.   Ries and Ries, 2002, pp. x–xvi offer a nice synopsis of the concept and this is also consistent with the argument made in the Salisbury piece that was cited in Chapter 1.

46.   For a thorough examination of the mainstream media's coverage of the Clinton scandals, see Kalb, 2001.

47.   Ries and Ries, 2002, pp. 44–55.

48.   Ibid., pp. 30–32.

49.   See Bennett, 1996, pp. 55–77 for a useful discussion of the 1992 Clinton campaign.

50.   For example, Toobin, 1999, p. 102 provides an example of Lucianne Goldberg's similar sentiments.

51.   Luntz, 1994, p. 32, unpublished document provided by anonymous source.

52.   See Newman, 1999a, pp. 97–98 and 112–117 for an analysis of the Clinton scandals from the perspective of analyzing the President's marketing performance.

53.   Ries and Ries, 2002, pp. 39–43 and 205–209.

54.   Ibid., p. 42.

55.   Ibid., pp. 164–171.

56.   See Trout and Rivkin, 2000, *Differentiate or Die,* for a book-length discussion on the importance of differentiation in brand building and marketing campaigns. This phenomenon is part of the above-noted problem of credentials.

57.   Ries and Ries, 2002, pp. 48–55, and Ries and Trout, 2001, pp. 101–113.

58.   Ries and Trout, 2001, pp. 53–60.

59.   Ries and Ries, 2002, pp. 97–104 discuss consistency in depth.

60.   In a fashion consistent with the argument made about tabloid versus mainstream journalism in Sabato, Stencel and Lichter, 2000.

61.   This is complementary to the overall argument about Conservative media made by Brock in his 2002 work and for a good background on the culture of scandal in America, see the chapter entitled "Scandal Times" in Johnson, 2001.

62.   Conason and Lyons, 2000, pp. 54 and 112–115 and Brock, 2002, pp. 134–159.

63.   Conason and Lyons, 2000, pp. 112–115.

64.   Ibid., p. 115.

65.   Ibid., p. 113.

66.   Moore, 1991, pp. 71; 73–74.

67.   Ibid., pp. 73–74; for a different analysis from the perspective of cascade effects and public opinion, see Sunstern in Kaplan and Moran, 2001, pp. 13–14.

68.   Conason and Lyons, 2000, p. 103 for a good background on the American Spectator; Schoenwald, 2001, p.167 for the origins of the National Review; and pp. 27–32 for an examination of the role that popularizers have played in spreading the Conservative message.

69.   For in-depth examinations of the business of Conservatism, see Brock, 2002 and 2004, and for an examination of the role that Conservative media plays in building the movement, see Rampton and Stauber, 2004.

70.   Viguerie and Franke, 2004, pp. 108–109, pp. 173–211, and pp. 277–292. See also Balz and Brownstein, 1996; p. 169, p. 171, for a second analysis of Limbaugh's role in introducing the public to modern Conservatism and its many political products.

71.   Hunter, 1992.

72.   Viguerie and Franke, 2004, pp. 178–181 discuss the evolution of these new technologies and their impact on Conservative marketing.

73.   Ibid., p. 183.

74.   See Brock, 2002, for a discussion of the advertising strategies of various Conservative media entrepreneurs relative to the Limbaugh program.

75.   Ibid., p. 77; For a thorough examination of the new channels that became available to Conservatives, see Viguerie and Franke, pp. 213–236.

76.   Ibid., pp. 261–275 examines the Conservative publishing business and its history in depth while Brock, 2002, discusses that plus its operation throughout his work.

77.   Smith and Clurman, 1998, provide these terms and excellent descriptions of them on pp. 15–117. not done yet

78.   Ibid., pp. 49–50.

79.   Ibid. describes the size of the boomer generation on pp. 42–69.

80.   See West, 2001, or Sabato, 1991, for thorough discussions of the role that increasing competition is having on journalistic standards.

81.   See Johnson's, 2001 chapter entitled "Scandal Times," for more on this era.

82.   See Kalb, 2001, pp. 216–220 for an analysis of the impact of the Clinton-Lewinsky hug on public opinion.

83.   Garment's, 1991, or Ginsberg and Shefter's, 1999, book-length treatments of scandals show that the early Clinton ones are very much this.

84.   See Ginsburg and Shefter, 1999, pp. 152–153.

85. Viguerie and Franke, 2004, pp. 181–92.

86. Conason and Lyons, 2000, profile these various groups, especially in Little Rock and the funders of the so-called "Arkansas Project" throughout their work while Brock provides very useful background and a personal history in his 2002 work.

87. Klein, 2002, p. 111 notes Fiske was appointed at Clinton's request.

88. "Whitewater Report Clears Clintons" UPI September 20, 2000, found at newsmax.com, link last visited June 1, 2006, as Newman, 1999a, notes on p. 118 Starr seemed to be his own worst enemy.

89. For a detailed examination of Whitewater, see Stewart, 1996.

90. Newman, 1999a, p. 118.

91. For example, Diamond, 1998, argues that the entire administration was tailor made for the kinds of marketing efforts of which I am arguing, among the Christian Right.

92. Newman, 1999a, p. 83.

93. Ibid., p. 119.

94. See Newman, 1999a, pp. 82–83 for an alternative analysis of these events.

95. See Morris, 2001, for an alternative theory of incumbent success in the 2000 House elections and Hibbing and Theiss-Morse, 1995, for an argument about how Congress has come to be seen in adversarial terms anyway by much of the American public in recent decades. Not done

96. Waldman, 2004, pp. 115–117 discusses as a series of events.

Chapter 5

1. For a study of the use of branding, positioning and product differentiation in the news business, see James T. Hamilton's *All the News That's Fit to Sell.*

2. http://www.pbs.org/wgbh/pages/frontline/shows/persuaders/interviews/luntz.html}, link last visited May 27, 2006, for an interview with Frank Luntz that is very useful in understanding language's role in brand building, as well as for insight into the Contract with America. The author was also provided with copies of two documents by anonymous sources that were written by Luntz. These were very useful in understanding the way in which language was practically applied in the case of the Contract with America, even if there was little that was specifically used in this chapter. They were, *"The Language of A New Majority"* written in 1996, and, *"Year 30: A Strategic and Tactical Campaign Plan for the Republican Majority,"* written in 1994. For an analysis of the Contract with America in terms of its political and policy goals, see *"The Contract with America: Implementing New Ideas in the U.S.,"* by Jeffrey B. Gaynor *www.heritage.org,* link last visited on July 7, 2004.

3. Trout and Rivkin, 2004, p. 14.

4. See Isserman and Kazin, 2000, for an examination of these events and their aftermath.

5. www.umich.edu/_nes/nesguid/toptable/tab3_2.htm, link last visited October 9, 2006.

6. Ibid.

7. Trout and Rivkin, 2004, pp. 41–42.

8. Sabato and Simpson, 1996, pp. 87–89.

9. For a detailed examination of the many facets of positioning, see Ries and Trout *Positioning*, and for a very useful examination of repositioning oneself and one's rivals, see pp. 61–69.

10. Sabato and Simpson, 1996, provide a detailed examination of the delegitimation activities of Newt Gingrich and they set the pattern of subsequent Conservative behavior on pp. 85–87.

11. Sabato and Simpson, 1996, pp. 26–27 and 270.

12. For details on Gingrich's organization building see Sabato and Simpson, 1996, pp. 73–140. For details on the structure of the Amway model, see www.amway.com, link last visited June 1, 2006, and for a solid journalistic account of the 1994 House Freshmen that supports many of the points being made herein about the events during this Congress, see Killian, 1998.

13. Sabato and Simpson, 1996, pp. 73–102.

14. Ibid.

15. Ibid., pp. 87–88.

16. Ibid., p. 85.

17. See Viguerie and Franke, 2004, pp. 107–347 for a detailed treatment of these phenomena.

18. See Newman, 1999b, p. 262.

19. Zyman and Brott, 2002, p. 72.

20. Sabato and Simpson, 1996, pp. 96–98.

21. Ibid., p. 47 and Interview with Vin Weber. www.pbs.org, *Frontline: The Long March of Newt Gingrich*. Link last visited May 28, 2006.

22. Sabato and Simpson, 1996, p. 87 present a list of Gingrich's activities in this area.

23. Ries and Trout, 2001, pp. 61–69.

24. Drew, 1996, p. 60.

25. Remarks June 11, 1995 at Claremont, NH. Source: http://www.ibiblio.org/pub/archives/whitehouse-papers/1995/Jun/1995–06–11-President-and-Speaker-Gingrich-at-NH-Senior-Centre. This link contains a transcript issued by the White House. Link last visited June 1, 2006.

26. Ibid.

27. Sabato and Simpson, 1996, pp. 33–48.

28. Ibid.

29. Interview with Frank Gregorsky, www.pbs.org, *Frontline: The Long March of Newt Gingrich*. {http://www.pbs.org/wgbh/pages/frontline/newt/newtintwshtml/gregorsky.html}, link last visited May 30, 2006.

30. Ibid.

31. Ibid., and Sabato and Simpson, 1996, p. 47.

32. Sabato and Simpson, 1996, p. 82.

33. For a useful introduction to the coordinated campaign, see Steven J. Jarding, *Extensions* "State Political Parties and Coordinated Campaigns: Organization Waiting to Happen," (Summer 1987), pp. 4–5 and 17.

34. Sabato and Simpson, 1996, p. 47.

35. Ibid., pp. 46–47.

36. Ibid., pp. 87–90

37. Drew, 1996, p. 30.

38. "Democrats Plan as Confidence Grows" by Jonathan Weisman, Boston Globe, May 8, 2006. {http://www.boston.com/news/local/politics/us_house/articles/2006/05/08/democrats_plan_as_confidence_grows/}, link last visited May 8, 2006. For a working link as of June 2006 see {http://www. contracostatimes.com/mld/cctimes/news/politics/14522799.htm?source =Rss &channel=cctimes_politics}.

39. Interview with Vin Weber, *PBS's Frontline, The Long March of Newt Gingrich*. {http://www.pbs.org/wgbh/pages/frontline/newt/newtintwshtml/weber.html}, link last visited May 28, 2006.

40. Newman, 1999a, pp. 77–79 and Luntz, 1994 pp.2–3, unpublished document provided by anonymous source.

41. For an analysis of the key role that term limits played in selling the Contract, see Wray in Newman, 1999a, pp. 754–755.

42. Ibid. notes this on p. 78.

43. Ries and Ries, 2002, p. 75.

44. Drew, 1996, p. 31, and for a book-length discussion of positioning see the 2001 book of that name by Ries and Trout.

45. Drew, 1996, p. 32.

46. {http://www.house.gov/house/Contract/CONTRACT.html}, link last visited June 1, 2006.

47. Something that, as we saw, Newman, 1999a, noted on p. 78.

48. Drew, 1996, p. 33.

49. Ibid.

50. Ibid.

51. In this sense, they did use it as a postelection tool as Newman, 1999a, p.78 suggests but had also run on it.

52. Drew, 1996, pp. 39–40 for details about the inaugural sessions of Congress and the Contract.

53. Ibid., p. 36.

54. Ibid., p. 33.

55. Ibid., p. 43.

56. Ibid., p. 100.

57. Ibid., p. 185.

58. Ibid., p. 187.

59. Ibid., pp. 122–123 and Newman, 1999a, p. 78 for an analysis of talk radio's import during the campaign.

60. See Zyman and Brott, 2002, pp. 7 and 174–185.

61. As quoted in A. B. Stoddard "Twelve Years Later, Myths About the Contract Persist," *The Hill*, April 5, 2006. http://www.hillnews.com/thehill/export/TheHill/News/Campaign/040506.html, link last visited May 25, 2006.

62. As quoted in "Beyond the Contract" by Major Garrett. *Mother Jones*, March/April 1995 issue. http://www.motherjones.com/news/feature/1995/03/garrett.html, link last visited May 25, 2006.

63. Luntz, 1994 unpublished document provided by an anonymous source, p. 2.

64. Ries and Trout 2001, pp. 66–67.

65. See particularly the interview with Howard Calloway, "www.pbs.org, *Frontline The Long March of Newt Gingrich*. {http://www.pbs.org/wgbh/pages/frontline/newt/newtintwshtml/callaway3.html.} Link last visited May 25, 2006.

66. Ibid.

67. Interview with Eddie Mahe, "The Long March of Newt Gingrich." www.pbs.org *Frontline: The Long March of Newt Gingrich. {*http://www.pbs.org/wgbh/pages/frontline/newt/newtintwshtml/mahe.html.} Link last visited May 25, 2006. This interview is particularly useful in understanding a variety of the marketing techniques employed during this period and supports many of the points made herein.

68. "Language: A Key Mechanism of Control." *FAIR Update,* February, 1995. http://www.fair.org/index.php?page=1276 Link last visited October 8, 2006.

69. Ibid.

70. For details, see Sabato and Simpson, 1996, pp. 116–117.

71. For details of the way in which this presented Bill Clinton with a marketing opportunity, see Newman, 1999a, pp. 117- 121 and 79–81 for an assessment of the damage that was done to Conservatives in 1996.

72. George W. Bush remarks to the 2000 Republican National Convention. www.cnn.com. {http://www.cnn.com/ELECTION/2000/conventions/republican/transcripts/bush.html,} link last visited June 1, 2006.

73.   http://www.fair.org/activism/vandal-update.html, link last visited June 1, 2006. For a synopsis of these events, see Waldman, 2004, pp. 113–115.

74.   Ibid.

75.   http://archives.cnn.com/2001/ALLPOLITICS/stories/01/26/whitehouse.pranks.02/, link last visited June 1, 2006.

76.   Ibid.

77.   Ibid.

78.   Ibid.

79.   Waldman, 2004, also examines this episode and presents many of the same facts but does not do so in context of the brand strategy.

80.   Carina Chocano "Decoding the White House Dress Code," April 16, 2001, www.slate.com, link last visited June 1, 2006.

81.   Ibid.

Chapter 6

1.   Rampton and Stauber, 2003, pp. 128–130 point out the advantages of defining this conflict so broadly.

2.   See Susskind, 2004, pp. 74–75 and 82–88, 87.

3.   See Waldman, 2004, 125–32 for an examination of Bush's legitimacy as a result of the 2000 election.

4.   William Grieder "Under the Banner of the 'War' on Terror." *The Nation,* June 21, 2004 argues that the point to the war on terror was that it relaunched the Cold War. http://www.thenation.com/doc/20040621/greider, link last visited May 2, 2006. This is similar to analysis by Snow, 2003.

5.   Ibid. see also Piven, 2005 for an analysis of many of these same events, as well as domestic policy from an agenda setting perspective.

6.   Something that Moore and Slater, 2003, show on pp. 308–311.

7.   Ibid., p. 307 shows that the White House was very concerned about its ability to find bin laden by 2002.

8.   www.pollingreport.com. The data is CBS News Polling data as posted but all of the posted polls show the similar trends. The link for Bush's approval was first visited April 14, 2006 and last visited October 9, 2006

9.   See Rampton and Stauber, 2003, pp. 143–145 for an examination of the impact that fear has on presidential popularity.

10.   Waldman, 2004, pp. 81–86.

11.   As Russ Baker notes in "Two Years Before 9/11, Candidate Bush Was Already Talking about Attacking Iraq According to His Former Ghostwriter." October

28, 2004, http://www.commondreams.org/headlines04/1028–01.htm link last accessed October 9, 2006.

12. For an examination of Bush's press coverage in the wake of 9/11 see Waldman, 2004, pp. 120–125 and 132–137.

13. For a parallel analysis of the Iraq War and in depth examination of the difference between the Bush rhetoric and the way in which Bush policies worked see Alterman and Greene, 2004.

14. Jamieson and Waldman, 2003, pp. 143–146.

15. For a good background on PNAC and a list of its members see Rampton and Stauber, 2003, pp. 46–48.

16. See "Ridge defends 'duct tape' tip Homeland agency plans more advice" By Frank James and Rick Pearson, Washington Bureau. Frank James reported from Washington and Rick Pearson from Chicago. *Chicago Tribune*, February 14, 2003. http://www.chicagotribune.com/news/nationworld/chi-0302140308feb14,0,6113119.story?coll=chi-news-hed. Link last accessed October 8, 2006

17. For background and an examination of the civil liberties implication of the Padilla case see Waldman, 2004, pp. 272–273.

18. "Sixth Man Arrested in Buffalo Terror Cell Bust" Associated Press, September 16, 2002.www.foxnews.com, site last visited June 1, 2006.

19. "Four accused of being in terrorist cell in Detroit" August 29, 2002, www.cnn.com, link last visited June 1, 2006.

20. For a good treatment see Waldman, 2004, pp. 118–126 and 133–137.

21. See for example Michael Isakoff and Mark Hosenball's "Dubious Link Between Atta and Saddam" Newsweek.com, December 19, 2003. http://www.msnbc.msn.com/id/3741646/ last visited October 19, 2006. For full-length examinations see Rampton and Stauber,2003, pp. 92–96 and Waldman,2004, p. 82.

22. "Poll: 70% Believe Saddam, 9/11 Link" *USA Today,* September 6, 2003. http://www.usatoday.com/news/washington/2003–09–06-poll-iraq_x.htm. Link last visited April 22, 2006. This is also cited in Waldman, 2004, p. 85.

23. See Rampton and Stauber, 2003, for a detailed examination of the Bush Administration's efforts to shape this perception especially pp. 37–63.

24. As Waldman, 2004, notes on p. 74.

25. Waldman, 2004, p. 81 argues the topic was raised within five hours.

26. Rampton and Stuaber, 2003, pp. 37–40.

27. For a number of specific examples please see the Carnegie Endowment for International Peace report, "WMD in Iraq:Evidence and Implications" link first visited March , 2004 and last visited October 9, 2006

28. Moore and Slater, 2004, p. 315.

29.   For details on the use of blue ink in Iraqi elections see "BIG TURNOUT BUOYS
       HOPES UNFLINCHING: Millions vote in defiance of rebel attacks" by Borzou
       Daragahi, *San Francisco Chronicle Foreign Service Monday,* January 31, 2005.
       h t t p : / / w w w . s f g a t e . c o m / c g i - b i n / a r t i c l e . c g i ? f i l e = / c / a /
       2005/01/31/MNG95B34K01.DTL, link last visited April 20, 2006.

30.   Eric Schmidtt and Thom Shanker "Washington Recasts Terror War as Struggle"
       New York Times, July 27, 2005. For a working link http://www.iht.com/arti-
       cles/2005/07/26/news/terror.php, link visited August 1, 2005.

31.   Especially pp. 94–100 but this work generally supports my point.

32.   Speech to Congress on September 20, 2001: http://www.whitehouse.gov/news/
       releases/2001/09/20010920–8.html, link last accessed on October 9, 2006.

33.   Ibid.

34.   Ibid.

35.   Ibid.

36.   Ibid.

37.   Ibid.

38.   Ibid.

39.   Ibid.

40.   Ibid.

41.   ibid.

42.   Moore and Slater, 2004, p. 13.

43.   http://en.wikipedia.org/wiki/USA_PATRIOT_Act. link visited on June 5, 2006.

44.   http://www.whitehouse.gov/news/releases/2001/10/20011026–5.html. Link
       last accessed October 8, 2006.

45.   See Rampton and Stauber, 2003, pp. 46–49 for a somewhat different analysis.

46.   http://www.newamericancentury.org/iraqclintonletter.htm, site last visited June
       1, 2006.

47.   Ibid.

48.   Ibid.

49.   Ibid.

50.   Ibid.

51.   Ibid.

52.   ibid.

53.   ibid.

54.   Ibid.

55.   Ibid.

56.   While the author compiled this chart independently and expanded it to include Bush's
       second term, Stauber and Rampton, 2003, pp. 47–48 present a similar chart

involving PNAC and Bush's first term. The author used a number of relevant Government websites and wikipedia (http://en.wikipedia.org/)to produce and confirm the information found in the chart. This was last done on October 18, 2006.

57.   Ricci, 1993.

58.   *The Weekly Standard.* pp. 26–29. as accessed through the Project For A New American Century Website, http://www.newamericancentury.org/defense-20010730.pdf#search=%22cowering%20superpower%22 last accessed October 9, 2006

59.   Examples of which can be found in Rampton and Stauber 2003, pp. 80–90.

60.   Matthew Rothschild October 22, 2001. "Iraq, Anthrax and the Hawks." www.commondreams.org, link last visited April 16, 2006.

61.   Ibid.

62.   Ibid.

63.   For example see "New Documents Reveal Saddam Hid WMD was Tied to Al Qaeda" by Karl Limbacher, November 16, 2005. www.newsmax.com, link last visited May 23, 2006.

64.   As Donald Rumsfeld hypothesized. See "Rumsfeld: Saddam May Have Destroyed WMD," *Pravda,* May 29, 2003. Link last visited October 9, 2006. The relevant quote reads "It is also possible that they decided that they would destroy them prior to a conflict"http://english.pravda.ru/opinion/columnists/29–05–2003/2948-rumsfelllld-0

65.   For example see "Iraq Official: Saddam Moved WMD to Syria" by Carl Limbacher, January 26, 2006. www.newsmax.com, link visited May 23, 2006

66.   http://www.guardian.co.uk/afghanistan/story/0,1284,617446,00.html and http://www.guardian.co.uk/september11/oneyearon/story/0,12361,785554,00.html last accessed on October 9, 2006

67.   "Bush Tells Bin Laden Cannot Hide, Tells Troops to Prepare." http://www.sptimes.com/News/091501/Worldandnation/Bush_says_bin_Laden_c.s html, link last visited June 1, 2006.

68.   "President Delivers State of the Union Address," January 29, 2002. www.whitehouse.gov. link last accessed October 8, 2006.

69.   Ibid.

70.   http://www.whitehouse.gov/news/releases/2002/01/20020129–11.html. link last accessed October 8, 2006.

71.   Ibid.

72.   See Rampton and Stauber, 2003, pp. 114–116.

73.   For a detailed version of these events see Moore and Slater, 2003, pp. 307–318

74.   *New York Times,* September 7, 2002.

75.   House J. Res 114.

76. Ibid.

77. Ibid.

78. Ibid.

79. Ibid.

80. Ibid.

81. *USA Today,* November 6, 2002, *Cleland Defeated By A Conservative* <http://www.usatoday.com/news/politicselections/2002-11-06-chambliss_x.htm, link last visited May 1, 2006.

82. http://www.whitehouse.gov/news/releases/2002/10/20021016-1.html last accessed October 9, 2006

83. For example see William M. Welch, "Republicans Using Iraq Issue to Slam Opponents," *USA Today,* October 13, 2002. http://www.usatoday.com/news/washington/2002-10-13-iraq-politics_x.htm, link last visited February 17, 2005.

84. http://www.whitehouse.gov/news/releases/2002/10/20021007-8.html, link last visited June 1, 2006.

85. Ibid.

86. James Carroll, personal discussions with author, 2006.

87. President's Remarks at the U.N. General Assembly, September, 12, 2002. http://www.whitehouse.gov/news/releases/2002/09/20020912-1.html, link last visited June 1, 2006.

88. Ibid.

89. Ibid.

90. Ibid.

91. Ibid.

92. Ibid.

93. http://www.albinoblacksheep.com/text/france.html link visited March, 2004.[last accessed October 8, 2006

94. "Outrage at Old Europe Remarks." http://news.bbc.co.uk/1/hi/world/europe/2687403.stm last accessed October 8, 2006

95. For an example of the roots of Conservative feelings toward the U.N. see Viguerie and Franke, 2004, p. 53.and McGirr, 2001, especially pp. 177–179 for an analysis of the way in which anti-UN feelings have been enduring in the Conservative movement.

96. For example Rampton and Stauber, 2003, p. 117 note the actual low-level of contributions in the same way that Democratic candidates eventually would.

97. http://news.bbc.co.uk/cbbcnews/hi/world/newsid_2866000/2866785.stm site last visited October 17, 2006.

98. John Kampfner "Saving Private Lynch" May 15, 2003. http://news.bbc.co.uk/1/hi/programmes/correspondent/3028585.stm, link last visited June 1, 2006.

99.　　Ibid.

100.　　See Rampton and Stauber, 2003, for a discussion of this as a media event aimed at Americans and for an analysis of this episode, as well as the entire Iraq affair from the perspective of communications' scholars.

Chapter 7

1.　　For an in-depth discussion, please see Turow, 1997, especially from p. 125 onward.

2.　　Turow, 1997, explains this concept of pp. 166–167.

3.　　Ibid., p. 167.

4.　　Interview with Matthew Dowd. *PBS's Frontline's The Architect.* http://www.pbs.org/wgbh/pages/frontline/shows/architect/rove/metrics.html link last accessed October 8, 2006

5.　　Turow, 1997, pp.44–47 and 136–137.

6.　　Something that Ibid. discussed in terms of corporate marketing. Ibid., p. 177

7.　　A trend that Ibid. discusses in a variety of brand based marketing on p. 177.

8.　　Ibid., p. 178 quotes Lester Wunderman as defining corporate brands in this way.

9.　　Ibid. discusses this in terms of corporate marketing p. 178.

10.　　Ibid.

11.　　Ibid. notes the importance of doing so for corporate marketers throughout his work.

12.　　Ibid. discusses this in terms of corporate marketing p. 173

13.　　Bush Strategist Mehlman Takes RNC Reigns: Manager of Reelection campaign vows to deliver a durable GOP Majority by John F. Harris Thursday January 20, 2005. http://www.washingtonpost.com/wp-dyn/articles/A22189–2005Jan19.html, link last visited June 5, 2006.

14.　　Ibid.

15.　　"Bush Strategist Mehlman Takes RNC Reigns: Manager of Reelction Campaign Vows to Deliver a Durable GOP Majority" by John F. Harris, Thursday January 20, 2005. http://www.washingtonpost.com/wp-dyn/articles/A22189–2005Jan19.html, link last visited June 5, 2006.

16.　　Ibid.

17.　　"Republicans and the Future" by Ken Mehlman. *Washington Times.* January 25, 2005. http://www.washtimes.com/op-ed/20050124–091842–4755r.htm, link last visited June 5, 2006.

18.　　Ibid.

19.　　Turow, 1997, p. 181–182 for a discussion of these techniques' use in corporate marketing.

20. Turow, 1997, p. 92 for the first point, and, p. 105 for the second. As outlined in the first chapter, Turow's study very much underlies the point to this one.

21. Ibid. discusses how this market segmentation is leading to the development of image tribes on pp. 184–200.

22. Ibid., p. 92.

23. Ibid., pp. 157–183 for a discussion of the impact that this is having in the worlds of media and advertising.

24. For a thorough journalistic analysis that supports the points being made in the next three chapters particularly about the way in which Kerry's personality and the Iraq War contributed to Bush's win please ,see "How Bush Really Won" by Mark Danner, *New York Review of Books,* January 13, 2005. http://www.nybooks.com/articles/17690, link visited November 10, 2005.

25. Interview with Grover Norquist *PBS's Frontline* "The Architect." Link and dates as noted in prior chapters.

26. As Waldman, 2004, pp. 1–22 discusses the dissonance between Bush's actual background and what his 2000 campaign talked about.

27. See Frank, 2004, for a discussion of the value of authenticity in Conservatism and Jamieson and Waldman for the way in which this can contribute to media coverage of a candidate.

28. For an in-depth examination of the uses of viral marketing in the Bush campaign see "The Multilevel Marketing of the President" by MATT BAI, *New York Times Magazine,* April 25, 2004, http://www.nytimes.com/2004/04/ 25/magazine/25GROUNDWAR.html?ex=1398225600&en=07c8203349fbd15a&e i=5007&partner=USERLAND, link last visited October 9, 2006.

29. For a nice analysis of these points see Danner, 2005, as noted above.

30. Remarks on "NBC News's 'Meet the Press'" on April 9, 2006. http://www.msnbc.msn.com/id/12169680/ last accessed on October 8, 2006.

31. As quoted in Moore and Slater, 2004, p. 273.

32. The author would like to extend special thanks to Bill Israel who prompted me to think about the different ways in which Conventions could be used. The thoughts on the technique are mine as are any flaws associated with them but his NPR interview planted a seed that caused me to ponder.

33. Klein, 2000, shows how corporate brands both seek to build identification for their products and relationships with their customers on pp. 15–26.

34. For a good examination of the way in which the internet can be used to promote a brand see Zyman and Miller, 2000. See pp. 153–226 for understanding the Bush internet strategy or Braunstein and Levin, 2000, pp. 207–180 for a discussion of brand building on the internet.

35. Zyman and Miller, 2000, p. 68 speak about this in terms of corporate branding activities.

36. Turow, 1997, p. 136.

37. Ibid., p. 137.

38.   Ibid.

39.   Ibid., p. 138.

40.   Ibid., p. 141.

41.   Something that Viguerie, 2004, pp. 329–333 discusses on the various ways in which Conservatives have used communications technologies to avoid the media's observation.

42.   For an example of the way in which other kinds of marketers have sought to use video to communicate with their audiences see Turow, 1997, pp. 160–177.

43.   Fineman, *Newsweek*, November 8, 2004 link first visited July 2005. http://www.msnbc.msn.com/id/3144249/site/newsweek/ link last visited October 8, 2006.

44.   Zyman and Miller, 2000, pp. 70–73 nicely breakdown they way in which marketers target undecided audiences.

45.   Ibid.

46.   "The Ground Game" by Howard Fineman, in *Newsweek*, October 4, 2004. http://www.msnbc.msn.com/id/6099426/site/newsweek/, link last visited July 7, 2005.

47.   For example, Sabato and Simpson, 1996, pp. 127–141 go into depth about the way in which voter guides became a key part of the Conservative campaign during the 1990s.

48.   Turow, 1997.

49.   Ralph Wilson, "The Six Simple Principles of Viral Marketing" *Web Marketing Today, Issue 70, February 1, 2000.* link last visited June 1, 2006. http://www.wilson-web.com/wmt5/viral-principles.htm

50.   Ibid.

51.   Ibid.

52.   Howard Fineman, "The Ground Game," *Newsweek*, October 4, 2004, as above

53.   Ibid.

54.   www.newsweek.com, "Inner Circle," November 15, 2004. http://www.msnbc.msn.com/id/6406880/site/newsweek/, link last accessed July 10, 2005.

55.   Turow, 1997, pp. 148–150 illustrates the ways in which product marketers do this in order to get rid of their worst performing segments.

56.   As Zyman and Miller, 2000, show has been a conscious corporate strategy on p. 72.

57.   Ibid., p. 61.

58.   Ibid., pp. 66–67.

59.   Bill Berkowitz, "Christian Zionists, Jews & Bush's Reelection Strategy," *WorkingForChange.* http://www.workingforchange.com/article.cfm?itemid=1702105.28.04, link last visited June 22, 2005.

60. "GOP Won With Accent On Rural and Traditional" by Paul Farhi and James V. Grimaldi, *Washington Post* Staff Writer, Thursday, November 4, 2004. http://www.washingtonpost.com/wp-dyn/articles/A23754-2004Nov3.html. link last accessed October 8, 2006

61. Ibid.

62. Ibid.

63. For a post-election analysis of the importance of values voting and an analysis of issue salience in 2004 election that very much supports the argument that I am making about brand loyalty, see D. Sunshine Hillygus and Todd G. Shields "Moral Issues and Voter Decision-making in the 2004 Presidential Election." *PS Political Science and Politics*, 38(2), pp. 201–210.

64. Inglehart, 1971, pp. 991–1017. "The Silent Revolution in Europe: Intergenerational Change in Post-Industrial Societies," *American Political Science Review*, 65(4), (1971) discusses post-materialism in depth.

65. By Jeff Zeleny, John McCormick , Tim Jones and Mark Silva. *Chicago Tribune,* "Broad Turnout Strategy Gave Bush Coveted Edge," November 7, 2004. http://www.chicagotribune.com/news/specials/elections/chi-0411070241nov07,1,4489779.story?coll=chi-electionsprint-hed. Link last accessed October 8, 2006.

66. Ibid.

67. Ibid.

68. Ibid.

69. For a post-election analysis of the Bush team's Hispanic outreach effort and its results please see "The Latino Vote in the 2004 Election" by Matt Bareto, David Leal, Jongho Lee and Rudolfo de la Garza, *PS: Political Science and Politics*, 38, pp. 41–49. 2006. 0. For a thorough examination of the Bush strategy toward Catholics please see " Using Catholicism' by Eleanor Clift. www.newsweek.com link visited June 6, 2005. "Bush versus Kerry on Israel Edward I. Koch," Commentary for Bloomberg Radio republished on www.newsmax.com Thursday, August 12, 2004. http://www.newsmax.com/archives/articles/2004/8/11/145903.shtml, link last accessed October 8, 2006.

71. Bush versus Kerry on Israel Edward I. Koch," Commentary for Bloomberg Radio republished on www.newsmax.com Thursday, August 12, 2004. http://www.newsmax.com/archives/articles/2004/8/11/145903.shtml, link last accessed October 8, 2006.

72. For a good examination of the Bush outreach effort to Jewish voters please see *Jews for Bush ?* by Dick Polman, *Jewish World Review,* June 15, 2004. http://www.jewishworldreview.com/0604/jewish_vote.php3, link last visited June 6, 2005. Kerry's unfamiliarity to voters and the problems that it causes for his campaign is also discussed in depth in Danner, 2005 as noted above.

73. A list of which can be found at: http://pc;/stanford.edu/campaigns/campaign2004/ archive.html, site visited October 22, 2006.

74. Cannon, 1991, pp. 470,473–474.

75. "Bush's Catholic Courtship Strategy" by Deborah Caldwell. http://www.beliefnet.com/story/146/story_14691_1.html, link last visited June 30, 2005.

76. David Gibson as quoted in ibid.

77. Ibid.

78. "The Five (or More) W's" by Mike Allen, *The Washington Post*, Thursday, May 13, 2004, p. A04. http://www.washingtonpost.com/wp-dyn/articles/A22399–2004 May12.html, link last visited July 1, 2005.

79. Ibid.

80. Ibid.

81. Ibid.

82. "Barbara Bush Tells Women What 'W' Stands For Run Date" by Jodi Enda *WeNews correspondent*, August 31, 2004. http://www.womensenews.org/article.cfm/ dyn/aid/1970, link last visited July 1, 2005.

83. Ibid.

84. Ibid.

85. Ibid.

86. Ibid.

87. Ibid.

88. Moore and Slater, 2003, pp. 295–296.

89. Ann Florini as quoted in Moore and Slater, 2003, p. 296.

90. "Four More Years" http://www.pollingreport.com/2004.htm#Four link first visited July 2005 and last visited June 1, 2006

91. Ibid.

92. www.mediamatters.org items/200405010002, link visited January 25, 2005 and last visited October 19, 2006.

93. Ibid.

94. http://www.businessweek.com/magazine/content/04_08/b3871044.htm, link last visited January, 25, 2005.

95. Ibid.

96. http://mediamatters.org/items/200405010002, link visited January 25, 2005 and last visited October 19, 2006. "Backdating the Recession," May, 2004 provides an in-depth analysis of the way in which the Conservatives built the Clinton Recession brand story.

97. Ibid.

98. Ibid.

99. http://www.newsmax.com/archives/articles/2001/3/20/190717.shtml, link last visited January 27, 2005.

100. Ibid.

101. Ibid.

102. Ibid.

103. Luskin, Donald, "*Truth* Matters The last Recession Began under Clinton, Despite Rewrites on the Left." *National Review,* May 5, 2004, 8:50 A.M. {http://www.nationalreview.com/nrof_luskin/luskin200405050850.asp}, link visited January 22, 2005 and last visited October 19, 2006. Media Matters for America's link took note of this and provided an in-depth response to Luskin that can be found at {http://mediamatters.org/items/200405060001}, link visited January 22, 2005 and last visited October 19, 2006. Both contributed to the analysis in this section.

104. Ibid.

105. Ibid.

106. Ibid.

107. {http://www.whitehouse.gov/news/inaugural-address.html,} link last visited June 15, 2005.

108. {http://www.whitehouse.gov/news/reports/taxplan.html}, link last visited June 16, 2005.

109. http://www.whitehouse.gov/news/releases/2004/10/20041009-2.html, link last visited October 8, 2006.

110. http://www.debates.org/pages/trans2004c.html, link last visited February 7, 2007.

111. Ibid.

112. http://www.whitehouse.gov/news/releases/2004/09/print/20040902-2.html

113. http://www.debates.org/pages/trans2004c.html, link last visited February 7, 2007.

114. Ad script for "Safer, Stronger" compiled by author from www.georgewbush.com, 2004. Working link as of October 17, 2006: http://www.gwu.edu/%-7Eaction/2004/ads04/bushad030404c.html.

115. Thomas et al., 2005, p. 45.

116. Source for the memo's major points. http://www.zephoria.org/lakoff/files/Luntz.pdf. The author has gotten this memo from a number of sources but this was the last on October 23, 2006.

117. Ibid.

118. The memo came to light after it fell into the hands of the Democrats. "Talking Iraq: Some Things are Better Left Unsaid" by John F. Harris and Brian Faler, *Washington Post,* June 20, 2004, link last visited May 17, 2006. http://www.washingtonpost.com/wp-dyn/articles/A54906-2004Jun19.html, the reason why I chose to use the above-noted memo is that it contains the full depth of the points instead of the very nice summary that the Post article carries.

119. A point also made by Danner, 2005 as noted above.

Chapter 8

1. Turow, 1997, p. 105 discusses this in terms of the signature shows of cable television networks.

2. The Republican National Convention schedules used herein can be found at http://www.gwu.edu/~action/2004/repconv04/, link last visited May 2, 2006.

3. http://www.gwu.edu/%7Eaction/2004/chrnconv.html, link visited October 26, 2006.

4. Turow, 1997, p. 129.

5. Ibid.

6. Turow, 1997, 129.

7. Ibid.

8. Ibid. and p. 164 for a discussion of the ways in which the dramatic changes in message distribution have affected the ad business.

9. *FK* See Turow, 1997, p. 129 for a useful discussion of infomercials and {{www.hawthornedirect.com/glossary/glossary_d.html}, link last visited May 30, 2006.

10. www.hawthornedirect.com/glossary/glossary_d.html, link last visited May 30, 2006.

11. For a description of the changing use and narrowing audience for political conventions, see Newman, 1999a, pp. 22–23.

12. Ibid.

13. Text remarks by Governor George Pataki at the republican national convention, {http://www.washingtonpost.com/wp-dyn/articles/A57276-2004Sep2.html}, September 2, 2004. link list visited October 17, 2006.

14. Ibid.

15. Viguerie and Franke, 2004, especially pp. 107–137; for an interesting examination of direct marketing's history and its uses during the 1990s, see Sherman in Newman, 1999b, pp. 365–388. For a discussion of the way in which this fits into the contemporary niche media environment, see Turow, 1997.

16. http://en.wikipedia.org/wiki/Infomercial, link last visited May 22, 2006.

17. Ibid.

18. Turow, 1997, p. 129.

19. http://www.forrelease.com/D20040829/nysu019.P2.08292004154528.08528.html, link last visited June 10, 2005.

20. Turow, 1997, p. 105.

21. Ibid., pp. 91–92 and 136–137.

22. 2004 Republican National Convention draws Black GOPers to New York City Jet, September 27, 2004 by Kevin Chappell, working link as of June 1, 2006, http://www.findarticles.com/p/articles/mi_m1355/is_12_106/ai_n6258667.

23. http://www.gwu.edu/~action/2004/chrnconv.html describes the selection process in detail and notes the media-driven nature of conventions. Link last visited October 26, 2006.

24. Newman, terms this the "situational contingency" writing in Newman, 1999b, p. 262.

25. http://www.gwu.edu/~action/2004/repconv04/, link last visited May 2, 2006.

26. Ibid.

27. Ibid.

28. Ibid.

29. ibid

30. Ibid.

31. "A Liberal Hollywood Actor Who Speaks Up for Bush" by Bruce Weber, *New York Times,* September 1, 2004, working link as of October 17, 2006, http://select.nytimes.com/search/restricted/article?res=F00D17FF3E550C728CDD A00894DC404482. .

32. Ibid.

33. "Infotainment at the Republican National Convention" by John Sayles, *The Nation,* September 27, 2004. http://www.thenation.com/doc/20040927/sayles, link visited June 6, 2005.

34. Monday, August 30, 2004; 8:53 P.M. August 30, 2004. http://www.washingtonpost.com/wp-dyn/articles/A47167–2004 Aug 30.html, link last visited June 10, 2005.

35. Ibid.

36. Ibid.

37. Ibid.

38. Ibid.

39. Monday, August 30, 2004; http://www.washingtonpost.com/wp-dyn/articles/A47236–2004Aug30.html, link last visited June 10, 2005.

40. Ibid.

41. Tuesday, August 31, 2004; 8:54 P.M. http://www.washingtonpost.com/wp-dyn/articles/A50426–2004Aug31.html, link last visited June 10, 2005.

42. Ibid.

43. Ibid.

44. Wednesday, September 1, 2004, http://www.washingtonpost.com/wp-dyn/articles/A54468–2004Sep1.html, link last visited June 10, 2005.

45. Monday, August 30, 2004, www.washingtonpost.com linked as noted above.

46. Wednesday, September 1, 2004, http://www.washingtonpost.com/wp-dyn/articles/A54468–2004Sep1.html, link last visited June 10, 2005.

47. Ibid.

48. Ibid.

49. Wednesday, September 1, 2004, 10:42 P.M. http://www.washingtonpost.com/wp-dyn/articles/A54300–2004Sep1.html, link last visited October 8, 2006.

50. http://www.whitehouse.gov/news/releases/2004/09/20040901–7.html, link last visited April 5, 2006.

51. Ibid.

52. Ibid.

53. Ibid.

54. Ibid.

55. Ibid.

56. Ibid.

57. The verbatim quote can be found at http://www.washingtonpost.com/wp-dyn/articles/A47236–2004Aug30.html, visited as noted above.

58. http://www.presidentialrhetoric.com/campaign/rncspeeches/mccain.html, link last visited, April 1, 2006.

59. http://www.washingtonpost.com/wp-dyn/articles/A47237–2004Aug30.html, link last visited June 29, 2005.

60. http://www.washingtonpost.com/wp-dyn/articles/A50470–2004Aug31.html, link last visited June 29, 2005.

61. http://www.presidentialrhetoric.com/campaign/rncspeeches/schwarzenegger.html, link last visited April 20, 2006.

62. Ibid.

63. Ibid.

64. Remarks by Barbara and Jenna Bush to the Republican National Convention, http://www.gop.com/Blog/BlogPost.aspx?BlogPostID=996, link last visited on October 8, 2006.

65. Ibid.

66. http://www.washingtonpost.com/wp-dyn/articles/A50438–2004Aug31.html, link last visited February 6, 2007.

67. Ibid.

68. http://www.whitehouse.gov/news/releases/2004/09/20040902–2.html, link last visited June 20, 2005.

69. Ibid.

70. Ibid.

71. Ibid.

72. Ibid.

73. Ibid.

74. Ibid.

75. Ibid.

76. Ibid.

77. Ibid.

78. Ibid.

79. Ibid.

80. Ibid.

81. Ibid.

82. Ibid.

83. Ibid.

84. "Bush Leads Kerry by 7 Points" by Susan Page, *USA Today,* September 7, 2004, http://www.usatoday.com/news/politicselections/nation/president/2004–09–06-poll_x.html, link last visited July 10, 2005.

85. Ibid.

86. Ibid.

87. "Bush's Vision for U.S.—Idealistic and Strong Priorities: National security stressed over domestic issues" by John Wildermuth, Zachary Coile, Carla Marinucci, *Chronicle Political Writers,* Friday, September 3, 2004, http://www.sfgate.com/cgibin/article.cgi?file=/chronicle/archive/2004/09/03/M NGL98JA9E1.DTL, link last visited July 11, 2005.

88. http://www.gwu.edu/~action/2004/repconv04/bushroadout.html, link last visited October 8, 2006.

89. Ibid.

90. Ibid.

91. Ibid.

92. Ibid.

93. Ibid.

94. Ibid.

95. Ibid.

96. For a good history of, as well as the strategy involved in presidential debates, see Kraus in Newman, 1999b, pp. 389–401 for a useful discussion of debates with a marketing focus.

97. For another example of the way in which the Bush administration used Luntz's work to sell its policies, see "Let Them Eat Words" by Deborah Tannen, *American Prospect Online,* http://www.prospect.org/print/V14/8/tannen-d.html, link last visited June 8, 2006.

98. For an examination of the media effects of the global test comment and a nice analysis of how the play into the Cold War aspects of what my analysis sees as a brand, see Danner, 2005 as noted above.

99. http://www.presidency.ucsb.edu/showdebate.php?debateid=29, link last visited February 1, 2007.

100. Remarks by President Bush and Senator Kerry in 2004 Presidential Debate. www.whitehouse.gov, October 1, 2004, link last visited October 1, 2006.

101. "Rumsfeld's War on Terror Memo," *USA Today*, October, 16, 2003, http://www.usatoday.com/news/washington/executive/rumsfeld-memo.htm, link last visited October 8, 2006.

102. Remarks by President Bush and Senator Kerry in First 2004 Presidential Debate. http://www.whitehouse.gov/news/releases/2004/10/20041001, link last visited October 1, 2006.

103. http://www.washingtonpostc.om/wpsrv/politics/debatereferee/debate_930.html. Site last visited February 1, 2007. Remarks by President Bush and Senator Kerry in First 2004 Presidential Debate http://www.whitehouse.gov/news/releases/2004/10/20041001, link last visited October 1, 2006.

105. Ibid.

106. Ibid.

107. http://www.washingtonpost.com/wpsrv/politics/debatereferee/debate_930.html. Link last visited February 1, 2007

108. Ibid.

109. Ibid.

110. www.debates.org/pages/trans2004a.html, link last visited February 1, 2007.

111. www.debates.org/pages/trans2004c.html, link last visited February 1, 2007.

112. Ibid.

113. Remarks by President Bush and Senator Kerry in First 2004 Presidential Debate, October 8, 2004, as noted above

114. Ibid.

115. http://www.presidency.ucsb.edu/showdebate.php?debateid=29

116. Ibid.

117. www.debates.org/pages/trans2004a.html, link last visited as noted above.

118. Ibid.

Chapter 9

1. The ad scripts were collected primarily by the author during Fall, 2004 campaign by visiting georgewbush.com regularly from the period 9/1 until just after the election. The scripts or good portions of them were usually contained in press releases. Most of them, plus a good number of Kerry and 527 group ads, can still be found at http://medialit.med.sc.edu/adwatchdatabase.htm, link last visited June

1, 2006. A second Website containing working links as of October 17, 2006 is http://www.gwu.edu/~action/2004/ads04/bushads04.html.

2. Trout and Rivkin, 2000, p. 107

3. Ibid.

4. Script for "Safer, Stronger." www.georgewbush.com. Compiled by author, Fall 2004, last visited November, 2004, and cross-checked at http://www.gwu.edu/%7Eaction/2004/ads04/bushad030404c.html, link last visited October 17, 2006.

5. Script for "Weapons." www.georgewbush.com. Compiled by author Fall 2004. A working link for which could be found as of October 17, 2006: http://www.gwu.edu/%7Eaction/2004/ads04/bushad042604.html.

6. Ibid.

7. Script for "Patriot Act." www.georgewbush.com. Compiled by author Fall 2004. Working link for which could be found as of October 17, 2006 at http://www.gwu.edu/%7Eaction/2004/ads04/bushad052604.html.

8. Ibid.

9. For a look at how Bush and Conservatives discuss Liberals, see Waldman, 2004, pp. 12–21.

10. "Troops Fog of War-Updated." Script compiled by the author from www.georgew.bush.com, Fall 2004 and a working link for which can be found as of October 17, 2006 at http://www.gwu.edu/ %7Eaction/2004/ads04/bushad041504.html.

11. Thomas et al., 2004, p. 63.

12. "Fog of War." Script compiled by the author from georgewbush.com. Fall 2004 and working link can be found as above.

13. Ibid.

14. Thomas et al., 2004, pp. 61–62 provide one version of this explanation as well as a good example of the way in which Kerry failed to make his actual position clear enough for the average voter to understand.

15. Thomas et al., 2004, p. 61.

16. For example see "Bush's Top Ten Flip-Flops," September 28, 2004. http://www.cbsnews.com/stories/2004/09/28/politics/main646142.shtml, link visited July 10, 2005 and last visited October 14, 2006.

17. http://www.cbsnews.com/stories/2004/09/28/politics/main646142.shtml, link visited as above.

18. Something that Waldman explores as a political but not as a marketing phenomenon in his 2004 work.

19. Script for "100 Days." Compiled by the author from www.georgewbush.com, Fall 2004 and a working link for which can be found as of October 17, 2006 at http://www.gwu.edu/%7Eaction/2004/ads04/bushad031204100.html.

20. Ibid.

21. Ibid.

22. Ibid.

23. "Despite Bush Flip-Flops, Kerry Gets Label" by John F. Harris, *Washington Post* Staff Writer, Thursday, September 23, 2004, p.A01. http://www.washingtonpost.com-/wp-dyn/ articles/A43093–2004Sep22.html, link visited June 2, 2006 and last visited October 14, 2006.

24. Ibid.

25. "Despite Bush Flip-Flops, Kerry Gets Label" by John F. Harris, *Washington Post* Staff writer, Thursday, September 23, 2004, p. A01. As visited above. The same point is made in Jamieson and Waldman, 2003 regarding the way in which what they call the frame around Gore's honesty was developed and spread. *Don't understand #/*

26. "Despite Bush Flip-Flops, Kerry Gets Label" by John F. Harris, *Washington Post* Staff Writer, Thursday, September 23, 2004, p. A01 accessed as noted above.

27. For more details, see Waldman, 2004, pp. 109–110 for a nice synopsis of Gore's Internet invention and pp. 87–104 for a discussion of the way in which Conservatives did the same to Clinton.

28. As quoted in "Despite Bush Flip-Flops, Kerry Gets Label" by John F. Harris, *Washington Post* Staff Writer, Thursday, September 23, 2004, p. A01. http://www.washingtonpost.com/wp-dyn/articles/A43093–2004Sep22.html, link last visited October 14, 2006.

29. Ibid.

30. Script for "Tell The Truth" compiled by the author from www.georgewbush.com, Fall 2004 and a working link for which can be found as of October 18, 2006 at http://www.gwu.edu/~action/2004/ads04/bushad042304i.html.

31. Ibid.

32. Ibid.

33. Ibid.

34. Ibid.

35. Ibid.

36. Ibid.

37. Script for "Unprincipled Chapter 1" compiled by the author from www.georgewbush.com, Fall 2004. A CNN story corroborating the ad's contents could be found as of October 17, 2006 at http://www.cnn.com/2004/ALLPOLITICS/02/13/elec04.prez.main/.

38. Script for "Unprincipled Chapter 1" compiled by the author from www.georgewbush.com, Fall 2004.

39. Ibid.

40. Ibid.

41. Script for "Medicare Hypocrisy" compiled by the author from www.georgewbush.com, Fall 2004 and a working link for which as of October 17, 2006 can be found at http://www.gwu.edu/%7Eaction /2004/ads04/bushad090904.html.

42. Ibid.

43. Ibid.

44. Script for "Thinking Mom" compiled by the author from www.georgewbush.com, Fall 2004 and a working link for which can be found at http://www.gwu.edu/~-action/2004/ads04/bushad100404tm.html.

45. Ibid.

46. Ibid.

47. Ibid.

48. Script for "Clockwork" compiled the author from georgewbush.com, Fall 2004 and for which a working link as of October 17, 2006 can be found at http://www.gwu.edu/~action/2004/ads04/bushad100404cl.html.

49. Ibid.

50. ibid.

51. Script for "Economy Common Sense versus Higher Taxes." Compiled by the author from georgewbush.com, Fall 2004. A working link to the short version of the ad as of October 17, 2006 can be found at http://www.gwu.edu/%7Eaction/2004/ads04/bushad091704.html.

52. Ibid.

53. Ronald Reagan Farewell Address to the Nation. January 11, 1989. http://www.reagan.utexas.edu/archives/speeches/1989/011189i.htm, last visited October 8, 2006.

54. Waldman, 2004, pp. 199–234 presents a thorough analysis of the distribution of the Bush tax cuts as well as the rhetoric used to promote it to the public.

55. Script for "Economy Common Sense versus Higher Taxes." Compiled by the author from georgewbush.com, Fall 2004 and a working link as of November 8, 2006 for which can be found at http://www.gwu.edu/%-7Eaction/2004/ads04/bushad091704.html.

56. Ibid.

57. Script for full-length version of above compiled by the author from georgewbush.com, site visited during the Fall 2004 campaign.

58. Script for "Tort Reform" as compiled by the author from georgewbush.com, Fall 2004 and a working link as of October 17, 2006 for which can be found at http://www.gwu.edu/~action/2004/ads04/bushad100504tr.html.

59. As Moore and Slater, 2003, show on pp. 224–227 that tort reform in Texas was driven by something similar. It is an example of what Lakoff, 2004 terms a strategic initiative.

60. Script for "Med Mal" as compiled by the author from georgewbush.com, Fall 2004 and a working link for which as of October 17, 2006 can be found at http://www.gwu.edu/~action/2004/ads04/bushad100504mm.html.

61. Ibid.

62. Script for "Lead" compiled by the author from georgewbush.com, Fall 2004 and a working link for which can be found at http://www.gwu.edu/%-7Eaction/2004/ads04/bushad030404a.html.

63. Both quotes ibid.

64. Ibid.

65. For a particularly useful example of the way in which the Bush team recycled ads, see the American Museum of the Moving Image online exhibition "The Living Room Candidate" at http://livingroomcandidate.movingimage.us/election/index.php?nav_action=election&nav_subaction=R&campaign_id=178&ad_id=, link last visited March 17, 2005. For an examination of the way in which the Bush effort to use what we're calling the Reagan heritage brand succeeded and for a similar examination of some of the same events covered herein, see John B. Judis, Ruy Teixeira and Marisa Katz, "How Bush Went Back to the 1970's," *New Republic,* November 15, 2004.

66. Script for "Safer, Stronger" as compiled by the author from georgewbush.com, Fall, 2004 and a working link for which can be see as noted above.

67. Ibid.

68. For a particularly useful example of the way in which the Bush team recycled ads, see the American Museum of the Moving Image online exhibition "The Living Room Candidate" at http://livingroomcandidate.movingimage.us/election/index.php?nav_action=election&nav_subaction=R&campaign_id=178&ad_id=, link last visited March 17, 2005.

69. Script for "Safer, Stronger" as compiled by the author from georgewbush.com, Fall, 2004 and a working link for which can be found as noted above.

70. Script for "Tested" as compiled by the author from georgewbush.com, Fall, 2004 and a working link for which as of October 17, 2006 can be found at http://www.gwu.edu/%7Eaction/2004/ads04/bushad030404b.html.

71. Ansolabehere, Behr, and Iyengar, 1993, p. 82.

72. Raw Data: President's remarks in Springfield, Missouri, Friday, July 30, 2004. http://www.whitehouse.gov/news/releases/2004/07/20040730-3.html, link last visited October 8, 2006.

73. Ibid.

74. Ibid.

75. http://www.whitehouse.gov/news/releases/2004/07/20040730-3.html

76. Ibid.

77. http://www.foxnews.com/story/0,2933,127583,00.html link last accessed February 1, 2007.

78. Ibid.

79. http://www.whitehouse.gov/news/releases/2004/07/20040730–3.html

80. Ibid.

81. http://www.foxnews.com/story/0,2933,127583,00.html

82. Ibid.

83. "Bush: Kerry Would 'Weaken' U.S. President Defends Iraq War in Run-Up to Second Debate" by Jim VandeHei, *Washington Post* Staff Writer, Thursday, October 7, 2004, p. A01. http://www.washingtonpost.com/wp-dyn/articles/A10573–20040ct6.html, link first visited July 7, 2005 and last visited October 19, 2006.

84. President's remarks in Wilkes-Barre, Pennsylvania, October 6, 2004. http://www.whitehouse.gov/news/releases/2004/10/20041006–9.html, link last visited October 8, 2006.

85. "Bush: Kerry Would 'Weaken' U.S. President Defends Iraq War in Run-Up to Second Debate" by Jim VandeHei, *Washington Post* Staff Writer, Thursday, October 7, 2004, p. A01 makes the point in terms of framing, as referenced above.

86. Ibid. notes the timing of these events.

87. Something ibid. notes as a series of events.

88. Ibid notes part of this but the passage is from www.whitehouse.gov. President's remarks in Wilkes-Barre, Pennsylvania October 6, 2004, as noted above.

89. The full passage is taken from http://www.washingtonpost.com/wp-dyn/articles/A11390–20040ct6.html, last visited February 7, 2007 and the sentiments of it are noted in "Bush: Kerry Would 'Weaken' U.S. President Defends Iraq War in Run-Up to Second Debate" by Jim VandeHei, *Washington Post* Staff Writer, Thursday, October 7, 2004, link as visited above.

90. President's remarks in Wilkes-Barre, Pennsylvania, October 6, 2004. http://www.whitehouse.gov/news/releases/2004/10/20041006–9.html, link last visited October 8, 2006.

91. Ibid.

92. Ibid.

93. Ibid.

94. "Bush: Kerry Would 'Weaken' U.S. President Defends Iraq War in Run-Up to Second Debate" by Jim VandeHei, *Washington Post* Staff Writer, Thursday, October 7, 2004, link as visited above.

95. President's remarks in Wilkes-Barre, Pennsylvania, October 6, 2004. www.whitehouse.gov, link last visited on October 8, 2006.

96. Ibid.

97. Ibid.

98. For a similar analysis see "Checking the Facts in Advance" by Paul Krugman. http://www.nytimes.com/2004/10/12/opinion/12krugman.html?ex=1255320000&en=01f498ac2764f&ei=5088&partner=rssnyt.

99. President's Remarks in Wilkes-Barre, Pennsylvania, October 6, 2004. www.whitehouse.gov, link last visited on October 8, 2006.

100. http://www.washingtonpost.com/wp-dyn/articles/A11290–20040ct6_5html, link last visited February 7, 2007.

101. "Bush: Kerry Would 'Weaken' U.S. President Defends Iraq War in Run-Up to Second Debate" by Jim VandeHei, *Washington Post* Staff Writer, Thursday, October 7, 2004, p. A01, link as accessed above.

102. President's remarks in Wilkes-Barre, Pennsylvania, October 6, 2004. www.whitehouse.gov, link last visited on October 8, 2006.

103. Ibid.

104. "Bush: Kerry Would 'Weaken' U.S. President Defends Iraq War in Run-Up to Second Debate" by Jim VandeHei, *Washington Post* Staff Writer, Thursday, October 7, 2004, p. A01, accessed as noted above.

105. President's remarks in Wilkes-Barre, Pennsylvania October 6, 2004. www.whitehouse.gov, link accessed as noted above.

106. President's remarks in Wilkes-Barre, Pennsylvania, October 6, 2004. www.whitehous link accessed as noted above.

107. Ibid.

108. Ibid.

109. Ibid.

110. http://www.washingtonpost.com/wp-dyn/articles/A11290–20040ct6_5html,link last visited February 7, 2007.

111. Ibid.

112. Thomas et al, 2005, p. 143.

113. Ibid.

114. President's Remarks in Wilkes-Barre, Pennsylvania, October 6, 2004. www.white-house.gov, link accessed as noted above.

115. Ibid.

116. Ibid.

117. Ibid.

118. Ibid.

119. Ibid.

120. Ibid.

121. Ansolabehere, Behr, and Iyengar, 1993 point out the importance of ratings points in building impressions.

122. President's remarks in Wilkes-Barre, Pennsylvania, October 6th, 2004. www.white-house.gov link last visited October 8, 2006.

123. Ibid.

124. Ibid.

125. Ibid.

126. Frank, 2004, p. 248 notes the way in which Conservatism depends on people not making connections between problems in order to succeed. Lakoff, 2004 notes Conservatism's impact on many areas of American life on pp. 91–95.

127. http://www.whitehouse.gov/news/releases/2004/07/20040730-3.html, site visited as above

128. For an alternative analysis of the campaign from the Democratic perspective, see "What Went Wrong ?" by Peter Beinart, *New Republic,* November 15, 2004. For a second such analysis, see Christopher Paine "And Another Thing" writing in the *Bulletin of the Atomic Scientist* , 61(1) (January 2005).

129. Poll taken October 10–29, 2004. www.pollingreport.com, link last visited June 1, 2006.

130. www.pollingreport.com link last visited June 1, 2006.

131. http://www.pollingreport.com/2004.htm#Four, link last visited June 1, 2006.

132. Ibid.

133. The source for all of the polling data is www.pollingreport.com. The link was visited from June 2005 until June 1, 2006.

Chapter 10

1.   Stauber and Rampton, 1995.

2.   Zyman, 2000, p. 133.

3.   Ibid., 1988.

4.   Lowi, 1996.

5.   Rumsfeld's War-On-Terror Memo, http://www.usatoday.com/news/washington/executive/rumsfeld-memo.htm, link last visited October 19, 2006

6.   All polling data can be found at http://www.pollingreport.com/bushjob2.htm. This particular link section was last visited on October 29, 2006.

7.   See particularly Waldman, 2004.

8.   Frank, 2004, pp. 89–109 goes into great depth on this topic.

9.   Ibid., pp. 157–178.

10. Something that Waldman, 2004 shows in his analysis of the Bush tax cuts and Johnson, 1991 shows throughout his examination of the Reagan administration's economic policies.

11. For a book-length critique of Conservative policies and their impact on American society see Greider, 2004.

12. Peter Singer *The President of Good and Evil,* 2004.

13. Ibid, p. 221.

14. Ibid.

15. See Ling and Glantz "Why and How the Tobacco Industry Sells Cigarettes to Young Adults: Evidence From Industry Documents," *American Journal of Public Health,* 92(6) (June 2002), pp. 908–916. Lakoff, 2004 notes the way in which the strong parent model influences the Conservative mind-set.

16. See Inglehart, "The Silent Revolution in Europe: Intergenerational Change in Post-Industrial Societies," *American Political Science Review,* 65(4) (December, 1971) pp. 991–1017.

17. See Richard Florida, 2003.

18. Berry, 1984.

19. Skocpol, 2003.

20. Ibid.

21. Singer, 2004, p. 221.

22. Rampton and Stauber, 2004.

23. Ibid.

24. Ibid. and Sabato and Simpson, 1996, pp. 103–117 show the way in which this dynamic works in the case of the Christian Right.

25. Brock, 2004, pp. 280–291 provides a nice explanation of the way in which Conservative activists use talk radio as a distribution channel.

26. "33 internal FOX editorial memos reviewed by MMFA reveal FOX News Channel's inner workings," www.mediamatters.org, July 14, 2004. http://mediamatters.org/items/200407140002. link last visited October 19, 2006.

27. Sabato and Simpson, 1996, p. 121 dub the faxing operation the "echo chamber" and note that the point is to get that day's message out through as many sympathetic channels as is possible.

28. For an in-depth examination of this phenomenon as well as the broader uses of media in distributing the Conservative brand story, see David Brock's *The Republican Noise Machine: Right-Wing Media and How It Corrupts Democracy,* 2004.

29. Berry, 2000.

30. Ibid.

31. Lakoff, 2004.

32. See Frank, 2004, p. 248 for a discussion of the highly segmented nature of the Conservative worldview.

33. Ibid.

34. See particularly Bob Woodward's *Bush At War* for an in-depth look at the way in which the Bush team intentionally constructed the conflict in as a broad a way as they possibly could. Two clear examples of which can be found on pp. 41 and 73.

It uses as a pretext for the Iraq War are specifically referenced on pp. 83, 84, and 328–329.

35. Ibid., p. 32.

36. Lakoff, 2004.

37. Teixeira and Rodgers, 2000 present a book-length examination of the way in which neither party really pays attention to the needs of working-class white Americans and what they could do to reach them.

38. "The Democratic Party is Toast" by Grover Norquist, *Washington Monthly*, (September 2004). http://www.washingtonmonthly.com/features/2004/0409.norquist.html, link last visited October 8, 2006.

39. Ibid.

40. For a trenchant discussion of the organization building activities of Conservative philanthropists in general and the so-called Kochtopus in particular, see Rampton and Stauber, 2004, pp. 20–30 and 35–41.

41. Lakoff, 2004.

42. For a discussion of Clinton's mass-media branding efforts, see Newman, 1999a.

43. See Schoenwald, 2001 and McGirr, 2001.

44. See Frank, 2004, pp. 89–109 for an examination of this dynamic in one state.

45. As noted by Waldman, 2004.

46. As Zyman and Miller, 2000, p. 33 show building relationships is a key part of brand building in the current age.

47. Zyman and Miller, 2000, pp. 41–43 examine the way in which Clinton used the positioning technique to come back from the disaster of 1994.

48. For an in-depth examination of Clinton see Newman, 1999a.

49. As Lakoff, 2004 makes clear.

50. Edsall and Edsall, 1992, p. 282.

51. Ibid.

52. Zyman and Miller, 2000, pp. 43 and 161–167 discuss the benefits of building customized relationships with customers in building brand loyalty.

53. This is described by Zyman and Miller, 2000, as organic marketing and his description nicely fits what Conservatives do in their branded campaigns.

54. Brock, 2004, pp. 23–37 outlines the early history and strategy behind this campaign and pp. 76–115 for its subsequent uses.

55. Skowronek, 1997.

56. Putnam, 2000 and Cohen, 2003.

57. Cohen, 2003.

58. Bennett, 2003, pp. 250–273 provides a very useful set of suggestions that could improve the media and civic environments within American politics.

59.   For an interesting argument about the chances of this happening given trends in society and media, see Turow, 1997, pp. 184–200.

Bibliography

Aldrich, John. *Why Parties: The Origin and Transformation of Party Politics in America.* Chicago, IL: University of Chicago Press, 1995.

Alterman, Eric and Mark Green. *How George W. Bush (Mis)Leads America.* New York: Viking, 2004.

Ansolabehre, Stephen, Roy Behr, and Shanto Iyengar. *The Media Game: American Politics in the Television Age.* Boston: Allyn and Bacon, 1993.

Balz, Daniel J. and Ronald Brownstein. *Storming the Gates: Protest Politics and the Republican Revival.* Boston: Little, Brown, 1996.

Bellah, Robert M., Richard Madsen, William M. Sullivan, Ann Swindler, and Steven M. Tipton. *Habits of the Heart: Individualism and Commitment in American Life.* Berkeley, CA: University of California Press, 1985.

Bennett, W. Lance. *The Governing Crisis: Media, Money and Marketing in American Elections.* New York: St. Martin's Press, 1996.

————. *News: The Politics of Illusion.* New York: Longman, 2003.

Berlant, Lauren and Lisa Duggan. *Our Monica Ourselves.* New York: New York University Press, 2001.

Berry, Jeffery M. *The Interest Group Society.* Boston: Little, Brown, 1984.

————. *The New Liberalism: The Rising Power of Citizen Groups.* Washington, DC: Brookings, 1999.

Braunstein, Mark and Edward H. Levine. *Deep Branding on the Internet: Applying Heat and Pressure Online to Build a Lasting Brand.* Roseville, CA: Prima Press, 2000.

Brock, David. *Blinded by the Right: The Conscience of an Ex-Conservative.* New York: Random House, 2002.

————. *The Republican Noise Machine: Right-Wing Media and How It Corrupts Democracy.* New York: Crown Publishers, 2004.

Campbell, Colin and Bert A. Rockman (eds.). *The Clinton Legacy.* Chatham, NJ: Seven Bridges Press, 1999.

Cannon, Lou. *Reagan.* New York: G.P. Putnam's Sons. 1982.

————. *President Reagan: The Role of a Lifetime.* New York: Simon and Schuster, 1991.

Cohen, Lisabeth. *A Consumer's Republic: The Politics of Mass Consumption in Post-War America.* New York: Knopf, 2003.

Combs, James. *The Reagan Range: The Nostalgic Myth in American Politics.* Bowling Green, OH: Bowling Green State University Popular Press, 1993.

Conason, Joe and Gene Lyons. *The Hunting of the President: The Ten Year Campaign to Destroy Bill and Hillary Clinton.* New York: Saint Martin's, 2000.

Czerniawski, Richard D. and Michael W. Maloney. *Creating Brand Loyalty: The Management of Power Positioning and Really Great Advertising.* New York: AMACOM, 1999.

Dallek, Robert. *Ronald Reagan: The Politics of Symbolism.* Cambridge, MA: Harvard University Press, 1999.

Deaver, Michael K. with Mickey Herskowitz. *Behind The Scenes: In Which the Author Talks about Ronald and Nancy Reagan and Himself.* New York: William Morrow, 1988.

————. *A Different Drummer: My Thirty Years with Ronald Reagan.* New York: Harper Collins/Perennial, 2001.

———— (ed.). *Why I Am a Reagan Conservative.* New York: William Morrow, 2005.

Diamond, Sara. *Roads to Dominion: Right-Wing Movements and Political Power in the United States.* New York: Guilford Press, 1995.

————. *Not by Politics Alone: The Enduring Influence of the Christian Right.* New York: Guilford Press, 1998.

Downs, Anthony. *An Economic Theory of Democracy.* New York: Addison-Wesley, 1997.

Drew, Elizabeth. *Showdown: The Struggle between the Gingrich Congress and the Clinton White House.* New York: Simon and Schuster, 1996.

Dugger, Ronnie. *On Reagan: The Man and His Presidency.* New York: McGraw-Hill, 1983.

Edelman, Murray. *The Symbolic Uses of Politics.* Urbana, IL: University of Illinois Press, 1964.

———. *Constructing the Political Spectacle.* Chicago, IL: University of Chicago Press, 1988.

Edsall, Thomas Byrne and Mary D. Edsall. *Chain Reaction: The Impact of Race, Rights and Taxes on American Politics.* New York: W.W. Norton, 1992.

Farnsworth, Stephen J. and Robert Lichter. *Nightly News Nightmare.* Lanham, MD: Rowman and Littlefield, 2003.

Feinstein, Stephen. *The 1970's from Watergate to Disco.* Berkeley Heights, NJ: Enslow, 2000.

Felten, Erik (ed.). *A Shining City: The Legacy of Ronald Reagan.* New York: Simon and Schuster, 1998.

Florida, Richard. *The Rise of the Creative Class and How Its Transforming Work, Leisure, Community and Everyday Life the Transformation of American Life.* New York: Basic, 2003.

Frank, Thomas. *What's The Matter With Kansas?: How Conservatives Won the Heart of America.* New York: Metropolitan Books, 2004.

Garment, Suzanne. *Scandal: The Culture of Mistrust in American Politics.* New York: Times Books, 1991.

Ginsburg, Benjamin and Martin Shefter. *Politics by Other Means: Politicians, Prosecutors and the Press from Watergate to Whitewater.* New York: W.W. Norton, 1999.

Greider, William. *The Soul of Capitalism: Opening Paths to A Moral Economy.* New York: Simon and Schuster, 2003.

Hamilton, James. *All the News That's Fit to Sell.* Princeton, New Jersey: Princeton University Press, 2004.

Hibbing, John and Elizabeth Theiss-Morse. *Congress as Public Enemy: Attitudes Toward American Political Institutions.* New York: Cambridge University Press, 1995.

Hunter, James Davison. *Culture Wars: The Struggle to Define America.* New York: Basic Books, 1992.

Isserman, Maurice and Michael Kazin. *America Divided: The Civil War of the 1960's.* New York: Oxford University Press, 2000.

Jamieson, Kathleen Hall. *Packaging the Presidency: A History and Criticism of Presidential Campaign Advertising.* New York: Oxford University Press, 1996.

Jamieson, Kathleen Hall and Paul Waldman. *The Press Effect: Politicians, Journalists and the Stories that Shape the Political World.* New York: Oxford University Press, 2003.

Johnson, Haynes. *Sleepwalking Through History: America in the Reagan Years.* W.W. Norton, 1991.

————. *The Best of Times: America in the Clinton Years.* Orlando, FL: Harcourt, 2001.

Kalb, Marvin. *One Scandalous Story: Clinton, Lewinsky and Thirteen Days that Shook American Journalism.* New York: Free Press, 2001.

Kaplan, Leonard V. and Beverly I. Moran. *Aftermath: The Clinton Impeachment and the Presidency in the Age of Spectacle.* New York: New York University Press, 2001.

Key, V. O. *Public Opinion and American Democracy.* New York: Knopf, 1963.

Killian, Linda. *The Freshmen: What Happened to the Republican Revolution?* Boulder, CO: Westview Press, 1998.

Kingdon, John. *Agendas, Alternatives, and Public Policy* (2nd ed). *New York:* Addison-Wesley Educational Publishers, 1997.

Klein, Joe. *The Natural: The Misunderstood Presidency of Bill Clinton.* New York: Doubleday, 2002.

Klein, Naomi. *No Logo: Taking Aim at the Brand Bullies.* New York: Picador Press, 2000.

Krugman, Paul. *Peddling Prosperity: Economic Sense and Nonsense in an Age of Diminished Expectations.* New York: W.W. Norton, 1994.

Lakoff, George. *Don't Think of An Elephant!: Know Your Values and Frame the Debate, the Essential Guide for Progressives.* White River Junction, Vermont: Chelsea Green Publishing, 2004.

Lowi, Theodore J. *The End of the Republican Era.* Norman, OK: University of Oklahoma Press, 1996.

Luntz, Frank I. *Candidates, Consultants and Campaigns: The Style and Substance of American Electioneering.* Oxford: Blackwell, 1988.

Manheim, Jarrol B. *The Death of a Thousand Cuts: Corporate Campaigns and the Attack on the Corporation.* Mahwah, NJ: Lawrence Earlbaum and Associates, 2001.

Maraniss, David. *First in His Class: A Biography of Bill Clinton.* New York: Simon and Schuster, 1996.

Mark, Margaret and Carol S. Pearson. *The Hero and the Outlaw: Building Extraordinary Brands Through the Power of Archetypes.* New York: McGraw-Hill, 2001.

Mayhew, David R. *Divided We Govern: Party Control, Lawmaking and Investigations, 1946-1990.* New Haven, Connecticut: Yale University Press, 1991.

McConnell, Ben, Jackie Huba, and Guy Kawasaki. *Creating Customer Evangelists: How Customers Become a Voluntary Sales Force.* Chicago: Dearborn Trade, Kaplan, 2003.

McGirr, Lisa. *Suburban Warriors: The Origin of the New American Right.* Princeton, NJ: Princeton University Press, 2001.

Micklethwait, John and Adrian Wooldridge. *The Right Nation: Conservative Power in America.* New York: Penguin, 2004.

Moore, Geoffrey A. *Crossing the Chasm: Marketing and Selling Technology Products to Mainstream Customers.* New York: Harper Business, 1991.

Moore, James. *Bush's War for Re-Election: Iraq, the White House and the People.* Hoboken, NJ: John Wiley and Sons, 2004.

Moore, James and Wayne Slater. *Bush's Brain: How Karl Rove Made George W. Bush Presidential.* New York: Wiley, 2003.

Morris, Edmund. *Dutch: A Memior of Ronald Reagan.* New York: Random House, 1999.

Morris, Irwin. *Votes, Money and the Clinton Impeachment.* Boulder, CO: Westview Press, 2001.

Newman, Bruce I. *The Mass Marketing of Politics: Democracy in an Age of Manufactured Images.* Thousand, Oaks, CA: Sage, 1999a.

―――― (ed.). *Handbook of Political Marketing.* Thousand Oaks, CA: Sage, 1999b.

Pemberton, William E. *Exit with Honor: The Life and Presidency of Ronald Reagan.* Armonk, NY: M.E. Sharpe, 1997.

Peters, Ronald M. *The American Speakership: The Office in Historical Perspective.* Baltimore, MD: Johns Hopkins University Press, 1990.

Phillips, Kevin. *The Politics of Rich and Poor: Wealth and the American Electorate in the Reagan Aftermath.* New York: Random House, 1990.

――――. *Arrogant Capital: Washington, Wall Street and the Frustration of American Politics.* Boston: Little, Brown, 1994.

Piven, Frances Fox *The War At Home:The Domestic Costs of Bush's Militarism.* New York: The New Press, 2004.

―――― and Richard Cloward. *Regulating the Poor: The Functions of Public Welfare.:* (2nd Updated Edition). New York: Vintage Press, 1993.

Postman, Neil. *Amusing Ourselves to Death: Public Discourse in the Age of Show Business.* New York: Penguin, 1986.

Putnam, Robert D. *Bowling Alone: The Collapse and Revival of American Community.* New York: Simon and Schuster, 2000.

Rampton, Sheldon and John Stauber. *Trust Us We're Experts: How Industry Manipulates Science and Gambles with Your Future.* New York: Jeremy P. Tarcher/Putnam; 1st Trade ed., 2002.

――――. *Weapons of Mass Deception: The Uses of Propaganda in Bush's War on Iraq.* New York: Penguin, 2003.

――――. *Banana Republicans.* New York: Penguin, 2004.

Rentschler, William. *Goldwater: Conservative Icon of Integrity.* Lincolnwood, IL: Contemporary Books, 2000.

Ricci, David M. *The Transformation of American Politics: The New Washington and the Rise of Think Tanks.* New Haven, CT: Yale University Press, 1993.

Ries, Al and Laura Ries. *The 22 Immutable Laws of Branding.* New York: Harper Business, 2002.

Ries, Al and Jack Trout. *Positioning: The Battle for Your Mind.* New York: McGraw-Hill, 2001.

Sabato, Larry. *Feeding Frenzy: How Attack Journalism Has Transformed American Politics.* New York: Free Press, 1991.

Sabato, Larry and Glenn R. Simpson. *Dirty Little Secrets: The Persistence of Corruption in American Politics.* New York: Times Books, 1996.

Sabato, Larry, Mark J. Stencel, and S. Robert Lichter. *Peepshow: Media and Politics in an Age of Scandal.* Lanham, MD: Rowman and Littlefield, 2000.

Stauber, John and Sheldon Rampton. *Toxic Sludge is Good For You: Lies, Damn Lies and the Public Relations Industry.* Monroe, ME: Common Courage Press, 1995.

Schieffer, Bob and Gary Paul Gates. *The Acting President: Ronald Reagan and the Supporting Players Who Helped Him Create the Illusion that Held America Spellbound.* New York: E.P. Dutton, 1989.

Schier, Steven E. *By Invitation Only: The Rise of Exclusive Politics in the United States.* Pittsburgh, PA: University of Pittsburgh Press, 2000.

Schoenwald, Jonathan M. *A Time for Choosing: The Rise of Modern American Conservatism.* New York: Oxford University Press, 2001.

Singer, Peter. *The President of Good and Evil: Questioning the Ethics of George W. Bush.* New York: Penguin, 2004. Skocpol, Theda. *Diminished Democracy: From Membership to Management in American Civic Life.* Norman, OK: University of Oklahoma Press, 2003.

Skowronek, Steven. *The Politics That Presidents Make: Leadership from John Adams to Bill Clinton.* Cambridge, MA: Belknap Press, 1997.

Smith, Hedrick. *The Power Game: How Washington Works.* New York: Harper-Collins, 1989.

Smith, J. Walker and Ann Clurman. *Rocking the Ages: the Yankelovich Report on Generational Marketing.* New York: Harper Business, 1997.

Snow, Donald T. *National Security Policy for A New Era: Globalization and Geopolitics.* New York: A.B. Longman, 2003.

Spitzer, Robert J. *The Politics of Gun Control.* Chatham, NJ: Chatham House, 1995.

Stewart, James B. *Bloodsport: The President and His Adversaries.* New York: Simon and Schuster, 1996.

Susskind, Ron. *The Price of Loyalty.* New York: Simon and Schuster, 2004.

Teixeira, Ruy and Joel Rodgers. *America's Forgotten Majority: Why the White Working Class Still Matters.* New York: Basic Books, 2000.

Thomas, Evan and the Staff of *Newsweek. Election 2004: How Bush/Cheney '04 Won and What You Can Expect in the Future.* New York: Public Affairs, *2004.*

Toobin, Jeffery. *A Vast Conspiracy: The Real Story of a Sex Scandal that Nearly Brought Down A President.* Carmichael, CA: Touchstone Books, 1999.

Travis, Daryl. *Emotional Branding: How Successful Brands Gain the Irrational Edge.* Roseville, CA: Prima Venture, 2000.

Trout, Jack. *Big Brands, Big Trouble: Lessons Learned the Hard Way.* New York: John Wiley, 2001.

Trout, Jack and Steve Rivkin. *Differentiate or Die: Survival in Our Era of Killer Competition.* New York: John Wiley, 2000.

Turow, Joseph. *Breaking Up America: Advertisers and the New Media World.* Chicago, IL: University of Chicago Press, 1997.

Twitchell, James. *Branded Nation: The Marketing of Megachurch, College Inc. and Museumworld.* New York: Simon & Schuster. Reprint ed., 2003.

Tye, Larry. *The Father of Spin: Edward Bernays and the Birth of Public Relations.* New York: Crown, 1998.

Viguerie, Richard and David Franke. *America's Right Turn: How Conservatives Used New and Alternative Media to Take Power.* Chicago: Bonus Books, 2004.

Waldman, Paul. *Fraud: The Strategy Behind the Bush Lies and What the Media Didn't Tell You.* Naperville, IL: Sourcebooks Inc., 2004.

West, Darrel M. *The Rise and Fall of the Media Establishment.* New York: Palgrave, 2001.

West, Darrel M. and John M. Orman. *Celebrity Politics.* Upper Saddle River, NJ: Prentice Hall, 2003.

Wolin, Sheldon. *The Presence of the Past: Essays on the State and the Constitution.* Baltimore, MD: Johns' Hopkins University Press, 1981.

Woodward, Bob. *Shadow: Five Presidents and the Legacy of Watergate.* New York: Simon and Shuster, 2000.

———. *Bush At War.* New York: Simon and Schuster, 2002.

Wymbs, Norman E. *A Place to Go Back To: Ronald Reagan in Dixon, Illinois.* New York: Vantage Press, 1987.

Zyman, Sergio. *The End of Marketing As We Know It.* New York: Harper Business, 2000.

Zyman, Sergio with Armin Brott. *The End of Advertising as We Know It.* Hoboken, NJ: John Wiley and Sons, 2002.

Zyman, Sergio and Scott Miller. *Building Brandwith: Closing the Sale on Line.* New York: Harper, Collins, 2000.

Index